BETWEEN BORDERS

Between Borders

PEDAGOGY AND THE
POLITICS OF CULTURAL STUDIES

edited by

Henry A. Giroux

and

Peter McLaren

ROUTLEDGE   NEW YORK   LONDON

Published in 1994 by

Routledge
29 West 35 Street
New York, NY 10001

Published in Great Britain by

Routledge
11 New Fetter Lane
London EC4P 4EE

Library of Congress Cataloging-in-Publication Data
Giroux, Henry A.
  Between borders : pedagogy and the politics of cultural studies / Henry A. Giroux,
Peter McLaren.
      p.   cm.
  Includes bibliographical references (p.   ) and index.
  ISBN 0-415-90777-2 (hb.)—ISBN 0-415-90778-0 (pbk.)
  1. Critical pedagogy. 2. Educational anthropology. I. McLaren, Peter. II. Title.
  LC196.G57   1993
  370.19—dc20   93-4919
                                                                          CIP

British Library Cataloguing-in-Publication Data also available.

To my three sons, Jack, Chris, and Brett, who are the greatest joy of my life, and who, I hope, will always recognize that to live dangerously is to live in the borderland where desire, justice and love meet. Ain't that the kick, guys?
—*Henry Giroux*

To Jenny, Laura and Marcelo, and Jon. For their patience, love, and understanding and for teaching me which borders to cross.
—*Peter McLaren*

CONTENTS

INSURGENT MULTICULTURALISM AND THE JOURNEY
INTO DIFFERENCE

NATIONALISM, POSTCOLONIALISM, AND
THE BORDER INTELLECTUAL

ACKNOWLEDGMENTS

During the last decade, the fields of cultural studies and critical pedagogy have been expanding within the United States and abroad. Within the university, both fields are developing in a diverse number of disciplines and are generating a boom industry in undergraduate and graduate courses. Moreover, critical pedagogy and cultural studies have found their way into publishers' book lists and a number of book series that have proliferated over the last decade. Of course, the proliferation of these two fields has not gone on unproblematically. There is an enormous debate over the central categories, premises, and practices that are being legitimated within various discourses that address these fields.

Our concern in this book is neither to chart out the various theoretical positions and practices that characterize the myriad versions of these fields nor to make a claim for another authoritative version of cultural studies. The latter terrain has been covered extensively by others and need not be repeated again. Instead, we have brought together a series of authors whose work attempts not only to address the importance of cultural studies as a pedagogical practice but also to rework the political grounds on which the content and context of pedagogy define the meaning of cultural studies.

In this case, cultural studies combines theory and practice in order to affirm and demonstrate pedagogical practices engaged in creating a new language, rupturing disciplinary boundaries, decentering authority, and rewriting the institutional and discursive borderlands in which politics becomes a condition for reasserting the relationship between agency, power, and struggle. The various authors in this collection make visible in different ways two intersecting concerns. In the first instance, they attempt to demonstrate a pedagogy of cultural studies. In other words, they undertake to make clear how cultural studies can deepen its own political possibilities by establishing pedagogical practices consistent with the principles that inform the wide-ranging concerns that have come to mark the multilayered and shifting field of cultural studies. Central to these concerns are issues regarding representation and the discourse of difference, desire and the pedagogy of commodification, cultural memory and the politics and cultural work, democracy and the discourse of the border intellectual, and eros and the politics of reception.

Second, a number of authors in this collection attempt to develop the broader implications of pedagogy in cultural studies by addressing how the production of knowledge, values, and collective identities takes place within particular social, historical, cultural, institutional, and textual formations. Departing from the traditional emphasis of cultural studies with a largely "white on white" textual orientation, a number of authors focus on diverse geographies of identity, representation, and place. This is a book that takes seriously Michel Foucault's notion that power is productive and diverse; it also addresses the assumption stressed in feminist theory that agency, though multilayered and fragmentary, is an essential category for developing a politics of and for democratic struggles.

Combining a language of history, critique, and possibility, *Between Borders* brings together scholars in the field of cultural studies and critical pedagogy for the first time; it also addresses issues regarding pedagogy, identity, and representation through a number of concerns that have not been adequately taken up in the forefront of current debates either in the academy or in broader cultural settings. Hence, *Between Borders* provides a "third space" for a number of cultural workers to engage the connection between pedagogy and cultural studies while simultaneously offering an analysis of feminist, gay/lesbian, postcolonial, and identity issues that have been largely ignored as *both* pedagogical and political considerations. Furthermore, this book gives new meaning to the attempt to demonstrate the broader implications of intellectuals as cultural workers and pedagogy as a form of cultural production that takes place in a variety of political and cultural spheres.

Earlier versions of chapters 1, 2, 4, 5, 6, 7, and 11 have appeared in *Cultural Studies* 17, no. 1 (1992). Simon Watney's "School's Out" first appeared in Diana Fuss, ed., *Inside/Out* (New York: Routledge, 1991); Chandra Mohanty's "On Race and Voice: Challenges for Liberal Education" was first published by Oxford University Press in *Cultural Critique* no. 14 (1989/1990); Nancy Fraser's "Rethinking the Public Sphere: A Contribution to the Critique of Actually Existing Democracy" was first published in Craig Calhoun, ed., *Habermas and the Public Sphere* (Cambridge: MIT Press, 1991); Michele Wallace's "Multiculturalism and Oppositionality" was first published in *Afterimage* (October 1991). We are thankful to the various authors and publishers for permission to reprint these articles.

INTRODUCTION:

BRINGIN' IT ALL BACK

HOME—PEDAGOGY

AND CULTURAL

STUDIES[1]

LAWRENCE GROSSBERG

Any consideration of the relationship between education and cultural studies must acknowledge that this intersection of interests has occurred at a particular moment in time and space, a moment in which, as Stuart Hall (1992b, 11) points out,

> cultural studies programs exist everywhere . . . where they've come to provide a focal point for interdisciplinary studies and research, and for the development of critical theory. Each program, in each place, as is appropriate, joins together a different range of disciplines in adapting itself to the existing academic and intellectual environment. Cultural studies, wherever it exists, reflects the rapidly shifting ground of thought and knowledge, argument and debate about a society and about its own culture.

There is a certain crucial ambiguity in the language of cultural studies' proliferation here, for it can be read as alternatively geographical and discursive. Still, Hall is certainly right that cultural studies is booming in both senses, although there is no guarantee, despite Hall's optimism, that every appearance of cultural studies is valuable or even progressive.[2]

Hall goes on to suggest that cultural studies represents "a point of disturbance . . . in at least two senses." First, in its interdisciplinarity, it operates at "the frontiers of intellectual life, pushing for new questions, new models and new ways of study." Second, and perhaps even more important, it is an intellectual, even a theoretical practice driven less by its own theoretical project than by its engagement with, its attempt to respond to the demands of, a world outside of the academy:

In thrusting onto the attention of scholarly reflection and critical analysis
the hurly burly of a rapidly changing, discordant, and disorderly world, in
insisting that academics sometimes attend to the practical life, where everyday social change exists out there, cultural studies tries in its small way to
insist on what I want to call the vocation of the intellectual life. That is
to say, cultural studies insists on the necessity to address the central, urgent
and disturbing questions of a society and a culture in the most rigorous
intellectual way we have available. (Hall 1992b, 11)

EDUCATION AND THE EMERGENCE OF CULTURAL STUDIES

In this introduction, I want to acknowledge, and try to contribute to, one of the
most pressing, promising, and paradoxical sites of cultural studies to have emerged
recently: education. I describe it as paradoxical because, despite a strong connection
between cultural studies and education at the former's beginnings, the concern
for education has apparently had only a limited impact until recently.

Contrary to popular wisdom, which locates the origins of cultural studies in
universities and in the production of a series of academic texts, Raymond Williams
(1989) offers a different version, based in pedagogy and a common interest in a
"democratic culture":

In the late 40s, people were doing courses in the visual arts, in music, in
town planning and the nature of community, the nature of settlement, in
film, in press, in advertising, in radio; courses which if they had not taken
place in that notably unprivileged sector or education [adult education]
would have been acknowledged much earlier. (154)

And here is Stuart Hall's (1990, 12) redescription of the traditionally acknowledged
founding figures of cultural studies:

We thus came from a tradition entirely marginal to the centers of
English academic life, and our engagement in the questions of cultural
change . . . we first reckoned within the dirty outside world. The Centre
for Contemporary Cultural Studies was the locus to which we *retreated*
when that conversation in the open world could no longer be continued;
it was politics by other means. Some of us—me, especially, had always
planned never to return to the university, indeed never to darken its doors
again. But then, one always has to make pragmatic adjustments to where
real work, important work, can be done.

All of the founding figures of cultural studies (including Richard Hoggart, Raymond Williams, E. P. Thompson, and Stuart Hall) started their careers, and their intellectual projects, in the field of education, outside the university, in extramural departments and adult working-class courses. It was in such adult education classes that Raymond Williams first started to look at the idea of culture. Such pedagogical contexts, which existed outside the formal educational institutions of the state, served people (primarily women and members of the working class) who were deprived of any opportunities for, indeed actively "blocked from," any higher education. What these students brought to the classes, according to Williams, was a very real desire to discuss what they read "in a context to which they brought their own situation, their own experience" (1989, 152).

Williams argues that some of this same energy that characterized his extramural students reappeared in the 1960s, when students confronted the various disciplines in relation to their own situations and experiences, forcing their teachers to acknowledge the fact that specific disciplines might have been inadequate to address the questions that students were raising. But Williams also suggests that this energy, going back to the 1960s, "lacks to this day that crucial process of interchange and encounter between the people offering the intellectual disciplines and those using them" (Williams 1989, 157). Here, Williams points to a crucial element, often lacking in many so-called democratic pedagogies: "the more basic right to define the questions . . . regardless of disciplinary boundaries" (157).

But even beyond the occasion of the emergence of cultural studies, education has played an important role in Williams's understanding of cultural studies. Starting with a common assumption of cultural studies—that the development of any cultural practice, including cultural studies itself, must be related "to the very precise formations and social institutions in which [the] consequences happened and had to happen" (Williams 1989, 161)—Williams concludes that we must ask what the role of cultural studies can be in a particular "educational conjuncture."[3] He argues that it "must be more than just a resented interruption from what is otherwise taught." It must offer "a persuasive, reasoned and practical proposal" (Williams 1989, 161). And he concludes (162), "If this is thought through now, if we fight for it, even if we fail we shall have done something to justify ourselves before the future. But I don't think we need fail at all; I think that the results will be uneven and scattered, but this is where the challenge is."

Given this challenge, the relative absence of education in the body of texts that have come to constitute (British) cultural studies, especially in the United States, becomes ironic at best. There is in fact very little explicit work published in either the "Occasional Papers" or the more formal *Working Papers* published by the Centre for Contemporary Cultural Studies during the 1970s.[4] In the mid-1970s, an Education Working Group was established which, in 1981, published *Unpopular Education: Schooling and Social Democracy in England since 1944* (Education Group/CCCS 1981). This work attempted to "understand the ways in which educational politics have been constructed in England during the post second world war period" (8). And, not surprisingly, it shared the model of incorporation and resistance which dominated the Centre and cultural studies during the 1970s.

Another line of work, with more visibility in both the Occasional Papers and the *Working Papers,* involved the "transition from the school to work."[5] This research, which connected as much to the Centre's interest in youth culture as to an interest in education, gave rise to one of the most influential books to come out of the Centre: Paul Willis's *Learning to Labour: How Working Class Kids Get Working Class Jobs* (1977).

The 1980s saw more activity from Centre members (and ex-members) in researching education, although this work was neither widely distributed nor apparently centrally recognized in contemporary discussions of cultural studies, especially outside of Britain.[6] This work continued the interest in the relations between state politics and educational policy, an interest that found its most sophisticated expression in the reforming of the Education Working Group in the 1980s, and the publication of *Education Ltd.: Schooling, Training and the New Right in England since 1979* (Education Group II 1990), which examines the transformation of public education under Thatcherism.

Of course, the Centre in Birmingham was not the only site of cultural studies and other important, albeit often scattered, work on education was done. Here one has to mention the Ideology and Consciousness Collective, which, besides the journal *Ideology and Consciousness* (later *I & C*), published an important collection entitled *Changing the Subject: Psychology, Social Regulation and Subjectivity* (Henriques et al. 1984). Additionally, one has to acknowledge the important, largely theoretical work organized by and around the journal *Screen Education,* and the Society for Education in Film and Television (SEFT).

Finally, one more thing needs to be said about the place of education in cultural studies, a point that is often ignored but is actually crucial to the history of the reception of cultural studies in the United States: the discipline of education was, as early as the 1970s, one of the only places to give cultural studies a home of sorts (communication was the other). I say "of sorts" because while scholars like Michael Apple and Henry Giroux read, taught, and talked about some of the British work, I do not think that they were yet quite moved to locate themselves within the cultural studies project, or to identify cultural studies with their own project of a critical pedagogy.

IN DEFENSE OF CULTURAL STUDIES

While the current boom in cultural studies has opened up new and exciting possibilities, it is, I believe, necessary to approach every claim to cultural studies with a certain skepticism. Williams's (1989) distinction between a project and a formation can be helpful here:

> The relation between a project and a formation is always decisive; and . . . the emphasis of Cultural Studies is precisely that it engages with both. . . . We have to look at what kind of formation it was from which

the project of Cultural Studies developed, and then the changes of formation that produced different definitions of that project. . . . [W]hat is happening each time is that a formation in a given general relationship to its society is taking what you could otherwise trace as a project with certain continuities, and in fact altering it, not necessarily for the better. There have been as many reversions as there have been advances. (151, 155)

In other words, not every formation of cultural studies remains faithful to the project, and not every project is possible within a specific formation. While the space of cultural studies is and must remain open to new projects and formations, new articulations and configurations, it is important to remember that in any specific place, it does matter what shape cultural studies takes, how it is defined. And consequently, not everything is—or need be—cultural studies. The insertion is important because cultural studies does not claim to hold any privileged position; it has never presented itself as the only important or valid sort of intellectual work that can be or should be done.

It is thus necessary to say something about the trajectory (the relation of project and formation) of cultural studies, and to go beyond the obvious claim that it encompasses a number of attempts to understand and intervene into the relations of culture and power. What distinguishes cultural studies, I would argue, is its radical contextualism. In fact, cultural studies, in its theoretical practice, might be described as a theory of contexts, or, in its political practice, as the practice of making contexts. This is the force of the concept of "articulation," which, starting from the assumption that there are no guaranteed relations in history, goes on to analyze history as the practice of deconstructing and reconstructing relations (contexts, effects, etc.).[7]

This radical contextualism has significant implications at a number of different levels. First, cultural studies approaches theory as a contextual intervention. It rejects both the application of a theory known in advance as well as an empiricism without theory. While it is committed to a detour through theory, it is not theory driven. Instead, it is driven by its own sense of history and politics. Theory is always a response to a particular context. In this sense, I agree with Manthia Diawara's (1992, 7) critique:

Unfortunately a good deal of U.S. cultural studies that invokes the Birmingham tradition disengages theory from its space of application. The perspectives of the Birmingham school cannot simply be lifted and applied to the U.S. . . . [T]he anti-essentialism of this cultural studies has become an essentialism of its own kind: the reification of discourse. . . . This abstract discourse belies the fact that they have been more influenced by certain strains of post-structuralism than by recent developments in the black studies strand of cultural studies.

Thus, David Bailey and Stuart Hall (1992a, 4–5) locate the important work in 1980s British cultural studies on race, ethnicity, and black cultural politics in "a period of rapid and turbulent change which encompassed several paradigm shifts in both theory and practice and was marked by a powerful synergy between race, politics and representation." They emphasize that "no single position can ever be secure in its correctness. Different strategies [and I might add theories] are right in different locations and at different moments."[8]

At the same time, the contextuality of theory in cultural studies also leads me to disagree with any effort to reduce cultural studies to a single theoretical insight, such as Patrick Brantlinger's decontextualized claim that the "main lesson of cultural studies" is that "in order to understand ourselves, the discourses of the Other— of all the others—is that which we most urgently need to know" (cited in Pfister 1991, 207). While this is, of course, a crucial lesson of cultural studies (as well as of other political interventions, including feminist theory), Brantlinger writes as if the "recognition and respect for difference" were sufficient to produce "an authentically democratic mass culture unifying people."

Second, for cultural studies, the very nature of the relation between culture and power depends upon the particular context or site into which it is attempting to intervene. Hence, cultural studies is never simply a theory of ideology, or of culture as the symbolic representation of powers which exist outside its domain. Cultural studies cannot be reduced to practices which constantly rediscover what we already know: for example, that particular practices reproduce either structures of domination and subordination or representation of identity, difference, and inequality. Such observations are not unimportant: we do, after all, need to be constantly reminded of the racist, sexist, xenophobic, and homophobic dimensions of our social and cultural lives. But cultural studies always tries to go beyond such "discoveries" to understand the complexities of how such structures and representations work within the field of forces that constitute the domain of cultural struggle.

Cultural studies also cannot be reduced to practices which constantly rediscover that the dominant powers, by incorporating the subordinate, always undermine (or deconstruct) their own stability. Nor can cultural studies be identified with a critical practice which is content to find the cracks in the processes of reproduction and representation. Too often, the assumption (and it is a crucial assumption for cultural studies) that people are active and capable of struggle and resistance (which of course does not guarantee that they are struggling or resisting in any particular instance) becomes a discovery sufficient unto itself. This raises an important distinction, and a common misunderstanding of cultural studies' optimism: while cultural studies refuses to assume that people are cultural dopes, it does not deny that they are often duped by culture.[9] While cultural studies often constructs "images of strength, courage and the will to survive in the face of overpowering hostility" (Bailey and Hall 1992a, 5), this does not mean that it erases that hostility or the systems of domination (which are never simply cultural) within which notions of empowerment and even resistance define the necessary conditions for any active and organized opposition. Cultural studies is committed to contestation, both as a fact of reality (although not necessarily in every instance) and as its own strategic practice. For cultural studies, the question of power must always be located within a field of struggle, not as a zero sum game in which one either simply wins or loses, but, rather, as a ongoing effort to change the balance and organization of forces. In this light, we can better understand cultural studies' commitment to the popular, not merely as a set of texts but as the terrain on which political struggle must be carried out in the contemporary world.

Third, the very concept of culture itself is contextual or at least polysemic. It is caught between social formations, everyday life, and representational practices (or, to use more common terms, between community, a whole way of life, and maps of meaning). Here we can take notice of a certain irony. On the other hand, some critics (such as Diawara) argue that cultural studies, at least in one of its strains, is often marked by a propensity to reduce culture to textuality. Yet on the other hand, other critics agree with Ellen Rooney's (1990, 24) characterization: "The resistance to textuality is announced as an effort to maintain a proper space for political action 'outside the text' but its actual effect is to depoliticize the very signifying practices which enable us to engage in any kind of politically motivated intellectual work whatsoever." Obviously, I do not agree with Rooney's argument, based in a feminist poststructuralism, that cultural studies depoliticizes discourse, but I do agree that cultural studies refuses to reduce culture, or the politics of culture, to questions of textuality. Cultural studies assumes a reality which is constantly reworked by and only made available through cultural practices.[10] In some cultural studies work, this has led to a rejection of the model of critical practice as a hermeneutic or interpretive act of theoretical self-reflection. Echoing Hebdige (1993), critical practice becomes a "witness" of the effects of reality, culture, and critical work on each other.[11] In effect, cultural studies denies the apparent autonomy of culture which is often reinforced by theories of textuality. It argues that cultural practices are not only the sites and the stakes of struggle, but also the weapons as well. In other words, cultural practices not only represent power, they deploy it as well.

Fourth, in cultural studies, the cultural practice (or text) itself and its effects are also contextual. Here I can do no better than to cite as an example a passage from one of the "canonical works" of British cultural studies, *Policing the Crisis* (Hall et al. 1978, 185), which examined the social constitution of the "event of mugging" and its political effectivity:

> There are, we argue, clear historical forces at work in this period, shaping so to speak, from the outside, the immediate transactions on the ground between "muggers," potential muggers, their victims and their apprehenders. In many comparable studies, these larger and wider forces are merely noted and cited; their direct and indirect bearing on the phenomenon analyzed is, however, left vague and abstract—part of the "background."

In our case, we believe that these so-called "background issues" are, indeed, exactly the critical forces which *produce* "mugging" in the specific form in which it appears. . . . It is to this shaping context, therefore, that we turn.

Hence, the cultural practice (or text or event) is neither simply a microcosmic representation of nor the embodiment of a meaning which is related to some social other (whether a totality or a specific set of relations). At the very least, it is the site of complex representational work. But it may be more useful to see it as a place where a multiplicity of forces (determinations and effects) are articulated to produce the practice, a place where different things can and do happen, where different possibilities of uses and effects intersect. A cultural practice is a complex and conflictual place which cannot be separated from the context of its articulation, since it has no existence outside of that context (Frow and Morris forthcoming).

Finally, as I have already suggested, politics—its sites, goals, and forms of struggle—is contextually defined in cultural studies. Here I want to consider one of the common, and I believe mistaken, criticisms of cultural studies. For example, Alan O'Connor (1989, 407) writes that "cultural studies in the U.S. is being sponsored by scholars who rarely have any connection to existing political and cultural movements and are somewhat surprised that this might be possible." Even more strongly, Ellen Rooney (1990, 20) asserts that

> cultural studies in the U.S. has a political problem insofar as its relationship
> to a specifically political struggle outside the university is at best contested.
> Practically speaking, women's studies has an enormous advantage over . . .
> cultural studies . . . its students offer a political conscious constituency
> before they enter the field. . . . I want to stress the theoretical importance
> of the political activities of women's studies students outside the university.

I certainly do not want to reject the model of intellectual politics suggested here. And while I agree that the origins of women's, black, and ethnic studies programs can be traced to oppositional social movements (in part located outside the university), I also agree with Chandra Mohanty (in this volume) that the origins of such programs were often "a defensive political move: the state's institutionalization of a discourse of reform in response to the civil rights movement." That is, for Mohanty, such programs must also be seen as part of a process of the "management" of race and difference.[12]

Cultural studies, however, offers a different model of intellectual politics: neither the organic intellectual, who has an already existing relation to an already existing constituency, nor the specific intellectual, who can only construct local and temporary constituencies based entirely on his or her expertise. Cultural studies attempts at least to construct a more flexible, more pragmatic, more modest, and more contextual model of the political function of the intellectual, connecting to, constructing, and reconstructing its conjunctural constituency. Cultural studies thinks constituencies are made, not given in advance, as if the relationship of social identity and politics were already inscribed on the walls of our social experiences. Raymond Williams (1989, 162) described the pedagogical responsibility of cultural studies as

> taking the best we can in intellectual work and going with it in this very open way to confront people for whom it is not a way of life, for whom it is not in all probability a job, but for whom it is a matter of their own intellectual interest, their own understanding of the pressures on them, pressures of every kind, from the most personal to the most broadly political.

Or, to quote Stuart Hall (1992b, 17–18) again:

> The work that cultural studies has to do is to mobilize everything that it can find in terms of intellectual resources in order to understand what keeps making the lives we live, and the societies we live in, profoundly and deeply anti-humane. . . . Cultural studies' message is a message for academics and intellectuals but fortunately, for many other people as well. In that sense I have tried to hold together in my own intellectual life, on the one hand, the conviction and passion and the devotion to . . . rigorous analysis and understanding, to the passion to find out, and to the production of knowledge that we did not know before. But, on the other hand, I am convinced that no intellectual worth his or her salt, and no university that wants to hold up its head in the face of the twenty-first century, can afford to turn dispassionate eyes away from the problems . . . that beset our world.

The question of cultural studies is not so much whom we are speaking to (audience) or even for (representation), but whom we are speaking against. And consequently, the resources we need, the strategies we adopt, and the politics we attempt to define must always take into account the particular context in which we are struggling. As Bailey and Hall (1992c, 15) argue,

> It is perfectly possible that what is politically progressive and opens up new discursive opportunities in the 1970s and 1980s can become a form of closure—and have a repressive value—by the time it is installed as the dominant genre. . . . It will run out of steam; it will become a style; people will use it not because it opens up anything but because they are being spoken by it, and at that point, you need another shift.

THE SPACE OF EDUCATION

No one can doubt that, not only the institutions and practices of education, but the very concept of education, have come under intense scrutiny and even attack in recent years. Most visibly, of course, this has been the result of education's being caught between the conflicting demands and critiques of two opposed discourses. On the one side there is a discourse of multiculturalism and liberation which calls for a democratic culture based on an acceptance of social difference and which is usually predicated on a theory of identity and representation. On the other side there is a discourse of conservatism based on canonical notions of general education and a desire to impose what it cannot justify—the existence of an illusory common culture. From this imaginary place, it has launched an attack, largely through the media, by articulating an identity between three distinct strands of work on the Left: the critique of the canon, the renewed power of theory, and the interest in radical pedagogy. These debates may be, as Michael Denning (1992, 33) has argued, "skirmishes over the forms and ownership of cultural capital, a war of intraclass position." Or they may be the current forms in which the contradictions in the very idea of a democratic and universal education are being played out (involving questions of appropriateness—of subjects and objects—as well as of normative standards and aims).

But as Paul Willis (1990, 147) has recently suggested,

> The field of education is likely to come under even more intense pressure. It will be further marginalized in most people's experience by common [read "popular" or "everyday"] culture. In so far as educational practices are still predicated on traditional liberal humanist lines and on the assumed superiority of high art, they will become almost totally irrelevant to the real energies and interests of most young people and have no part of their identity formation. Common culture will, increasingly, undertake in its own ways, the roles that education has vacated.
>
> Insofar as education/training becomes ever more subordinated to technical instrumentalism and to the "needs" of industry, it will be seen as a necessary evil to be tolerated in order to obtain access to the wage in order to obtain access to leisure and consumption and their cultural energies. . . .
>
> . . . We need an altogether new approach in education.

Without intending to sound too paranoid, it seems fair to say that education is surrounded on all sides: from the Left, by the concerns of multiculturalism and radical pedagogy; from the Right, by the demand for a reinstantiation of general education, which Denning (1992, 41) describes as "a key part of middlebrow culture," using the mass media and culture industries to distribute a packaged translation of the classical curriculum; from the top, by the increasing economic and technological rationality imposed on educational institutions; and from below, by the microapparatuses and macroalliances of popular culture.

In this context, the recent conjunction of cultural studies and educational theory has produced a wide range of questions, positions, and practices; it has provoked some of the most interesting explorations and some of the most troubling speculations. And it has expanded our understanding of education, so that, at its most problematic, education becomes identified with culture itself, leaving open the task that it be rearticulated, respecified. Compare for example, two views. First, Roger Simon (in this volume) defines pedagogy as "a term which signals the practical synthesis of the question 'what should be taught and why?' with considerations as to how that teaching should take place." This rather narrow view contrasts sharply with Willis's (1990, 137) claim that

> making (not receiving) messages and meanings in your own context and from materials you have appropriated is, in essence, a form of education in the broadest sense. It is the specifically developmental part of symbolic work, an education about "the self" and its relation to the world and to others in it. Where everyday symbolic work differs from what is normally thought of as "education" is that it "culturally produces" from its own chosen symbolic resources.

What we actually have here is not the equation of education and culture, an equation which would erase the specificity of schooling altogether, but a space which extends from the pedagogy of culture to the culture of pedagogy. At one extreme, we can locate Michael Dyson's concern (in this volume) with Michael Jordan as a public pedagogue, as a "figure of . . . authority whose career educates us." Or Roger Simon's attempt (in this volume) to understand the pedagogy of a particular T-shirt as part of a larger process, which includes schooling, of the production of popular memory, "a pedagogy of historical reformation" which elucidates the "different educative forms of reciprocal relation between present and past."

At the other extreme, cultural practices have to be located in the institutional and technological conditions which regulate specific fields. Here we can locate an even broader range of projects (all included in this volume): Ava Collins's attempt to bring popular culture into the classroom while respecting its existence in a discursive space outside the academy, by finding systems of evaluation inherent within popular texts themselves; David Trend's arguments for media education as the teaching of skills or literacies that value difference; Carol Becker's original effort to think about both the possibilities of educating the audience of art about its often mystifying and discomforting effects, and the need to educate young art students to understand the effects of their work in relation to particular audiences; or Henry Giroux's trenchant investigations into "how particular forms of authority are secured through the organization of the curriculum at all levels of schooling."

In the space between these extremes, we move from the important issue of the relation between teachers and students to questions about the relation of the classroom to the outside world. Here we can consider (all in this volume): bell hooks's important argument that an empowering pedagogy must reconsider (and admit) the place of passion, emergy, and eros (which is not merely sexual) in the classroom. hooks calls for a pedagogy in which teachers openly care about and even love, not only their subject matter, but their subjects (students) as well. David

Trend similarly proposes the educational relation as a model for other relationships, while both Chandra Mohanty and Nancy Fraser seem to call for the school to become the agent or site (respectively) of a "public culture of dissent." All of these are attempts to elucidate the often taken for granted assumption that education should lead our students to live their lives differently.

In the space between the extremes described above, in the new space of educational discourse, the very concept of pedagogy has been exploded and multiplied. No longer satisfied with a pedagogy of knowledge, we now must consider the possibilities of a pedagogy of voices (Mohanty) and of liberation (McLaren), a pedagogy of place (Giroux), of desire, style, and presence (Dyson), of desiring machines (McLaren). The taken for granted site of pedagogy has opened up and what we have begun to explore are the pedagogies of border intellectuals (Giroux, JanMohamed) and the possibilities of postmodern pedagogies.

Yet for all of the excitement that this new space produces, I think we must take seriously the possibility that something is also being lost. It is not just that our confidence that we know what the question of pedagogy or education is about has been rendered uncertain. It is that, having given up the assumption that we know in advance the relationship between education and culture, we have still to do the work necessary to theorize and politicize that relationship. I do not want to suggest that the current intersection of cultural studies and educational theory represents some kind of failure. On the contrary, I want to point to an apparent irony: that precisely by approaching the apparent equivalence of education and culture, we are actually moving closer to their differentiation, a differentiation which takes us beyond the commonsensical notion of education as the production and dissemination of knowledge.

CULTURE AND IDENTITY

Perhaps the most visible trajectory that the encounter between cultural studies and education has taken is through contemporary work on identity. Here the work, not only of cultural studies, but of feminists, postcolonial critics, and critics of race, has been very influential. But this work can also be traced back to the sociological work of the 1960s (e.g., labeling theory) which identified schooling as a crucial element in the processes of identity formation. Today, such work is often predicated on the distinction between two forms of the struggle over, two forms of the production of, identity, a distinction which is often credited to Stuart Hall, among others.

Let me briefly elaborate these two forms. The first assumes that there is some intrinsic and essential content to any particular identity which can be traced back to some authentic common origin or structure of experience. Struggle then takes the form of contesting negative (distorting) images with positive (more accurate) ones, of trying to discover the authentic and original content of the identity, of offering one fully constituted, separate and distinct identity (only this time a good one) in place of another (bad) one.

The second emphasizes the impossibility of such fully constituted, separate and distinct identities. It denies the existence of authentic and originary content based in a universally shared origin or experience. Struggles over identity no longer involve questions of adequacy or distortion but, rather, of the politics of difference and representation. According to Hall, the relevant questions concern how identities are produced and taken up through practices of representation. Identity is always a temporary and unstable effect of difference: "Identity is a structured representation which only achieves its positive through the narrow eye of the negative. It has to go through the eye of the needle of the other before it can construct itself" (Hall 1991a, 21).

This position, which has quickly gained authority in black and postcolonial cultural studies in the U.S., maintains a strong notion of difference, in which "X" is equal to, defined by the fact of its being, not Y, not Z, etc., and a weak notion of the other (since the other is also measured by its difference, with the occasional allowance for some indeterminable excess). That is, the identity of any term depends, for all practical purposes, totally on its relation to, its difference from, its constitutive other.

This emphasis on identit*ies* and differences, rather than on a singular identity, points then to the connection between the fragments, to the articulations between the differences, and, hence, to the necessity of what Kobena Mercer (1992b) has called the mantra of race, class, and gender: "The challenge is to be able to theorize more than one difference at once" (Mercer 1992a, 34). This suggests a much more difficult politics, because the sides (good and bad) cannot be given in advance, nor even in neat distributions. As Michele Wallace says (in this volume), echoing the writings of June Jordan, "the thing that needs to be said first—women are not to be trusted just because they're women, any more than blacks are to be trusted because they're black, or gays because they're gay and so on." Similarly, Roger Simon (in this volume) argues against "mindlessly accepting all contesting counter-memories," but also calls for "learning how to hear what is being asserted within them and seriously considering the claim they make on our understanding of the present."

This second notion of identity has fueled important work in educational theory; for example, it has helped shape the call for a "border pedagogy" as a critical practice which would enable people to examine their own conditions of existence by adopting "a position of nonidentity with their own positions" (Giroux, in this volume) and, in the process, empower them to create new positions or identities. And it has helped give rise to Henry Giroux's notion (in this volume) of a "representational pedagogy" which "make[s] the political more pedagogical by addressing how a critical politics can be developed between a struggle over access to regimes of representation and using them to re-present different identities. . . ." One final word of caution, however, needs to be added to the discussion of these two views of identity and identity politics: the relation between them is not merely theoretical; it is as much a question of political strategy. Thus, the relationship is also not merely one of supersession, the latter replacing the former. As I have argued already, for cultural studies, such theoretical and political choices are always a matter of contexts and strategies. The first view of identity was not and is not simply mistaken; it was and in certain instances continues to be a vital political force.

The second view of identity as an effect of difference, which Hall has at times put forth, has to be distinguished from a third view which, while Hall has never advocated it, might be read into his work. In fact, a number of writers have already begun to express some dissatisfaction with both theories of identity and difference.[13] For example, Kobena Mercer (1992a, 34, 33) has written: "There is nothing remotely groovy about difference and diversity as political problems. . . . The management of diversity and difference through the bureaucratic mantra of race, class and gender encouraged the divisive rhetoric of being more marginal, more oppressed and therefore more righteous than thou." Similarly, Michael Denning (1992, 38) argues that "race, class and gender are not the answers in cultural studies, the bottom line explanation to which all life may be reduced; they are precisely the problems posed—their history, their formation, their 'articulation' with particular historical events or artistic works." Peter McLaren (in this volume) concurs: "Educators need to do more than to help students redescribe or represent themselves in new ways." And Chandra Mohanty (in this volume) offers the beginnings of a way out of this dilemma: "The central issue, then, is not one of merely *acknowledging* difference; rather, the more difficult question concerns the kind of difference that is acknowledged and engaged."

The suggestion that there are different kinds of difference can lead us to recognize that there is a third sense of identity being proposed, unintentionally perhaps, in Hall's discourse of identity and difference.[14] Or perhaps it would be better to see it as a theory of agency—of identification and belonging (or in Hall's term, "ethnicity"). Here, difference itself, as much as identity, is an effect of power, of other social and cultural practices and processes (Said 1979). As Bailey and Hall (1992c, 21) write,

> Identities can, therefore, be contradictory and are always situational. . . .
> In short, we are all involved in a series of political games around fractured
> or decentered identities. . . . [S]ince black signifies a range of experiences,
> the act of representation becomes not just about decentering the subject
> but actually exploring the kaleidoscopic conditions of blackness.

The notion of the "kaleidoscopic conditions of blackness" suggests that identity is related to a distributive map of the social terrain. Similarly, Hall has recently redescribed the power and practice of racism in ways that suggest that difference itself is the product or effect of such distributive relations (1992b, 16):

> Contrary to the superficial evidence, there is nothing simple about the
> structure and dynamics of racism. . . . It is racism's very rigidity that is

due to its complexity. Its capacity to punctuate the universe into two great opposites masks something else; it masks the complexes of feelings and attitudes, beliefs and conceptions, that are always refusing to be so neatly stabilized and fixed. . . . All that symbolic and narrative energy and work is directed to secure us "over here" and them "over there," to fix each in its appointed species place. It is a way of masking how deeply our histories actually intertwine and interpenetrate; how necessary "the Other" is to our own sense of identity; how even the dominant, colonizing, imperializing power only knows who and what it is and can only experience the pleasure of its own power of domination in and through the construction of the Other.

This third model is built on a weak notion of difference (simply asserting that "X" is not the same as Y or Z) and a strong sense of otherness (which argues that each term exists somehow independently of its relationship to the other terms, that it has its own positivity which is not merely an excess). A strong sense of otherness recognizes that the other exists in its own place, independent of any *specific* relation. This sense of difference/otherness is more akin to Gilles Deleuze and Felix Guattari's (1987) notion of multiplicity, which they oppose to fragmentation since the latter still leaves the trace of totality and unity, the trace of "the one." Here we are talking about plural identities which are never fixed and never settle into a fixed pattern. Hall has on another occasion described this as the problem of citizenship (Hall and Held [1989], cited in Giroux in this volume): "the diverse communities to which we belong, the complex interplay of identity and identification in modern society, and the differentiated ways in which people participate in social life." And Kobena Mercer's (1992a, 33) description of "what was important" about the politics of race of the last decade, similarly points to such a politics of multiplicity, of identification and belonging: "that we actively constructed an elective community of belonging through a variety of practices."

This structure of agency or ethnicity involves a more explicitly spatial territorialization; it involves an organization of places and spaces, of people, practices, and commodities. It is in this sense that discourse is always placed, because people are always anchored or invested in specific sites. Hence, it matters how and where practices and people are placed, since the place determines from and to where one can speak (or act). Ethnicity involves lines of intensity which construct and map structures of mobility and placement; it describes where and how people can stop and locate themselves; such locations are temporary points of identification and belonging and orientation. Such sites define the possibilities of mobility and practice, of change and security. But the maps which describe the accessibility and distribution of such places, and the ability to connect different places, are never constructed solely out of the will of individuals or groups. They are themselves socially determined, the sites of struggles for power. The relations of ethnicity or agency are determined, not merely by ideological practices of representation, but also by affective practices of investment.

Some of the most important work in education has already begun to enter this terrain. Here I would mention not only bell hooks's call for an affective pedagogy, but Henry Giroux's concept (in this volume) of a critical pedagogy of representations which would explore "how students, teachers, and other cultural workers actively produce and mobilize their own desires within particular historical and social contexts as forms of identification and agency." Such a pedagogy examines how "representations work as desiring machines to secure particular forms of affective investment." Similarly, Peter McLaren (in this volume) calls for a pedagogy which would provide students with the opportunity "to devise different assemblages of the self," to develop "nomadic forms of individual and collective agency."

THE POLITICS OF EDUCATION

Finally, I want to consider some of the implications of cultural studies for questions of pedagogy. If we take seriously Michael Denning's (1992, 41) statement that "it is necessary that we begin to imagine cultural studies not simply as the critique of the disciplines [or, I might add, as simply another discipline] but as an alternative to the humanities themselves, a reformation of general education," then it has consequences, not only in terms of our objects of study and our aims, but also in terms of our practice. Cultural studies requires us to consider, not only pedagogy as a cultural practice, but the pedagogy of cultural practices. There is a double articulation here, which must always be located in the specific historical conjuncture and institutional context in which the articulations are both enabled and constrained.

It is responsible to identify three models of a progressive pedagogical practice. The first, a hierarchical practice, assumes that the teacher already understands the truth to be imparted to the student. Of course, sometimes such a practice is quite appropriate and can truly contribute to emancipatory struggles. But the problems with such a practice become more apparent when the teacher assumes that he or she understands the real meanings of particular texts and practices, the real relations of power embodied within them, and the real interests of the different social groups brought together in the classroom or in the broader society. Then it is the teacher who draws the line between the good, the bad, and the ugly, between the politically correct and the politically incorrect.

The second, a dialogic practice, aims to allow the silenced to speak; only when absolutely necessary does it claim to speak for them. But this assumes that they are not already speaking simply because we, the teachers, do not hear them, perhaps because they are not speaking the right languages or not saying what we would demand of them. Moreover, such a practice fails to see that there are often real material and social conditions that have disenabled people from speaking at particular places, in particular ways, at particular moments.

The third, a praxical pedagogy, attempts to offer people the skills that would enable them to understand and intervene into their own history. Hopefully, such skills would enable them to move beyond the realm of discursive struggles to challenge the institutional relations to power by connecting themselves up with "the broader struggles of communities to democratize and reconstruct the public sphere" (Fraser in this volume). The problem with this practice is not only that it assumes that people are not already trying to intervene into their own history but, more important, that it assumes that the teacher already understands the right skills which would enable emancipatory and transformative action, as if such skills were themselves not contextually determined. In my opinion, this is the problem with identifying an emancipatory pedagogy with the practice of reading texts in order to develop interpretive skills for the analysis of the construction of difference. To put it another way, such a pedagogy only gets half of cultural studies' practice right. It does grasp the fact that "theory is only a detour on the way to something more important" (Hall 1991, 42), but it fails to see that its political stakes as well must be context-specific. There are no universal skills which we can offer independent of the context into which we want to intervene, and, more important, into which our students want to intervene.

It seems to me that all three of these pedagogical strategies avoid the really difficult question: not of the elitism which all three continue to deploy, but of the possibility of an "earned elitism." It is too easy to say that the task of becoming critical is not something we can give to or perform for our students. But this does not mean that we as teachers can give up the need to construct positions of authority for ourselves, as teachers. We need to locate places from which we can construct and disseminate knowledge in relation to the materiality of power, conflict, and oppression. It is here then that we can return to the question of the specificity of the pedagogical in terms of "the politics and ethics of criticism" (Bailey and Hall 1992c, 21). Recognizing that pedagogies are themselves always institutionalized, placed, as it were, we must look into the social relations of discourse, into the ethics of enunciation and of the different possible enunciative positions, the places of authority we construct for ourselves and our students.

Here it may be useful to turn to a different formation of cultural studies, particularly strong in Australia, which sees particular cultural practices and formations as technologies of power, apparatuses that deploy power in organizing the relations between people, practices, and things.[15] In particular, the "technology of the humanities"—which was put into place as the modern formation of literary education and critical reading, and which also positioned the teacher as the intellectual and moral model (supposedly lived out in his or her ability to reconcile the contradictions of social existence such as reason versus the. will)—is, Ian Hunter (1988) argues, a central part of the machinery of modern power. It is part of a larger system of disciplinization which produces the "civil-ized" student or what Toby Miller (forthcoming), following Johann Sebastian Bach, has called the "well-tempered" or "well-tuned" subject. Unfortunately, this machinery is often reproduced in contemporary instantiations of cultural studies and even critical pedagogy. We can glean some further evidence of the too common complicity of pedagogical practices, even radical ones, with contemporary forms of power if we recognize that the distance which such practices often assume or demand (from the text at least) is really a demand for disinvestment, an indifference, a "refusal to invest oneself and take things seriously." This sense of difference is, of course, precisely what Pierre Bourdieu (1984) has described as the dominant aesthetic sensibility.

I want to suggest here the possibility of a fourth model of pedagogy, a pedagogy of articulation and risk. Such a practice, while refusing the traditional forms of intellectual authority, would not abandon claims to authority. Refusing to assume ahead of time that it knows the appropriate knowledge, language, or skills, it is a contextual practice which is willing to take the risk of making connections, drawing lines, mapping articulations, between different domains, discourses, and practices, to see what will work, both theoretically and politically. It employs the rhizomatic "methods" of Deleuze and Guattari, "the freaky method of experiment and collage" (Mercer 1992a, 37). Kobena Mercer (1992a, 38-39) describes such a practice as one which seeks not to "save the world" but, more modestly, to "multipl[y] connections between things that have [apparently] nothing to do with each other. . . . [R]hizomatic thinking invites research for routes out of the common predicaments we share here and now." Mercer sees this method as somehow more appropriate to the stakes of contemporary cultural and pedagogical struggles: it

> speaks to the conditions of exile and displacement . . . to conditions of
> homelessness and restlessness in terms of a renewed commitment to theory
> that is motivated by the desire to displace established orthodoxies; to keep
> on moving, from soul to soul, from station to station, on the dark side of
> the political imaginary. Diaspora is a doman of dissemination and dispersal,
> where seeds are scattered along diverse vectors and trajectories. (Mercer
> 1992a, 39)

This is an affective pedagogy, a pedagogy of possibilities (but every possibility has to risk failure) and of agency. It refuses to assume that either theory or politics, theoretical or political correctness, can be known in advance. It is a pedagogy which aims not to predefine its outcome (even in terms of some imagined value of emancipation or democracy) but to empower its students to begin to reconstruct their world in new ways, and to rearticulate their future in unimagined and perhaps even unimaginable ways. It is a pedagogy which demands of students, not that they conform to some image of political liberation nor even that they resist, but simply that they gain some understanding of their own involvement in the world, and in the making of their own future. Consequently, it neither starts with nor works within a set of texts but, rather, deals with the formations of the popular, the cartographies of taste, stability, and mobility within which students are located. It does not take for granted the context of specific cultural practices nor the terms within which they produce effects. It is a pedagogy which draws unexpected maps of the possibilities of and constraints on agency as it intersects with both everyday life and the social formation.[16]

Of course, such a pedagogy does not deny that the teacher must take responsibility for the production of knowledge in the classroom. But now, the teacher is no longer expected to provide an ethical model of authority but, rather, what Cameron McCarthy has called a model of thoughtfulness. This is obviously riskier, both pedagogically and politically. It offers a risky politics of risk, a politics of contextuality which attempts to offer new positions and forms of authority. (In that sense, it is as much a reconfiguration of the first practice described above as anything else.) It is also a practice which, I believe, constantly traverses the line between teaching and research, allowing them to rearticulate one another, opening knowledge up to new questions, spoken from elsewhere. It is here that our critical and pedagogical practice is inevitably transformed from a reflective and distant relation to both the subjects and objects of our authority to an active and passionate articulation. Such a pedagogy however can only be a politicizing engagement in the last instance, for it must leave the field of articulations as open as possible. And it is here as well that we will always encounter the limits of our claim to authority, at just the moment when the claim is legitimated.

This leads me to the question of our political intervention as teachers and of the aims of possibilities of pedagogy. I will approach this in terms of two final issues: the place of the popular in education and the articulation of a political vision in education. If political struggles are won and lost in the space between people's everyday lives and the material production and distribution of values and power, in the space where people and groups are articulated, both ideologically and affectively, to social identities, cultural practices, and political projects, then it is here that pedagogy must operate. The task of a politically engaged pedagogy is, after all, never to convince a predefined subject—whether empty or full, whether essential or fragmented—to adopt a new position. Rather, the task is to win an already positioned, already invested individual or group to a different set of places, a different organization of the space of possibilities.

If there are no guarantees in history, there can be no secure knowledge which predefines people's interests or the parameters of a progressive politics. If people are neither totally unaware nor totally passive in the face of their own interests, needs, and subordinations, they are not waiting to be told where and how to struggle. To repeat what I said earlier, people are not cultural dopes. After all, if they were, how could we teach them (other than through manipulation as grotesque as that which we claim to be struggling against)? But this is not to say that we must simply accept or celebrate where people are, their common sense, their sense of who they are, for that is precisely what the struggle over culture is about. On the other hand, if people are not being "duped," if their positions are not sometimes being articulated "behind their backs," there would be no need to teach them, to make them aware of their existence as both a stake and a possible agent in the struggle. Moreover, we must recognize that as teachers we are not separated from "the people," and our authority, while it may be temporarily and contextually legitimated, is always institutionally and discursively located. I might sum this up by saying that we must give up the too easy model of domination and resistance, built on a logic of either/or.

Cultural studies starts where people are but it does not assume that either they or we know the answers in advance. It is perhaps not surprising to hear echoes of Williams in Mostern's statement (in this volume) that

> the critical pedagogue is always someone who teaches from where the student is at, rather than from where the teacher is at. This does not mean that the teacher denies his or her pedagogical intentions or specific expertise, but merely that s/he respects the myriad expertise of the students that s/he does not share.

Such a pedagogy must go against the all too common tendency on the Left to propose alternative media or cultural practices to replace those in which students are already invested, inventing marginal and populist counterdiscourses. Instead, I would argue that the critical pedagogue must listen for the "stutterings," the unexpected dialects and misspeakings, the unpredicted articulations, within the hegemonic culture, which are capable of producing a minor and popular remapping (Deleuze and Guattari 1987), which may enable the mobilization of people's memories, fantasies, and desires, and redirect their investments in politics and the other.

Keeping this in mind, I think it is possible to see that the elitism of so much critical work is not defined by its theory or even by its esoteric vocabulary. People are uninterested, not because they can't do the work—in most cases, the so-called jargon is in the dictionary—but because they don't see any reason to; they don't care about the questions we ask. The elitism of intellectuals comes, not merely from our assumption that we already know the answers, but even more from our assumption that we already know the questions. It would, however, be too easy to assume that we simply need to ask our students what the questions are. We need to use our authority, mobilized through a pedagogy of risk and experimentation, to discover what the questions can be in the everyday lives of our students, and what political possibilities such questions open up. We have to be willing to enter the terrain of everyday life, the terrain of dispersed Others, in order to make sense of the realities of their (our) lives. Only then can we prize open already existing contradictions, "thereby renovating and making critical an already existing activity" (Gramsci 1971, 331).

But then it also follows that we cannot tell our students what ethics or politics— obviously the two are intimately connected although not identical—to embrace. Again, we must connect to the ethics and politics they already embrace and then struggle to rearticulate them to a different position (without necessarily knowing in advance that we will be successful, or even what that different position will actually be). At the same time, we must collectively articulate a common affective vision of a shared political future based on a politics of practice (what people do, what they invest in, where they belong) rather than on a politics of identity. This must go beyond the mere invocation of an ideal such as democracy; we must invoke and bear witness to the concrete meanings of such political values, and to the concrete possibilities of human life.[17]

If we are to imagine a different, a better, future, we need to consider the different ways people participate in social, cultural, economic, and political life. We need to recognize not only that these are related but that they are themselves the sites of struggle, that it is here, right here, in the practices of educators (in our practices) that, in part, hegemony is constructed. And it is for this reason that pedagogy must always remains a central and yet a modest site of struggle. For it is here, as teachers, that we can examine how people make history and articulate what history we would—collectively—hope to make.

NOTES

1. This introduction is a revision of my inaugural lecture of the Waterbury Forum for Education and Cultural Studies at Pennsylvania State University. I want to thank Henry Giroux for inviting me to give the lecture and to write this introductory lecture, and for his generous support and insightful comments.

2. A number of questionable appearances might be mentioned here. Both the conservative think tank Family Research Council and the corporatist East-West Center have recently appointed directors of cultural studies. More ambiguously, my friend and colleague Andrew Goodwin recently sent me a copy of his son's second-grade timetable, which includes a two-hour work period, every Wednesday, for cultural studies and grammar.

3. In *Politics and Letters* (Williams 1979, 78–83), Williams offers us a very specific example of such contextual thinking (particularly relevant to contemporary debates) drawn from his own extramural teaching. In the period between the two world wars, when he was teaching, there was a particularly heated split between the National Council of Labour Colleges (defending consciously affiliated socialist workers' education) and the Worker's Education Association (which argued that a distinct class affiliation "had to be mediated by a kind of education that made no presumptions," that explored all positions rather than teaching only the party line). While the former risked subordinating education to party politics, the latter risked incorporation, by accepting the academic standards of the universities to which its classes were attached. Here is Williams's personal response to this conflict: "I agreed that it would have been wholly wrong in class not to declare your position; and equally that you made no assumption at the beginning of the class that you shared anything else than an interest in the subject." He describes the danger of "teaching declining into a propaganda exercise." However, he quickly adds that "in fact increasingly through the 50s the dangers were the opposite."

4. There is, however, one noteworthy exception: In *Working Papers* no. 10 (1977), Dan Finn, Neil Grant, and Richard Johnson authored "Social Democracy, Education and the Crisis." This paper was revised and published in 1978 as an Occasional Paper. These three authors, together with Steven Baron and Michael Green, published *Unpopular Education* in 1981. Other Occasional Papers include: Merilyn Moos, "Government Youth Training Policy and Its Impact on Further Education" (1979); Brian Doyle, "Some Uses of English: Denys Thompson and the Development of English

in Secondary Schools" (1981); James Avis, "Curriculum Innovation in F.E.: A Case Study" (1983); and Mariette Clare, "Ideologies of Adult Literacy" (1985).

5. Although this literature is absent from *Working Papers,* the Occasional Papers include the following: Paul Willis, "Transition from School to Work Bibliography" (1973); Paul Willis, "The Main Reality: Transition School/Work: SSRC Report" (1975); Paul Willis, "How Working Class Kids Get Working Class Jobs," (1975). Also relevant is Janice Winship, "Women and Work Bibliography" (1978).

6. See, for example, Finn 1987 and Bates et al. 1984.

7. For a discussion of articulation, see Grossberg 1992, chapter 1.

8. Diawara's binary division of the terrain (abstract poststructuralism versus black cultural studies) is, however, inadequate, and his celebration of "the black studies strand of cultural studies" fails to acknowledge that much of this work not only also follows poststructuralism in its "fetishism of difference" (a term I borrow from Keya Ganguly), but also often underestimates the necessary contextuality of theory and of its political possibilities. As much as some writers looking at questions of, e.g., popular culture and hegemony fail to adequately contextualize their work, the same may be said of a certain proportion of those working in "black cultural studies." Some of this latter group, in fact, not only fail to recognize the gap between theories of difference and hybridity, they also ignore the contextual specificity of such notions as hybridity, fragmentation, and otherness.

9. In part, this misunderstanding is often the result of reducing cultural studies to a model of communication, as if articulation were the same as decoding. See Grossberg forthcoming.

10. This is the site of a significant theoretical debate within cultural studies, over two readings, as it were, of Foucault's notion of the positivity of discourse. On the one hand, there are those (generally following Ernesto Laclau) who see the outside, the real, as a constitutive and indeterminate other. On the other, there are those (generally following Deleuze and Guattari) who argue that the real is a contingent and effective configuration of material effects. A second dimension of this dispute concerns the theory of hegemony, which, according to Laclau, involves the organization of the social into a struggle between "the people" and the power bloc, a difference which is then mapped onto the cultural terrain as well. Deleuzeans tend to reject this binary model. See Grossberg 1992.

11. For a critique of interpretive practices, see Bennett 1990.

12. But, as Mohanty points out, this is not the fault of these intellectual and political formations themselves: "this process of individualization of histories of dominance is . . . characteristic of educational institutions and processes in general." Such programs then must often set themselves to fight against what Henry Giroux has called a pedagogy of normative pluralism. Where race and gender are treated in terms of personal or individual experiences, where individuals are treated as representatives of cultural groups, whatever legitimation is offered to traditionally subordinated groups "takes place purely at an attitudinal, interpersonal level rather than in terms of a fundamental challenge to hegemonic knowledge and history" (Mohanty in this volume).

13. See Giroux 1992 and Grossberg 1993. The critique of a view of identity as difference (negativity) must acknowledge the complex ways in which difference is figured in

such theories. Grossberg (1993) describes three such figures: fragmentation, hybridity, and differance.

14. The difference between a weak and a strong sense of otherness can be understood as reenacting the debate between Derrida and Foucault (Grossberg 1993). The failure to see this third sense may be partly explained by the different connotations and forces of the term "difference" in the U.S. and Britain. In the U.S., "difference" almost inevitably draws one into the discourses of poststructuralism. It is also worth pointing out that Hall (1992a) has also recently described three views of identity: the Enlightenment subject or a notion of essential identity; the sociological subject, based in symbolic interaction theory, which still predicates a unified and stable subject although it is constructed only in social relations; and the postmodern hybrid subject. Although Hall's triad does not correspond exactly to the distinctions offered here, I believe it points to the same conclusions.

15. See, e.g., Bennett 1992; the important work of the journal *Culture and Policy;* and the debate "Culture, Policy and Beyond" in *Meanjin* 51, no. 3 (Spring 1992).

16. See Grossberg 1992 for a more elaborate description of one approach to such a pedagogical project.

17. Consequently, I think it takes more work than we have often been willing to perform to define the real stakes of our pedagogical strategies. We cannot take for granted the affective and ideological resonances which appeals to values like "democracy" will have for our students. In the abstract, "democracy" is a useful basis for a critique of existing political relations, but it often remains vague and unspecified. While I don't want to deny the importance of an "educated and participatory democracy," I am uneasy about the wholesale adoption of "self-management" as a model for all of life, and of "collective decision making" as a solution to all problems. We not only need to rethink the meaning of democracy and the possibilities of its relocation from the domain of the state to that of culture, but even more we need to think about whether democracy is sufficient by itself, or whether there are in fact limits that have to be thought through in its relation to questions of liberty, justice, and other forms of equality. After all, even Laclau and Mouffe (1985, 189), the leading advocates of "democracy" as a central principle of struggle, suggest that "no hegemonic project can be based exclusively on a democratic logic, but must also consist of a set of proposals for the positive organization of the social."

WORKS CITED

Bailey, David, and Hall, Stuart, eds. (1992a). *Critical Decade: Black British Photography in the 80s.* Ten–8 2, no. 3 (spec. issue).

Bailey, David, and Hall, Stuart (1992b). "Critical Decade: An Introduction." In Bailey and Hall 1992a: 4–7.

Bailey, David, and Hall, Stuart (1992c). "The Vertigo of Displacement: Shifts within Black Documentary Practices." In Bailey and Hall 1992a: 15–23.

Bates, Inge; Clarke, John; Cohen, Philip; Finn, Dan; Moore, Robert; and Willis, Paul (1984). *Schooling for the Dole? The New Vocationalism.* London: Macmillan.

Bennett, Tony (1990). *Outside Literature.* New York: Routledge.

Bennett, Tony (1992). "Putting Policy into Cultural Studies." In Grossberg, Nelson, and Treichler 1992. 23–34.

Bourdieu, Pierre (1984). *Distinction: A Social Critique of the Judgement of Taste.* Trans. R. Nice. Cambridge: Harvard University.

Deleuze, Gilles, and Guattari, Felix (1987). *A Thousand Plateaus: Capitalism and Schizophrenia.* Trans. B. Massumi. Minneapolis: University of Minnesota.

Denning, Michael (1992). "The Academic Left and the Rise of Cultural Studies." *Radical History Review* 54:21–48.

Diawara, Manthia (1992). "Black Studies, Cultural Studies: Performative Acts." *Afterimage* 20:6–7.

Education Group, Centre for Contemporary Cultural Studies (1981). *Unpopular Education: Schooling and Social Democracy in England Since 1944.* London: Hutchinson.

Education Group II (1990). *Education Ltd.: Schooling, Training and the New Right in England Since 1979.* London: Routledge.

Finn, Dan (1987). *Training without Jobs: New Deals and Broken Promises.* London: Macmillan.

Frow, John, and Morris, Meaghan (forthcoming). Introduction. In Frow and Morris, eds, *Australian Cultural Studies: A Reader.*

Giroux, Henry A. (1992). *Border Crossings: Cultural Workers and the Politics of Education.* New York: Routledge.

Gramsci, Antonio (1971). *Selections from the Prison Notebooks.* Trans. Q. Hoare and G. Nowell Smith. New York: International Publishers.

Grossberg, Lawrence (1991). "From Media to Popular Culture: A Question of Pedagogy." *Metro* no. 86:20–26.

Grossberg, Lawrence (1992). *We Gotta Get Out of This Place: Popular Conservatism and Postmodern Culture.* New York: Routledge.

Grossberg, Lawrence (1993). "Cultural Studies and/in New Worlds." *Critical Studies in Mass Communication* 10:1–22.

Grossberg, Lawrence (forthcoming). "Can Cultural Studies Find True Happiness in Communication?" *Journal of Communication.*

Grossberg, Lawrence; Nelson, Cary; and Treichler, Paula, eds. (1992). *Cultural Studies.* New York: Routledge.

Hall, Stuart (1990). "The Emergence of Cultural Studies and the Crisis of the Humanities." *October* 53:11–23.

Hall, Stuart (1991a). "The Local and the Global: Globalization and Ethnicity." In King 1991:19–39.

Hall, Stuart (1991b). "Old and New Identities, Old and New Ethnicities." In King 1991:41–68.

Hall, Stuart (1992a). "The Question of Cultural Identity." In Hall, Stuart; Held, David; and McGrew, Tony, eds., *Modernity and its Futures.* Cambridge: Polity, 1992. 273–325.

Hall, Stuart (1992b). "Race, Culture and Communications: Looking Backward and Forward at Cultural Studies." *Rethinking Marxism* 5:10–18.

Hall, Stuart; Critcher, Charles; Jefferson, Tony; Clarke, John; and Roberts, Brian (1978). *Policing the Crisis: Mugging, the State, and Law and Order.* New York: Holmes and Meier.

Hall, Stuart, and Held, David (1989). "Citizens and Citizenship." In Stuart Hall and Martin Jacques, eds., *New Times: The Changing Face of Politics in the 1990s.* London: Lawrence and Wishart. 173–88.

Hebdige, Dick (1993). "The Machine Is *Unheimlich*: Krzysztof Wodiczko's Homeless Vehicle Project." *Cultural Studies* 7:173–223.

Henriques, Julian; Looway, Wendy; Urwin, Cathy; Venn, Couze; and Walkerdine, Valerie (1984). *Changing the Subject: Psychology, Social Regulation and Subjectivity.* London: Methuen.

Hunter, Ian (1988). *Culture and Government: The Emergence of Literary Education*. London: Macmillan.

King, Anthony, ed. (1991). *Culture Globalization and the World-System*. London: Macmillan.

Laclau, Ernesto, and Mouffe, Chantal (1985). *Hegemony and Socialist Strategy*. London: Verso.

Mercer, Kobena (1992a). "Back to My Routes: A Postscript to the 80s." In Bailey and Hall 1992a: 32–39.

Mercer, Kobena (1992b). " '1968': Periodizing Postmodern Politics and Identity." In Grossberg, Nelson, and Treichler 1992. 424–38.

Miller, Toby (forthcoming). *The Well-Tempered Self: Formations of the Cultural Subject*.

O'Connor, Alan (1989). "The Problem of American Cultural Studies." *Critical Studies in Mass Communication* 6:405–13.

Pfister, Joel (1991). "The Americanization of Cultural Studies." *Yale Journal of Criticism* 4:199–229.

Rooney, Ellen (1990). "Discipline and Vanish: Feminism, the Resistance to Theory, and the Politics of Cultural Studies." *Differences* 2:14–27.

Said, Edward W. (1979). *Orientalism*. New York: Vintage.

Williams, Raymond (1979). *Politics and Letters*. London: New Left Books.

Williams, Raymond (1989). "The Future of Cultural Studies." In Raymond Williams, *The Politics of Modernism: Against the New Conformists*. London: Verso.

Willis, Paul (1977). *Learning to Labour: How Working Class Kids Get Working Class Jobs*. Westmead: Saxon House.

Willis, Paul (1990). *Common Culture*. Boulder: Westview.

RACISM,

DEMOCRACY, AND

THE PEDAGOGY OF

REPRESENTATION

CHAPTER 1

LIVING DANGEROUSLY:

IDENTITY POLITICS

AND THE NEW

CULTURAL RACISM

HENRY A. GIROUX

THE CULT OF ETHNICITY AND ITS ZEAL-
OTS HAVE PUT AT STAKE THE AMERICAN TRADITION OF A SHARED COMMITMENT
TO COMMON IDEALS AND ITS REPUTATION FOR ASSIMILATION, FOR MAKING A
"NATION" OF NATIONS. —C. VAN WOODWARD, "EQUAL BUT SEPARATE"

AT THE END OF THE 20TH CENTURY, U.S.
SOCIETY IS BECOMING MORE RACIALLY AND ETHNICALLY DIVERSE; MORE POLAR-
IZED ALONG CLASS LINES; MORE ALARMED BY LESBIANS, GAY MEN, AND OTHER
SEXUAL MINORITIES; MORE CONSCIOUS OF GENDER DIFFERENCES; AND, AS A RE-
SULT, INCREASINGLY PREOCCUPIED WITH POLITICAL CONFLICT OVER ISSUES OF REP-
RESENTATION. —JEFF ESCOFFIER, "THE LIMITS OF MULTICULTURALISM"

LIVING DANGEROUSLY IN THE AGE OF IDENTITY POLITICS

As old borders and zones of cultural difference become more porous or eventually collapse, questions of culture increasingly become interlaced with the issues
of power, representation, and identity. Dominant cultural traditions once self-
confidently secure in the modernist discourse of progress, universalism, and ob-
jectivism are now interrogated as ideological beachheads used to police and contain
subordinate groups, oppositional discourses, and dissenting social movements.
Struggles over the academic canon, the conflict over multiculturalism, and the
battle for either extending or containing the rights of new social groups dominate

the current political and ideological landscape (Giroux 1992). What is at stake in these struggles far exceeds the particular interests that structure any one of them or the specific terrains in which they are subject to debate, whether they be the academy, the arts, schools, or other spheres of public life. Underlying the proliferation of these diverse and various battles is a deeper conflict over the relationship between democracy and culture on the one hand, and identity and the politics of representation on the other.

Central to this debate is an attempt to articulate the relationship among identity, culture, and democracy in a new way. For the Left, this has generally meant launching an assault on monumentalist views of Western culture, a one-dimensional Eurocentric academic canon, the autonomous subject as the sovereign source of truth, and forms of high culture which maintain sexist, racist, homophobic, and class-specific relations of domination. More specifically, the challenges raised by feminism, postmodernism, and postcolonialism have contributed to a redefinition of cultural politics that addresses representational practices in terms that analyze not only their discursive power to construct common sense, textual authority, and particular social and racial formations, but also the "institutional conditions which regulate different fields of culture" (Bennett 1992, 25). While many of the implications of such a cultural politics are still unclear, it has at the very least rendered visible, as Rita Felski (1989) points out, a number of important political/cultural projects. These include:

> the proliferation of information technologies and the gradual shift towards a postindustrial (although not postcapitalist) society, the declining authority of liberalism and Marxism as symptomatic of an increasing skepticism towards metanarratives, the reemergence of feminism and other social movements which have foregrounded difference and exposed the patriarchal, heterosexist, and ethnocentric nature of dominant Western ideals, an expanding aestheticization of everyday life through the mass dissemination of signs and images and a simultaneous questioning of the art/life opposition inherent in high modernism, a shift in philosophical and social theory towards linguistic paradigms accompanied by a sustained critique of foundationalist thought. (Felski 1989, 36).

The central challenge for educators and other cultural workers attempting to address these problems is to redefine the relationship between culture and politics in order to deepen and extend the basis for transformative and emancipatory practice. As part of such a challenge, the political side of culture must be given primacy as an act of resistance and transformation by addressing issues of difference, identity, and textuality within rather than outside of the problematics of power, agency, and history. The urgent issue here is to link the politics of culture to the practice of a substantive democracy (Giroux 1988). Stuart Hall and David Held (1990) foreground the importance of this task by arguing that any radical politics of representation and struggle must be situated within what they call "a contemporary politics of citizenship."

The value of such a politics is that it makes the complicated issue of difference fundamental to addressing the discourse of substantive citizenship; moreover, it favors looking at the conflict over relations of power, identity, and culture as central to a broader effort to advance the critical imperatives of a democratic society. Central to such a struggle is rethinking and rewriting difference in relation to wider questions of membership, community, and social responsibility.

> A contemporary "politics of citizenship" must take into account the role which the social movements have played in expanding the claims to rights and entitlements to new areas. [This means addressing] questions of membership posed by feminism, the black and ethnic movements, ecology and vulnerable minorities like children. But it must also come to terms with the problems posed by "difference" in a deeper sense: for example, the diverse communities to which we belong, the complex interplay of identity and identification in modern society, and the differentiated ways in which people now participate in social life. The diversity of arenas in which citizenship is being claimed and contested today is essential to any modern conception of it because it is inscribed in the very logic of modern society itself. (176)

Identity politics since the 1960s has played a significant role in refiguring a variety of human experiences within a discourse in which diverse political views, sexual orientations, races, ethnicities, and cultural differences are taken up in the struggle to construct counternarratives and create new critical spaces and social practices. Yet, the history of identity politics is not one that has moved unproblematically from resistance to a broader politics of democratic struggle. While identity politics was central to challenging the cultural homogeneity of the 1950s and providing spaces for marginal groups to assert the legacy and importance of their diverse voices and experiences, it often failed to move beyond a notion of difference structured in polarizing binarisms and an uncritical appeal to a discourse of authenticity. Identity politics enabled many formerly silenced and displaced groups to emerge from the margins of power and dominant culture to reassert and reclaim suppressed identities and experiences; but in doing so, they often substituted one master narrative for another, invoked a politics of separatism, and suppressed differences within their own "liberatory" narratives. Ellen Willis provides a severe but insightful critique of the theoretical and political dead end in which identity politics found itself in the 1970s and 1980s, and the legacy she believes must be challenged in the 1990s.

> The appeal of "identity politics" is that it arises from a radical insight— that domination is systematically structured into the relations between social groups. The problem is that [identity politics] gives rise to a logic that

chokes off radicalism and ends up by supporting domination. If the present obsession with group identity as the basis of politics is hard to imagine, much less build, a broad-based radical collectivity, it has even more tellingly stood in the way of a principled commitment to the freedom and happiness of individuals, without which no genuine radicalism is possible. (Willis 1991, 58)

Despite the moralism, anti-intellectualism, and suspect romanticization of authentic experience associated with issues of identity politics, these issues have begun to occupy the center of academic and popular debates around concerns regarding culture, difference, and democratic renewal. Moreover, identity politics is no longer simply a one-dimensional, discursive feature of left-wing theory and practice. At the same time, the radical possibilities associated with the link between democracy and the politics of cultural difference have not been lost on the New Right in the United States. In what has turned into a cultural blitz, the New Right of the Reagan/Bush era has continuously chipped away at the legal, institutional, and ideological spheres necessary to the existence of a democratic society. During the last decade, conservatives have rolled back civil rights legislation, waged antitpor-nography campaigns against the arts in order to eliminate public funding for "politically offensive" groups, and attempted to replace state provision and public service with privatization programs designed to expand the power of capital, individual competitiveness, and corporate freedom (Giroux 1992). One result has been the salvaging of funds for public schools, health care programs, and an overall assault on the most basic presumptions of democratic life (Kozol 1991).

Central to the new conservative offensive has been a renewed interest in addressing the radical politics that inform recent developments in the emerging discourses on culture and democracy. In particular, the New Right has focused on postmodernist, feminist, postcolonialist and other minority discourses that have raised serious questions regarding how particular forms of authority are secured through the organization of the curriculum at all levels of schooling. The radical call to reclaim the legacy of substantive democracy by reappropriating the language of equality, justice, and cultural difference has not been lost on conservative ideologues and public intellectuals. For example, Samuel Lipman (1989), writing in *the New Criterion,* argues that

culture and democracy cannot co-exist, for democracy by its nature represents the many, and culture, by its nature is created by the few. What the many cannot immediately comprehend, they destroy. . . . What is necessary are definitions of culture and democracy based . . . less on inclusions and more on exclusions, less on finding similarities between conflicting realities, concepts, and goals and more on recognizing the differences between them. (15–16)

Lipman is not alone in viewing the extension of democratic ideology and political representation as a serious threat to dominant configurations of power and control. Conservative columnist and former presidential hopeful Patrick Buchanan openly embraces an authoritarian populism which views cultural democracy as a threat to the "American way of life." What is interesting for our purposes is the way in which Buchanan embraces the language of difference. For Buchanan, the reality of cultural difference, with its plurality of languages, experiences, and histories, poses a serious threat to both national unity and what he defends as Judeo-Christian values. According to Buchanan, calls for expanding the existing limits of political representation and self-determination are fine as long as they allow Americans to "take back" their country. In this conservative discourse, difference becomes a signifier for racial exclusivity, segregation, or, in Buchanan's language, "self-determination." For Buchanan, public life in the United States has deteriorated since 1965 because "a flood tide of immigration has rolled in from the Third World, legal and illegal, as our institutions of assimilation . . . disintegrated." Rewriting the discourse of nativism, Buchanan asks: "Who speaks for the Euro-Americans? Is it not time to take America back?" (quoted in Krauthammer 1990, A4).

Similarly, right-wing whites in America now echo a view of difference not as a marker for racial superiority but as a signifier for cultural containment, homogeneity, and social and structural inequality. The appeal is no longer to racial supremacy but to cultural uniformity parading under the politics of nationalism and patriotism. In this case, difference is removed from the language of biologism and firmly established as a cultural construct only to be reworked within a hegemonic project that connects race and nation against the elimination of structural and cultural inequality. In the same spirit of displaying difference in order to displace it within a hegemonic project of national unity, Frank Kermode, writing in *the New York Times*, dismisses some of the more articulate advocates of a progressive politics of difference as "a noisy crowd of antihomophobes, antiracists and antiwhites" (Kermode 1992, 33). This is a remarkable statement that conjures up the specter of race as an ideological signpost for an assault on whites. Race in this context is invoked not to eliminate differences but to preserve them within self-contained cultural and social borders that prevent either crossing borders or forging new identities within new spaces or spheres of cultural difference. Of course, the Los Angeles uprising at the end of April 1992 not only ruptures the legitimacy of the new racial politics of containment, it also reveals how liberal and conservative discourses become complicitous with the underlying conditions that created the uprising by refusing to link race and class, by refusing to recognize that racism in the United States is deeply embedded in a politics of social, economic, and class divisions.

Renato Rosaldo (1989) focuses on the issue in arguing that "questions of culture seem to touch a nerve because they quickly become anguished questions of identity" (ix). The struggles emerging over "anguished questions of identity" have taken a new turn in the last decade. The "culture wars" that have beset American politics since the advent of the Reagan/Bush reign have become increasingly dominated by a politics of representation rooted in an authoritarian populist discourse that is powerfully refiguring the relationship between identity and culture, particularly as it is addressed in the discourse of racial difference.

There is a certain irony in the fact that at this current historical conjuncture, when many left critics appear to be fed up with identity politics, conservatives have seized upon it with a vengeance.[1] Writing in *Tikkun* magazine, left social critic Ilene Philipson reduces identity politics to the discourse of anxiety, alienation, and inadequacy. In this view, attempts on the part of various social groups to combat racism, homophobia, or sexism are overly determined by psychological concerns with self-identity, self-esteem, and anomie. Philipson makes the point succinctly:

> Identity politics provides a way of avoiding self-blame for feelings of power-lessness and anomie that are, at their root, politically and socially constructed. But as such, the politics of identity inevitably misdirects our attention away from the fact that, apart from a tiny group at the top of the class hierarchy (to use a forgotten term), alienation, a sense of not being recognized for who one is, and feelings of impotence and failure affect us all—certainly to different degrees and with different repercussions. . . . [I]dentity politics is not sufficiently radical to speak to this distress, to get at the root sources of our alienation and individually experienced lack of social recognition. (1991, 54)

Philipson's reductionism is disturbing. Identity politics covers a complex and diverse terrain of theoretical positions and discourses concerned with questions of subjectivity, culture, difference, and struggle. In its hard and soft versions, this terrain extends from the cultural politics of black nationalists like Louis Farrakhan to the more radically progressive discourses of ethnicity and cultural difference in the works of Stuart Hall and Homi K. Bhabha. But there is more at stake here than a species of theoretical carelessness on the part of left critics who simply dismiss identity politics as separatist, elitist, and reactionary; there is also the politically shortsighted willingness to abandon identity politics at a time when right-wing conservatives are reappropriating progressive critiques of race, ethnicity, and identity and using them to promote rather than dispel a politics of cultural racism. This is a serious mistake. While the end of identity politics is something that left critics and cultural workers seem to be endlessly debating, they do not appear to have fully come to grips with its political and racial consequences. As Stuart Clarke (1991) points out, the issue of identity politics will not go away in the 1990s. Identity politics has become one of the more powerful commonsense constructions developed by the right wing in its attempt to "blunt progressive political possibilities. . . . [by privileging] race as a sign of social disorder and civic decay" (Clarke 1991, 37).

Rather than merely dismissing identity politics, left cultural workers need to engage the issue more dialectically. In this case, a critical perspective on identity politics should be seen as fundamental to any discourse or social movement that believes in the radical renewal of democratic society. With this qualification in mind, the relationship between identity and politics can be reformulated within a politics of representation which is open to contingency, difference, and self-reflexivity but still able to engage in a hegemonic project that reconstructs public life through a politics of democratic solidarity. Not to do so is to place left social movements and cultural workers outside rather than inside of the public debate about identity, difference, and culture. Stuart Clarke puts it well:

> The point of this is to indicate that the complex, even contradictory, character of identity politics must be accounted for in efforts to develop a politically effective critical perspective. Identity politics will remain a persistent feature of our political landscape in part because it produces limited but real empowerment for its participants. (1991, 46)

In part, Clarke's concern is legitimated by the ideological shift that has taken place among cultural conservatives in the last few years. With the advent of the assault by a wide range of conservative groups on "political correctness," multiculturalism, and radical intellectuals in the academy, identity politics has replaced the Cold War signifier of "communism" as the most serious domestic threat to the New World Order.[2] Moreover, in response to this threat, pedagogy and the issue of cultural representation have become strategic forces used by the New Right and other conservative groups in mobilizing an authoritarian populist movement. Three important issues are at stake here. First, the New Right has developed a powerful new strategy for abstracting cultural difference from the discourse of democracy and social justice. Central to such a discourse is the attempt to fuse culture within a tidy formation that equates the nation, citizenship, and patriotism with a racially exclusive notion of difference. Second, it is crucial to recognize that conservatives have given enormous prominence to waging a cultural struggle over the control and use of the popular media and other spheres of representation in order to "articulate contemporary racial meanings and identities in new ways, to link race with more comprehensive political and cultural agendas, to interpret social structural phenomena (such as inequality or social policy) with regard to race" (Winant 1990; 125). Third, it is imperative that the Left not only construct a new politics of difference but extend and deepen the possibilities of critical cultural work by reasserting the primacy of the pedagogical as a form of cultural politics.

In what follows, I will analyze more specifically the ideological contours of the old and new politics of difference. I will then analyze how the some of the basic assumptions of the new politics of difference are used in the film *Grand Canyon* to refigure dominant social and racial identities. I will conclude by considering the implications the above discussion has for a critical pedagogy of representation. In doing so, I will stress the importance of reworking the relationship between cultural workers and pedagogy as part of a broader politics of representation, political practice, and emancipatory change.

REPRESENTATION, DIFFERENCE, AND THE NEW POLITICS OF RACE

THE CULTURALISM OF THE NEW RACISM HAS GONE HAND IN HAND WITH A DEFINITION OF RACE AS A MATTER OF DIFFERENCE RATHER THAN A QUESTION OF HIERARCHY. IN ANOTHER CONTEXT [FRANTZ] FANON REFERS TO A SIMILAR SHIFT AS A PROGRESSION FROM VULGAR TO CULTURAL RACISM. . . . CULTURE IS CONCEIVED ALONG ETHNICALLY ABSOLUTE LINES, NOT AS SOMETHING INTRINSICALLY FLUID, CHANGING, UNSTABLE, AND DYNAMIC, BUT AS A FIXED PROPERTY OF SOCIAL GROUPS RATHER THAN A RELATIONAL FIELD IN WHICH THEY ENCOUNTER ONE ANOTHER AND LIVE OUT SOCIAL, HISTORICAL RELATIONSHIPS. WHEN CULTURE IS BROUGHT INTO CONTACT WITH RACE IT IS TRANSFORMED INTO A PSEUDOBIOLOGICAL PROPERTY OF COMMUNAL LIFE. — PAUL GILROY, "ONE NATION UNDER A GROOVE"

· ·

The old racism developed within the historical legacy of colonialism and modern slavery and rested on a blatant ideological appeal to pseudobiological and scientific theories of racism to justify inequality, hierarchies, and exploitation as part of the universal order. In this racism, the Other's identity warrants its very annihilation because it is seen as impure, evil, and inferior. Moreover, whiteness represents itself as a universal marker for being civilized and in doing so posits the Other within the language of pathology, fear, madness, and degeneration (Gilman 1985).

Within dominant regimes of representation, the old racism trades in classic stereotypes, grounds Otherness in fixed, transhistorical and cultural categories, and refuses to address the structural and ideological foundations of racist cultural practices (Goldberg 1990). Racist ideology in this case collapses the meaning of being the Other into the representation of Otherness.[3] In its various forms, there is little effort to make inequality, racism, or powerlessness problematic, open to discussion—in other words, this is a racism that refuses to critically engage in ethical and political terms its own privileged site of enunciation. It is the racism of *The Birth of a Nation,* the black exploitation films of the 1960s, the school textbooks filled with grotesque stereotypes of blacks. It is a racist practice that offers no apologies and focuses on how one inhabits dominant representations/ beliefs rather than on the beliefs themselves as the basis for constructing common sense. In the words of Stuart Hall (1988), the old racism is organized through the epistemic discourse of the violence of the Other. Based on fear and desire, the old racism attempts to construct blacks as the object rather the subject of representation—a process that allows whiteness to remain unproblematic even as it projects onto the black subject its own fantasies of noble primitiveness and reckless violence. The old racism "operates by constructing impassable symbolic boundaries between racially constituted categories, and its typically binary system of representation constantly marks and attempts to fix and naturalize the difference between belong-ingness and Otherness"(Hall 1988, 28).

We are now witnessing in the United States (and in Europe) the emergence of a new racism and politics of cultural difference expressed both in the reconfigura-tion of the relationship between Otherness and difference, on the one hand, and meaning and the politics of representation on the other (Winant 1990; Policar 1990; Taguieff 1990; Clarke 1991). Underlying the emergence of the new politics of racism and difference is a deep ambivalence on the part of liberals and conserva-tives about the traditional categories that have been used to defend racist practices. Identifications grounded in the racial superiority of whites, the fixing of Anglo-European culture as synonymous with civilization itself, and the civilizing mission of patriarchal, Eurocentric discourse are no longer easily maintained within main-stream ideologies and regimes of representation. The new social movements of the 1960s, the reception of feminist, postmodernist, and postcolonialist discourses in the 1970s, the development of critical popular cultural forms in the 1980s, and the rise of the new ethnicities with their challenge to liberal pluralism in the 1990s, have necessitated a new politics of difference and representation of racial politics on the part of both the Left and the New Right (West 1990). As American life becomes more hybridized, the distinctions between what Emily Hicks (1991) calls "original and alien cultures" have become more difficult to maintain theoretically and politically. As new cultural boundaries and spaces emerge crisscrossed with a diversity of Otherness, dominant strategies of representation are abrogated and struggled over through an ongoing process of negotiation, translation, and transfor-mation. The sensibility that informs the relationship between cultural borders reorders the codes of reference for engaging cultural differences and their related networks of hierarchy, power, and struggle.

With these qualifications in mind, any analysis of the new cultural politics of difference and race must acknowledge the shift in the "dominant regimes of representation" (Hall 1988) around race and multiculturalism that has occurred in the national and popular press within the last few years. In theoretical terms, this points to a proliferation of competing discourses that not only challenge the old vocabulary on race but also expand the sites from which notions of whiteness and blackness, among others, are made visible, rewritten, and circulated. At the same time, since there is no longer any single articulating principle defining the racial dimensions of cultural work and life, the audiences which are the subject and object of racial enunciations have become more complex, contradictory, and multilayered. On one level this has led to what Stuart Hall (1988, 1991) calls the end of the innocent black subject. At stake here is the recognition that " 'black' is essentially a politically and culturally constructed category, which cannot be grounded in a set of fixed trans-cultural or transcendental racial categories and which therefore has no guarantees in Nature" (Hall 1988, 28). Hence, issues of being black are abstracted from the language of essentialism and scientism and shifted to the terrain of representation. As Hall puts it, "The end of the essential black subject . . . entails a recognition that the central issues of race always appear historically in articulation, in a formation, with other categories and divisions and are constantly crossed and recrossed by the categories of class, of gender, and ethnicity" (1988, 28).

Within this discourse the relationship between identity and being "black" is no longer fixed, static, or secure. Hall's position offers cultural workers new opportunities to rewrite the politics of representation around race and difference by deconstructing in historical and relational terms not only the central categories of "Otherness," but also the dominant discourses and representations that secure "whiteness" as a universalizing norm (Young 1990; Dyer 1988; hooks 1990). At stake here is the need to create a new political vocabulary and project for rethinking a politics of cultural difference predicated on broader conceptions of race and identity. In this case, cultural workers need to construct a notion of border identity that challenges any essentialized notion of subjectivity while simultaneously demonstrating that the self as a historical and cultural formation is shaped in complex, related, and multiple ways through its interaction with numerous and diverse communities (Fraser 1992). Needless to say, such a project has and does pose a serious threat to the hegemonic politics of race and representation practiced by Reagan/Bush conservatives. The challenge has not been lost on the New Right.

Whereas the Bush era began with the image of Willie Horton and the implication that black criminality offered the principal signifier to underscore the cultural concerns of racism, the new cultural racism has shifted the emphasis from a notion of difference equated with deviance and cultural deprivation to a position that acknowledges racial diversity only to proclaim that different racial formations, ethnicities, and cultures pose a threat to national unity. Racial privilege is no longer maintained primarily through the use of terror or other traditional neofascist techniques. The struggle for racial privilege based on an implicit model of white supremacy or cultural nationalism takes many forms among conservatives and right-wing liberals, but underlying all of these efforts is an attempt to "rearticulate racial meanings, to reinterpret the content of 'whiteness' and the politics that flows from it" (Winant 1990, 126). One instance of this hegemonic project is a politics of representation that suggests that whites are the victims of racial inequality. In this discourse the social gravity of poverty, economic exploitation, and class divisions is removed from any analysis of race. The strategy for such a politics gathered a powerful momentum during the Reagan era with the practice of "coding" racial meanings so as to mobilize white fears. Hence, the use of terms such as quotas, busing, welfare, and multiculturalism as signifiers to arouse the insecurities and anger of whites. Another instance of the new politics of racism is expressed in displaying racial difference as a significant aspect of American life, but doing so only to pose it as a threat that has to be overcome. This strategy became particularly clear in the aftermath of the Los Angeles uprising. The dominant press repeatedly labeled the uprising as a riot, and consistently referred to the events that took place as acts of lawlessness. In this case, the politics of the new racism revealed itself shamelessly in the Bush administration's efforts to respond to the L.A. uprising by claiming that it was caused by the failed liberal social programs inaugurated by President Lyndon Johnson in the 1960s. What is really under assault here are not the social, economic, and political conditions that made the uprising possible, but the Voting Rights Act of 1965, and various programs that launched Aid to Families with Dependent Children, Head Start, Chapter 1, Food Stamps, and other public reform efforts. The most disgraceful response to the uprising, one which fully embodied the sentiments of the new racism, came from the *National Review,* which claimed that the main lesson of the insurrections was that law-abiding people (read whites) need more police to protect themselves, and that the real cause of the uprising was "bitterness nursed by many blacks [which] is largely the bequest of people like Reverend Jackson and Representative Waters, who have a stake in fomenting divisive race-consciousness" (Johnson 1992, 17).

Surprisingly, these two strategies are not fundamentally at odds with each other. In the first instance, conservatives invoke racial separation in order to mobilize white fears and to organize a constituency for implementing mainstream policy initiatives. In the second instance, racial difference is attacked as something to be overcome. In this discourse, whiteness as a signifier of power and privilege becomes the unspoken referent for naming and passing judgment on the continuing efforts of radicals, minorities, and others to organize around racial and class differences in pressing for political, educational, cultural, and social reforms. Evoking the racially coded language and images of national unity, conservative groups have attempted to dismantle the progressive elements of racial politics by advocating standardized testing in the public schools, attacking multiculturalism as a threat to a "common culture," and deploying cultural pluralism as a slogan which displays difference without mentioning dominant relations of power and class oppression. Winant (1990) argues that the new racial politics of the New Right and Neoconservatism articulate with a wider cultural and political agenda that resists any policy which threatens "the fundamentally integrative, if not assimilationist, character of the 'American ethnic pattern,' market rationality, anti-statism, the merits of individualism, and respect for the 'high culture' of the West" (Winant 1990, 132).

In what follows, I want to analyze the film *Grand Canyon* in order to illustrate how the new politics of difference and race is being constructed within a Hollywood version of identity politics. This analysis is intended to examine how a representational politics actively marks its subjects through racially coded forms of address and enunciation in which subject positions are made available and desires mobilized and where "spectacles of identity politics interact with the construction of common sense" (Clarke 1991, 47). In the last section of the essay, I will develop some central elements of a pedagogy of representation that offers possibilities for developing a decolonizing educational practice in which the act of representing can be addressed historically and semiotically as a part of an emancipatory attempt to situate relations between the self and others within a broader struggle for a more just and democratic society.

NEW AGE WHITENESS AND THE POLITICS OF DIFFERENCE

> **A**MERICA'S SENSE OF ITS OWN "RADICAL
> INNOCENCE" HAS ITS MOST PROFOUND ORIGINS IN [THE] BELIEF THAT THERE IS A
> BASIC HUMANITY UNALTERED BY THE DIVERSITY OF THE CITIZENS WHO SHARE
> IN IT. DEMOCRACY IS THE UNIVERSAL QUANTIFIER BY WHICH AMERICA—THE
> "MELTING POT," THE "NATION OF IMMIGRANTS"—CONSTITUTES ITSELF AS A NA-
> TION. IF *ALL* OUR CITIZENS CAN BE SAID TO BE AMERICANS, THIS IS NOT BECAUSE
> WE SHARE ANY POSITIVE CHARACTERISTICS, BUT RATHER BECAUSE WE HAVE ALL
> BEEN GIVEN THE RIGHT TO *SHED* THESE CHARACTERISTICS, TO PRESENT OURSELVES
> AS DISEMBODIED BEFORE THE LAW. I DIVEST MYSELF OF MY POSITIVE IDENTITY,
> THEREFORE I AM A CITIZEN. —JOAN COPJEC, "THE UNVERMOGENDER OTHER"

· ·

As we move into an age in which cultural space becomes unfixed, unsettled, porous, and hybrid, it becomes increasingly difficult either to defend notions of singular identity or to deny that different groups, communities, and people are increasingly bound to each other in a myriad of complex relationships. Modes of representation that legitimated a world of strict cultural separation, collective identities, and rigid boundaries seem hopelessly outdated as the urban landscape is being rewritten within new and shifting borders of identity, race, and ethnicity. New cultural spaces, borderlands, identities, texts, and crossings have created some-thing of a panic among those groups who control dominant regimes of representa-tion. Whereas in the past, the response to racial inequality was to pretend it didn't exist, the current reaction is to re-present it without changing the social, economic, and political conditions that create it. Indifference and silence, or even worse, an appeal to outright racial supremacy, have reluctantly given way to forms of negotia-tion and translation as varied ethnicities, races, and cultural differences assert them-selves both within and between diverse communities. Dominant society no longer resorts to exterminating or silencing Others; nor can it simply erase them. Cultural difference has descended on America like a fog. Dominant groups are now driving very carefully through a cultural terrain in which whiteness can no longer remain invisible as a racial, political, and historical construction. The privilege and practices of domination that underscore being white in America can no longer remain invisible through either an appeal to a universal norm or a refusal to explore how whiteness works to produce forms of "friendly" colonialism.[4]

Los Angeles seems to exemplify the changing nature of the metropolitan urban terrain and the cultural politics that appear to besiege it.[5] The hybridized cultural landscape of Los Angeles has been mythologized in Dennis Hopper's depiction of gang life in *Colors,* rendered as a borderland where cyborgs and humans rewrite the meaning of identity and difference in Ridley Scott's *Bladerunner,* and brilliantly taken up through the complex relations that constitute the coming of age experi-ences of mostly black young men in a neighborhood in South Central Los Angeles in John Singleton's *Boyz N the Hood*. In all of these films, Los Angeles is portrayed against a gritty reality in which cultural differences produce a borderland where an apocalyptic vision of the future is played out amid growing forms of daily violence, resistance, fear, and struggle. Difference in these films is neither innocent nor removed from wider social and political articulations.

In *Grand Canyon,* directed by Lawrence Kasdan, Los Angeles once again becomes a prophetic site for understanding how the language and relations of cultural differences are reshaping public culture in the happy boutique neighborhoods of the rich and the privileged. As in the films mentioned above, Los Angeles becomes an important signifier in order to comment about fear, violence, and racial politics as they are rewritten within the changing understanding of Otherness and the growing self-consciousness of what it means to be white in America. What is interesting about *Grand Canyon* is that it goes beyond the empty pluralism that always racializes the Other but never makes whiteness visible. In fact, Kasdan presents a narrative in which whiteness becomes the major referent for defining and acknowledging the responsibility that whites have in a world in which they define themselves as racially and culturally under siege.

Grand Canyon embodies the reactionary side of identity politics, but it does not echo the shrill fanaticism of a Pat Buchanan, Jesse Helms or Pat Robertson. Instead, it mobilizes the fears and desires of white folks who recognize that cultural differences are here to stay but don't want to be positioned so as to call their own racism or complicity with economic, social, and political inequalities into question. The central white characters in Kasdan's film want to exercise good conscience, retain their property values, and still be able to jog without being mugged. Their racism is more subtle, clean, and New Age. Racial Otherness represents a pragmatic rather than an ethical dilemma for them. Border crossings become an excuse for acknowledging the collapse of public life without having to take responsibility for it.

Kasdan's *Grand Canyon* attempts to erase the problem and politics of representation by refusing to portray the complexity of social, political, and cultural forces that structure relationships between whites and blacks on the one hand and men and women on the other. But it is important to note, particularly with regard to white/black relations, that Kasdan does not rely on traditional modes of representation. That is, he does not resort to addressing the issue of cultural difference by simply including the Other in the script. He does not attempt to secure filmic legitimacy simply by covering the story and including the requisite number of blacks. On the contrary, Kasdan is more vigilant and intent on rewriting and reimaging how Otherness is presented in ways that don't "permit or make for interventions on the part of those (Others) represented" (Mariani and Crary 1990, 97). In this case, Kasdan's view of racial conflict, poverty, sexism, and public life is defined within a monolithic notion of whiteness which fails to question the place of white racism as a historical and social construction. Consequently, Kasdan provides a celluloid mapping of racial conflict and cultural differences that are resolved in a dystopian politics that subordinates human agency to the grand forces of nature and allows whites to feel good about themselves while simultaneously absolving them of any responsibility in either constructing or maintaining those ideological and structural forces that privilege agency for some groups and greatly limit it for others. Goodwill and choice combine in this film to create a New Age sense of possibility which in the final analysis collapses irreducible differences among blacks, whites, and women into the airy recognition that we are all secondary to the larger natural forces of good and evil that shape the planet and thus provide a common ground on which to recognize how goodness can flow out of despair, how agency is limited by nature, and how ethics is powerless against nature's unfolding.

What is missed in Kasdan's New Age ideology, as Michael Dyson (1991) points out in a different context, is "how choice itself is not a property of autonomous moral agents acting in an existential vacuum, but rather something that is created and exercised within the interaction of social, psychic, political, and economic forces of everyday experiences" (75). Of course, it could be argued, since Kasdan refuses in *Grand Canyon* to disrupt the ideological, textual, and structural codes that inform race relations in this country, that his approach simply reflects the traditional colonial policy of reinscribing potentially disruptive social relations in order to contain them. But where Kasdan takes a different theoretical and political twist is in his attempt to produce forms of cultural self-representation in which whites are simultaneously portrayed as both the victims of cultural change and the only gatekeepers of a society which appears to be on the verge of self-destruction. In this form of cultural representation, radical innocence becomes the signifier for a hegemonic practice that colonizes the normal through a notion of common sense in which race, inequality, and power are eventually erased in a New Age vision of goodwill where luck and chance rather than struggle and agency police the present and predict the future. Though willing to admit that the landscape of cultural difference has radically changed in America in the last twenty years, Kasdan presents his audiences with a hegemonic notion of cultural "innocence" in which it is argued that there "still exists a precious, universal, 'innocent' instance in which we can all recognize ourselves" (Copjec 1991, 30).

ENCOUNTERS WITH OTHERNESS

HISTORICALLY-SPEAKING, EVERY COMMUNITY HAS FELT FORCED TO ACCEPT CHANGE, TO AT LEAST COME TO TERMS WITH OTHER COMMUNITIES. THE QUESTION IS, WHEN DO COMMUNITIES BECOME FROZEN? WHEN DO THEY SAY THAT THEY WILL NOT CHANGE ANY MORE? I THINK THAT HAPPENS WHEN THEY FEEL BESIEGED, THREATENED, WHEN NO SPACE IS LEFT FOR THEM TO GROW. —HOMI BHABHA AND BHIKHU PAREKH, "IDENTITIES ON PARADE"

Grand Canyon is most importantly about whites becoming self-conscious of race and Otherness as central determinants in shaping the existing social, political, and cultural landscape, but also in providing a referent for a new politics and form of ethical address. This referent combines for whites the opportunity to acknowledge this new landscape without having to give up their power or privilege. At the heart of the story is an attempt to define what being white, male, and privileged means when the encounter with the harsh colonial terrain of American society can no longer be avoided by the rich and the powerful. *Grand Canyon* attempts to mediate the traditional white phobia of race mixing through the liberal assertion of the right to be different. Couched in the discourse of pluralism, this particular notion of cultural difference presents whiteness "more as a case of historical acci- dent, rather than a characteristic cultural/historical construction, achieved through white domination" (Dyer 1988, 46). Whiteness as a category is rendered invisible as a symbol of ethnicity, while simultaneously avowed as a major category to normalize definitions of class, race, gender, heterosexuality, and nationality (Lloyd 1992). Similarly, *Grand Canyon* does not address cultural differences by acknowledg- ing the wider grid of social relations marked by existing systems of inequality and discrimination. Hence, there is no sense in this film of how "different groups are related to each other within networks of hierarchy and exploitation" (Welch 1989, 128). Understood in these terms, the film attempts first to renegotiate the possibilities for whites to acknowledge those Others who have been marginalized in American society less as human beings caught in the vice of oppression and exploitation than as a threat to a unitary sense of white identity and national unity. Second, *Grand Canyon* attempts to develop an articulation between unity and difference that reinforces whiteness as a discourse, referent, and practice of power. Third, the film uses racism as the basis for white self-criticism but in doing so is silent about the mutuality of responsibility between whites and blacks in addressing issues of ethnicity and social change. These points can be more fully developed by analyzing how the overarching narrative that structures *Grand Canyon* is organized around three different sets of relations: the social divisions between whites and blacks; the relationship between men and women; and the relationship between human beings and nature.

Black and white relationships are primarily developed between the encounter that Mack (Kevin Kline), a wealthy immigration lawyer, has with Simon (Danny Glover), a mechanic who virtually saves Mack from being assaulted by a black gang after he gets lost while driving home from a Lakers basketball game. The context of the meeting is central to the relationship.

In order to avoid heavy traffic after the game, Mack tries taking a shortcut and drives into a black neighborhood that immediately appears to be both alien and menacing. Difference looms up before Mack as strange, unfamiliar, and ominous. As Mack drives along the streets of the neighborhood with its boarded-up houses, numerous liquor stores, and mix of homeless, poor, and roaming youth, he hears the sound of rap music exploding all around him. A car drives by filled with four black youths who wave menacingly to him. Suddenly, his new Lexus dies and he is trapped in a zone of difference coded with racial fear and danger. He uses his car phone to call for a tow truck, but the phone stops working and he is forced to leave the safety of his Lexus and use a public phone. His fear at this point rises to the point of desperation. He tells the tow truck dispatcher that if a driver doesn't show up soon he may lose his life and not just his car. His fear has reached the point of desperation, and he races back to his car to wait for the tow truck. Within minutes, the car playing the rap music, surely a signifier of danger to the yuppie lawyer, pulls up behind Mack's Lexus. Four young men get out of the car and begin to taunt him. Clearly, Mack's life is in danger. One of the young men has a gun tucked in his belt and gestures to it while telling Mack to get out of the car. Mack gets out and tells them they can have whatever they want. The young man snarls at him. The binarism between Mack as the model of decency and the young black men as a threatening symbol of social savagery skillfully works to portray whites as a besieged group while simultaneously portraying inner-city black youths as a signifier of danger and social decay.

Chance and danger, another major subtext of the film, emerges when Simon, the black tow truck driver arrives on the scene. Exhibiting street-wise savvy and courage, Simon convinces the young men to cool out and go back to roaming the streets. Simon is the model of the cool, tough, yet responsible, black man. He lives alone. Not only does he support a deaf daughter who attends a college in Washington, D.C., he also helps support his sister, who lives with a son who is gradually being lost to the L.A. black gang culture. Simon's life is complicated. Trapped within the limits imposed by poverty, racism, and the culture of survival, Simon maintains a view of society that allows him to go on with his life but undercuts his own sense of individual and collective agency.

Sitting with Mack while the Lexus is being repaired, Simon tells him that he once visited the Grand Canyon. He recalls how it made him realize how insignificant life is in the long haul. For Simon, the message is clear: humans within the larger scheme of nature are minute and transitory. Humbled before the long duration of history and time that inscribes the vastness and wonder of the Grand Canyon, Simon substitutes a New Age naturalism for a notion of critical agency and social possibility.

Mack is so grateful to Simon for saving his car and life that he later takes him out to breakfast, develops a friendship with him, and in doing so crosses over a racial boundary that allows him to recognize difference as part of daily life, but at the same time he refrains from questioning his own place in the larger economy of power and privilege that largely relegates blacks to a subaltern status in contemporary American society.

The relationship between Simon and Mack is mutually reinforced through their sense that the world is organized through a random sense of chance, luck, and danger. For Mack, this is an important insight that allows him to assuage his liberal conscience by helping Simon's sister find an apartment in a safer neighborhood, and fixing Simon up with a black women who works for Mack's law firm. In this context, Mack's whiteness is not understood through the evocation of a critical reading of history, an invocation of dangerous memory, or an understanding of how social relations that reproduce privileges and power must be unlearned and transformed. On the contrary, whiteness for Mack becomes a referent for self-sacrifice buttressed by the liberal assumption that as a privileged white man he can solve the problems of marginalized and subordinate Others. For Simon, Mack exemplifies how history turns merely on luck and circumstance. After all, what are the chances of an inner-city black mechanic either meeting or becoming friends with a high-powered, privileged yuppie white lawyer. Simon displays his gratitude to Mack at the end of the film by driving his sister and her young boy along with Mack and his family to the Grand Canyon. It is here in the face of the wonder of nature that the immensity of the racial, cultural, political, economic, and social differences that separate these families are erased in a New Age notion of unity and spirituality.

The relationship between whites and blacks/Others is also revealed through the coming of age narrative of two young men in the film. Mack and Claire's son, named after Roberto Clemente, the famous Puerto Rican baseball player, is portrayed in terms that suggest he leads a relatively untroubled life. Roberto is from a rich family, goes to a decent school, develops a romance with a young woman in summer camp, and appears to be on his way to a successful future. The most serious tension in his life appears to be learning how to drive and coping with a name that contradicts his own refusal to view himself as ethnic. Learning how to make a left turn in traffic appears to be the most pressing test he will face in the near future.

On the other hand, Simon's nephew is portrayed as a young male black who has given his life up to the L.A. gang culture. This black teenage boy's problems come from living with a single parent who cannot contain him and residing in a community filled with crime and despair over which he has no control. Kasdan presents the film audience with a view of black urban life that is as one-dimensional as the stereotypes and tropes he uses to construct the coming of age odyssey of a black youth growing up in a poor inner-city neighborhood. The suffocating conditions of urban decay, rampant poverty, and random violence are frozen by Kasdan in a series of images that refuse to analyze the historical, cultural, economic, and political conditions that provide some dialectical grounding for understanding how domination, power, resistance, and identity come together to reveal the complexity of life in such a setting. The binarism created by Kasdan of growing up "black" and "white" does not suggest what these two young men have in common, how one form of life relates to the other, or how new identities might be constructed by transforming these related sites of privilege and oppression. In this scenario, whiteness is not only privileged, it is also the only referent for social change, hope, and action. Within the rigid binarism portraying these two very different coming-of-age experiences cast in racial terms, blacks are equated with lawlessness while whites are seen as paragons of rationality, compassion, and stability. Once again, what is revealed here is a fundamental disrespect for marginalized Others manifest in the refusal to analyze what whiteness as a category of power means (or suggests) in terms of its ethical relations with Others. This type of disrespect for the Other is also manifested throughout the film in the refusal of allowing those who are oppressed, blacks, women, and children to speak for themselves, to be the subject of resistance and historical agency, and to be complexly represented within rather than outside of the specificity of their daily lives.

Otherness as both a marker of deficit and a resource to redefine whiteness as a universal symbol of unity and hope is displayed in a number of other relations throughout the film. Race and gender intersect in a dominating fashion through the portrayal of Mack's wife, Claire (Mary MacDonnell). Caught in a mid-life crisis, Claire appears to solve her problem while taking her daily jog. Passing the nearby woods, she finds an abandoned Third World baby. Ignoring the concrete identity of the child (why was she abandoned? what history, memories, and pain inform this act? what does such an act suggest about the ethical relations between the wealthy and the poor in terms of their respective problems, hopes, and plans for the future?). Kasdan uses this intersection of "chance and luck" to suggest that Claire's identity is entirely dependent on her providing nurturance to Others, particularly since she can no longer provide such nurturance to her husband and teenage son. Claire eventually adopts a baby and in doing so not only secures her own identity but also affirms the notion of self-sacrifice, guilt, and duty that appears to be endemic to Kasdan's conception of how responsible action is constituted for whites. A subtext of this relationship is that Third World families are not responsible enough to raise their own children. Conversely, in this case, colonialism is seen as having its benefits.

Claire is not much different than all of the women who inhabit the celluloid landscape of *Grand Canyon*. Mack's mistress, Simon's lover, and Claire are women whose identities are largely shaped in the images of men. Kasdan suggests that their only desires are rooted in the patriarchal demands for women (not men) to nurture, raise children, or find a "good" man. Deprived of a complex identity and voice, all of the women in this film lack any sense of agency or the need to redefine their lives outside of the imperatives of a patriarchal culture. Moreover, Kasdan also uses a debilitating binarism in framing the differences among the women in *Grand Canyon*. Either they are viewed as little more than prostitutes, as is the case with Kline's mistress, Dee (Mary-Louise Parker), or they are viewed as selfless saints, an image embodied in Claire (who is viewed in a number of scenes through the figure of the Madonna rocking the baby Jesus).

Finally, all of the main characters in this film share the belief that some miraculous force establishes connections between people who inhabit the planet and that this force expresses itself through the circumstances of luck, chance, and fate. Mack tells Simon, for instance, that he believes that God once appeared to him in the form of a woman wearing a baseball cap and saved him from being hit by a bus. Clearly, his time to die had not come. Simon reveals his own infatuation with nature and the insignificance of human life and agency in the face of the wonder and awe of the Grand Canyon. Claire believes that finding the baby she adopted was orchestrated by some higher force. Thus, she doesn't have to bother with the social, political, and ideological consequences of either the abandonment of a Third World child or her adopting a baby under such circumstances. In the end, the primacy of the social, political, and cultural as they are manifested in various problems informing cultural differences, gender issues, and the problematic of ethnicity are wiped away in a New Age adoration of the mysteries and wonders of nature. All of life's riddles are seemingly resolved when all the central players end up in the final scene of the film staring with amazement and awe at the aesthetic wonder of the Grand Canyon. Clearly, in this scenario, nature and social Darwinism are on the side of white domination as all of the differences that brought together these various men, women, and children are removed from the systemic injustices which influence their respective lives. History, power, and agency now dissolve into the abyss of liberal goodwill, New Age uplift thinking, and a dead-end pastoralism; and cultural differences dissolve into a regime of representations that universalize harmonizing systems while eliminating the discourse of power, conflict, and struggle.

TOWARD A PEDAGOGY OF REPRESENTATION AND REPRESENTATIONAL PEDAGOGY

The question I want to take up here is how cultural workers might extend and deepen the politics of representation by addressing what I call a critical pedagogy of representation and a representational pedagogy. In the first instance, I am referring to the various ways in which representations are constructed as a means of comprehending the past through the present in order to legitimate and secure a particular view of the future. Pedagogically, this raises the question of how students can learn to interrogate the historical, semiotic, and relational dynamics involved in the production of various regimes of representations and their respective politics. In other words, a pedagogy of representation focuses on demystifying the act and process of representing by revealing how meanings are produced within relations of power that narrate identities through history, social forms, and modes of ethical address that appear objective, universally valid, and consensual. At issue here is the task of both identifying how representational politics works to secure dominant modes of authority and mobilize popular support while also interrogating how the act of presenting is developed within forms of textual authority and relations of power "which always involve choice, selectivity, exclusions, and inclusions" (Said in Mariani and Crary 1990, 96).

Central to a pedagogy of representation is providing students with the opportunities to deconstruct the mythic notion that images, sounds, and texts merely express reality (Simon 1992). More specifically, a critical pedagogy of representation recognizes that students inhabit a photocentric, aural, and televisual culture in which the proliferation of photographic and electronically produced images and sounds serve to actively produce knowledge and identities within particular sets of ideological and social practices (Giroux and McLaren in Schwoch, White, and Reily 1992). By granting the concept of representation a formative and not merely an expressive place in the constitution of social and political life, questions of subjectivity, power, and politics take on an increasing significance as a pedagogical practice in which the relationship between difference and identity must be located within rather than outside of the mediations of history, culture, and ideology (Giroux and McLaren in Schwoch, White, and Reily 1992).

On one level, this suggests that students must analyze those institutions that constantly work through the power of representations and social practices to "produce, codify, and even rewrite histories of race and colonialism in the name of difference" (Mohanty 1989/90, 184). Representations are not simply forms of cultural capital necessary for human beings to present themselves in relation to others and human nature, they also inhabit and sustain institutional structures that need to be understood and analyzed within circuits of power that constitute what might be called a political economy of representations. In this case, a pedagogy and politics of representation would highlight historically how "machineries of representation" within the growth of new mass communication and information technologies are inextricably linked to the emergence of corporate-controlled and knowledge-based societies in which a politics of representation must be partly understood within the imperatives of the newly emerging transnational market economies of the postmodern age (Schiller 1986, 1989; Schneider and Wallis 1988). This insight has provoked Trinh T. Minh-Ha to remark:

> To address the question of production relations . . . is endlessly to reopen the question: how is the real (or the social ideal of good representation) produced? Rather than catering to it, striving to capture and discover its truth as a concealed or lost object, it is therefore important also to keep asking: how is truth being ruled? (1990, 85)

In part, Stuart Hall (1988) further extends this insight in arguing that cultural workers must address not only the relations of representations, how their machineries work to actively produce commonsense notions of identity and difference, but also how dominant regimes of representation actively "structure conditions of existence . . . outside of the sphere of the discursive" (27). By providing students with critical tools to decode dominating machineries of representation, their own locations and social formations can be understood in terms that allow them to introduce into their discourse "a sense of the political which ultimately leads to a consideration of power" (Borsa 1990, 31).

Drawing on the work of Abigail Solomon-Godeau (1991), I want to argue that there are three principle elements at work in a pedagogy of representation. First, cultural workers must identify the historically contingent nature of the form and content of a particular form of representation. In the case of a *Grand Canyon* this can be done by having students read historical accounts which challenge the liberal view of black/white relations that are allegedly constructed outside of the dynamics of power and ideology in the film. *Grand Canyon* may be problematized for the ways in which it covers over forms of cultural self-representation that are constituted within dominant historical, hierarchical, and representational systems. This is not merely a matter of recovering lost historical narratives, it is a pedagogical practice which addresses the issue of how forms of cultural identity are learned in relation to the ordering and structuring of dominant practices of representation. At stake here is not only how representational practices efface the "marks of [their] making" but also how those excluded from the means of representation are actually re-presented (Solomon-Godeau 1991).

Second, cultural workers must do more than insist on the complicity of representations doing violence to those who are either represented or misrepresented. Cultural workers also refuse the pedagogical practices which support a voyeuristic reception of texts by providing students with a variety of critical methodologies and approaches to understand how issues regarding audience, address, and reception configure within cultural circuits of power to produce particular subject positions and secure specific forms of authority (Grossberg 1989). In other words cultural workers must make problematic those pedagogical practices that inform particular systems of representation in order to legitimate certain strategies of inclusion and exclusion, practices of subject formation, and the ratification of selective modes of affective investment and expression. Of particular interest here is how particular forms of representation create, mobilize, and secure particular desires, that is, how such representations work as desiring machines to secure particular forms of affective investment. This suggests more than taking up how representations work to police desires; it points more importantly to how students, teachers, and other cultural workers actively produce and mobilize their own desires within particular historical and social contexts as forms of identification and agency.

Third, representations are always produced within cultural limits and theoretical borders, and as such are necessarily implicated in particular economies of truth, value, and power. In relation to these larger axes of power in which all representations are embedded, it is necessary to remind the student: Whose interests are being served by the representations in question in, for example, *Grand Canyon*? Where can we situate such representations ethically and politically with respect to questions of social justice and human freedom? What moral, ethical, and ideological principles structure our reactions to such representations?

Turning to the issue of representational pedagogy, I want to argue that such an approach goes beyond analyzing the structuring principles that inform the form and content of the representation of politics; instead, it focuses on how students and others learn to identify, challenge, and rewrite such representations. More specifically, it offers students the opportunity to engage pedagogically the means by which representational practices can be portrayed, taken up, and reworked subjectively so as to produce, reinforce, or resist certain forms of cultural representation and self-definition. Central to such a pedagogy is the need for cultural workers to accentuate the mutually reinforcing moments of pedagogy and politics as primary to the practice of representing as an act of resistance and transformation. Richard Kearney (1991) has addressed, in part, this issue by posing the postmodern problematic of representation as an interrelated issue of politics, ethics, and pedagogy. The central question for him is: "how to imagine a set of relations which will do justice to the post-modern imaginary? . . . to render due account of the complexities of our civilization of images; and to judge it justly according to adequate ethical criteria?" (211). In attempting to partially answer Kearney's query, I would propose that a representational pedagogy take up the following issues:

First, this pedagogical approach would give students the opportunity not simply to discover their hidden histories but to recover them. This means "retrieving the betrayed stories of history . . . through a critical deployment of imagination . . . able to discriminate between reality as a fact and existence as a possibility" (Kearney 1991, 215–16). As part of the pedagogy of cultural representation and identity formation, this would suggest that cultural workers offer students the tools to challenge any notion of subjectivity grounded in a view of history as unchanging, monolithic, or static. Identities are always subject as Stuart Hall points out "to the 'play' of history, culture, and power" (1990, 225). Consequently, identities undergo constant transformations.

The relationship between history and identity is a complex one and cannot be reduced to unearthing hidden histories that are then mined for positive images. On the contrary, educators need to understand and develop in their pedagogies how identities are produced differently, how they take up the narratives of the past through the stories and experiences of the present. Understood in these terms, a representational pedagogy is not wedded to the process of narrating an authentic history, but to the dynamics of cultural recovery, which involves rewriting the relationship between identity and difference through a retelling of the historical past. A representational pedagogy is rooted in making the political more pedagogical by addressing how a critical politics can be developed between a struggle over access to regimes of representation and using them to re-present different identities as part of the reconstruction of democratic public life. Stuart Hall (1988) alludes to this problem as the struggle around positionalities and the struggle for a politics of difference. For him, the important issue here is how a

> politics can be constructed which works with and through difference, which is able to build those forms of solidarity and identification which make common struggle and resistance possible but without suppressing the real heterogeneity of interests and identities, and which can effectively draw the political boundary lines without which political contestation is impossible, without fixing those boundaries for eternity.(28)

Second, critical educators need to understand more clearly how to construct a representational pedagogy that is attentive to how the incorporation of the everyday is mobilized within the text of mass culture to produce particular relations between the margins and the centers of power (Grossberg 1992). In part, this means providing students with the analytical tools to challenge those representations that produce racism, sexism, and colonialism through the legacy of ethnocentric discourses and practices. But more is demanded here than an understanding of the new technologies of representation and how they are used to fix identities within relations of domination and subordination. At issue here is the need to develop pedagogical practices that do more than read off ideologies as they are produced within particular texts. Central to such an approach is understanding how knowledge and desire come together to promote particular forms of cultural production, investments, and counternarratives that invoke communities of memory that are lived, felt, and interrogated. Critical educators also need to use these technologies as part of a counternarrative of emancipation in which new visions, spaces, desires, and discourses can be developed that offer students the opportunity for rewriting their own histories differently within rather than outside of the discourse of critical citizenship and cultural democracy. Within this discourse, students would study their own ethnicities, histories, and gain some sense of those complex and diverse cultural locations that have provided them with a sense of voice, place, and identity. In this way, students could be made more attentive to both the struggles that inform their own identities and also to other struggles around culture and voice that often seem to have no relationship to their own lives. I am particularly concerned here about a representational pedagogy that makes whiteness visible as an ethnic category. About making white students understand how their own identities are beyond neither ethnicity, history, privilege, nor struggle. Cultural difference, in this case, must be taken up as a relational issue and not as one that serves to isolate and mark particular groups. This has important pedagogical implications. For example, Bob Suzuki (1991) discovered that in a class he was teaching on multicultural education, many of his white students were ignorant of their own Irish, working-class histories. He writes:

> When I asked my students to share what they knew about their ethnic and cultural backgrounds with the rest of the class, students of color—especially African-American students—usually had the most knowledge of their family histories. White ethnic students were generally the least knowledgeable, and after they listened to the long narratives of the students of color, they would be somewhat intimidated and say—sometimes rather forlornly—"I Wish I had something to contribute, but I don't even know much about my background. In fact, I don't even have a culture." At first, I found such statements astonishing because I hadn't realized the extent to which ethnic experience has been literally obliterated for many white ethnics. Once I gained that realization, however, I could deal much more effectively with these students. (34)

The representational pedagogy illustrated by Suzuki rejects the notion that the systemic violence of racism and difference as negative identity can only be addressed by focusing on alleged Others. Ethnicity becomes a constantly traversed borderland of differences in which identities are fashioned in relationship to the shifting terrains of history, experience, and power (Hall 1990). Ethnicity as a representational politics pushes against the boundaries of cultural containment and becomes a site of pedagogical struggle in which the legacies of dominant histories, codes, and relations become unsettled and thus open to being challenged and rewritten. This suggests at the most general level that a representational pedagogy must be a pedagogy of place, that is, it must address the specificities of the experiences, problems, languages, and histories that students and communities rely upon to construct a narrative of collective identity and possible transformation. At the very least, a representational pedagogy must renounce the notion of aesthetic autonomy and fully engage the social and political realities that shape the larger society (Bennett 1990); moreover, the knowledge, skills, and values that students acquire in rewriting the relationship between pedagogy and a representational politics must also be used to constantly interrogate the politics of their own locations, voices, and actions. One pedagogical qualification needs to be made here. A representational pedagogy and politics of representation must do more than promote self-understanding and an understanding of others, it must also work to create the institutional, political, and discursive conditions necessary in which power and privilege are not merely exposed or eliminated but are "consciously rendered reciprocal (and put to good use)" (Khare 1992, 5).

In conclusion, I want to reiterate that if a representational pedagogy and a pedagogy of representation are to address the challenge of the new cultural racism, they will have to rework the relationship between identity and difference as part of a broader struggle over institutions and ideologies designed to extend and deepen greater forms of political, economic, and cultural democracy. Such a struggle demands a profoundly more sophisticated understanding of how cultural workers can address the productive dynamics of pedagogy within a utopian discourse that can bear witness to representations that narrate cultural legacies which favor emancipatory possibilities, and offer students the opportunity to represent them-selves in ways which suggest that they can imagine differently in order to act otherwise. Finally, any attempt to connect the issues of agency, ethical responsibil-ity, and representational pedagogy must work self-consciously within the often overlooked tension between being politically committed and pedagogically wrong. At the very least, this might suggest that any pedagogy of representation and representational pedagogy be rooted in a politics which is simultaneously utopian but always distrustful of itself.

NOTES

1. This is not to suggest that questions of identity are not addressed in a progressive way by left cultural critics. On the contrary, writers such as Diana Fuss (1989), Judith Butler (1990), bell hooks (1990), Jonathan Rutherford (1990), Michele Wallace (1990), Lawrence Grossberg (1992), Stanley Aronowitz (1992), Emily Hicks (1991) and too many others to name here are attempting to rethink a politics of identity within a broader conception of cultural difference. But in doing so, many of these critics have failed to address how the construction of identity politics works as part of a broader pedagogical discourse to shape popular commonsense conceptions of identity, culture, and difference. What is often at stake in this work is exploring the intersection and relationship between different identities, ethnicities, and political experiences within a particular field of domination. What is generally ignored is how these identities are taken up and engaged within particular histories, locations, and zones of everyday life as both a pedagogical and political issue.

2. Examples of this perspective can be found in Berman 1992.
3. I take this distinction from a lecture that Paul Smith delivered on "Clint Eastwood and Being Black" at Miami University in February of 1991.
4. This issue is taken up in Dyer 1988, hooks 1990, and Young 1990.
5. One of the most important analyses of Los Angeles in cultural and political terms can be found in Mike Davis 1990. Of course, in light of the recent uprising, L.A. signifies more than postmodern hybridity, it also signifies, I believe, a "wake-up call" to the rest of America. The message seems clear: the economic, political, and social conditions that have come to characterize the inner cities in the last decade cannot continue. L.A. signifies the call for new leadership, new alliances, and the need for massive social, economic, and cultural reforms. But L.A. also makes visible the real legacy of the Reagan/Bush era, one which was aptly characterized by Ralph Nader when asked how he would grade Bush's first term:

> I'd give him an F. All the trends that began under Reagan have accelerated under Bush: precipitous economic decline, staggering deficits, lopsided balance of trade, growing unemployment, declining quality of life, rising personal-income taxes, failing banks, reeling real estate, unaffordable medical costs, fourth-rate schools, rampant street crime, unchecked corporate crime, an ignorant energy policy and abuses of the public trust by a government increasingly unaccountable for its actions—except to big business. (Nader cited in Donahue 1992, 10).

WORKS CITED

Aronowitz, Stanley (1992). *The Politics of Identity*. New York: Routledge.
Bennett, Tony (1990). *Outside Literature*. New York: Routledge.
Bennett, Tony (1992). "Putting Policy into Cultural Studies." In Grossberg, Nelson, and Treichler 1992, 23–34.
Berman, Paul, ed. (1992). *Debating P.C.: The Controversy over Political Correctness on College Campuses*. New York: Laurel.
Bhabha, Homi K., and Parekh, Bhikhu (1989). "Identities on Parade: A Conversation." *Marxism Today* (June): 2–5.
Borsa, Joan (1990). "Freda Khalo: Marginalization and the Critical Female Subject." *Third Text* 12 (Autumn): 21–40.
Butler, Judith (1990). *Gender Trouble: Gender and the Subversion of Identity*. New York: Routledge.
Clarke, Stuart Alan (1991). "Fear of a Black Planet." *Socialist Review* 21 (3/4): 37–59.
Copjec, Joan (1991). "The Unvermogender Other: Hysteria and Democracy in America." *New Formations* 14 (Summer): 27–41.
Davis, Mike (1990). *City of Quartz*. London: Verso.
Donahue, Deirdre (1992). "Nader Rates, Berates Bush in *Playboy*." *USA Today* May 8: 10.
Dyer, Richard (1988). "White." *Screen* 29 (4): 44–64.
Dyson, Michael (1991). "Growing Up under Fire: *Boyz N the Hood* and the Agony of the Black Man in America." *Tikkun* 6 (5) (November/December): 74–78.
Escoffier, Jeff (1991). "The Limits of Multiculturalism." *Socialist Review* 21 (3/4): 61–73.
Felski, Rita (1989). "Feminism, Postmodernism, and the Critique of Modernity." *Cultural Critique* 13 (Fall): 33–56.

Fraser, Nancy (1992). "The Uses and Abuses of French Discourse Theories for Feminist Politics." *Theory, Culture and Society* 9:51–71.

Fuss, Diana (1989). *Essentially Speaking: Feminism, Narrative, and Difference.* New York: Routledge.

Gilman, Sander L. (1985). *Difference and Pathology: Stereotypes of Sexuality, Race, and Madness.* Ithaca: Cornell.

Gilroy, Paul (1990). "One Nation under a Groove: The Cultural Politics of 'Race' and Racism in Britain." In Goldberg 1990. 263–82.

Giroux, Henry A. (1988). *Schooling and the Struggle for Public Life.* Minneapolis: University of Minnesota Press.

Giroux, Henry A. (1992). *Border Crossings: Cultural Workers and the Politics of Education.* New York: Routledge.

Giroux, Henry A., and McLaren, Peter (1992). "Media Hegemony: Towards a Critical Pedagogy of Representation." In Schwoch, White, and Reily 1992. xv–xxxiv.

Goldberg, Theo, ed. (1990). *Anatomy of Racism.* Minneapolis: University of Minnesota Press.

Grossberg, Lawrence (1989). "The Context of Audience and the Politics of Difference." *Australian Journal of Communication* 16:13–35.

Grossberg, Lawrence (1992). *We Gotta Get Out of This Place: Popular Conservatism and Postmodern Culture.* New York: Routledge.

Grossberg, Lawrence; Nelson, Cary; and Treichler, Paula, eds. (1992). *Cultural Studies.* New York: Routledge.

Hall, Stuart (1988). "New Ethnicities." In *ICA Document* 7. London: ICA. 27–31.

Hall, Stuart (1990). "Cultural Identity and Diaspora." In Rutherford 1990. 222–37.

Hall, Stuart (1991). "Ethnicity: Identity and Difference." *Radial America* 13 (4): 9–20.

Hall, Stuart, and Held, David (1990)."Citizens and Citizenship."In Hall and Jacques 1990. 173–88.

Hall, Stuart, and Jacques, Martin, eds. (1990). *New Times: The Changing Face of Politics in the 1990s.* London: Verso.

Hicks, Emily (1991). *Border Writing: The Multidimensional Text.* Minneapolis: University of Minnesota Press.

hooks, bell (1989). *Talking Back.* Boston: South End Press.

hooks, bell (1990). *Yearnings.* Boston: South End Press.

Johnson, Harold (1992). "The Fire This Time." *National Review* 44 (10): 17–18.

Kearney, Richard (1991). *Poetics of Imagining: From Husserl to Lyotard.* New York: Harper Collins.

Kermode, Frank (1992). "Whose History Is Bunk?" *New York Times Book Review* February 23: 3, 33.

Khare, R. S. (1992). "The Other's Double—The Anthropologist's Bracketed Self: Notes on Cultural Representation." *Oxford Literary History* 23:1–23.

Kozol, Jonathan (1991). *Savage Inequalities.* New York: Crown.

Krauthammer, Charles (1990). "The Real Buchanan Is Surfacing." *Cincinnati Enquirer* March 3: A4.

Laclau, Ernesto, and Mouffe, Chantal (1985). *Hegemony and Socialist Strategy.* London: Verso.

Lipman, Samuel (1989). "Redefining Culture and Democracy." *New Criterion* 8 (4): 10–18.

Lloyd, David (1991). "Race under Representation." *Oxford Literary Review* 13 (1/2): 62–94.

Mariani, Phil, and Crary, Jonathan, eds. (1990). *Discourses: Conversations in Postmodern Art and Culture.* Cambridge: MIT Press.

Minh-ha, Trinh T. (1990). "Documentary Is/Not a Name." *October* 52:76–100.

Mohanty, Chandra T. (Winter 1989/90). "On Race and Voice: Challenges for Liberal Education in the 1990s." *Cultural Critique*: 179–208.

Policar, Alain (1990). "Racism and Its Mirror Image." *Telos* 83 (Spring): 99–108.

Philipson, Ilene (1991). "What's the Big I.D.? The Politics of the Authentic Self." *Tikkun* 6 (6): 51–55.

Rosaldo, Renato (1989). *Culture and Truth*. Boston: Beacon.

Rutherford, Jonathan, ed. (1990). *Identity, Community, Culture, Difference*. London: Lawrence and Wishart.

Said, Edward (1990). "In the Shadow of the West: An Interview with Edward Said." In Mariani and Crary. 1990 93–103.

Schiller, Herbert (1986). *Information and the Crisis Economy*. New York: Oxford University Press.

Schiller, Herbert (1989). *Culture Inc.: The Corporate Takeover of Public Expression*. New York: Oxford University Press.

Schneider, Cynthia, and Wallis, Brian, eds. (1989). *Global Television*. Cambridge: MIT Press.

Schwoch, James; White, Mimi; and Reily, Susan (1992). *Media Knowledge: Readings in Popular Culture, Pedagogy and Critical Citizenship*. Albany: SUNY Press.

Simon, Roger I. (1992). *Teaching against the Grain*. New York: Bergin and Garvey.

Solomon-Godeau, Abigail (1991). *Photography at the Dock: Essays on Photographic History, Institutions, and Practices*. Minneapolis: University of Minnesota Press.

Suzuki, Bob H. (1991). "Unity with Diversity: Easier Said than Done." *Liberal Education* 77 (1): 30–35.

Taguieff, Pierre-André (1990). "The New Cultural Racism in France." *Telos* 83(Spring): 109–122.

Tomlinson, John (1991). *Cultural Imperialism*. Baltimore: Johns Hopkins University Press.

Wallace, Michele (1990). *Invisibility Blues: From Pop to Theory*. London: Verso Press.

Welch, Sharon (1989). *A Feminist Ethic of Risk*. Minneapolis: Fortress Press.

West, Cornel (1990). "The New Cultural Politics of Difference." *October* 53 (Summer): 93–109.

Willis, Ellen (1991). "Multiple Identities." *Tikkun* 6(6): 58–60.

Winant, Howard (1990). "Postmodern Racial Politics in the U.S." *Socialist Review* 20 (1): 121–45.

Woodward, C. Van (1991). "Equal but Separate." *New Republic* (July 15 and 22): 42–43.

Young, Robert (1990). *White Mythologies*. London: Routledge.

CHAPTER 2

INTELLECTUALS, POWER

AND QUALITY

TELEVISION

AVA COLLINS

In the struggle over educational ideology and the ideology of education—the famous "storm" over the university (Searle) that has intensified within the last decade—one presupposition emerges as common to all positions across the spectrum of debate, from radical Right to radical Left: popular culture presents an urgent, fundamental, and undeniable challenge to pedagogical theory and practice. Of course, how this challenge is understood by various partisans of the debate over the canon and curricular reform is at the very center of the controversies provoked by these issues of reform. The effects of popular culture are generally viewed apocalyptically by both the Left and the Right, signifying the end of educational practice as we know it. We can only hope so. However, the Right wants to "reclaim the legacy" (Bennett), quite literally reinstituting an educational system based on nineteenth-century models that ignore changed conditions of circulation of information and knowledge in the technologically sophisticated twentieth-century public arena, and in effect banish popular cultural forms from the classroom. The Left is struggling to develop analytical models that take into account changed social, cultural, and material conditions, but ironically they often fail to extend their analyses to the very system within which they are developing those models, thus frequently reproducing the very relations of cultural and social power that they seek to investigate, rarely questioning their own positions within an educational system that produces, organizes, and legitimates certain means or methods of the transmission of knowledge and power. I want to argue here that the models that the Left is developing are much more productive than those of the Right, but in order to keep from ultimately reproducing the same mistakes of the Right (albeit from a different perspective), they need to incorporate a self-critical dimension that allows the intellectual—the teacher—to understand that the readings he or she produces make up one part of a whole arena of evaluative activity, a part that is not necessarily privileged once we begin to question the traditional relations of information, knowledge, and power as they circulate within the classroom. The last part of this essay applies and critiques a particular model for the study of popular culture, Ien Ang's influential audience response study of "Dallas" viewers. Through a reading of a contemporary "Quality Television"[1] program, "thirtysomething," I hope to suggest how other evaluative mechanisms that are operative outside the academy are put into play, complicating the relations of "reading," interpretation, response, and knowledge that intellectuals activate within the classroom to justify the study of popular culture.

TECHNOLOGY, LITERACY, AND PEDAGOGY: WHY NOW?

Within the curricular reform/canon debates, the very form that education will take in the future is up for grabs, so the stakes could hardly be higher. My aim in this first section is to lay the foundation for a more nuanced understanding of the challenge popular culture presents to curricular reform and the pedagogical responses to it that have stimulated such heated debate in recent years. Since popular culture is hardly a new concept, we probably should begin by asking why it recently has become so central to pedagogical debates. A thorough answer to this question involves a complex relation of social, economic, intellectual, and political factors that are clearly beyond the scope of this essay, but here I would like to adumbrate and discuss some of these factors, in order ultimately to suggest how we can productively start to come to terms *pedagogically* with popular culture in ways that don't simply co-opt its discursive space as a cultural form situated outside the academy, which is in fact one of its principle defining characteristics.

With very few exceptions,[2] the debate over the place of popular culture within the curriculum has produced more heat than light, with very little reflection on why this issue is so "hot" right now. At least, in part, it must be linked to its immediate social and cultural context, to specific material conditions, which are taken for granted, rarely explicitly addressed or engaged,[3] by most critics who have taken up the pedagogical debate about curriculum and the canon. I am referring here to the technological "revolution" that has encompassed students' and teachers' lives, both inside and outside the educational institutions where they meet, embodied in the shift of the technology of culture from print to electronic media. This revolution began to escalate and to manifest itself in very particular ways, not coincidentally, at the very time that William Bennett prepared and issued the infamous report, "To Reclaim a Legacy," that invigorated the current canon debate. The proliferation of cable TV channels (augured, significantly, in the opening broadcast of MTV in 1981), the breathtaking growth in the home video technologies,[4] the personal computer "explosion" and the attendant networking of those computers, the increasing prevalence of the fax machine, etc.—all profoundly affect the way that information is disseminated, exchanged, and circulated within the culture, with profound ramifications for those institutions involved in the cultural production and exchange of information and knowledge. The growth of electronic media cultures has changed the nature and function of popular culture, for talking about popular culture in the 1990s necessarily involves talking about the new mass communication and information technologies. *New York Times* classical music reviewer Edward Rothstein recently bemoaned this state of affairs, grudgingly acknowledging that "popular culture today is quite different from popular cultures of other periods even in the West. Electronic media, assisted by disintegrating folk cultures, have created enormous interconnected markets; commercial low musics reach wider than ever before . . ." (H31). Rothstein understands but wants to negate the fact that such changed material conditions also necessarily challenge prevailing assumptions about the cultural production of knowledge, the relation of information to knowledge and power, and force an analysis of "how relations of pedagogy and relations of power are inextricably tied not only to what people know but how they come to know it in a particular way within the constraints of specific social forms" (Giroux and Simon 2). When students step into a classroom, they do not shed their cultural and social context; they understand that these technological changes affect the dynamics of an institution whose central work has been the definition and circulation of information and knowledge. The dynamics of interaction among students, teachers, and texts has been altered within the classroom itself by the increasing permeation of technological hardware and software, with which students are often more proficient than their teachers precisely because of their popular cultural experiences[5] (a situation which implicitly undermines traditional roles of power and authority in the classroom).

As Henry Giroux and Roger Simon point out, a productive response to such a situation would be to "retheorize the importance of popular culture as a central category for developing a theory and practice of critical pedagogy" (4), a pedagogy that is attentive to

> how students actively construct the categories of meaning that prefigure their production of and response to classroom knowledge. By ignoring the cultural and social forms that are authorized by youth and simultaneously empower or disempower them, educators risk complicitly silencing and negating their students. . . . Educators who refuse to acknowledge popular culture as a significant basis of knowledge often devalue students by refusing to work with the knowledge that students actually have and so eliminate the possibility of developing a pedagogy that links school knowledge to the differing subject relations that help to constitute their everyday lives. (3)

Such a task involves developing a means of incorporating student experience of cultural forms into pedagogical theory, which has proved a hinge point in the curriculum/canon debate, and a sticking point in the development of a critical pedagogy that incorporates an adequate politics of popular culture, largely because there are no existing theoretical paradigms to address the central issue of evaluation. How can we address the issue of how students assign value to texts, of how they construct their own evaluative paradigms in relation to the evaluative paradigms they encounter in the classroom and what that relation is, when we have not explicitly addressed the issue of how value is assigned to any text by anyone, including teachers and critics, except in reference to the accepted wisdom of the canon? The assignation of value rests on a myriad of untested assumptions about the properties of texts, reading processes, and the accumulation of experience that lead many to unquestioningly accept that teacher knows best, as well as *what* is best.

Barbara Herrnstein Smith points out the questionable set of assumptions on which such a notion of value is based: "namely, that literary value was a determinate property of texts and that the critic, by virtue of certain innate and acquired capacities (taste, sensibility, etc, . . .), was someone specifically equipped to discriminate it" (7). In a complexly argued historical survey of literary criticism, she demonstrates how positivistic philological scholarship that privileged scientism and objectivity was wedded to a humanistic pedagogy that was dedicated to preserving and transmitting the cultural values presumably embodied in "the culture's esteemed objects—in this case its canonized texts" (6). This marriage provided a spurious objectivist base for a Platonic conception (i.e., transcendent, enduring, universal) of literature that effectively banished the problematic of value and evaluation from the academy, allowing critics to simply pronounce or assume what was valuable: "One of the major effects of prohibiting or inhibiting explicit evaluation is to forestall the exhibition and obviate the possible acknowledgement of divergent systems of value and thus to ratify, by default, established evaluative authority" (11).

Much of the force of conservative support of the traditional curriculum and the canon derives from a perceived lack of students' abilities to discern value at all precisely because of their inability to distance themselves either literally or figuratively from their culture, most especially their popular culture.[6] According to these conservative critics (see most especially Bloom, Hirsch, D'Souza), they boogie into classrooms attached to Walkmans, tabloids in hand to keep them entertained while the Professor tries valiantly but vainly to introduce them to true Culture (as in "the best that has been thought and said"). Their heads filled with tabloid trash, their ears ringing with the pulsating, sexually titillating beat of rock music, their eyes blinded by blatantly commercial film, television, and advertising images, these students simply cannot make distinctions, much less the refined distinctions that mark the erudite person. Tenured conservative Roger Kimball loftily asserts:

> The notion that some works are better and more important than others, that some works exert a special claim on our attention, that "being educated" requires thoughtful acquaintance with these works and an ability to discriminate between greater and lesser—all this is anathema to the forces arrayed against the traditional understanding of the humanities. The very

idea that the works of Shakespeare might be indisputably greater than the collected cartoons of Bugs Bunny is often rejected as antidemocratic and an imposition on the freedom and political interests of various groups. (xii)

Thus begins the argument for the purging of student experience from the classroom, the reinstatement of the absolute authority of the Professor within that domain, and the revision—or reversion—of the curriculum to encompass the Western classics that embody the Values of Civilization.

The problems with such a position are legion, but for the purposes of my argument here I would like to address two in particular. The first problem is how strikingly this vision is rooted in a nineteenth-century model of cultural transmission of the values of civilization from generation to generation through carefully selected representative texts—a model based on a certain notion of literacy that maintains the primacy of print in the processes of critical thinking. Jack Goody most specifically expresses this teleological argument in his book *The Domestication of the Savage Mind,* claiming that the acquisition of alphabetic literacy manifested in writing leads directly to critical and analytic thinking. Goody himself seems unaware of the cultural imperialism inherent in his dismissal of the critical reasoning abilities of prealphabetic cultures; he is also unaware of the ideological nature of his claim that critical thinking as we know it, which he privileges as an absolute value central to "civilized" culture, is a function of alphabetic literacy. Gregory Ulmer points out in his development of "teletheory" ("the application of grammatology to television in the context of schooling") that

it is a mistake to hypostatize "critical thinking" as an absolute value, transcending specific historical and social conditions. Academic discourse will continue to be "critical" to the extent that it continues—as it will—to exercise the forms of literacy. But that is not all it will be. Against the critics of the new technology who charge it with being "uncritical" or incapable of representing critical cognition, teletheory offers this proposition: video can do the work of literacy, but no better than literacy can do the work of speech. It has its own features and capacities that are fully cognitive, whether or not they are "critical." . . . School is the institutionalization of literacy, writing as an "on-going activity," which does not mean that speech and video are to be excluded. Similarly television is the institutionalization of video in our civilization, which does not mean that the technology is limited to the purposes of entertainment or information. (3)

The desire to maintain a specific form of "critical thinking" rooted in one technology—print—simply does not respect the mutability and diversity of institutions, or of various cultural forms—oral, written, imaged, electronic, in short all that traditionally constitutes popular culture—of transmission of information and value.

Ulmer warns that failure to consider "the cognitive capacities of video reflect [the] failure to acknowledge the changed status of the image and story in the field of cognitive science over the past fifteen years or so." He goes on to say that

> there is no technological determinism that dictates what will become of video in our culture, even if that technology is now institutionalized in television. Television is indeed a rival didactic institution, promoting an alternative mode of thought, just as the critics warn. But what should the response of the schools be?" (ix)

The representatives of the conservative faction in education in this country seem to believe that the appropriate response is warring institutions, which compete for the hearts and minds of students either through entertainment or education, which can never cognitively coincide.

The second problem with Kimball's position, closely related to the desire to maintain and promote nineteenth-century models of education and perhaps arising out of it, is the awesome disregard that Kimball and others demonstrate of the exigencies of the cultural situation that has arisen along with the new technologies. The proliferation of cable channels and VCRs has indeed made it possible to access Bugs Bunny and Shakespeare simultaneously, but it is Kimball's absurdist rhetoric that locks these texts into a dichotomy that is constructed *only* in and through that very rhetoric. Students are faced with a cultural complexity involving an entire array of texts, genres, artistic forms, and media that force them to make more difficult and subtle distinctions both intellectually and affectively than ever before. In a given context, students are rarely asked to choose between Bugs Bunny and Shakespeare—indeed one would be hard-pressed to imagine a scenario in which a student would need to make such a choice (perhaps a more plausible scenario would have been between *Tenured Radicals* and Bugs Bunny as cartoon visions of the struggle between good and evil). They are faced rather with choices between texts like a Shakespeare play and *The Gospel at Colonus,* a much less easily denigrated pairing. Any reader of this essay can certainly provide any number of pairings of choices that they themselves have faced within, between, and among various media as they stood in a bookstore or videostore or library. Kimball and Bloom and others simply ignore the complexity of choosing and choice in an electronic world that *within a specific context* puts whole ranges of choice literally at a fingertip, fixing instead as central one set of dominant ahistorical and acontextual values that is completely at odds with a late twentieth-century social, cultural, and institutional context.

The leftist project to define a critical pedagogy that can come to terms with popular forms has always been especially sensitive to this context, but has rarely been any more effective in dealing with issues of student experience and evaluation.[7] As Giroux and Simon point out,

> Radical analyses [of culture] usually focus either on deconstructing the ideologies at work in particular cultural forms or on how readers organize

texts according to their own meanings and experiences. In both cases
pedagogy is subordinate to and subsumed within a rather limited notion
of ideology production. In this approach, the concern over ideology is
limited to a particular view of consent in which the study of popular culture
is reduced to analysis of texts or to popular culture as a form of consumption.
(15)

This passage neatly encapsulates the two predominant leftist positions emanating
from the Frankfurt School and the British Culturalist School, which ironically
reproduce many of the same evaluative problems of their counterparts on the
Right: the privileging of interpretive paradigms that "reveal" the true ideological
meanings and messages of texts for audiences, or paradigms that show how audiences
resist this ideological domination through "resistant readings." The privileging of
interpretive paradigms carries with it the same consequences for the Left as it does
for the Right, namely that critics who can discern true Culture demonize popular
culture as pure commodity product, inauthentic, mindlessly repetitive, imposed
from above by a cabalistic culture industry that threatens civilization as we know
it. The "resistant readings" approach tends to a celebratory, but often uncritical
pluralism that privileges difference without any sense of the complex theoretical,
political, and social implications of such a position. And certainly the same primacy
is given to a particular conception of "critical thinking" deriving out of a print-
based culture that does not recognize other types of cognition and reaction. The
practical pedagogical consequences of these positions are perhaps best exemplified
by a passage from an article by Paul Smith, who is reflecting precisely on the
theory and practice of his own teaching of popular culture. Smith writes:

Meaning is often already understood by students to reside within texts
of a traditional kind (novels, poems, stories) but is not always recognized
by them as a component of the [Popular Culture Commodity Text].
Students already think of PCCTs as texts which do not need to be analyzed;
rather they often seem self-evident or obvious, texts which, to adopt a
distinction of Roland Barthes, signal rather than signify. The first pedagogical task, then, can be conceived as the production of contradiction in and
among students' views of the PCCT, simply by treating it as meaningful
and significant. The text, any text, delimits a particular field of meaning,
displays internal contradictions, offers particular interpretive choices, alludes
to given histories and circumstances. These need to be put into play in all
their contradictions, not necessarily as contradictions which need to be
resolved, but as contradictions which the students should be encouraged
to puzzle. Similarly, the conflict among different students' receptions of
the PCCT can be encouraged, further undermining the text's previously
silent, unanalyzed passage through their lives and marking it as the site of
disagreement, not to say struggle. (34)

Who is the hero of this narrative? Smith assumes that the students do not understand their popular cultural texts as meaningful or significant until they are treated as such within certain discursive frameworks that define the relation of knowledge and power located only within certain institutional boundaries. Their experience of the texts is allegedly uncritical, shaped only by the specific institutions within which they encounter them—the school involves texts with intellectual but not affective meaning, the realm of commodified culture produces affective, but not intellectually meaningful, texts, until, that is, the proper evaluative forms are activated and applied, guided by the benevolent presence of the teacher. He assumes like Kimball that a certain kind of critical thinking, which is limited to the classroom, is the key to unlocking texts. And while Smith is careful in the beginning of his article to make the popular culture texts he studies in his classroom the site of the *intersection* of "our interaction and as objects for which we are consumers" (leading him to term them popular-cultural-commodity texts), he concludes that the

> PCCT, however internally conflictual it might be or however it might accommodate itself to changing social conditions, always contains the specific interests that underpin it and produce it. My claim is that those specific interests cannot be brought out in the classroom by any straightforward kind of encounter with the texts nor, in other words, by the unmediated pedagogical plan of offering the students the opportunity to react to them. This would be to adopt a pedagogical approach which is ultimately too text-centered and leaves too much unbroached. The task is, instead, to direct attention and learned skills to something outside texts. (43)

While I understand that the impetus for Smith's pedagogical approach here is a response to an anti-intellectualism that privileges an uncritical affectivity, and an attempt to reinscribe students' experience into the institutional, discursive spaces that shape it, in doing so he reinscribes himself into the unresolvable debate over the place of evaluation in pedagogical politics. The debate is unresolvable because the very terms within which it is framed pose it as a binary opposition between what is approachable and unapproachable in texts and in students' responses to them. How can an academic speak as a cultural worker possessed of a certain knowledge and expertise without falling into an elitist posture in which the academic is always necessarily wiser than her/his students? The assumption that students' affective responses are "uncritical," and that the texts themselves are always already invested with the politics of commodification, smacks dangerously of an inherent value, hidden from the view of all but interpretive "seers," residing in the text due to its means of production. The very designation "PCCT" places all such texts into a monolithic category that simply ignores the potential complexity of their use value in favor of a tainted "intrinsic value," thereby founding a materialist critique on a thoroughly amaterialist presupposition regarding inherent value. In order to avoid the "taint" of the specific interests that underpin it (a kind of commodified intentional fallacy), we must direct our attention to something outside texts—that is, responses, but responses are not really responses until they are given a particular voice—resistant voice—in the classroom. In effect, we are led away from any notion of a literacy that exists outside the walls of the academy, or of responses that can be "critical" in a way not yet approachable in the classroom itself, because the pedagogical approaches that have been developed up to now continue to obscure the fact that, as Smith has argued, "evaluation is not merely an aspect of formal academic criticism but a complex set of social and cultural activities central to the very nature of [artistic cultural products and production]" (10).

In what follows, I hope to suggest through an analysis of a popular television text how we can begin to deal with the evaluation of popular cultural texts that takes us out of the limiting binarisms that plague the popular culture/curriculum debate by examining how a television text can create its own hierarchy for response based on a very different standard of evaluation arising from the medium itself. In the process we can begin to comprehend the expanded literacy, the kind of developing cognition necessary to be able to "read" these images, not as we would "critically" read a written text, but in their visual and cultural situation precisely outside of an academic "critical" attitude that applies almost exclusively to the written text.

"THIRTYSOMETHING" AND THE IDEOLOGY OF POPULAR ENTERTAINMENT

Over the past two decades television texts have been the subject of increasingly sophisticated textual analysis, and reception theory has stimulated equally sophisticated approaches to audience research and analysis. What has not grown increasingly sophisticated in television study is the issue of evaluation, which remains in the dark ages of mass communication research, based on the evaluative principle of television as "bad object." It is not so much that television has not been subject to constant evaluation as that the critical paradigms used to evaluate television have not been able to account for the very complexity of the television experience that the analysis of television has revealed. As one of the least legitimate forms of popular culture, television is seemingly the easiest to evaluate.

Ien Ang, in her ground-breaking study, *Watching Dallas,* argues that there are really only two ideologies used in the evaluation of television, the "ideology of mass culture" and the "ideology of populism." The former is the predominant mode of academic criticism, which sees television as precisely that which is opposed to "authentic art." The ideology of mass culture offers two positions for the viewer to adopt: the refusal of television as a "bad object," or an ironic position in which viewers distance themselves from television by making it an object of derision, the ironic detachment itself becoming the source of the pleasure. This position is exemplified in Ang's quote of the statement, "I find Dallas amusing because it is so bad." Ang presents the latter, the ideology of populism, as the single alternative, which constructs itself only in opposition to the ideology of mass culture, offering one position to the viewer, namely that there is "no accounting for taste." Viewers who adopt this position find it is not one of strength or confidence, precisely because it is constructed only negatively, against the rational discourse of mass culture criticism which denies it any claim to rational expression. Those viewers who dislike television find the rational discourse of intellectual tradition at their disposal, whereas those who enjoy it can only say, "I like it," an intensely personal statement that implies a lack of generalizable standards.

While Ang sets up the two ideologies as separate modes of evaluating the pleasure that TV offers a viewer, when they are placed against each other it becomes clear that only one offers a true mode of evaluation; there is only one way of truly accounting for taste, which is encompassed by the ideology of mass culture. This ideology provides the language of explanation and evaluation, while the populist position is an utter rejection of evaluation. It can make no appeal to "formal, universalized criteria which are devoid of subjective passions and pleasures," (Ang. 113) because it is rooted in those very passions and pleasures. In short, the viewer has available either the critical discourse of the professional intellectual, which sets the standard for evaluating cultural artifacts, or the discourse of the "common" viewer, which abstains from evaluation. Ang insists that the power of the ideology of mass culture to dominate the way people evaluate TV is not absolute in that it finally does not necessarily prescribe people's cultural practices. That is, people may express guilt about the practice, but they continue to watch TV. This crucial point is rendered inconsequential in short order, however, when Ang points out that the commercial culture industry

> employs the populist ideology for its own ends by reinforcing the cultural eclecticism underlying it and propagating the idea that indeed there's no accounting for taste, that in other words, no objective aesthetic judgments are possible. It sells it products by propagating the idea that everyone has the right to his or her own taste and has the freedom to enjoy pleasure in his or her own way. (115)

Ang correctly implies that the power of the ideology of mass culture may not be strong enough to keep people from watching—and even enjoying—television, but then implies that it is powerful enough to keep the producers of television from producing shows that can stand up to an accounting for taste, and the viewer is right back to consumer (as opposed to producer) of low-quality texts, the television is right back to "bad cultural object," which people may watch, but which offers little in the way of anything to talk about.

Ang's analysis, then, presupposes a preexisting, independent, and unitary hierarchy of evaluation largely derived from scholarly criticism, which is awarded pride of place, given proprietorial rights over the construction of taste in the cultural arena. Either the viewer accepts the hierarchy, which specifically condemns that pleasure as irrational and therefore forces the viewer to repudiate it; or the viewer may acknowledge pleasure, but renounce evaluation and accept a place on the lower rung of the hierarchy as the owner, in Pierre Bourdieu's scenario of the "aristocracy of culture," of the naive gaze against which the aesthetic gaze is constructed. Ang notes that these naive viewers are not in a position to form an equally negative view of those viewers who dislike television, but can only offer resistance to the negative identities that others (i.e., the aristocracy, or more sophisticated and aware intellectual viewers) ascribe to them.

But does Ang's hierarchical scenario apply to the American viewing experience? American viewers are rarely apologetic or dismissive about their viewing experiences—to the contrary there seems to be an extremely high level of engagement with TV in American audiences, evident through both the amount of television the pollsters tell us they watch and the range of choices available to them in programming and channels, and through the impressive marketing industry that has built up around TV, from the mind-boggling array of mass market publications devoted to television and television stars to the clothing industry which produces a range of licensed and unlicensed apparel, from T-shirts to entire fashion lines, derived from a particular program's styles. Viewers literally wear their engagement with TV on their sleeves. What all this indicates is that the unitary hierarchy of value that Ang posits is not acknowledged by American audiences. This is not to suggest that they are indiscriminate viewers, thoroughly inculcated with the ideology of populism.

Instead, they are viewers continuously making distinctions, but outside of the rigid hierarchy of values that places all interpretive and evaluative power in the hands of the professional intellectual. Contrary to Ang's contention, American audiences do form negative images of those who dislike popular television, and the professional intellectuals who have been largely responsible for a negative assessment of television are a favorite target, generally portrayed as unable to deal with television in any comprehensible way because of their inability to understand the medium on its own terms. I will return to this point later, but for now it is sufficient to note that implicit in such a portrayal, of course, is the idea that the medium does in fact have its own terms to set standards for taste, which cannot fit into the imposed-from-without hierarchy of the intelligentsia because these standards are not fixed in the same way, and therefore do not necessarily apply in any hierarchical fashion.

Thus, to Ang's two categories—which do in fact describe types of viewing experience—there needs to be added a third, what I would like to call the "ideology of popular entertainment," to account for this strain in American television that, rather than "propagating the idea that indeed there's no accounting for taste," is preoccupied with constructing and accounting for taste, which viewers can recognize as deriving from their own ability to choose, and which the program must acknowledge in order to be chosen. So while "America's Funniest Home Videos" may appeal to the ideology of populism at its most explicit, that ideology does not explain, say, Quality Television programs like "Hill Street Blues," "St. Elsewhere,"

"Moonlighting," "L.A. Law," or "thirtysomething," programs which explicitly try to account for taste by making their own taste distinctions that separate them from other programs of the same ilk, and both implicitly and explicitly address the issue of why they should be chosen and by whom. The latter quality programs differentiate themselves from those that Jane Feuer analyzes in her watershed work on Quality TV in that they no longer proclaim both their difference from and their likeness to other television, but insist on their difference from other television in specifically evaluative terms derived exclusively from television. Through an analysis of two sequences from two different "thirtysomething" shows which aired in 1989–90 season, I'd like to begin to give an idea of how the show begins to account for taste, and asserts that its taste really *is* better. This kind of TV does not merely repudiate the ideology of mass culture, but appropriates it and puts it to use for its own ideological ends.

The first sequence opens the "Mike Van Dyke Show" episode, which aired as the Christmas special in both 1988 and 1989. The first shot is a close-up of a Trivial Pursuit game, which is revealed to be on the floor of the yuppie couple Michael and Hope Steadman's living room as the camera draws back. The lighting is "atmospheric," with the fireplace providing the greatest light source, the light flickering over the characters and the game board, so that the very first shot distinguishes this show as a "quality" show, borrowing its lighting, camera, and editing technique from film, not from the studio sitcom; this is "thirtysomething," and not a cheesy studio sitcom, say, "Married With Children." As the scene progresses, this distinction becomes increasingly clearly drawn. Gary, the college professor character who represents "the intellectual," rolls the dice and draws a question on television, and immediately gripes, in a self-reflexive statement that is a significant marker of quality television, "Why do I always land on TV?" He complains that his generation seems incapable of defining itself other than by old television songs remembered from old television shows, while the other characters—Hope, Michael, and Ellen—provide a background rendition of the theme song from the "Dick Van Dyke Show." The question "Who played Buddy and Sally?" stimulates a series of reminiscences and comments about old TV shows, all of which work to distinguish "thirtysomething" as a new and different kind of television. "thirtysomething" is not the naive television programs of the fifties, where, as Hope says, "everybody is always nice and everybody is always happy," and the contrived formulas, such as mothers who are always dead (Ellen's remark), and contrived situations that have no continuity from week to week (Michael), have no reference to reality. This is, rather, an ensemble show, where characters intersect in continual but consistently varying situations, facing crises in their domestic and working lives (and mothers are very much alive and part of those crises), which are not necessarily resolved in one easy episode.

But the sequence doesn't simply reject its televisual precursors as naive and set itself up as the preferred "aesthetic." They talk about these shows fondly, realizing and acknowledging the crucial role they play in establishing the identity of this show and of the individual characters. The point of this self-conscious reflection on earlier shows is to demonstrate that these shows are interwoven into the fabric of consciousness as a vital component of cultural memory and cannot be easily discredited, no matter how much the characters or we laugh at them. That television provides the standard of its own value becomes apparent both within the sequence, through the character of Gary, and in the playing out of the rest of this particular episode. Gary is a college professor, who bemoans having "wasted his time reading Ivanhoe," and he finally is unable to answer the question. His answer, "Julius and Ethel Rosenberg played Buddy and Sally," is a particularly telling response. Gary cannot draw on his intellectual background here, because that has nothing to do with this subject. All he can do is what all intellectuals do—make absurd elisions using "historical" or "real" texts that figure only marginally as an element of popular cultural memory, and therefore seem to have some kind of relevance that others can't quite figure out, except that they reveal his political correctness and his complete inability to function within this sphere or to make it function within his.

The rest of the episode is devoted to demonstrating how relevant these shows really are to the fabric of our consciousness. As he goes through a series of crises— the specter of his business failing, Hope's car crash and apparently resulting illness, and a crisis of religious conviction—Michael envisions his life as the "Dick Van Dyke Show," where he can imagine the resolutions to these crises in the happy fashion of the Fifties sitcom. Michael literally projects himself and the other people in his life onto the TV screen he is watching; he "becomes" Rob Petrie, Hope "becomes" Laura, and the problems he is experiencing are thematized and begin to be resolved within the diegesis of the "Dick Van Dyke Show." But, of course, his life does not actually work that way, and at some point he can no longer contain his anxieties within the parameters of the sitcom, and he abandons it. Jim Collins points to this moment where Michael walks out of the diegesis of the earlier show, and back into the "thirtysomething" diegesis as a moment of complex "trancontextualization,"[8] in which

> television does indeed become a part of the family in that the intertextual referencing of *thirtysomething* functions as a comic "talking out" process in which we confront our televisual past, our relationship to the medium being roughly analogous to that which many enjoy with their actual families; both are characterized by the same ambivalence, the same sense of ironic denial of the absurd past alongside the recognition that, like it or not, these characters who wander through our unconscious have played far too prominent a role in the forging of our identity. (269)

This transcontextualization is made even more complex by the scene which closes the episode. Earlier in the show, Michael goes to temple, and wanders into the rabbi's office, where he runs into Jack Gilbert, whom he has previously envisioned as the Santa Claus character in his fantasy of the Van Dyke show. It appears that Michael has unconsciously projected a character from his past—the rabbi of the temple he used to attend—into his fantasy, until on a repeat visit to the temple, Michael discovers that the rabbi he saw apparently does not exist, rather it was a projection of his televisual memory into his actual existence in a way that reveals the continual working of one upon the other. The transcontextualization cuts both ways. Is the Jack Gilbert figure really Michael's guardian angel, his Clarence, who finally does deliver the ultimate happy ending (not only is Hope not dying of the aftereffects of her car crash, she is pregnant, and there really is a Santa Claus!)? This projection is the exact opposite of Michael's continuing fantasy of the Van Dyke show, where he places himself within the diegesis of that sitcom in order to allow for happy resolutions. Here a happy resolution is made to appear very real by virtue of its dissimilarity to the sitcom—in the Van Dyke show, Hope/Laura's disappearance and failure to show up on time would not play as potentially anxiety-producing, signifying possible tragedy, while in "thirtysomething," it is entirely possible that she is out there somewhere dying—but the happy resolution also emphasizes the similarity of "thirtysomething" to other fictional forms like the sitcom and the inspirational Christmas film, in both its use of them and the attendant acknowledgment of its debt to them—a debt made even more explicit by the Bedford Falls production logo at the end of every show, with the house and song from *It's a Wonderful Life*. We find those shows and this show affecting precisely because of their ability to make things come out right.

But this ideology of popular entertainment, which restructures and resolves the conflict of popular entertainment versus high art standards in a self-legitimation process, which exploits the ideology of mass culture to its own ends, must eventually also resolve the charge that popular entertainment is advertiser-driven, nothing more than a commodity (a PCCT) created to be sold as mere entertainment, a backdrop for selling products. "thirtysomething" specifically thematizes this issue. Within the program, advertising is consistently presented as a creative activity, produced in an interactive environment where Michael and Elliott transfer their own experience and sensibility onto the screen as advertisements. The episodes that deal with the first project that Michael and Elliott undertake at an agency where they've just been hired depict this process from conception to final product. Elliott and Michael are given a candy bar account, and they devise the idea of selling candy bars to adults utilizing the concept of "retro-snacking," i.e., encouraging consumers to rediscover the pleasures of the foods of their youth by re-orienting their adult presuppositions to allow the rediscovery of that pleasure. The uncanny relevance this has to the attempt by "thirtysomething" to encourage us to rediscover the pleasures of the television of our youth is reinforced by the continual self-referencing that goes on in the ad that Michael and Elliott write and shoot. The ad is a simple reduplication of the scene that we watched as Michael and Elliott brainstormed to come up with an idea for the ad—their experience translated directly into an ad. In another, later brainstorming session with the head of the agency, he tells them that *they are* the demographic, "the spokesmen for the late eighties" and laughingly says, "Look at them. They're the commercial."

But this is not a negative comment within the program—it is in fact a celebratory one. The creativity of this commercial and the show is that it is able to translate and make accessible that "real" experience. This show goes so far as to expose the mechanisms of production of the show itself, but keeps that exposure within the frame of the diegesis. When they shoot the ad, they seem to be shot on the same sets that are used as the agency offices of "thirtysomething," and for a disorienting moment it looks as if we are getting a behind the scenes view of "thirtysomething" itself. Elliott is seen on long shot, talking to what we could assume is his own director or crew member of the "thirtysomething" set. But then the two actors who have been hired by the agency to play Elliott and Michael appear, and we watch the ad being shot, exposing the process that went into the creation of the original (and originary) scene between Michael and Elliott, showing that indeed "thirtysomething" itself is grounded in both reality and the creativity that translates that moment.

The most striking and self-referential sequence, though, is the focus group response to the ad. They hate it, and the criticism they level at the ad is precisely the criticism that is often leveled at "thirtysomething": the characters are whiny yuppies without real problems, the men don't act like men, there is too much male-bonding crap. The most telling response—"I enjoyed it. . . I enjoyed hating it"—echoes Ang's ironic viewer of "Dallas," who adopts the ideology of mass culture to turn illicit enjoyment into more acceptable mockery. But here the show is responding ironically itself, clearly rejecting this as a valid response. The focus group members are themselves whiny and obnoxious, obviously unable to accept new or different ideas, evidenced by the statement "men should be men," and they timidly parrot the words of pseudopsychological analysis, "This touchy-feely male-bonding crap makes me sick." In this form, the accounting for their taste is no more coherent or articulate than those who just know what they like. Michael and Elliot cannot use this information to develop a new approach, or even to condemn the ad the focus group so inexplicably hates. The expressions of the mass culture ideology are not creative, or new, they are merely derivative, and validate an existing status quo. The viewers are dupes, not of an advertising industry that lulls them into either torpor or a passion for consumption, but rather victims of their own inability to articulate their responses in a language that actually expresses their attitudes about the medium they love to hate and yet cannot condemn.

The ideology of popular entertainment, then, positions itself against the ideology of mass culture and the ideology of populism in such a way as to expose their limitations in the evaluation of television texts. My use of the "thirtysomething" examples attempts to demonstrate how television texts can appropriate both ideologies and turn them to its own uses, offering in its own turn a range of positions for a viewer to occupy, from scornful rejection of old TV shows to an ironic attitude, but with other positions available as well, and this ideology recognizes the ambivalence of those positions without necessarily opposing them or "resolving" them. I am not arguing that "thirtysomething" is necessarily a socially progressive program, but I am arguing that television is engaged in a process of self-evaluation in which it constantly re-presents its own cultural capital in an attempt to introduce its own "gold standard" that circulates alongside other standards.

In terms of the larger stakes of the politics of interpretation, the ideology of popular entertainment also provides a third alternative to the binarism inherent in the textual analysis versus audience research debate which is at the foundation of Ang's influential work. This third ideology veers away from a politics of interpretation that forces the rejection of TV as bad object in the first place or forces the critic to look for "something outside the texts," both of which still ultimately locate the struggle as between only the intellectual and the "common viewer." The ideology of popular entertainment provides a significant challenge to the evaluative power of "the intellectuals," that portion of the audience that is able most cogently to theorize its position, and therefore, by its own standards, is in the best position to provide evaluation, of either text or audience. This third ideology demonstrates that there are other agents involved in evaluating popular media—the text itself, a range of viewers who are neither "intellectuals" nor "common," the advertising industry, the production industry, various other institutions too numerous to mention.

I do not wish to suggest that intellectuals—like Gary—have no place or function within the evaluative arena, but rather that theirs is not a necessarily privileged position that shows us how to interpret and evaluate all texts. Henry Giroux warns that

> rather than providing a place for young people to speak, the study of popular culture becomes a form of border crossing in which the Other becomes a resource for academic appropriation and valorization. What begins as a critical project is often reduced to an intellectual practice that merely privileges the authoritative persona of the "seer." This peculiarly Western tradition, so valorized in cultural professions has contributed to the regressively monolithic views of literacy we seek to dismantle. (243)

In pedagogical terms, avoidance of this trap involves injecting a note of self-criticism, a constant vigilance and awareness of our own politics in performing textual analysis. This metaevaluative perspective may be the only perspective that allows for any kind of claim to special status—a special status that depends not on the intrinsic genius of the academic, but on the academic's ability to delineate the multiple processes of evaluation that are operative simultaneously, among which the academic process is merely *one*. Adopting this metaevaluative position may be the only way we can hope to understand those processes from both within and without, able to step outside and remain imbricated at the same time in the social and textual processes of evaluation, both describing and inventing new electronic languages of thought that will make us and our students "literate" in entirely new, productive, and potentially powerful ways.

NOTES

1. This term comes from a pivotal work in television study by Jane Feuer, Paul Kerr, and Tise Vahimagi. The term will be discussed more fully later in this paper, but this work

is central to much of the critical and analytical work currently being produced about television.

2. See most especially Giroux and Simon, which is truly one of the very few articles that develops a pedagogical theory that incorporates a politics of popular culture. It heavily influences this essay. While many of the other essays in the volume with the Giroux and Simon essay attempt to come to terms with popular culture, I believe those essays fall into many of the traps that I will sketch out in the remainder of this essay. The Giroux and Simon essay has the virtue of being much more self-conscious about its own politics.

3. In a few cases the technological revolution is mentioned explicitly, most notably in Joshua Meyrowitz, Neil Postman, and Gregory Ulmer. Again, the only one of these three who develops a pedagogical theory which incorporates rather than dismisses a politics of popular culture is Ulmer. I believe his project is both unprecedented and necessary.

4. "During the 1980s, the number of U.S. households with VCRs climbed from 1.85 million (one home in 40) to 62 million (two-thirds of all homes). Prerecorded video cassette sales rose from only three million in 1980 to 220 million in 1990—an increase of 6,500 percent—while the number of cable households rose from 19.6 million in 1980 to 55 million in 1990, with pay subscriptions increasing from 9 million to 42 million during the decade" (Schatz).

5. Many of the students in my ten-year-old daughter's class are more proficient than the parent volunteers who teach them "keyboarding." Their mastery of the educational computer games has proved so quick that the school has had to scramble to buy new software that challenges their level of proficiency. Recently, when I asked one student why he was so good at the math games on the computer, when he struggles with them on paper, he shrugged and gave the one-word answer, "Nintendo."

6. See especially Bloom, who is perhaps the most derisive critic of student abilities among the representatives of the conservative pedagogues. Then see Aronowitz and Giroux for a devastating and elegant reply.

7. See Giroux and Simon, Aronowitz and Giroux, and the essays in Cary Nelson's book, especially Grossberg's; and Grossberg's *We Gotta Get Out of This Place,* where he deals substantively with issues of affectivity.

8. This is a concept developed by Linda Hutcheon in *A Theory of Parody,* where she focuses on a kind of parody that "is an integrated structural modeling process of revising, replacing, inverting and 'trans-contextualizing' previous works of art" (11). Transcontextualization is far more than simple quotation or inversion of an earlier work of art by a text, it is "repetition with a difference" involving critical distance. See especially chapter 2 for her fleshing out of this concept.

WORKS CITED

Ang, Ien. *Watching Dallas: Soap Opera and the Melodramatic Imagination.* New York: Methuen, 1985.

Aronowitz, Stanley, and Henry Giroux. "Textual Authority, Politics, and the Politics of Literacy." *Postmodern Education: Politics, Culture and Social Criticism.* Minneapolis: U of Minnesota P, 1991. 24–56.

Bennett, William. "To Reclaim a Legacy: Text of the Report of Humanities in Higher Education." *Chronicle of Higher Education.* Nov. 28, 1984: 16–21.

Bloom, Allan. *The Closing of the American Mind: How Higher Education Has Failed Democracy and Impoverished the Souls of Today's Students.* New York: Simon and Schuster, 1987.

Bourdieu, Pierre. "The Aristocracy of Culture." In Collins et al. 164–93.

———. "The Production of Belief: Contribution to an Economy of Symbolic Goods." In Collins et al. 131–63.

Collins, Jim. "Watching Ourselves Watch Television, or Who's Your Agent?" *Cultural Studies* 3.3 (1989): 261–81.

Collins, Richard et al. *Media, Culture and Society.* London: Sage, 1986.

D'Souza, Dinesh. *Illiberal Education: The Politics of Race and Sex on Campus.* New York: Free Press, 1991.

Feuer, Jane, Paul Kerr, and Tise Vahimagi. *MTM: Quality Television.* London: BFI Publications, 1984.

Giroux, Henry. *Border Crossings: Cultural Workers and the Politics of Education.* New York: Routledge, 1992.

Giroux, Henry, and Roger Simon. "Popular Culture as a Pedagogy of Pleasure and Meaning." In Giroux and Simon, *Popular Culture.* 1–29.

Giroux, Henry, and Roger Simon. *Popular Culture, Schooling and Everyday Life.* Granby, MA: Bergin and Garvey, 1989.

Goody, Jack. *Domestication of the Savage Mind.* New York: Cambridge UP, 1977.

Grossberg, Lawrence. *We Gotta Get Out of This Place: Popular Conservatism and Postmodern Culture.* New York: Routledge, 1992.

Hirsch, E.D., Jr. *Cultural Literacy: What Every American Needs to Know.* New York: Vintage, 1988.

Hutcheon, Linda. *A Theory of Parody.* New York: Methuen, 1985.

Kimball, Roger. *Tenured Radicals: How Politics Has Corrupted Our Higher Education.* New York: Harper and Row, 1990.

Meyrowitz, Joshua. *No Sense of Place.* New York: Oxford UP, 1985.

Nelson, Cary, ed. *Theory in the Classroom.* Urbana: U of Illinois P, 1986.

Postman, Neil. *Amusing Ourselves to Death.* New York: Penguin, 1985.

Rothstein, Edward. "Mr. Berry, Say Hello to Ludwig." *New York Times,* Sunday, April 12, 1992: H31.

Schatz, Thomas. "The New Hollywood." *Film Theory Goes to the Movies.* Ed. Jim Collins, Hilary Radner, Ava Collins. New York: Routledge, 1992.

Searle, John. "The Storm over the University." *Debating P.C.* Ed. Paul Berman. New York: Dell, 1992. 85–123.

Smith, Barbara Herrnstein. "Contingencies of Value." *Canons.* Ed. Robert von Hallberg. Chicago: U of Chicago P, 1984.

Smith, Paul. "The Popular-Cultural-Commodity Text." In Giroux and Simon, *Popular Culture.* 31–46.

Ulmer, Gregory. *Teletheory: Grammatology in the Age of Video.* New York: Routledge, 1989.

CHAPTER 3

RETHINKING THE

PUBLIC SPHERE: A

CONTRIBUTION TO THE

CRITIQUE OF ACTUALLY

EXISTING DEMOCRACY[1]

NANCY FRASER

INTRODUCTION

Today in the U.S. we hear a great deal of ballyhoo about "the triumph of liberal democracy" and even "the end of history." Yet there is still a great deal to object to in our own "actually existing democracy," and the project of a critical social theory of the limits of democracy in late capitalist societies remains as relevant as ever. In fact, this project seems to me to have acquired a new urgency at a time when "liberal democracy" is being touted as the *ne plus ultra* of social systems for countries that are emerging from Soviet-style state socialism, Latin American military dictatorships, and southern African regimes of racial domination.

Those of us who remain committed to theorizing the limits of democracy in late capitalist societies will find the work of Jürgen Habermas as an indispensable resource. I mean the concept of "the public sphere," originally elaborated in his 1962 book, *The Structural Transformation of the Public Sphere,* and subsequently resituated but never abandoned in his later work.[2]

The political and theoretical importance of this idea is easy to explain. Habermas's concept of the public sphere provides a way of circumventing some confusions that have plagued progressive social movements and the political theories associated with them. Take, for example, the long-standing failure in the dominant wing of the socialist and Marxist tradition to appreciate the full force of the distinction between the apparatuses of the state, on the one hand, and public arenas of citizen discourse and association, on the other. All too often it was assumed in this tradition that to subject the economy to the control of the socialist state was to subject it to the control of the socialist citizenry. Of course that was not so. But the conflation of the state apparatus with the public sphere of discourse and association provided ballast to processes whereby the socialist vision became institutionalized in an authoritarian statist form instead of in a participatory democratic form. The result has been to jeopardize the very idea of socialist democracy.

A second problem, albeit one that has so far been much less historically momentous and certainly less tragic, is a confusion one encounters at times in contemporary feminisms. I mean a confusion that involves the use of the very same expression "the public sphere," but in a sense that is less precise and less useful than Habermas's. This expression has been used by many feminists to refer to everything that is outside the domestic or familial sphere. Thus, "the public sphere" in this usage conflates at least three analytically distinct things: the state, the official economy of paid employment, and arenas of public discourse.[3] Now, it should not be thought that the conflation of these three things is a "merely theoretical" issue. On the contrary, it has practical political consequences, for example, when agitational campaigns against misogynist cultural representations are confounded with programs for state censorship, or when struggles to deprivatize housework and child care are equated with their commodification. In both these cases, the result is to occlude the question whether to subject gender issues to the logic of the market or the administrative state is to promote the liberation of women.

The idea of "the public sphere" in Habermas's sense is a conceptual resource that can help overcome such problems. It designates a theater in modern societies in which political participation is enacted through the medium of talk. It is the space in which citizens deliberate about their common affairs, hence, an institutionalized arena of discursive interaction. This arena is conceptually distinct from the state; it a site for the production and circulation of discourses that can in principle be critical of the state. The public sphere in Habermas's sense is also conceptually distinct from the official economy; it is not an arena of market relations but rather one of discursive relations, a theater for debating and deliberating rather than for buying and selling. Thus, this concept of the public sphere permits us to keep in view the distinctions between state apparatuses, economic markets, and democratic associations, distinctions that are essential to democratic theory.

For these reasons, I am going to take as a basic premise for this essay that something like Habermas's idea of the public sphere is indispensable to critical social theory and to democratic political practice. I assume that no attempt to understand the limits of actually existing late capitalist democracy can succeed without in some way or another making use of it. I assume that the same goes for urgently needed constructive efforts to project alternative models of democracy.

If you will grant me the general idea of the public sphere is indispensable to critical theory, then I shall go on to argue that the specific form in which Habermas has elaborated this idea is not wholly satisfactory. On the contrary, I contend that his analysis of the public sphere needs to undergo some critical interrogation and reconstruction if it is to yield a category capable of theorizing the limits of actually existing democracy.

Let me remind you that the subtitle of *Structural Transformation* is "An Inquiry into a Category of Bourgeois Society." The object of the inquiry is the rise and decline of a historically specific and limited form of the public sphere, which Habermas calls the "liberal model of the bourgeois public sphere." The aim is to identify the conditions that made possible this type of public sphere and to chart their devolution. The upshot is an argument that, under altered conditions of late-twentieth-century "welfare state mass democracy," the bourgeois or liberal model of the public sphere is no longer feasible. Some new form of public sphere is required to salvage that arena's critical function and to institutionalize democracy.

Oddly, Habermas stops short of developing a new, postbourgeois model of the public sphere. Moreover, he never explicitly problematizes some dubious assumptions that underlie the bourgeois model. As a result, we are left at the end of *Structural Transformation* without a conception of the public sphere that is sufficiently distinct from the bourgeois conception to serve the needs of critical theory today.

That, at any rate, is the thesis I intend to argue. In order to make my case, I shall proceed as follows: I shall begin, in section one, by juxtaposing Habermas's account of the structural transformation of the public sphere to an alternative account that can be pieced together from some recent revisionist historiography. Then, I shall identify four assumptions underlying the bourgeois conception of the public sphere, as Habermas describes it, which this newer historiography renders suspect. Next, in the following four sections, I shall examine each of these assumptions in turn. Finally, in a brief conclusion, I shall draw together some strands from these critical discussions that point toward an alternative, postbourgeois conception of the public sphere.

THE PUBLIC SPHERE: ALTERNATIVE HISTORIES, COMPETING CONCEPTIONS

Let me begin by sketching some highlights of Habermas's account of the structural transformation of the public sphere. According to Habermas, the idea of a public sphere is that of a body of "private persons" assembled to discuss matters of "public concern" or "common interest." This idea acquired force and reality in early modern Europe in the constitution of "bourgeois publics spheres" as counter-weights to absolutist states. These publics aimed to mediate between "society" and the state by holding the state accountable to "society" via "publicity." At first this meant requiring that information about state functioning be made accessible so that state activities would be subject to critical scrutiny and the force of "public opinion." Later, it meant transmitting the considered "general interest" of "bour-geois society" to the state via forms of legally guaranteed free speech, free press, and free assembly, and eventually through the parliamentary institutions of represen-tative government.

Thus, at one level, the idea of the public sphere designated an institutional mechanism for "rationalizing" political domination by rendering states accountable to (some of) the citizenry. At another level, it designated a specific kind of discursive interaction. Here the public sphere connoted an ideal of unrestricted rational discussion of public matters. The discussion was to be open and accessible to all; merely private interests were to be inadmissible; inequalities of status were to be bracketed; and discussants were to deliberate as peers. The result of such discussion would be "public opinion" in the strong sense of a consensus about the common good.

According to Habermas, the full utopian potential of the bourgeois conception of the public sphere was never realized in practice. The claim to open access in particular was not made good. Moreover, the bourgeois conception of the public sphere was premised on a social order in which the state was sharply differentiated from the newly privatized market economy; it was this clear separation of "society" and state that was supposed to underpin a form of public discussion that excluded "private interests." But these conditions eventually eroded as nonbourgeois strata gained access to the public sphere. Then, "the social question" came to the fore; society was polarized by class struggle; and the public fragmented into a mass of competing interest groups. Street demonstrations and back room, brokered compromises among private interests replaced reasoned public debate about the common good. Finally, with the emergence of "welfare state mass democracy," society and the state became mutually intertwined; publicity in the sense of critical scrutiny of the state gave way to public relations, mass-mediated staged displays, and the manufacture and manipulation of public opinion.

Now, let me juxtapose to this sketch of Habermas's account an alternative account that I shall piece together from some recent revisionist historiography. Briefly, scholars like Joan Landes, Mary Ryan, and Geoff Eley contend that Habermas's account idealizes the liberal public sphere. They argue that, despite the rhetoric of publicity and accessibility, that official public sphere rested on, indeed was importantly constituted by, a number of significant exclusions. For Landes, the key axis of exclusion is gender; she argues that the ethos of the new republican public sphere in France was constructed in deliberate opposition to that of a more woman-friendly salon culture that the republicans stigmatized as "artificial," "effeminate," and "aristocratic." Consequently, a new, austere style of public speech and behavior was promoted, a style deemed "rational," "virtuous," and "manly." In this way, masculinist gender constructs were built into the very conception of the republican public sphere, as was a logic that led, at the height of Jacobin rule, to the formal exclusion from political life of women.[4] Here the republicans drew on classical traditions that cast femininity and publicity as oxymorons; the depth of such traditions can be gauged in the etymological connection between "public" and "pubic," a graphic trace of the fact that in the ancient world possession of a penis was a requirement for speaking in public. (A similar link is preserved, incidentally, in the etymological connection between "testimony" and "testicle.")[5]

Extending Landes's argument, Geoff Eley contends that exclusionary operations were essential to liberal public spheres not only in France but also in England and

Germany, and that in all these countries gender exclusions were linked to other exclusions rooted in processes of class formation. In all these countries, he claims, the soil that nourished the liberal public sphere was "civil society," the emerging new congeries of voluntary associations that sprung up in what came to be known as "the age of societies." But this network of clubs and associations—philanthropic, civic, professional, and cultural—was anything but accessible to everyone. On the contrary, it was the arena, the training ground, and eventually the power base of a stratum of bourgeois men, who were coming to see themselves as a "universal class" and preparing to assert their fitness to govern. Thus, the elaboration of a distinctive culture of civil society and of an associated public sphere was implicated in the process of bourgeois class formation; its practices and ethos were markers of "distinction" in Pierre Bourdieu's sense,[6] ways of defining an emergent elite, setting it off from the older aristocratic elites it was intent on displacing, on the one hand, and from the various popular and plebeian strata it aspired to rule, on the other. This process of distinction, moreover, helps explain the exacerbation of sexism characteristic of the liberal public sphere; new gender norms enjoining feminine domesticity and a sharp separation of public and private spheres functioned as key signifiers of bourgeois difference from both higher and lower social strata. It is a measure of the eventual success of this bourgeois project that these norms later became hegemonic, sometimes imposed on, sometimes embraced by, broader segments of society.[7]

Now, there is a remarkable irony here, one that Habermas's account of the rise of the public sphere fails fully to appreciate.[8] A discourse of publicity touting accessibility, rationality, and the suspension of status hierarchies is itself deployed as a strategy of distinction. Of course, in and of itself, this irony does not fatally compromise the discourse of publicity; that discourse can be, indeed has been, differently deployed in different circumstances and contexts. Nevertheless, it does suggest that the relationship between publicity and status is more complex than Habermas intimates, that declaring a deliberative arena to be a space where extant status distinctions are bracketed and neutralized is not sufficient to make it so.

Moreover, the problem is not only that Habermas idealizes the liberal public sphere but also that he fails to examine other, nonliberal, nonbourgeois, competing public spheres. Or rather, it is precisely because he fails to examine these other public spheres that he ends up idealizing the liberal public sphere.[9] Mary Ryan documents the variety of ways in which nineteenth-century North American women of various classes and ethnicities constructed access routes to public political life, even despite their exclusion from the official public sphere. In the case of elite bourgeois women, this involved building a counter–civil society of alternative woman-only voluntary associations, including philanthropic and moral reform societies; in some respects, these associations aped the all-male societies built by these women's fathers and grandfathers; yet in other respects the women were innovating, since they creatively used the heretofore quintessentially "private" idioms of domesticity and motherhood precisely as springboards for public activity. Meanwhile, for some less privileged women, access to public life came through participation in supporting roles in male-dominated working-class protest activities.

Still other women found public outlets in street protests and parades. Finally, women's rights advocates publicly contested both women's exclusion from the official public sphere and the privatization of gender politics.[10]

Ryan's study shows that, even in the absence of formal political incorporation through suffrage, there were a variety of ways of accessing public life and a multiplicity of public arenas. Thus, the view that women were excluded from the public sphere turns out to be ideological; it rests on a class- and gender-biased notion of publicity, one which accepts at face value the bourgeois public's claim to be *the* public. In fact, the historiography of Ryan and others demonstrates that the bourgeois public was never *the* public. On the contrary, virtually contemporaneous with the bourgeois public there arose a host of competing counterpublics, including nationalist publics, popular peasant publics, elite women's publics, and working-class publics. Thus, there were competing publics from the start, not just from the late nineteenth and twentieth centuries, as Habermas implies.[11]

Moreover, not only were there always a plurality of competing publics but the relations between bourgeois publics and other publics were always conflictual. Virtually from the beginning, counterpublics contested the exclusionary norms of the bourgeois public, elaborating alternative styles of political behavior and alternative norms of public speech. Bourgeois publics, in turn, excoriated these alternatives and deliberately sought to block broader participation. As Eley puts it, "the emergence of a bourgeois public was never defined solely by the struggle against absolutism and traditional authority, but . . . addressed the problem of popular containment as well. The public sphere was always constituted by conflict."[12]

In general, this revisionist historiography suggests a much darker view of the bourgeois public sphere than the one that emerges from Habermas's study. The exclusions and conflicts that appeared as accidental trappings from his perspective, in the revisionists' view become constitutive. The result is a gestalt switch that alters the very meaning of the public sphere. We can no longer assume that the bourgeois conception of the public sphere was simply an unrealized utopian ideal; it was also a masculinist ideological notion that functioned to legitimate an emergent form of class rule. Therefore, Eley draws a Gramscian moral from the story: the official bourgeois public sphere is the institutional vehicle for a major historical transformation in the nature of political domination. This is the shift from a repressive mode of domination to a hegemonic one, from rule based primarily on acquiescence to superior force to rule based primarily on consent supplemented with some measure of repression.[13] The important point is that this new mode of political domination, like the older one, secures the ability of one stratum of society to rule the rest. The official public sphere, then, was—indeed, is—the prime institutional site for the construction of the consent that defines the new, hegemonic mode of domination.[14]

Now, what conclusions should be draw from this conflict of historical interpretations? Should we conclude that the very concept of the public sphere is a piece of bourgeois masculinist ideology, so thoroughly compromised that it can shed no genuinely critical light on the limits of actually existing democracy? Or should we conclude, rather, that the public sphere was a good idea that unfortunately was not realized in practice but that retains some emancipatory force? In short, is the idea of the public sphere an instrument of domination or a utopian ideal?

Well, perhaps both. But actually neither. I contend that both of those conclusions are too extreme and unsupple to do justice to the material I have been discussing.[15] Instead of endorsing either one of them, I want to propose a more nuanced alternative. I shall argue that the revisionist historiography neither undermines nor vindicates "*the* concept of the public sphere" *simpliciter,* but that it calls into question four assumptions that are central to a specific—*bourgeois masculinist*—conception of the public sphere, at least as Habermas describes it. These are:

1. the assumption that it is possible for interlocutors in a public sphere to bracket status differentials and to deliberate "as if" they were social equals; the assumption, therefore, that societal equality is not a necessary condition for political democracy;

2. the assumption that the proliferation of a multiplicity of competing publics is necessarily a step away from, rather than toward, greater democracy, and that a single, comprehensive public sphere is always preferable to a nexus of multiple publics;

3. the assumption that discourse in public spheres should be restricted to deliberation about the common good, and that the appearance of "private interests" and "private issues" is always undesirable;

4. the assumption that a functioning democratic public sphere requires a sharp separation between civil society and the state.

Let me consider each of these in turn.

OPEN ACCESS, PARTICIPATORY PARITY, AND SOCIAL EQUALITY

Habermas's account of the bourgeois conception of the public sphere stresses its claim to be open and accessible to all. Indeed, this idea of open access is one of the central meanings of the norm of publicity. Of course, we know, both from the revisionist history and from Habermas's account, that the bourgeois public's claim to full accessibility was not in fact realized. Women of all classes and ethnicities were excluded from official political participation precisely on the basis of ascribed gender status, while plebeian men were formally excluded by property qualifications. Moreover, in many cases, women and men of racialized ethnicities of all classes were excluded on racial grounds.

Now, what are we to make of this historical fact of the nonrealization in practice of the bourgeois public sphere's ideal of open access? One approach is to conclude that the ideal itself remains unaffected, since it is possible in principle to overcome these exclusions. And, in fact, it was only a matter of time before formal exclusions based on gender, property, and race were eliminated.

This is convincing enough as far as it goes, but it does not go far enough. The question of open access cannot be reduced without remainder to the presence or absence of formal exclusions. It requires us to look also at the process of discursive interaction within formally inclusive public arenas. Here we should recall that the bourgeois conception of the public sphere requires bracketing inequalities of status. This public sphere was to be an arena in which interlocutors would set aside such characteristics as differences in birth and fortune and speak to one another as if they were social and economic peers. The operative phrase here is "as if." In fact, the social inequalities among the interlocutors were not eliminated, but only bracketed.

But were they really effectively bracketed? The revisionist historiography suggests they were not. Rather, discursive interaction within the bourgeois public sphere was governed by protocols of style and decorum that were themselves correlates and markers of status inequality. These functioned informally to marginalize women and members of the plebeian classes and to prevent them from participating as peers.

Here we are talking about informal impediments to participatory parity that can persist even after everyone is formally and legally licensed to participate. That these constitute a more serious challenge to the bourgeois conception of the public sphere can be seen from a familiar contemporary example. Feminist research has documented a syndrome that many of us have observed in faculty meetings and other mixed-sex deliberative bodies: men tend to interrupt women more than women interrupt men; men also tend to speak more than women, taking more turns and longer turns; and women's interventions are more often ignored or not responded to than men's. In response to the sorts of experiences documented in this research, an important strand of feminist political theory has claimed that deliberation can serve as a mask for domination. Theorists like Jane Mansbridge have argued that

the transformation of "I" into "we" brought about through political deliberation can easily mask subtle forms of control. Even the language people use as they reason together usually favors one way of seeing things and discourages others. Subordinate groups sometimes cannot find the right voice or words to express their thoughts, and when they do, they discover they are not heard. [They] are silenced, encouraged to keep their wants inchoate, and heard to say "yes" when what they have said is "no."[16]

Mansbridge rightly notes that many of these feminist insights into ways in which deliberation can serve as a mask for domination extend beyond gender to other kinds of unequal relations, like those based on class or ethnicity. They alert us to the ways in which social inequalities can infect deliberation, even in the absence of any formal exclusions.

Here I think we encounter a very serious difficulty with the bourgeois conception of the public sphere. Insofar as the bracketing of social inequalities in deliberation means proceeding as if they don't exist when they do, this does not foster
participatory parity. On the contrary, such bracketing usually works to the advantage of dominant groups in society and to the disadvantage of subordinates. In
most cases, it would be more appropriate to unbracket inequalities in the sense of
explicitly thematizing them—a point that accords with the spirit of Habermas's
later "communicative ethics."

The misplaced faith in the efficacy of bracketing suggests another flaw in the
bourgeois conception. This conception assumes that a public sphere is or can be
a space of zero-degree culture, so utterly bereft of any specific ethos as to accommodate with perfect neutrality and equal ease interventions expressive of any and
every cultural ethos. But this assumption is counterfactual, and not for reasons that
are merely accidental. In stratified societies, unequally empowered social groups
tend to develop unequally valued cultural styles. The result is the development of
powerful informal pressures that marginalize the contributions of members of
subordinated groups both in everyday life contexts and in official public spheres.[17]
Moreover, these pressures are amplified, rather than mitigated, by the peculiar
political economy of the bourgeois public sphere. In this public sphere, the media
that constitute the material support for the circulation of views are privately owned
and operated for profit. Consequently, subordinated social groups usually lack
equal access to the material means of equal participation.[18] Thus, political economy
enforces structurally what culture accomplishes informally.

If we take these considerations seriously, then we should be led to entertain
serious doubts about a conception of the public sphere that purports to bracket,
rather than to eliminate, structural social inequalities. We should question whether
it is possible even in principle for interlocutors to deliberate as if they were social
peers in specially designated discursive arenas, when these discursive arenas are
situated in a larger societal context that is pervaded by structural relations of
dominance and subordination.

What is at stake here is the autonomy of specifically political institutions vis-
à-vis the surrounding societal context. Now, one salient feature that distinguishes
liberalism from some other political-theoretical orientations is that liberalism assumes the autonomy of the political in a very strong form. Liberal political theory
assumes that it is possible to organize a democratic form of political life on the basis
of socioeconomic and sociosexual structures that generate systemic inequalities. For
liberals, then, the problem of democracy becomes the problem of how to insulate
political processes from what are considered to be nonpolitical or prepolitcal
processes, those characteristic, for example, of the economy, the family, and informal everyday life. The problem for liberals, thus, is how to strengthen the barriers
separating political institutions that are supposed to instantiate relations of equality
from economic, cultural, and sociosexual institutions that are premised on systemic
relations of inequality.[19] Yet the weight of circumstance suggests that in order to
have a public sphere in which interlocutors can deliberate as peers, it is not
sufficient merely to bracket social inequality. Instead, it is a necessary condition

for participatory parity that systemic social inequalities be eliminated. This does not mean that everyone must have exactly the same income, but it does require the sort of rough equality that is inconsistent with systemically generated relations of dominance and subordination. *Pace* liberalism, then, political democracy requires substantive social equality.[20]

So far, I have been arguing that the bourgeois conception of the public sphere is inadequate insofar as it supposes that social equality is not a necessary condition for participatory parity in public spheres. What follows from this for the critique of actually existing democracy? One task for critical theory is to render visible the ways in which societal inequality infects formally inclusive existing public spheres and taints discursive interaction within them.

EQUALITY, DIVERSITY, AND MULTIPLE PUBLICS

So far I have been discussing what we might call "intrapublic relations," that is, the character and quality of discursive interactions within a given public sphere. Now I want to consider what we might call "interpublic relations," that is, the character of interactions among different publics.

Let me begin by recalling that Habermas's account stresses the singularity of the bourgeois conception of the public sphere, its claim to be *the* public arena in the singular. In addition, his narrative tends in this respect to be faithful to that conception, casting the emergence of additional publics as a late development to be read under the sign fragmentation and decline. This narrative, then, like the bourgeois conception itself, is informed by an underlying evaluative assumption, namely, that the institutional confinement of public life to a single, overarching public sphere is a positive and desirable state of affairs, whereas the proliferation of a multiplicity of publics represents a departure from, rather than an advance toward, democracy. It is this normative assumption that I now want to scrutinize. In this section, I shall assess the relative merits of single, comprehensive publics versus multiple publics in two kinds of modern societies—stratified societies and egalitarian multicultural societies.[21]

First, let me consider the case of stratified societies, by which I mean societies whose basic institutional framework generates unequal social groups in structural relations of dominance and subordination. I have already argued that in such societies, full parity of participation in public debate and deliberation is not within the reach of possibility. The question to be addressed here, then, is: what form of public life comes closest to approaching that ideal? What institutional arrangements will best help narrow the gap in participatory parity between dominant and subordinate groups?

I contend that, in stratified societies, arrangements that accommodate contestation among a plurality of competing publics better promote the ideal of participatory parity than does a single, comprehensive, overarching public. This follows from the argument of the previous section. There I argued that it is not possible to insulate special discursive arenas from the effects of societal inequality; and that where societal inequality persists, deliberative processes in public spheres will tend to operate to the advantage of dominant groups and to the disadvantage of subordinates. Now I want to add that these effects will be exacerbated where there is only a single, comprehensive public sphere. In that case, members of subordinated groups would have no arenas for deliberation among themselves about their needs, objectives, and strategies. They would have no venues in which to undertake communicative processes that were not, as it were, under the supervision of dominant groups. In this situation, they would be less likely than otherwise to "find the right voice or words to express their thoughts," and more likely than otherwise "to keep their wants inchoate." This, would render them less able than otherwise to articulate and defend their interests in the comprehensive public sphere. They would be less able than otherwise to expose modes of deliberation that mask domination by "absorbing the less powerful into a false 'we' that reflects the more powerful."

This argument gains additional support from the revisionist historiography of the public sphere, up to and including very recent developments. This history records that members of subordinated social groups—women, workers, peoples of color, and gays and lesbians—have repeatedly found it advantageous to constitute alternative publics. I propose to call these *subaltern counterpublics* in order to signal that they are parallel discursive arenas where members of subordinated social groups invent and circulate counterdiscourses, which in turn permit them to formulate oppositional interpretations of their identities, interests, and needs.[22] Perhaps the most striking example is the late-twentieth-century U.S. feminist subaltern counterpublic, with its variegated array of journals, bookstores, publishing companies, film and video distribution networks, lecture series, research centers, academic programs, conferences, conventions, festivals, and local meeting places. In this public sphere, feminist women have invented new terms for describing social reality, including "sexism," "the double shift," "sexual harassment," and "marital, date, and acquaintance rape." Armed with such language, we have recast our needs and identities, thereby reducing, although not eliminating, the extent of our disadvantage in official public spheres.[23]

Let me not be misunderstood. I do not mean to suggest that subaltern counterpublics are always necessarily virtuous; some of them, alas, are explicitly antidemocratic and antiegalitarian; and even those with democratic and egalitarian intentions are not always above practicing their own modes of informal exclusion and marginalization. Still, insofar as these counterpublics emerge in response to exclusions within dominant publics, they help expand discursive space. In principle, assumptions that were previously exempt from contestation will now have to be publicly argued out. In general, the proliferation of subaltern counterpublics means a widening of discursive contestation, and that is a good thing in stratified societies.

I am emphasizing the contestatory function of subaltern counterpublics in stratified societies in part in order to complicate the issue of separatism. In my view, the concept of a counterpublic militates in the long run against separatism because it assumes an orientation that is *publicist*. Insofar as these arenas are *publics* they are by definition not enclaves—which is not to deny that they are often involuntarily enclaved. After all, to interact discursively as a member of a public— subaltern or otherwise—is to disseminate one's discourse into ever widening arenas. Habermas captures well this aspect of the meaning of publicity when he notes that however limited a public may be in its empirical manifestation at any given time, its members understand themselves as part of a potentially wider public, that indeterminate, empirically counterfactual body we call "the public-at-large." The point is that, in stratified societies, subaltern counterpublics have a dual character. On the one hand, they function as spaces of withdrawal and regroupment; on the other hand, they also function as bases and training grounds for agitational activities directed toward wider publics. It is precisely in the dialectic between these two functions that their emancipatory potential resides. This dialectic enables subaltern counterpublics partially to offset, although not wholly to eradicate, the unjust participatory privileges enjoyed by members of dominant social groups in stratified societies.

So far, I have been arguing that, although in stratified societies the ideal of participatory parity is not fully realizable, it is more closely approximated by arrangements that permit contestation among a plurality of competing publics than by a single, comprehensive public sphere. Of course, contestation among competing publics supposes interpublic discursive interaction. How, then, should we under- stand such interaction? Geoff Eley suggests we think of the public sphere [in stratified societies] as "the structured setting where cultural and ideological contest or negotiation among a variety of publics takes place."[24] This formulation does justice to the multiplicity of public arenas in stratified societies by expressly acknowl- edging the presence and activity of "a variety of publics." At the same time, it also does justice to the fact that these various publics are situated in a single "structured setting" that advantages some and disadvantages others. Finally, Eley's formulation does justice to the fact that, in stratified societies, the discursive relations among differentially empowered publics are as likely to take the form of contestation as that of deliberation.

Let me now consider the relative merits of multiple publics versus a singular public for egalitarian, multicultural societies. By egalitarian societies I mean nonstra- tified societies, societies whose basic framework does not generate unequal social groups in structural relations of dominance and subordination. Egalitarian societies, therefore, are classless societies without gender or racial divisions of labor. However, they need not be culturally homogeneous. On the contrary, provided such societies permit free expression and association, they are likely to be inhabited by social groups with diverse values, identities, and cultural styles, hence to be multicultural. My question is: under conditions of cultural diversity in the absence of structural inequality, would a single, comprehensive public sphere be preferable to multiple publics?

To answer this question we need to take a closer look at the relationship between public discourse and social identities. *Pace* the bourgeois conception, public spheres are not only arenas for the formation of discursive opinion; in addition, they are arenas for the formation and enactment of social identities.[25]

This means that participation is not simply a matter of being able to state propositional contents that are neutral with respect to form of expression. Rather, as I argued in the previous section, participation means being able to speak "in one's own voice," thereby simultaneously constructing and expressing one's cultural identity through idiom and style.[26] Moreover, as I also suggested, public spheres themselves are not spaces of zero-degree culture, equally hospitable to any possible form of cultural expression. Rather, they consist in culturally specific institutions— including, for example, various journals and various social geographies of urban space. These institutions may be understood as culturally specific rhetorical lenses that filter and alter the utterances they frame; they can accommodate some expressive modes and not others.[27]

It follows that public life in egalitarian, multicultural societies cannot consist exclusively in a single, comprehensive public sphere. That would be tantamount to filtering diverse rhetorical and stylistic norms through a single, overarching lens. Moreover, since there can be no such lens that is genuinely culturally neutral, it would effectively privilege the expressive norms of one cultural group over others, thereby making discursive assimilation a condition for participation in public debate. The result would be the demise of multiculturalism (and the likely demise of social equality). In general, then, we can conclude that the idea of an egalitarian, multicultural society only makes sense if we suppose a plurality of public arenas in which groups with diverse values and rhetorics participate. By definition, such a society must contain a multiplicity of publics.

However, this need not preclude the possibility of an additional, more comprehensive arena in which members of different, more limited publics talk across lines of cultural diversity. On the contrary, our hypothetical egalitarian, multicultural society would surely have to entertain debates over policies and issues affecting everyone. The question is: would participants in such debates share enough in the way of values, expressive norms, and, therefore, protocols of persuasion to lend their talk the quality of deliberations aimed at reaching agreement through giving reasons?

In my view, this is better treated as an empirical question than as a conceptual question. I see no reason to rule out in principle the possibility of a society in which social equality and cultural diversity coexist with participatory democracy. I certainly hope there can be such a society. That hope gains some plausibility if we consider that, however difficult it may be, communication across lines of cultural difference is not in principle impossible—although it will certainly become impossible if one imagines that it requires bracketing of differences. Granted such communication requires multicultural literacy, but that, I believe, can be acquired through practice. In fact, the possibilities expand once we acknowledge the complexity of cultural identities. *Pace* reductive, essentialist conceptions, cultural identities are woven of many different strands, and some of these strands may be common to people whose identities otherwise diverge, even when it is the divergences that are most salient.[28] Likewise, under conditions of social equality, the porousness, outerdirectedness, and open-endedness of publics could promote intercultural communication. After all, the concept of a public presupposes a plurality of perspectives among those who participate within it, thereby allowing for internal differences and antagonisms, and likewise discouraging reified blocs.[29] In addition, the unbounded character and publicist orientation of publics allows for the fact that people participate in more than one public, and that the memberships of different publics may partially overlap. This in turn makes intercultural communication conceivable in principle. All told, then, there do not seem to be any conceptual (as opposed to empirical) barriers to the possibility of a socially egalitarian, multicultural society that is also a participatory democracy. But this will necessarily be a society with many different publics, including at least one public in which participants can deliberate as peers across lines of difference about policy that concerns them all.

In general, I have been arguing that the ideal of participatory parity is better achieved by a multiplicity of publics than by a single public. This is true both for stratified societies and for egalitarian, multicultural societies, albeit for different reasons. In neither case is my argument intended as a simple postmodern celebration of multiplicity. Rather, in the case of stratified societies, I am defending subaltern counterpublics formed under conditions of dominance and subordination. In the other case, by contrast, I am defending the possibility of combining social equality, cultural diversity, and participatory democracy.

What are the implications of this discussion for a critical theory of the public sphere in actually existing democracy? Briefly, we need a critical, political sociology of a form of public life in which multiple but unequal publics participate. This means theorizing the contestatory interaction of different publics and identifying the mechanisms that render some of them subordinate to others.

PUBLIC SPHERES, COMMON CONCERNS, AND PRIVATE INTERESTS

I have argued that in stratified societies, like it or not, subaltern counterpublics stand in a contestatory relationship to dominant publics. One important object of such interpublic contestation is the appropriate boundaries of the public sphere. Here the central questions are, what counts as a public matter and what, in contrast, is private? This brings me to a third set of problematic assumptions underlying the bourgeois conception of the public sphere, namely, assumptions concerning the appropriate scope of publicity in relation to privacy.

Let me remind you that it is central to Habermas's account that the bourgeois public sphere was to be a discursive arena in which "private persons" deliberated about "public matters." There are several different senses of privacy and publicity in play here. "Publicity," for example, can mean: 1) state-related; 2) accessible to everyone; 3) of concern to everyone; and 4) pertaining to a common good or shared interest. Each of these corresponds to a contrasting sense of "privacy." In addition, there are two other senses of "privacy" hovering just below the surface here: 5) pertaining to private property in a market economy; and 6) pertaining to intimate domestic or personal life, including sexual life.

I have already talked at length about the sense of "publicity" as open or accessible to all. Now I want to examine some of the other senses,[30] beginning with 3) of concern to everyone. This is ambiguous between what objectively affects or has an impact on everyone, as seen from an outsider's perspective, on the one hand, and what is recognized as a matter of common concern by participants, on the other hand. Now, the idea of a public sphere as an arena of collective self-determination does not sit well with approaches that would appeal to an outsider perspective to delimit its proper boundaries. Thus, it is the second, participant's perspective that is relevant here. Only participants themselves can decide what is and what is not of common concern to them. However, there is no guarantee that all of them will agree. For example, until quite recently, feminists were in the minority in thinking that domestic violence against women was a matter of common concern and thus a legitimate topic of public discourse. The great majority of people considered this issue to be a private matter between what was assumed to be a fairly small number of heterosexual couples (and perhaps the social and legal professionals who were supposed to deal with them). Then, feminists formed a subaltern counterpublic from which we disseminated a view of domestic violence as a widespread systemic feature of male-dominated societies. Eventually, after sustained discursive contestation, we succeeded in making it a common concern.

The point is that there are no naturally given, a priori boundaries here. What will count as a matter of common concern will be decided precisely through discursive contestation. It follows that no topics should be ruled off-limits in advance of such contestation. On the contrary, democratic publicity requires positive guarantees of opportunities for minorities to convince others that what in the past was not public in the sense of being a matter of common concern should now become so.[31]

What, then, of the sense of "publicity" as pertaining to a common good or shared interest? This is the sense that is in play when Habermas characterizes the bourgeois public sphere as an arena in which the topic of discussion is restricted to the "common good" and in which discussion of "private interests" is ruled out.

This is a view of the public sphere that we would today call civic republican, as opposed to liberal-individualist. Briefly, the civic republican model stresses a view of politics as people reasoning together to promote a common good that transcends the mere sum of individual preferences. The idea is that through deliberation the members of the public can come to discover or create such a common good. In the process of their deliberations, participants are transformed from a collection of self-seeking, private individuals into a public-spirited collectivity, capable of acting together in the common interest. On this view, private interests have no proper place in the political public sphere. At best, they are the prepolitical starting point of deliberation, to be transformed and transcended in the course of debate.[32]

Now, this civic republican view of the public sphere is in one respect an improvement over the liberal-individualist alternative. Unlike the latter, it does not assume that people's preferences, interests, and identities are given exogenously

in advance of public discourse and deliberation. It appreciates, rather, that preferences, interests, and identities are as much outcomes as antecedents of public
deliberation, indeed are discursively constituted in and through it. However, as
Jane Mansbridge has argued, the civic republican view contains a very serious
confusion, one which blunts its critical edge. This view conflates the ideas of
deliberation and the common good by assuming that deliberation must be deliberation about the common good. Consequently, it limits deliberation to talk framed
from the standpoint of a single, all-encompassing "we," thereby ruling claims of
self-interest and group interest out of order. Yet, this works against one of the
principal aims of deliberation, namely, helping participants clarify their interests,
even when those interests turn out to conflict. "Ruling self-interest [and group
interest] out of order makes it harder for any participant to sort out what is going
on. In particular, the less powerful may not find ways to discover that the prevailing
sense of 'we' does not adequately include them."[33]

In general, there is no way to know in advance whether the outcome of a
deliberative process will be the discovery of a common good in which conflicts
of interest evaporate as merely apparent or, rather, the discovery that conflicts of
interests are real and the common good is chimerical. But if the existence of a
common good cannot be presumed in advance, then there is no warrant for
putting any strictness on what sorts of topics, interests, and views are admissible
in deliberation.[34]

This argument holds even in the best-case scenario of societies whose basic
institutional frameworks do not generate systemic inequalities; even in such relatively egalitarian societies, we cannot assume in advance that there will be no real
conflicts of interest. How much more pertinent, then, is the argument to stratified
societies, which are traversed with pervasive relations of dominance and subordination. After all, when social arrangements operate to the systemic profit of some
groups of people and to the systemic detriment of others, there are prima facie
reasons for thinking that the postulation of a common good shared by exploiters
and exploited may well be a mystification. Moreover, any consensus that purports
to represent the common good in this social context should be regarded with
suspicion, since this consensus will have been reached through deliberative processes
tainted by the effects of dominance and subordination.

In general, critical theory needs to take a harder, more critical look at the
terms "private" and "public." These terms, after all, are not simply straightforward
designations of societal spheres; they are cultural classifications and rhetorical labels.
In political discourse, they are powerful terms that are frequently deployed to
delegitimate some interests, views, and topics and to valorize others.

This brings me to two other senses of privacy, which often function ideologically to delimit the boundaries of the public sphere in ways that disadvantage
subordinate social groups. These are sense 5) pertaining to private property in a
market economy; and sense 6) pertaining to intimate domestic or personal life,
including sexual life. Each of these senses is at the center of a rhetoric of privacy that
has historically been used to restrict the universe of legitimate public contestation.

The rhetoric of domestic privacy seeks to exclude some issues and interests from public debate by personalizing and/or familiarizing them; it casts these as private-domestic or personal-familial matters in contradistinction to public, political matters. The rhetoric of economic privacy, in contrast, seeks to exclude some issues and interests from public debate by economizing them; the issues in question here are cast as impersonal market imperatives or as "private" ownership prerogatives or as technical problems for managers and planners, all in contradistinction to public, political matters. In both cases, the result is to enclave certain matters in specialized discursive arenas and thereby to shield them from general public debate and contestation. This usually works to the advantage of dominant groups and individuals and to the disadvantage of their subordinates.[35] If wife battering, for example, is labeled a "personal" or "domestic" matter and if public discourse about this phenomenon is canalized into specialized institutions associated with, say, family law, social work, and the sociology and psychology of "deviance," then this serves to reproduce gender dominance and subordination. Similarly, if questions of workplace democracy are labeled "economic" or "managerial" problems and if discourse about these questions is shunted into specialized institutions associated with, say, "industrial relations" sociology, labor law, and "management science," then this serves to perpetuate class (and usually also gender and race) dominance and subordination.

This shows once again that the lifting of formal restrictions on public sphere participation does not suffice to ensure inclusion in practice. On the contrary, even after women and workers have been formally licensed to participate, their participation may be hedged by conceptions of economic privacy and domestic privacy that delimit the scope of debate. These notions, therefore, are vehicles through which gender and class disadvantages may continue to operate subtextually and informally, even after explicit, formal restrictions have been rescinded.

STRONG PUBLICS, WEAK PUBLICS: ON CIVIL SOCIETY AND THE STATE

Let me turn now to my fourth and last assumption underlying the bourgeois conception of the public sphere, namely, the assumption that a functioning democratic public sphere requires a sharp separation of civil society and the state. This assumption is susceptible to two different interpretations, depending on how one understands the expression "civil society." If one takes that expression to mean a privately ordered, capitalist economy, then to insist on its separation from the state is to defend classical liberalism. The claim would be that a system of limited government and laissez-faire capitalism is a necessary precondition for a well-functioning public sphere.

We can dispose of this (relatively uninteresting) claim fairly quickly by drawing on some arguments of the previous sections. I have already shown that participatory parity is essential to a democratic public sphere and that rough socioeconomic equality is a precondition of participatory parity. Now I need only add that laissez-faire capitalism does not foster socioeconomic equality and that some form of politically regulated economic reorganization and redistribution is needed to achieve that end. Likewise, I have also shown that efforts to "privatize" economic issues and to cast them as off-limits with respect to state activity impede, rather than promote, the sort of full and free discussion that is built into the idea of a public sphere. It follows from these considerations that a sharp separation of (economic) civil society and the state is not a necessary condition for a well-functioning public sphere. On the contrary, and *pace* the bourgeois conception, it is precisely some sort of interimbrication of these institutions that is needed.[36]

However, there is also a second, more interesting, interpretation of the bourgeois assumption that a sharp separation of civil society and the state is necessary to a working public sphere, one which warrants more extended examination. In this interpretation, "civil society" means the nexus of nongovernmental or "secondary" associations that are neither economic nor administrative. We can best appreciate the force of the claim that civil society in this sense should be separate from the state if we recall Habermas's definition of the liberal public sphere as a "body of private persons assembled to form a public." The emphasis here on "private persons" signals (among other things) that the members of the bourgeois public are not state officials and that their participation in the public sphere is not undertaken in any official capacity. Accordingly, their discourse does not eventuate in binding, sovereign decisions authorizing the use of state power; on the contrary, it eventuates in "public opinion," critical commentary on authorized decision making that transpires elsewhere. The public sphere, in short, is not the state; it is rather the informally mobilized body of nongovernmental discursive opinion that can serve as a counterweight to the state. Indeed, in the bourgeois conception, it is precisely this extragovernmental character of the public sphere that confers an aura of independence, autonomy, and legitimacy on the "public opinion" generated in it.

Thus, the bourgeois conception of the public sphere supposes the desirability of a sharp separation of (associational) civil society and the state. As a result, it promotes what I shall call *weak publics,* publics whose deliberative practice consists exclusively in opinion-formation and does not also encompass decision making. Moreover, the bourgeois conception seems to imply that an expansion of such publics' discursive authority to encompass decision making as well as opinion making would threaten the autonomy of public opinion—for then the public would effectively become the state, and the possibility of a critical discursive check on the state would be lost.

That, at least, is suggested by Habermas's initial formulation of the bourgeois conception. In fact, the issue becomes more complicated as soon as we consider the emergence of parliamentary sovereignty. With that landmark development in the history of the public sphere, we encounter a major structural transformation, since sovereign parliament functions as a public sphere within the state. Moreover, sovereign parliaments are what I shall call *strong publics,* publics whose discourse encompasses both opinion formation and decision making. As a locus of public deliberation culminating in legally binding decisions (or laws), parliament was to be the site for the discursive authorization of the use of state power. With the achievement of parliamentary sovereignty, therefore, the line separating (associational) civil society and the state is blurred.

Clearly, the emergence of parliamentary sovereignty and the consequent blurring of the (associational) civil society/state separation represents a democratic advance over earlier political arrangements. This is because, as the terms "strong public" and "weak public" suggest, the "force of public opinion" is strengthened when a body representing it is empowered to translate such "opinion" into authoritative decisions. At the same time, there remain important questions about the relation between parliamentary strong publics and the weak publics to which they are supposed to be accountable. In general, these developments raise some interesting and important questions about the relative merits of weak and strong publics and about the respective roles that institutions of both kinds might play in a democratic and egalitarian society.

One set of questions concerns the possible proliferation of strong publics in the form of self-managing institutions. In self-managed workplaces, child care centers, or residential communities, for example, internal institutional public spheres could be arenas both of opinion formation and decision making. This would be tantamount to constituting sites of direct or quasi-direct democracy wherein all those engaged in a collective undertaking would participate in deliberations to determine its design and operation.[37] However, this would still leave open the relationship between such internal public spheres-cum-decision-making-bodies and those external publics to which they might also be deemed accountable. The question of that relationship becomes important when we consider that people who are affected by an undertaking in which they do not directly participate as agents may nonetheless have a stake in its *modus operandi;* they therefore also have a legitimate claim to a say, through some other (weaker or stronger) public sphere, in its institutional design and operation.

Here we are again broaching the issue of accountability. What institutional arrangements best ensure the accountability of democratic decision-making bodies (strong publics) to *their* (external, weak or, given the possibility of hybrid cases, weaker) publics?[38] Where in society are direct democracy arrangements called for and where are representative forms more appropriate? How are the former best articulated with the latter? More generally, what democratic arrangements best institutionalize coordination among different institutions, including among their various co-implicated publics? Should we think of central parliament as a strong superpublic with authoritative discursive sovereignty over basic societal ground rules and coordination arrangements? If so, does that require the assumption of a single weak(er) external superpublic (in addition to, not instead of, various other smaller publics)? In any event, given the inescapable global interdependence manifest in the international division of labor within a single shared planetary biosphere, does it make sense to understand the nation-state as the appropriate unit of sovereignty?

I do not know the answers to most of these questions and I am unable to explore them further in this essay. However, the possibility of posing them, even in the absence of full, persuasive answers, enables us to draw one salient conclusion: any conception of the public sphere that requires a sharp separation between (associational) civil society and the state will be unable to imagine the forms of self-management, interpublic coordination, and political accountability that are essential to a democratic and egalitarian society. The bourgeois conception of the public sphere, therefore, is not adequate for contemporary critical theory. What is needed, rather, is a postbourgeois conception that can permit us to envision a greater role for (at least some) public spheres than mere autonomous opinion formation removed from authoritative decision making. A postbourgeois conception would enable us to think about strong *and* weak publics, as well as about various hybrid forms. In addition, it would allow us to theorize the range of possible relations among such publics, thereby expanding our capacity to envision democratic possibilities beyond the limits of actually existing democracy.

CONCLUSION: RETHINKING THE PUBLIC SPHERE

Let me conclude by recapitulating what I believe I have accomplished in this essay. I have shown that the bourgeois conception of the public sphere, as described by Habermas, is not adequate for the critique of the limits of actually existing democracy in late capitalist societies. At one level, my argument undermines the bourgeois conception as a normative ideal. I have shown, first, that an adequate conception of the public sphere requires not merely the bracketing, but rather the elimination, of social inequality. Second, I have shown that a multiplicity of publics is preferable to a single public sphere both in stratified societies and egalitarian societies. Third, I have shown that a tenable conception of the public sphere would countenance not the exclusion, but the inclusion, of interests and issues that bourgeois masculinist ideology labels "private" and treats as inadmissible. Finally, I have shown that a defensible conception would allow both for strong publics and for weak publics and that it would theorize the relations among them. In sum, I have argued against four constitutive assumptions of the bourgeois conception of the public sphere; at the same time, I have identified some corresponding elements of a new, postbourgeois conception.

At another level, my argument enjoins four corresponding tasks on the critical theory of actually existing democracy. First, this theory should render visible the ways in which social inequality taints deliberation within publics in late capitalist societies. Second, it should show how inequality affects relations among publics in late capitalist societies, how publics are differentially empowered or segmented, and how some are involuntarily enclaved and subordinated to others. Next, a critical theory should expose ways in which the labeling of some issues and interests as "private" limits the range of problems, and of approaches to problems, that can be widely contested in contemporary societies. Finally, our theory should show

how the overly weak character of some public spheres in late capitalist societies denudes "public opinion" of practical force.

In all these ways, the theory should expose the limits of the specific form of democracy we enjoy in contemporary capitalist societies. Perhaps it can thereby help inspire us to try to push back those limits, while also cautioning people in other parts of the world against heeding the call to install them.

NOTES

1. ©Nancy Fraser. Reprinted with permission from *Habermas and the Public Sphere,* ed. Craig Calhoun (Cambridge MA: M.I.T. Press, 1991). I am grateful for helpful comments from Craig Calhoun, Joshua Cohen, Tom McCarthy, Moishe Postone, Baukje Prins, David Schweikart, and Rian Voet. I also benefited from the inspiration and stimulation of participants in the conference on "Habermas and the Public Sphere," University of North Carolina, Chapel Hill, September 1989.

2. Jürgen Habermas, *The Structural Transformation of the Public Sphere: An Inquiry into a Category of Bourgeois Society,* tr. Thomas Burger with Frederick Lawrence (Cambridge MA: The M.I.T. Press, 1989). For Habermas's later use of the category of the public sphere, see Jürgen Habermas, *The Theory of Communicative Action,* vol 2, *Lifeworld and System: A Critique of Functionalist Reason,* tr. Thomas McCarthy (Boston: Beacon Press, 1987). For a critical secondary discussion of Habermas's later use of the concept, see Nancy Fraser, "What's Critical about Critical Theory? The Case of Habermas and Gender," in Fraser, *Unruly Practices: Power, Discourse and Gender in Contemporary Social Theory* (Minneapolis: University of Minnesota Press, 1989).

3. Throughout this paper, I refer to paid workplaces, markets, credit systems, etc. as "*official* economic system institutions" so as to avoid the androcentric implication that domestic institutions are not also "economic." For a discussion of this issue, see Nancy Fraser, "What's Critical about Critical Theory? The Case of Habermas and Gender," op. cit.

4. Joan Landes, *Women and the Public Sphere in the Age of the French Revolution* (Ithaca NY: Cornell University Press, 1988).

5. For the "public"/"pubic" connection, see the *Oxford English Dictionary* (second edition, 1989), entry for "public." For the "testimony"/"testicle" connection see Lucie White, "Subordination, Rhetorical Survival Skills and Sunday Shoes: Notes on the Hearing of Mrs. G.," *Buffalo Law Review,* vol. 38, no. 1 (Winter 1990) p. 6.

6. Pierre Bourdieu, *Distinction: A Social Critique of the Judgment of Pure Taste* (Cambridge MA: Harvard University Press, 1979).

7. Geoff Eley, "Nations, Publics, and Political Cultures: Placing Habermas in the Nineteenth Century," in *Habermas and the Public Sphere,* ed. Craig Calhoun. See also Leonore Davidoff and Catherine Hall, *Family Fortunes: Men and Women of the English Middle Class, 1780–1850* (Chicago: University of Chicago Press, 1987).

8. Habermas does recognize that the issue of gender exclusion is connected to a shift from aristocratic to bourgeois public spheres, but, as I argue below, he fails to notice the full implications of this recognition.

9. I do not mean to suggest that Habermas is unaware of the existence of public spheres other than the bourgeois one; on the contrary, in the preface to *Structural Transformation* (p. xviii), he explicitly states that his object is the liberal model of the bourgeois public

sphere and that therefore he will discuss neither "the plebian public sphere" (which he understands as an ephemeral phenomenon that existed "for just one moment" during the French Revolution) nor "the plebiscitary-acclamatory form of regimented public sphere characterizing dictatorships in highly developed industrial societies." My point is that, although Habermas acknowledges that there were alternative public spheres, he assumes that it is possible to understand the character of the bourgeois public by looking at it alone, in isolation from its relations to other, competing publics. This assumption is problematic. In fact, as I shall demonstrate, an examination of the bourgeois public's relations to alternative counterpublics challenges the bourgeois conception of the public sphere.

10. Mary P. Ryan, *Women in Public: Between Banners and Ballots, 1825–1880* (Baltimore: John Hopkins University Press, 1990) and "Gender and Public Access: Women's Politics in Nineteenth Century America," in *Habermas and the Public Sphere,* ed. Craig Calhoun.

11. Geoff Eley, "Nations, Publics, and Political Cultures."

12. Geoff Eley, "Nations, Publics, and Political Cultures."

13. I am leaving aside whether one should speak here not of consent tout court but rather of "something approaching consent," or "something appearing as consent," or "something constructed as consent" in order to leave open the possibility of degrees of consent.

14. The public sphere produces consent via circulation of discourses that construct the "common sense" of the day and represent the existing order as natural and/or just, but not simply as a ruse that is imposed. Rather, the public sphere in its mature form includes sufficient participation and sufficient representation of multiple interests and perspectives to permit most people most of the time to recognize themselves in its discourses. People who are ultimately disadvantaged by the social construction of consent nonetheless manage to find in the discourses of the public sphere representations of their interests, aspirations, life problems, and anxieties that are close enough to resonate with their own lived self-representations, identities, and feelings. Their consent to hegemonic rule is secured when their culturally constructed perspectives are taken up and articulated with other culturally constructed perspectives in hegemonic sociopolitical projects.

15. Here I want to distance myself from a certain overly facile line of argument that is sometimes made against Habermas. This is the line that ideological functions of the public spheres in class societies simply undermine the normative notion as an ideal. This I take to be a non sequitur, since it is always possible to reply that under other conditions, say, the abolition of classes, genders, and other pervasive axes of inequality, the public sphere would no longer have this function, but would instead be an institutionalization of democratic interaction. Moreover, as Habermas has himself often pointed out, even in existing class societies, the significance of the public sphere is not entirely exhausted by its class function. On the contrary, the idea of the public sphere also functions here and now as a norm of democratic interaction we use to criticize the limitations of actually existing public spheres. The point here is that even the revisionist story and the Gramscian theory that cause us to doubt the value of the public sphere are themselves only possible because of it. It is the idea of the public sphere that provides the conceptual condition of possibility for the revisionist critique of its imperfect realization.

16. Jane Mansbridge, "Feminism and Democracy," *American Prospect* no. 1 (Spring 1990) p. 127.

17. In *Distinction* Pierre Bourdieu has theorized these processes in an illuminating way in terms of the concept of "class habitus."

18. As Habermas notes, this tendency is exacerbated with the concentration of media ownership in late capitalist societies. For the steep increase in concentration in the U.S. in the late twentieth century, see Ben H. Bagdikian, *The Media Monopoly* (Boston: Beacon Press, 1983). This situation contrasts in some respects with countries with state-owned and operated television. But even there it is doubtful that subordinated groups have equal access. Moreover, political-economic pressures have recently encouraged privatization of media in several of these countries. In part, this reflects the problems of state networks having to compete for "market share" with private channels airing U.S.-produced mass entertainment.

19. This is the spirit behind, for example, proposals for electoral campaign financing reforms aimed at preventing the intrusion of economic dominance into the public sphere. Needless to say, within a context of massive societal inequality, it is far better to have such reforms than not to have them. However, in light of the sorts of informal effects of dominance and inequality discussed above, one ought not to expect too much from them. The most thoughtful recent defense of the liberal view comes from someone who in other respects is not a liberal. See Michael Walzer, *Spheres of Justice: A Defense of Pluralism and Equality* (New York: Basic Books, 1983). Another very interesting approach has been suggested by Joshua Cohen. In response to an earlier draft of this essay, he argued that policies designed to facilitate the formation of social movements, secondary associations, and political parties would better foster participatory parity than would policies designed to achieve social equality, since the latter would require redistributive efforts that carry "deadweight losses." I certainly support the sort of policies that Cohen recommends, as well as his more general aim of an "associative democracy"—the sections of this paper on multiple publics and strong publics make a case for related arrangements. However, I am not persuaded by the claim that these policies can achieve participatory parity under conditions of social inequality. That seems to me to be another variant of the liberal view of the autonomy of the political, which Cohen otherwise claims to reject. See Joshua Cohen, "Comments on Nancy Fraser's 'Rethinking the Public Sphere,' " (unpublished manuscript presented at the meetings of the American Philosophical Association, Central Division, New Orleans, April 1990).

20. My argument draws on Karl Marx's still unsurpassed critique of liberalism in part 1 of "On the Jewish Question." Hence, the allusion to Marx in the title of this essay.

21. My argument is this section is deeply indebted to Joshua Cohen's perceptive comments on an earlier draft of this paper in "Comments on Nancy Fraser's 'Rethinking the Public Sphere.' "

22. I have coined this expression by combining two terms that other theorists have recently used with very good effects for purposes that are consonant with my own. I take the term "subaltern" from Gayatri Spivak, "Can the Subaltern Speak?" in *Marxism and the Interpretation of Culture,* ed. Cary Nelson and Larry Grossberg (Chicago: University of Illinois Press, 1988) pp. 271–313. I take the term "counterpublic" from Rita Felski, *Beyond Feminist Aesthetics* (Cambridge MA: Harvard University Press, 1989).

23. For an analysis of the political import of oppositional feminist discourses about needs,

see Nancy Fraser, "Struggle over Needs: Outline of a Socialist-feminist Critical Theory of Late-Capitalist Political Culture," in Fraser, *Unruly Practices*.

24. Geoff Eley, "Nations, Publics, and Political Cultures." Eley goes on to explain that this is tantamount to "extend[ing] Habermas's idea of the public sphere toward the wider public domain where authority is not only constituted as rational and legitimate, but where its terms are contested, modified, and occasionally overthrown by subaltern groups."

25. It seems to me that public discursive arenas are among the most important and underrecognized sites in which social identities are constructed, deconstructed, and reconstructed. My view stands in contrast to various psychoanalytic accounts of identity formation, which neglect the formative importance of post-Oedipal discursive interaction outside the nuclear family and which therefore cannot explain identity shifts over time. It strikes me as unfortunate that so much of contemporary feminist theory has taken its understanding of social identity from psychoanalytic models, while neglecting to study identity construction in relation to public spheres. The revisionist historiography of the public sphere discussed earlier can help redress the balance by identifying public spheres as loci of identity reconstruction. For an account of the discursive character of social identity and a critique of psychoanalytic approach to identity see Nancy Fraser, "The Uses and Abuses of French Discourse Theories for Feminist Politics," *Boundary 2*, vol. 17, no. 2 (1990).

26. For another statement of this position, see Nancy Fraser, "Toward a Discourse Ethic of Solidarity," *Praxis International,* vol. 5, no. 4 (January 1986) pp. 425–29. See also Iris Young, "Impartiality and the Civic Public: Some Implications of Feminist Critiques of Moral and Political Theory" in *Feminism as Critique*, ed. Seyla Benhabib and Drucilla Cornell (Minneapolis: University of Minnesota Press, 1987) pp. 56–76.

27. For an analysis of the rhetorical specificity of one historical public sphere, see Michael Warner, *The Letters of the Republic: Publication and the Public Sphere in Eighteenth Century America* (Cambridge, MA: Harvard University Press, forthcoming).

28. One could say that at the deepest level, everyone is mestizo. The best metaphor here may be Wittgenstein's idea of family resemblances, or networks of crisscrossing, overlapping differences and similarities, no single thread of which runs continuously throughout the whole. For an account that stresses the complexity of cultural identities and the salience of discourse in their construction, see Nancy Fraser, "The Uses and Abuses of French Discourse Theories for Feminist Politics." For accounts that draw on concepts of *métissage*, see Gloria Anzaldúa, *Borderlands: La Frontera* (San Francisco: Spinsters/Aunt Lute, 1987) and Françoise Lionnet, *Autobiographical Voices: Race, Gender, Self-Portraiture* (Ithaca NY: Cornell University Press, 1989).

29. In these respects, the concept of a public differs from that of a community. "Community" suggests a bounded and fairly homogeneous group, and it often connotes consensus. "Public," in contrast, emphasizes discursive interaction that is in principle unbounded and open-ended, and this in turn implies a plurality of perspectives. Thus, the idea of a public, better than that of a community, can accommodate internal differences, antagonisms, and debates. For an account of the connection between publicity and plurality, see Hannah Arendt, *The Human Condition* (Chicago: University of Chicago Press, 1958). For a critique of the concept of community, see Iris Young, "The Ideal of Community and the Politics of Difference," in *Feminism and Postmodernism*, ed. Linda J. Nicholson (New York: Routledge, Chapman and Hall, 1989) pp. 300–23.

30. In this essay, I do not directly discuss sense 1) state-related. However, in the next section of this essay I consider some issues that touch on that sense.

31. This is the equivalent in democratic theory of a point that Paul Feyerabend has argued in the philosophy of science. See Feyerabend, *Against Method* (New York: Verso, 1988).

32. In contrast, the liberal-individualist model stresses a view of politics as the aggregation of self-interested, individual preferences. Deliberation in the strict sense drops out altogether. Instead, political discourse consists in registering individual preferences and in bargaining, looking for formulas that satisfy as many private interests as possible. It is assumed that there is no such thing as the common good over and above the sum of all the various individual goods, and so private interests are the legitimate stuff of political discourse.

33. Jane Mansbridge, "Feminism and Democracy," p. 131.

34. This point, incidentally, is in the spirit of a more recent strand of Habermas's normative thought, which stresses the procedural, as opposed to the substantive, definition of a democratic public sphere; here, the public sphere is defined as an arena for a certain type of discursive interaction, not as an arena for dealing with certain types of topics and problems. There are no restrictions, therefore, on what may become a topic of deliberation. See Seyla Benhabib's account of this radical proceduralist strand of Habermas's thought and her defense of it as the strand that renders his view of the public sphere superior to alternative views. Benhabib, "Models of Public Space: Hannah Arendt, the Liberal Tradition, and Jürgen Habermas," in *Habermas and the Public Sphere,* ed. Craig Calhoun.

35. Usually, but not always. As Josh Cohen has argued, exceptions are the uses of privacy in *Roe v. Wade,* the U.S. Supreme Court decision legalizing abortion, and in Justice Blackmun's dissent in Bowers, the decision upholding state antisodomy laws. These examples show that the privacy rhetoric is multivalent rather than univocally and necessarily harmful. On the other hand, there is no question but that the weightier tradition of privacy argument has buttressed inequality by restricting debate. Moreover, many feminists have argued that even the "good" privacy uses have some serious negative consequences in the current context and that gender domination is better challenged in this context on other discursive grounds. For a defense of "privacy" talk, see Joshua Cohen, "Comments on Nancy Fraser's 'Rethinking the Public Sphere.' "

36. There are many possibilities here, including such mixed forms as market socialism.

37. I use the expression "quasi-direct democracy" in order to signal the possibility of hybrid forms of self-management involving the democratic designation of representatives, managers, or planners held to strict standards of accountability through, for example, recall.

38. By hybrid possibilities I mean arrangements involving very strict accountability of representative decision-making bodies to their external publics through veto and recall rights. Such hybrid forms might in some, though certainly not all, circumstances be desirable.

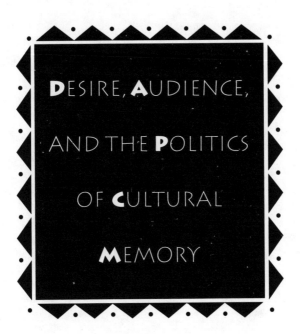

DESIRE, AUDIENCE,

AND THE POLITICS

OF CULTURAL

MEMORY

CHAPTER 4

THE EDUCATION OF

YOUNG ARTISTS AND

THE ISSUE OF

AUDIENCE

CAROL BECKER

WITHIN THE DOMINATOR SYSTEM, ART HAS BEEN ORGANIZED AROUND THE PRIMACY OF OBJECTS RATHER THAN RELATIONSHIPS, AND HAS BEEN SET APART FROM RECIPROCAL OR PARTICIPATIVE INTERACTIONS. (SUZI GABLIK, *THE REENCHANTMENT OF ART*)

As an educator who has weathered the censorship battles of the last five years, I have been forced to rethink the repercussions of the art world's isolation and to consider how we who are involved in training the next generation of artists might begin to incorporate into this process a fundamental concern for the particularities of audience and the placement of art work within a societal context.

Because these deeper questions about the relationship of the artist to society and the conflict between the artist's sense of art and the general public's sense of art have not been adequately addressed by the art world or within the art school environment, a cavernous rift has developed. Work which artists find unproblematic and barely controversial seems blasphemous, pornographic, or mean-spirited to those outside. While art which artists hope will be an interesting and even welcome challenge to society is often met with little or no response. In such ill-fated interchanges, the audience has often believed that artists were being unnecessarily obscure or confrontational at the same time that artists have felt misunderstood and unappreciated. The result has been mutual disappointment and hostility. In part the serious debates artists are now engaged in, in their work, remain hidden to those still caught within conventional notions of what art will do, what it will be, how far it can go, what subject matter it should address. In our inclusion or exclusion of such discrepancies within the educational process, we directly influence the art-making practices of the next generation of artists and the place they will be able to assume within a democratic society—either encouraging our students' engagement with a larger arena or perpetuating the isolation which has allowed art to become a vulnerable subject of narrow-minded attacks.

To understand why most art which grapples with serious issues generates hostility in non–art world viewers, it is important to characterize the conventional Western expectation of what function art will serve, and to understand how far this expectation is from the intention of most contemporary art work. At the core of such a discussion must be the concern with conventions of beauty—that experience of pleasure so many have come to associate with the phenomena of art.

The often unconscious expectations of a non–art world, non–visually trained audience are that art will be somewhat familiar yet also transcendent, that it will be able to catapult its viewers outside their mundane lives, provide therapeutic resolution to emotional ills, and, most significantly, that it will end in wonder. In an article titled "The Repression of Beauty" (1991), psychologist/philosopher James Hillman provides a useful understanding of the desire for beauty and of its emotional effect on the organism.

When you see something exquisite, Hillman writes, so much so that it arrests motion,

> you draw in your breath and stop still. This quick intake of breath, this little hshshs as the Japanese draw between their teeth when they see something beautiful in a garden—this *ahahah* reaction is the aesthetic response just as certain, inevitable, objective and ubiquitous, as wincing in pain and moaning in pleasure. Moreover, this quick intake of breath is also the very root of the word aesthetic, *aisthesis* in Greek, meaning sense-perception. *Aisthesis* goes back to the Homeric *aiou* and *aisthou* which means both "I perceive" as well as "I gasp, struggle for breath . . . *aisthmoai, aisthanomai,*" "I breathe in." (63)

Many still bring this traditional expectation to the art object; a hope that something basic will occur to jolt the viewer with an experience of beauty, or the shock of pain. In an escapist sense this represents a desire to find a rarified place of abandonment which makes few crossovers with the real world, which remains housed in the museum, or the pristine whiteness of the gallery, forever hidden from the course of history. In the best sense, this desire for the beautiful pertains to the notion, not unlike that held by members of the Frankfurt School, that beauty is itself subversive, especially in a world suffering from narcolepsy, that that which arouses desire, stimulates the senses, spurs the imagination—not in a simple, pretty, mindless way, but in a profound and therefore unsettling way—must inevitably challenge the normal course of life, which can never satisfy deepest desires or a longing for completeness.

Hillman also contends that "the work of art allows repressed districts of the world and the soul to leave the ugly and enter into beauty" (63) to transform the horrific, as do Goya's Black Paintings, into something which has shape, line, internal integrity—aesthetics. Many audience members do not realize that what we call art, that which has aesthetics, can manifest itself in a wide range of incarnations and serve many functions. "Every well constructed object and machine has form," says John Dewey, "but there is aesthetic form only when the object having this external form fits into a larger experience" (1934, 341). But how can we characterize the range of that expanded experience?

If it is successful, the art object resonates within its own history while also entering the ongoing debates in the art historical world. It speaks to a finely tuned intellect as well as to the collective unconscious. It can operate in images and at times in language or challenge the origin of language with its exploration of images. The work may address national identity as well as that which is subversive to that identity. It may try to articulate the complexity of the past, the remembrance of what is lost, to uncover that which is hidden, layer what is complex, speak the unspeakable, reveal collective fears, unseat personal anxieties, intersect the individual with the universal, challenge the collective dream. It can defy notions of progress and utility—the anchors of the reality principle—suspend linear time, immerse us in pleasure, irrelevance, irreverence, outrageousness. In Kant's sense it creates "purposiveness without purpose"—concentration for concentration's sake. It might play with, make fun of, denounce the prevailing ideology, mirror back the absurdities of commodification, push and torture the limits of technology, invert what is known until it becomes strange, bombard us with what is strange until it becomes known, return us to a longed-for, if only imagined, childhood, propel us into a visionary future with the child self intact and equip us to function more healthily in the adult world. Artists re-present the culture from which their identity has been constructed—their race, class, ethnicity, their sexuality, the complex combination of forces which have shaped the way in which they see the world. And they help us to understand, through images and language, the particularity of an individual psyche as it intersects with that of the collective.

These aforementioned are some of the best examples of what art and artists have done, and yet for a general public the comprehension and appreciation of art is still often limited to a more simplistic notion that art will bring joy, that it will transform pain.

There is something wonderful about art which can create happiness in a direct way, but increasingly artists can only make reference to contentment and the sensuality of an idyllic life in their negation. This type of work is most irritating to those with conventional expectations. They feel deprived of catharsis and the healing effect of beauty, yet, in fact, such work has everything to do with beauty precisely because beauty, as a static value-ridden entity, is so conspicuously absent. In its place is conflict, deconstruction—the taking apart and analysis of what there is and the mourning for a joyousness which no longer seems attainable.

Like Hillman (1991), the contemporary art world also is concerned with lifting repression, but its sense of how you do that contradicts Hillman's proposal. It is seen as reactionary in most art world circles to make work which does not challenge conventional notions of beauty. In other words, when lushness and exquisiteness do exist it is often within the framework of postmodern appropriation and pastiche. There must be some irony in the presentation—the reminder, always that we are not now seduced by what once reduced us and that we are able to stand outside the work with some critical distance and ask: From what ideological position was it formed? For whom was it made? Whose interests does it represent? Whose does it serve? What underlying questions does it ask? What implicit power relations frame it? The unintervened-with object is now rarely accepted on its own terms. A disruptive discourse enters into the experience and the work becomes a locus for serious debate. If this intervention is understood by the viewer, it can help clarify that art lives in the continuum of history, engages with contemporary issues and can be transformed by their demands.

But although art and artists increasingly do try to comment on the historical moment, their discourse is still often hermetic and incomprehensible to those outside. The uncertainty about how clear art needs to be and who is responsible for that clarity, has been the source of much debate and antagonism. According to John Dewey, "The language of art has to be acquired" (1934, 335). It is a learned discourse that may be accessed only through an immersion in art and the art world. But the existence of such a barrier is not acknowledged by those who present art to viewers. The mystification of contemporary art could be lifted in part if the general museum-going audience were cautioned when entering an exhibit that the work they are about to see might elude, confuse, and unnerve them if its language is not decoded, and that in fact the dislocation they may experience is crucial to the work's intent. It is often not understood that a good deal of contemporary work is referenced to art history—the signified is the history of art itself—and is not, as many still believe, the so-called life or emotional experience they expect art to address. Therefore, one cannot always "get" the work intuitively, unless the allusions, spoofs, and comments about other contemporary work and intra–art world debates are made apparent. Also, the environment of the gallery or the museum designed to create a fake neutrality, does not always allow the work to establish an adequate context. Why should we expect that an isolated image can reconstruct an entire world around itself? Suzi Gablik (1991, 18), quotes Sherry Levine on the "uneasy death of modernism." Levine says that the work in which artists are now often engaged ". . . only has meaning in relation to everyone else's project. . . . It has no meaning in isolation." Its context, then, is the spectrum of contemporary artistic creation, yet it is often presented in isolation so that it must generate its own meaning, even for those who cannot recreate the absent part of the dialogue.

In practice what often occurs when a person walks into the sterile museum setting and tries to grapple with a difficult piece of contemporary work, is that the viewer is left with the questions "What does this work mean?" "Why don't I understand it?" and then, if the work generates a bit of uneasiness or anger, as it often does, the question becomes, "Is it art?" In Chicago's Museum of Contemporary Art I have heard such queries directed at pieces by such artists as Joseph Beuys, Rebecca Horn, Christian Boltanski. Recently, standing in front of a Rauchenberg painting, I heard a man say, "I could make something like that." Those expressing such often-heard statements likely feel a great deal of frustration. For them the work is not serving the function they assume it should. Often these audience members question the incorporation of "found objects," the way the work is constructed; to them somehow the craft is not precise enough, the materials too mundane, or the representation too minimal. The work appears not to have taken enough labor. These viewers therefore suspect they have been duped and that they too could construct something of equal merit. Because they are able to step outside, to question its authenticity, it is clear that this work does not satisfy their need to be entranced, amazed, or swept away. They may or may not be sympathetic to the notion that the work might intentionally wish to transcend preciousness by negating the experience of its own rarification and that it is in fact successful in these terms. Not only might we say that the viewer has found the experience of the work wanting and in this sense has not "gotten" the artist's intention, but also that the viewer has not understood why this work has been called "art" at all. The hostility is directed to the artist, but also to the entire art apparatus—gallery owners, museum curators, collectors, critics—those who sanction certain work, position it in the museum or gallery context, and, in so doing, raise a certain level of expectation.

When Scott Tyler placed the U.S. flag on the gallery floor at the School of the Art Institute of Chicago, all these issues were raised. The initial reaction of many viewers was fury generated by the placement of the flag in such a compromised position. And this rage was followed by a series of questions: What is this strange thing called "installation"—a form that is neither painting, sculpture, nor photography but in Tyler's case an amalgam of all three? Why was this piece shown within the confines of the Art Institute of Chicago—a well-respected and prestigious venue? In reference to this last query, the location of the exhibit was an issue that needed immediate clarification. Tyler's installation, "What Is the Proper Way to Display a U.S. Flag?" was not chosen for exhibition by the twentieth-century curator of the museum but rather by a faculty committee selecting work for a student exhibition. Misinformed, thousands of Chicagoans in protest thought it was time to stop contributing their tax dollars to the Art Institute. The School of the Art Institute insisted on making the distinction between the function of a school and that of a museum, in the hope that it would change the perception of the work, but the damage was already done. Within these incidents rest the contradictions that artists, educators, and young art students are up against. Unfortunately, the pedagogical value of these subtexts often has remained unknown to those not trained to read the questions or to find their complexity exhilarating.

When art causes such a public furor it is often because the work conflates innovation in form with radicalness in content. A layperson may not easily understand the genre of installation or performance art. These have evolved out of other forms—sculpture, theater, dance—liberating the artist from conceptual and physical constraints. But without having knowledge of the restrictions such categories and contentions of form placed on the artist, a more general audience might have little access to, or sympathy for, the work. Once the parameters governing artistic activity have been lifted, the artist may be freer to create, but the audience is often lost.

When Karen Finley smears her naked body with chocolate and then covers it with sprouts to represent shit and sperm respectively, there is quite a bit to explain to those who can neither understand the humiliation she experiences as a woman, or the form with which she chooses to express it. She uses monologues, she also uses her body, yet her work is neither theater nor dance. The simple devices she has found for communicating terribly complicated issues of power and submission are actually extremely effective. When described out of context, however, the work can easily sound banal and crude, an easy target for literalists of the imagination, those hung up on profanity and those unable or unwilling to acknowledge the depth of personal pain that this work attempts to convey. "Aesthetic experience is a manifestation, a record and celebration of the life of a civilization, a means of promoting its development, and is also the ultimate judgement upon the quality of a civilization" (Dewey 1934, 326). Finley's work embodies a scathing critique of society, yet few outside the art world are interested in exploring the value of such work.

Right-wing politicians like Jesse Helms and Pat Buchanan, supposedly focused on issues of pornography, in part actually have been punishing artists for the seriousness of their work's content, the inventiveness of its form, and the articulated indictments of society it contains. Had Andres Serrano chosen to present the contradictions of Catholicism in a less unconventional way, had he not submerged a plastic crucifix in a tank filled with urine to photograph it as romantically and mysteriously as he did, or had he chosen to communicate the corruption of the church and the denigration of the teachings of Christ without the use of imagery, perhaps no one would have paid attention. If Karen Finley had simply talked about abuses to the female body and had not attempted to recreate them symbolically, perhaps she would not have been as readily criticized. If performance artist Tim Miller had said the same things about being a gay man in American society during the last twenty years—from the joys of sensual discovery to AIDS—without dramatizing the pain, and without taking off his clothes, his National Endowment for the Arts grant might not have been revoked. Or if David Wojnarovich, in writing about the Artists Space exhibition inspired by the nightmares of AIDS, had kept his rage in check and hadn't mentioned those government officials whom he holds responsible for apathy in the face of this epidemic, Frohnmayer might not have noticed. These artists, and many others, have paid for their radicalness. They have been punished for the political content of their vision and the degree to which they have had to resort to extreme forms to communicate the passion of their positions. But such work has received little support from those outside the art world because its meaning is not understood and its significance as a pedagogical tool and as an analysis of contemporary society cannot be grasped by those who are only familiar with "high art" or mainstream mass culture.

However oblivious to its audience such work may seem, there is an important function served by difficult, innovative art which refuses to be assimilated. It does jar the senses, challenges normal perception and destroys the illusion that the world in which we live can be easily understood. "It can be argued," Terry Eagleton writes, "that the unreadability of literature is precisely its radicalism. . . . Literature entices only to refuse, appears complicitous only to cold-shoulder. Literature is always somewhere else" (Eagleton 1975, 165). Art, in the same vein, can be utterly familiar and yet its opposite. It can baffle where one expects recognition, reject where one longs for acceptance, or be incomprehensible where one desperately seeks understanding. It can also be argued that the difficulty many have trying to grasp the meaning of contemporary art demonstrates the unnecessary exclusivity of the art world—its isolation from most people's lives. But the inability of many "to read" the visual work that is in front of them, is also a mark of how uneven the cultural life of American society actually is. Undoubtedly the fact that art has been obliterated from the public school system is at the source of the problem. Those who are attending or recently have attended public schools, for the most part, are visually illiterate. And even when art is taught within the school system, those who teach it rarely stretch beyond the traditional humanistic goals of art education, which focuses on genius, masterpiece, divine inspiration, and predominantly white Western art that ends with Impressionism. Most who teach at the public school level have not been trained to reflect upon the issues with which contemporary artists actually engage. Like literature, art now often presents itself as "threat, mystery, challenge, and insult" (Eagleton 1975, 18). "Literacy admits us to reading," Eagleton writes, "so that we can take the full measure of our exclusion" (18) . Those able to read are actually unable to read. Those able to see are nonetheless unable to see. But to an audience which has not been taught the pedagogical value of such frustration, this exclusion is a source of great hostility.

Artists and the art world seek to provoke in this way, but are then unwilling to deal with their audience's resultant anger. One could of course argue that the exclusivity of the art world is precisely the point and art should indeed always refuse to blend into mass culture, where images and issues often are flattened to banality. But artists, for the most part, do want their work to be understood and a stated goal for many is accessibility. Some artists talk about their desire to reach a larger audience, one outside the art world, and this has become a more significant issue as art is increasingly more charged with political concerns; some feel an almost moral obligation to reach out and extend to a larger, albeit unnamed, undifferentiated audience beyond that which is familiar.

Yet when one seeks models for a more accessible kind of work, few names come to mind. On everyone's list would be Barbara Kruger and Jenny Holzer, perhaps because their work is language-based and its messages seemingly explicit. What is interesting about their work in relationship to this discussion is the way in which they both position the audience within their discourse and reveal or do not reveal themselves in the process. I watched Jenny Holzer's impressive digital electronic signboards revolving around the curved spaces of the Guggenheim Museum in splendid red, white, and amber and wondered, almost out loud, who is this artist and what does she really think about life, art, politics? Is she as paranoid as these aphorisms would have us believe or is this nonspecified identity, manifested through these words, a creation, a persona? At whom is this voice directed? And does her desired audience actually "get it"?

The aphorisms warn us about private property, sex, love, passion, crimes of the heart, an unnatural Big Brother about whom we should concern ourselves. We wonder what can be made of statements like the following:

It's better to be a good person than a famous person.

It's better to be naive than jaded.

It's better to study the living fact than to analyze history.

It's crucial to have an active fantasy life.

Or:

What urge will save us now that sex won't?

Put food out in the same place every day and talk to the people who come to eat and organize them.

These distillations, arguments, bits of conversation, political wisdom, unsolicited advice, fly by us. What is their context? The power of the electronic billboards, the simultaneous arrogance and diffidence of the voice behind the text leave us breathless. Should we accept the confusion we experience as an essential component of the work? Or can we criticize the nonspecificity of the subject and object of such discourse? What might an average viewer deduce? What is the actual effect?

At a Barbara Kruger gallery exhibit in New York I experienced a similar confusion but for different reasons. Obviously Kruger's work has a much more clearly defined point of view—an explicitly political feminist stance. In this particular installation, her work was angry and that anger was focused around issues of power, domination, and gender-related inequities. The rage was palpable in red, black, and white, surrounding the viewer at every turn, even on the floor. But how are we supposed to understand Kruger's intent? Were these messages for the art world? If so, the art audience has already heard them. Are they for the average gallery goer? And if so should we assume that the audience shares Kruger's analysis? Or are these questions irrelevant and should we simply be grateful for this forceful surrogate voice enraged for all who feel anger and have no voice of their own?

Both Jenny Holzer and Barbara Kruger speak as the embodiment of reason in an unreasonable world, as truth in an untruthful world, and most assuredly as anger in a world which generates injustice and humiliation but offers few forms of expression for it. Jenny Holzer's aphoristic phrases have appeared on billboards, hat brims, T-shirts, placards. They have allowed the artist, here appearing as disembodied voice, to find a site-specific way to rivet her discourse. She has successfully taken it out of the gallery context and put it on the streets. Even were this work designed only to feed those in the intellectual vanguard it still would have a purpose. In a sense, a great deal of what appears as political work and seems as if it should stretch beyond the normal art world context may actually have a more useful function as theory. It appeals to those able and willing to grapple with art as an expression of ideas and to understand it philosophically—beyond, in spite of, instead of the fixation with the object. How much or how little of this is grasped by those outside the ranks of the initiated, those exiled from the communication—the excommunicated—can only be imagined.

The complexity of these issues poses a pedagogical challenge for those engaged in the education of young art students. How might this next generation be taught to grapple with these concerns? Can they be encouraged to serve as a bridge between the cutting edge of art world ideas and a less art-sophisticated audience? In truth, the issue of audience is rarely raised in the art-school pedagogical process, and by its omission it is usually assumed that work is being made to take its place within the art world context. This assumption usually becomes self-fulfilling. Yet among people with political consciousness, work which does not reach beyond the gallery world is often thought to have failed. Somehow it is hoped that there will be another venue, a larger arena, a new audience who will be interested in and affected by such work. But even the most political work is often unable to transcend its category as art. And work which is thought to cross over—move between the art world and a more mass audience—is often co-opted by art world recognition. This fashionable assimilation is a contradiction for work whose goal is social criticism and criticism of the exclusivity and elitism of the art world from which it has emerged. But because most artists cannot survive economically, intellectually, or emotionally without the approval of the academic art world for grants, teaching positions, exhibitions, critical reviews, and ego survival, they set their sites within the art world and are satisfied making a political statement about the hermeticism or corruption of that small arena. It would be ideal if work could break out of categorical boundaries and be simultaneously avant-garde and popular, but in practice, this is difficult to achieve. Given these hurdles, educators must set out clear programmatic goals to help students think about their work within a larger societal context and to imagine who their audience might be.

In practice, these fundamental questions about audience only arise when students make work which has an overt political agenda or has some other deliberate message to communicate, work that is after some specific result. Often the reason politically oriented work is so didactic is that it is attempting to "prove" to viewers in a moral way that they should accept the artist's point of view, see the world or at least a particular aspect of it as the artist does. In its attempt to convince— its sense of its own correctness and also its own isolation—the work often goes overboard, becomes heavy-handed. And that which is designed to persuade, to demonstrate that art can educate, concern itself with the issues of the world, succeeds instead in pushing its viewers away.

Mature artists like Jenny Holzer, Barbara Kruger, and Hans Haacke can bring to this challenge a good deal of humor and irony, but student artists grappling with the seriousness of the issues, perhaps for the first time, often lack this ability to step outside and to comment on the absurdity and even futility while nonetheless waging a strong battle against that which disturbs, unnerves, infuriates them. When students make issue-oriented work they try to tell others what to think. They often assume that their audience knows very little about the question they are addressing and must therefore be educated, or they assume a conservative audience that should be radicalized, or a puritanical one that needs to shocked. They rarely see, in an objective way, how confrontational and alienating the form of the work actually might be to those outside. At times this work projects their feelings about the world from which they come—about their parents, about the values presented to them which students now feel they need to combat. These points of reference become the object of their attack. The result, at its worst, may take the form of a generic rebellion—nudity for nudity's sake, anarchism for anarchism's sake. The ultimate effect of the work is not thought through. Students rarely step outside their own subjectivity long enough to measure the result. Even when they do study theory and develop strong philosophical principles, they are rarely taught strategy. And they are given little historical sense of how artists have functioned at other moments in American society or when they have successfully aligned with social movements committed to change.

In the same vein, because students need to be helped to understand not only the subject of their work but its objective, they must learn to ask themselves who would be their ideal viewer and who, most likely, will be their actual viewer. What might their audience need to know to understand the work? How much information should they offer? At a time when the issue of identity is being discussed in all areas of the art world, it is important to challenge the notion of a universal subject, to ask students about the particularities of audience and how much they actually know about the groups they have targeted. In practice, art deliberately designed for a larger audience becomes hermetic when these questions are not asked. Such inquiries, which seem pro forma in other disciplines, are truly confrontational within the art world because they smash the absoluteness of a subjectivity which is so treasured and goes unchallenged in the traditional art school environment.

I am not arguing that artists should simplify their work. I believe strongly in the tension created by that which cannot be easily absorbed and therefore engenders struggle. Moreover, I am committed to the notion that the traditional expectations for the place of art in society must be challenged, and that young artists must be taught to ask themselves how far they are willing to go to make certain vital connections apparent to a more diverse audience. Without such assistance even postmodern work seems caught in a modernist paradigm—as it waits for its inherent genius and universal appeal to be discovered and to trickle down to the masses. To assist a more direct and honest comprehension, artists simply have to make some attempt to help the viewer through the work's complexity. This is what students in particular find difficult to actualize. Because they themselves don't as yet know how they arrived at their own images, they are not sure what would be necessary to bring other people along with them. And yet, the amount of information disclosed by the piece itself becomes the measure for how much power one bestows on the audience. As we offer students our knowledge and experience, we extend to them the ability to communicate to as large an audience as they choose. In so far as we show them that their arrogance is unstrategic, however principled its intent, we give them the ability to assert control over the response their work might elicit. As we encourage or discourage the art school tendency toward hermeticism, we either free young artists from the confines of the art world's terminally hip subculture, or circumscribe them within its discourse forever.

The obscurity and postmodern nihilism that characterized a great deal of the 1980s art world has already begun to be transformed in the 1990s. There is no doubt that student artists are already pushing against the limits that have been handed down to them. They are increasingly committed to finding ways to represent issues like homelessness, the degradation of the environment, AIDS, child abuse. And they are struggling to find new forms within which to present their work. In the face of the gallery system's monetary crisis and the serious degeneration of the urban infrastructure, many have already abandoned the desire for a conventional career as a gallery artist and have instead focused on site-specific installation, performance, and work which is more community-based. These young artists who have seen through the illusion of the marketplace, are not easily seduced by its prestige.

So much of what is wrong, so much of what accounts for the massive gap between artists, writers, intellectuals, theorists, and the general public is historical. There has never been, and there is not now, a significant place for artists and intellectuals within American society. This is perhaps the biggest problem the artistic community faces. No matter how well we prepare our students, no matter how much we all attempt to reach beyond the narrow confines within which we have been trained, we nonetheless struggle against the fundamentally anti-intellectual nature of American society and the visual illiteracy the educational system perpetuates.

As I write this and Pat Buchanan's campaign ads rant on, it seems clear that we are probably watching the death of the NEA as we have known it. But as the economy collapses around us, perhaps artists will reach out to align themselves with other groups who also have been seriously disenfranchised. And one hopes the insights, perceptions, and brilliance of artists will be sought out in the 1990s to solve, in unique ways, problems that appear to be frighteningly unsolvable. Such solicitations could break down the artist's sense of isolation and help heal the censorship wounds of the last five years. They could transform the popular perception of art and the artist and help create compassion for those who attempt to articulate a personal vision, even when such efforts are met with misunderstanding and opposition. Out of the urgency we are now experiencing, caused by the greed of those without imagination who have been allowed to rule for too long, will come the search for languages and images rich and complex enough to represent the economic and spiritual pain many are experiencing, and visionary enough to help construct a sense of renewed passion and expectation for the future. We can only hope that the satisfaction artists might derive from constructing such images will be matched by the audience's pleasure in experiencing them.

WORKS CITED

Dewey, John (1934). *Art as Experience*. New York: Putnam.

Eagleton, Terry (1975). *Criticism and Ideology*. New York: Verso.

Gablik, Suzi (1991). *The Reenchantment of Art*. New York: Thames and Hudson.

Hillman, James (1991). "The Repression of Beauty." *Tema Celeste* (international edition) 4, no. 31 (May): 58–64.

Steinberg, Leo (1972). *Other Criteria: Confrontations with Twentieth-Century Art*. London: Oxford University Press.

CHAPTER 5

....

EROS, EROTICISM, AND

THE PEDAGOGICAL

PROCESS

....

BELL HOOKS

As professors we rarely speak of the place of eros or the erotic in our classrooms. Trained in the philosophical context of Western metaphysical dualism, many of us have accepted the notion that there is a split between the body and the mind. Believing this, individuals enter the classroom to teach as though only the mind is present and not the body. To call attention to the body is to betray the legacy of repression and denial that has been handed down to us by our professorial elders, who have usually been white and male. But our nonwhite elders were just as eager to deny the body. The predominantly black college has always been a bastion of repression. The public world of institutional learning was a site where the body had to be erased, go unnoticed. When I first became a teacher and needed to use the restroom in the middle of class, I had no clue as to what my elders did in such situations. No one talked about the body in relation to teaching. What did one do with the body in the classroom? Trying to remember the bodies of my professors, I find myself unable to recall them. I hear voices, remember fragmented details but very few whole bodies.

Entering the classroom determined to erase the body and give ourselves over more fully to the mind, we show by our beings how deeply we have accepted the assumption that passion has no place in the classroom. Repression and denial make it possible for us to forget and then desperately seek to recover ourselves, our feelings, our passions in some private place—after class. I remember reading an article in *Psychology Today* years ago when I was still an undergraduate, reporting a study which revealed that every so many seconds while giving lectures many male professors were thinking about sexuality—were even having lustful thoughts about students. I was amazed. After reading this article, which as I recall was shared and talked about endlessly in the dormitory, I watched male professors differently, trying to connect the fantasies I imagined them having in their minds with lectures, with their bodies which I had so faithfully learned to pretend I did not see. During my first semester of college teaching, there was a male student in my class whom I always seemed to see and not see at the same time. At one point in the middle of the semester, I received a call from a school therapist who wanted to speak with me about the way I treated this student in the class. The therapist told me that the student had said I was unusually gruff, rude, and downright mean when I related to him. I did not know exactly who the student was, could not put a face or body with his name, but later when he identified himself in class, I realized that I was erotically drawn to this student. And that my naive way of coping with feelings in the classroom that I had been taught never to have was to deflect (hence my harsh treatment of him), repress, and deny. Overly conscious then about ways such repression and denial could lead to the "wounding" of a student, I was determined to face whatever passions were aroused in the classroom setting and deal with them.

Writing about Adrienne Rich's work, connecting it to the work of men who thought critically about the body, in her introduction to *Thinking through the Body* Jane Gallop comments:

> Men who do find themselves in some way thinking through the body are more likely to be recognized as serious thinkers and heard. Women have first to prove that we are thinkers, which is easier when we conform to the protocol that deems serious thought separate from an embodied subject in history. Rich is asking women to enter the realms of critical thought and knowledge without becoming disembodied spirit, universal man (Gallop 1988, 7).

Beyond the realm of critical thought, it is equally crucial that we learn to enter the classroom "whole" and not as "disembodied spirit." In the heady early days of women's studies classes at Stanford University, I learned by the example of daring, courageous women professors (particularly Diane Middlebrook) that there was a place for passion in the classroom, that eros and the erotic did not need to be denied for learning to take place. One of the central tenets of feminist critical pedagogy has been the insistence on not engaging the mind/body split. This is one of the underlying beliefs that has made women's studies a subversive location in the academy. While women's studies over the years has had to fight to be taken seriously by academics in traditional disciplines, those of us who have been intimately engaged as students and/or teachers with feminist thinking have always recognized the legitimacy of a pedagogy that dares to subvert the mind/body split and allow us to be whole in the classroom, and, as a consequence, wholehearted.

Recently, Susan B., a colleague and friend, whom I taught in a women's studies class when she was an undergraduate, stated in conversation that she felt she was having so much trouble with her graduate courses because she has come to expect a quality of passionate teaching that is not present where she is studying. Her comments made me think anew about the place of passion, of erotic recognition in the classroom setting because I believe that the energy she felt in our women's studies classes was there because of the extent to which the women professors teaching those courses dared to give fully of ourselves, going beyond the mere transmission of information in lectures. Feminist education for critical consciousness is rooted in the assumption that knowledge and critical thought engaged with in the classroom should inform our habits of being and ways of living outside the classroom. Since so many of our early classes were taken almost exclusively by female students, it was easier for us not to be disembodied spirits in the classroom. Concurrently, it was expected that we would bring a quality of care and even "love" to our students. Eros, as a motivating force, was present in our classrooms. As critical pedagogues we were teaching students ways to think differently about gender, understanding fully that this knowledge would also lead them to live differently.

To understand the place of eros and eroticism in the classroom we must move beyond thinking of these forces solely in terms of the sexual, though that dimension need not be denied. Sam Keen, in his book *The Passionate Life,* urges readers to remember that in its earliest conception "erotic potency was not confined to sexual power but included the moving force that propelled every life-form from a state of mere potentiality to actuality" (Keen 1983, 5). Given that critical pedagogy seeks to transform consciousness, to provide students with ways of knowing that enable them to now themselves better and live in the world more fully, to some extent it must rely on the presence of the erotic in the classroom to aid the learning process. Keen continues:

> When we limit 'erotic' to its sexual meaning, we betray our alienation from the rest of nature. We confess that we are not motivated by anything like the mysterious force that moves birds to migrate or dandelions to spring. Furthermore, we imply that the fulfillment or potential toward which we strive is sexual—the romantic-genital connection between two persons.(5)

Understanding that eros is a force that enhances our overall effort to be self-actualizing, that it can provide an epistemological grounding informing how we know what we know, enables both professors and students to use such energy in a classroom setting in ways that invigorate discussion and excite the critical imagination.

Suggesting that this culture lacks a "vision or science of hygeology" (health and well-being) Keen asks, "What forms of passion might make us whole? To what passions may we surrender with the assurance that we will expand rather than diminish the promise of our lives?"(19). The quest for knowledge that enables us to unite theory and practice is one such passion. To the extent that professors bring this passion, which has to be fundamentally rooted in a love for ideas, we are able to inspire. The classroom becomes a dynamic place where transformation in social relations are concretely actualized and the false dichotomy between the world outside and the inside world of the academy disappears. In many ways this is frightening. Nothing about the way I was trained as a teacher really prepared me to witness my students transforming themselves.

It was during the years that I taught in the African-American studies department at Yale, a course on black women writers, that I witnessed the way education for critical consciousness can fundamentally alter our perceptions of reality and our actions. During one course we collectively explored in fiction the power of internalized racism, seeing how it was described in the literature as well as critically interrogating our experiences. However, one of the black female students who had always straightened her hair because she felt deep down that she would not look good if it were not processed changed. She came to class after a break and told everyone that this class had deeply affected her, so much so that when she went to get her usual "perm" some force within said no. I still remember the fear I felt when she testified that the class had changed her. Though I believed deeply in the philosophy of education for critical consciousness that empowers, I had not yet comfortably united theory with practice. Some small part of me still wanted us to remain disembodied spirits. And her body, her presence, her changed look was a direct challenge that I had to face and affirm. She was teaching me. Now, years later, I read again her final words to the class and recognize the passion and beauty of her will to know and to act:

> I am a black woman. I grew up in Shaker Heights, Ohio. I cannot go back and change years of believing that I could never be quite as pretty or intelligent as many of my white friends—but I can go forward learning pride in who I am. . . . I cannot go back and change years of believing that the most wonderful thing in the world would be to be Martin Luther King, Jr.'s wife—but I can go on and find the strength I need to be the revolutionary for myself rather than the companion and help for someone else. So no, I don't believe that we change what has already been done but we can change the future and so I am reclaiming and learning more of who I am so that I can be whole.

Attempting to gather my thoughts on eroticism and pedagogy, I have reread student journals covering a span of ten years. Again and again I read notes that could easily be considered "romantic" as students express their love for me, our class. Hear an Asian student offer her thoughts about a class:

> White people have never understood the beauty of silence, of connection and reflection. You teach us to speak, and to listen for the signs in the wind. Like a guide, you walk silently through the forest ahead of us. In the forest everything has sound, speaks. . . . You too teach us to talk, where all life speaks in the forest, not just the white man's. Isn't that part of feeling whole—the ability to be able to talk, to not have to be silent or performing all the time, to be able to be critical and honest—openly? This is the truth you have taught us: all people deserve to speak.

Or a black male student writing that he will "love me now and always" because our class has been a dance, and he loves to dance:

I love to dance. When I was a child, I danced everywhere. Why walk there when you can shuffle-ball-change all the way? When I danced my soul ran free. I was poetry. On my Saturday grocery excursions with my mother, I would flap, flap, flap, ball change the shopping cart through the aisles. Mama would turn to me and say, "boy stop that dancing. White people think that's all we can do anyway." I would stop but when she wasn't looking I would do a quick high bell kick or two. I didn't care what white people thought, I just loved to dance—dance—dance. I still dance and I still don't care what people think white or black. When I dance my soul is free. It is sad to read about men who stop dancing, who stop being foolish, who stop letting their souls fly free. . . . I guess for me, surviving whole means never to stop dancing.

These words were written by O'Neal LaRone Clark in 1987. We had a passionate teacher/student relationship. He was taller than six feet and I remember the day he came to class late and came right up to the front, picked me up and whirled me around. The class laughed. I called him "fool" and laughed. It was by way of apology for being late, for missing any moment of classroom passion. And so he brought his own moment. I too love to dance. And so we danced our way into the future as comrades and friends bound by all we had learned in class together. Those who knew him remember the times he came to class early to do funny imitations of the teacher. He died unexpectedly last year—still dancing, still loving me now and always.

When eros is present in the classroom setting then love is bound to flourish. Well-learned distinctions between public and private make us believe that love has no place in the classroom. Even though many viewers could applaud a movie like *The Dead Poet's Society,* possibly identifying with the passion of the professor and his students, rarely is such passion institutionally affirmed. As professors we are expected to publish, but no one really expects or demands of us that we really care about teaching in uniquely passionate and different ways. Teachers who love students and are loved by them are still "suspect" in the academy. Some of the suspicion is that the presence of feelings, of passions, may not allow for objective consideration of each student's merit. But this very notion is based on the false assumption that education is neutral, that there is some "even" emotional ground we stand on that enables us to treat everyone equally dispassionately. In reality, special bonds between professors and students have always existed but traditionally they have been exclusive rather than inclusive. To allow one's feeling of care and one's will to nurture particular individuals in the classroom to expand and embrace everyone goes against the notion of privatized passion. In student journals from various classes I have taught there would always be complaints about the perceived special bonding between myself and particular students. Realizing that my students were uncertain about expressions of care and love in the classroom, I found it necessary to teach on the subject. I asked students once: "Why do you feel that the regard I extend to a particular student cannot also be extended to each of you? Why do you think there is not enough love or care to go around?" To answer these questions they had to think deeply about the society we live in, how we are taught to compete with one another. They had to think about capitalism and how it informs the way we think about love and care, the way we live in our bodies, the way we try to separate mind from body.

There is not much passionate teaching or learning taking place in higher education today. Even when students are desperately yearning to be touched by knowledge, professors still fear the challenge, allow their worries about losing control to override their desires to teach. Concurrently, those of us who teach the same old subjects in the same old ways are often inwardly bored—unable to rekindle passions we may have once felt. If, as Thomas Merton suggests in his essay on pedagogy, "Learning to Live," the purpose of education is to show students how to define themselves "authentically and spontaneously in relation" to the world, then we can best teach if we are self-actualized. Merton reminds us that "the original and authentic 'paradise' idea, both in the monastery and in the university, implied not simply a celestial store of theoretic ideas to which the Magistri and Doctores held the key, but the inner self of the student" who would discover the ground of his or her being in relation to him- or herself, to higher powers, to community. That the "fruit of education . . . was in the activation of that inmost center" (1949, 9). To restore passion to the classroom or to excite it in classrooms where it has never been, we must find again the place of eros within ourselves and together allow the mind and body to feel and know and desire.

WORKS CITED

Gallop, Jane (1988). *Thinking Through the Body*. New York: Columbia University Press.
Keen, Sam (1983). *The Passionate Life*. San Francisco: Harper & Row.
Merton, Thomas (1979). "Learning to Live." In Naomi Burton Stone and Brother Patrick Hart (eds.) *Love and Learning*, New York: Farrar, Strauss & Giroux, Inc. 3-14.

CHAPTER 6

BE LIKE MIKE? MICHAEL

JORDAN AND THE

PEDAGOGY OF DESIRE

MICHAEL ERIC DYSON

Michael Jordan is perhaps the best and most well-known athlete in the world today. He has attained unparalleled cultural status because of his extraordinary physical gifts, his marketing as an icon of race-transcending American athletic and moral excellence, and his mastery of a sport which has become the metaphoric center of the black cultural imagination. But the Olympian sum of Jordan's cultural meaning is greater than the fluent parts of his persona as athlete, family man, and marketing creation. There is hardly cultural precedence for the character of his unique fame which has blurred the line between private and public, between personality and celebrity, and between substance and symbol. Michael Jordan stands at the breach between perception and intuition, his cultural meaning perennially deferred from closure because his career symbolizes possibility itself, gathering into its unfolding narrative the shattered remnants of previous incarnations of fame and yet transcending their reach.

Jordan has been called "the new DiMaggio" (Boers 1990, 30) and "Elvis in high tops," indications of the Herculean cultural heroism he has come to embody. There is even a religious element to the near worship of Jordan as a cultural icon of invincibility, as he has been called a "savior of sorts" (O'Brien 1990–91, 82), "basketball's high priest" (Bradley 1991–92, 60), and "more popular than Jesus," except with "better endorsement deals" (Vancil 1992, 51). But the quickly developing canonization of Michael Jordan provokes reflection about the contradictory uses to which Jordan's body is put as a cultural text and ambiguous symbol of fantasy, and the avenues of agency and resistance available especially to black youth who make symbolic investment in Jordan's body as a means of cultural and personal possibility, creativity, and desire.

I understand Jordan in the broadest sense of the term to be a public pedagogue, a figure of estimable public moral authority whose career educates us about the convergence of productive and disenabling forms of knowledge, desire, interest, consumption, and culture in three spheres: the culture of athletics, which thrives on skill and performance; the specific expression of elements of African-American culture; and the market forces and processes of commodification expressed by, and produced in, advanced capitalism. By probing these dimensions of Jordan's cultural importance, we may gain a clearer understanding of his function in American society.

Athletic activity has shaped and reflected important sectors of American society. First, it produced communities of common athletic interest organized around the development of highly skilled performance. The development of norms of athletic excellence evidenced in sports activities cemented communities of participants who valorized rigorous sorts of physical discipline in preparation for athletic competition and in expressing the highest degree of athletic skill. Second, it produced potent subcultures that inculcated in their participants norms of individual and team accomplishment. Such norms tapped into the bipolar structures of competition and cooperation that pervade American culture. Third, it provided a means of reinscribing Western frontier myths of exploration and discovery-as-conquest onto a vital sphere of American culture. Sports activities can be viewed in part as the attempt to symbolically ritualize and metaphorically extend the ongoing quest for mastery of environment and vanquishing of opponents within the limits of physical contest.

Fourth, athletic activity has served to reinforce habits and virtues centered in the collective pursuit of communal goals which are intimately connected to the common good, usually characterized within athletic circles as "team spirit." The culture of sport has physically captured and athletically articulated the mores, folkways, and dominant visions of American society, and at its best it has been conceived as a means of symbolically embracing and equitably pursuing the just, the good, the true, and the beautiful. And finally, the culture of athletics has provided an acceptable and widely accessible means of white male bonding. For much of its history, American sports activity has reflected white patriarchal privilege, and it has been rigidly defined and socially shaped by rules that restricted the equitable participation of women and people of color.

Black participation in sports in mainstream society, therefore, is a relatively recent phenomenon. Of course, there have existed venerable traditions of black sports such as the Negro Baseball Leagues, which countered the exclusion of black bodies from white sports. The prohibition of athletic activity by black men in mainstream society severely limited publicly acceptable forms of displaying black physical prowess, an issue that had been politicized during slavery and whose legacy extended into the middle of the twentieth century. Hence, the potentially superior physical prowess of black men, validated for many by the long tradition of slave labor that built American society, helped reinforce racist arguments about the racial regimentation of social space and the denigration of the black body as an inappropriate presence in traditions of American sport.

Coupled with this fear of superior black physical prowess was the notion that inferior black intelligence limited the ability of blacks to perform excellently in those sports activities which required mental concentration and agility. These two forces—the presumed lack of sophisticated black cognitive skills and the fear of superior black physical prowess—restricted black sports participation to thriving but financially handicapped subcultures of black athletic activity. Later, of course, the physical prowess of the black body would be acknowledged and exploited as a supremely fertile zone of profit as mainstream athletic society literally cashed in on the symbolic danger of black sports excellence.

Because of its marginalized status within the regime of American sports, black athletic activity often acquired a social significance that transcended the internal dimensions of game, sport, and skill. Black sport became an arena not only for testing the limits of physical endurance and forms of athletic excellence—while reproducing or repudiating ideals of American justice, goodness, truth, and beauty—but it also became a way of ritualizing racial achievement against socially imposed barriers to cultural performance.

In short, black sport activity often acquired a heroic dimension, as viewed in the careers of figures such as Joe Louis, Jackie Robinson, Althea Gibson, Wilma Rudolph, Muhammad Ali, and Arthur Ashe. Black sports heroes transcended the narrow boundaries of specific sports activities and garnered importance as icons of cultural excellence, symbolic figures who embodied social possibilities of success denied to other people of color. But they also captured and catalyzed the black cultural fetishization of sport as a means of expressing black cultural style, as a means of valorizing craft as a marker of racial and self-expression, and as a means of pursuing social and economic mobility.

It is this culture of black athletics, created against the background of social and historical forces that shaped American athletic activity, that helped produce Jordan and help explain the craft that he practices. Craft is the honing of skill by the application of discipline, time, talent, and energy toward the realization of a particular cultural or personal goal. American folk cultures are pervaded by craft, from the production of cultural artifacts that express particular ethnic histories and traditions, to the development of styles of life and work that reflect and symbolize a community's values, virtues, and goals. Michael Jordan's skills within basketball are clearly phenomenal, but his game can only be sufficiently explained by understanding its link to the fusion of African-American cultural norms and practices, and the idealization of skill and performance that characterize important aspects of American sport. I will identify three defining characteristics of Jordan's game that reflect the influence of African-American culture on his style of play.

First, Jordan's style of basketball reflects the *will to spontaneity*. I mean here the way in which historical accident is transformed into cultural advantage, and the way acts of apparently random occurrence are spontaneously and imaginatively employed by Africans and African-Americans in a variety of forms of cultural expression. When examining Jordan's game, this feature of African-American culture clearly functions in his unpredictable eruptions of basketball creativity. It was apparent, for instance, during game two of the National Basketball Association 1991 championship series between Jordan's Chicago Bulls and the Los Angeles Lakers, in a shot that even Jordan ranked in his all-time top ten (McCallum 1991, 32). Jordan made a drive toward the lane, gesturing with his hands and body that he was about to complete a patent Jordan dunk shot with his right hand. But when he spied defender Sam Perkins slipping over to oppose his shot, he switched the ball in midair to his left hand to make an underhanded scoop shot instead, which became immediately known as the "levitation" shot. Such improvisation, a staple of the will to spontaneity, allows Jordan to expand his vocabulary of athletic spectacle, which is the stimulation of a desire to bear witness to the revelation of truth and beauty compressed into acts of athletic creativity.

Second, Jordan's game reflects the *stylization of the performed self*. This is the creation and projection of a sport persona that is an identifying mark of diverse African-American creative enterprises, from the complexly layered jazz experimentation of John Coltrane, the trickstering and signifying comedic routines of Richard Pryor, and the rhetorical ripostes and oral significations of rapper Kool Moe Dee. Jordan's whole game persona is a graphic depiction of the performed self as flying acrobat, resulting in his famous moniker "Air Jordan." Jordan's performed self is rife with the language of physical expressiveness: head moving, arms extending, hands waving, tongue wagging, and legs spreading.

He has also developed a resourceful repertoire of dazzling dunk shots which further specify and articulate his performed self, and which have garnered him a special niche within the folklore of the game: the cradle jam, rock-a-baby, kiss the rim, lean in, and the tomahawk. In Jordan's game, the stylization of a performed self has allowed him to create a distinct sports persona that has athletic as well as economic consequences, while mastering sophisticated levels of physical expression and redefining the possibilities of athletic achievement within basketball.

Finally, there is the subversion of perceived limits through the use of *edifying deception,* which in Jordan's case centers around the space/time continuum. This moment in African-American cultural practice is the ability to flout widely understood boundaries through mesmerization and alchemy, a subversion of common perceptions of the culturally or physically possible through the creative and deceptive manipulation of appearance. Jordan is perhaps most famous for his alleged "hang time," the uncanny ability to remain suspended in midair longer than other basketball players while executing his stunning array of improvised moves. But Jordan's "hang time" is technically a misnomer, and can be more accurately attributed to Jordan's skillful athletic deception, his acrobatic leaping ability, and his intellectual toughness in projecting an aura of uniqueness around his craft than to his defiance of gravity and the laws of physics.

No human being, including Michael Jordan, can successfully defy the law of gravity and achieve relatively sustained altitude without the benefit of machines. As Douglas Kirkpatrick points out, the equation for altitude is $1/2g \times t2 = VO \times t$ (Editors 1990, 28). However, Jordan appears to hang by *stylistically* relativizing the fixed coordinates of space and time through the skillful management and manipulation of his body in midair. For basketball players, "hang time" is the velocity and speed a player takes off with combined with the path her/his center of gravity follows on her/his way up. At the peak of a player's vertical jump, the velocity and speed are close to, or at, zero; hanging motionless in the air is the work of masterful skill and illusion (Editors 1990, 28). Michael Jordan, through the consummate skill and style of his game, only appears to be hanging in space for more than the one second that human beings are capable of remaining airborne.

But the African-American aspects of Jordan's game are indissolubly linked to the culture of consumption and the commodification of black culture.[1] Because of Jordan's past mastery of basketball, his squeaky-clean image, and his youthful vigor in pursuit of the American Dream, he has become, along with Bill Cosby, the quintessential pitch man in American society. Even his highly publicized troubles with gambling, his refusal to visit the White House after the Bulls' championship season, and a book which purports to expose the underside of his heroic myth have barely tarnished his All-American image.[2] Jordan eats Wheaties, drives Chevrolets, wears Hanes, drinks Coca-Cola, consumes McDonald's, guzzles Gatorade, and, of course, wears Nikes. He and his shrewd handlers have successfully produced, packaged, marketed, and distributed his image and commodified his symbolic worth, transforming cultural capital into cash, influence, prestige, status, and wealth. To that degree, at least, Jordan repudiates the sorry tradition of the black athlete as the naif who loses his money to piranhalike financial wizards, investors, and hangers-on. He represents the New Age athletic entrepreneur who understands that American sport is ensconced in the cultural practices associated with business, and that it demands particular forms of intelligence, perception, and representation to prevent abuse and maximize profit.

From the very beginning of his professional career, Jordan was consciously marketed by his agency, Pro-Serv, as a peripatetic vehicle of American fantasies of capital accumulation and material consumption tied to Jordan's personal modesty and moral probity. In so doing, Pro-Serv skillfully avoided attaching to Jordan the image of questionable ethics and lethal excess that plagued inside traders and corporate raiders on Wall Street during the mid-1980s, as Jordan began to emerge as a cultural icon. But Jordan is also the symbol of the spectacle-laden black athletic body as the site of commodified black cultural imagination. Ironically, the black male body that has been historically viewed as threatening and inappropriate in American society (and remains so outside of sports and entertainment) is made an object of white desires to domesticate and dilute its more ominous and subversive uses, even symbolically reducing Jordan's body to dead meat (McDonald's McJordan hamburger), that can be consumed and expelled as waste.

Jordan's body is also the screen upon which is projected black desires to emulate his athletic excellence and replicate his entry into reaches of unimaginable wealth and fame. But there is more than vicarious substitution and the projection of fantasy onto Jordan's body that is occurring in the circulation and reproduction of black cultural desire. There is also the creative use of desire and fantasy by young blacks to counter, and capitulate to, the forces of cultural dominance that attempt to reduce the black body to a commodity or text that is employed for entertainment, titillation, or financial gain. Simply said, there is no easy correlation between the commodification of black youth culture and the evidences of a completely dominated consciousness.

Even within the dominant cultural practices that seek to turn the black body into pure profit, disruptions of capital are embodied, for instance, in messages circulated in black communities by public moralists who criticize the exploitation of black cultural creativity by casual footwear companies. In short, there are instances of both black complicity and black resistance in the commodification of the black cultural imagination, and the ideological criticism of exploitative cultural practices must always be linked to the language of possibility and agency in rendering a complex picture of the black cultural situation. As Henry Giroux observes,

> The power of complicity and the complicity of power are not exhausted simply by registering how people are positioned and located through the production of particular ideologies structured through particular discourses. . . . It is important to see that an overreliance on ideology critique has limited our ability to understand how people actively participate in the dominant culture through processes of accommodation, negotiation, and even resistance. (Giroux 1992, 194–95)

In making judgments about the various uses of the black body, especially Jordan's symbolic corporeality, we must specify how both consent and opposition to exploitation are often signalled in expressions of cultural creativity.

In examining his reactions to the racial ordering of athletic and cultural life, one can see that the ominous specificity of the black body creates anxieties for Jordan. His encounters with the limits of culturally mediated symbols of race and racial identity have occasionally mocked his desire to live beyond race, to be "neither black nor white" (Patton 1986, 52), to be "viewed as a person" (Vancil 1992, 57). While Jordan chafes under indictment by black critics who claim that he is not "black enough," he has perhaps not clearly understood the differences between enabling versions of human experience that transcend the exclusive gaze of race and disenabling visions of human community that seek race neutrality.

The former is the attempt to expand the perimeters of human experience beyond racial determinism, to nuance and deepen our understanding of the constituent elements of racial identity and to understand how race, along with class, gender, geography, and sexual preference shape and constrain human experience. The latter is the belief in an intangible, amorphous, nonhistorical, and raceless category of "person," existing in a zone beyond not simply the negative consequences of race, but beyond the specific patterns of cultural and racial identity that constitute and help shape human experience. Jordan's unclarity is consequential, weighing heavily on his apolitical bearing and his refusal to acknowledge the public character of his private beliefs about American society and the responsibility of his role as a public pedagogue.

Indeed, it is the potency of black cultural expressions which have not only helped influence his style of play, but which have also made the sneaker industry in which he lucratively participates a multibillion-dollar business. Michael Jordan has helped seize upon the commercial consequences of black cultural preoccupation with style, and the commodification of the black juvenile imagination at the site of the sneaker. At the juncture of the sneaker, a host of cultural, political, and economic forces and meanings meet, collide, shatter, and are reassembled to symbolize the situation of contemporary black culture.

The sneaker reflects at once the projection and stylization of black urban realities linked in our contemporary historical moment to rap culture and the underground political economy of crack, and reigns as the universal icon for the culture of consumption. The sneaker symbolizes the ingenious manner in which black cultural nuances of cool, hip, and chic have influenced the broader American cultural landscape. It was black street culture that influenced sneaker companies' aggressive invasion of the black juvenile market in taking advantage of the increasing amounts of disposable income of young black men as a result of legitimate and illegitimate forms of work.

Problematically, though, the sneaker also epitomizes the worst features of the social production of desire, and represents the ways in which the moral energies of social conscience about material values are drained by the messages of undisciplined acquisitiveness promoted by corporate bastions of the culture of consumption. These messages, of rapacious consumerism supported by cultural and personal narcissism, are articulated on Wall Street and are related to the expanding inner-city juvenocracy, where young black men rule over black urban space in the culture of crack and illicit criminal activity, fed by desires to "live large" and to reproduce capitalism's excesses on their own terrain. Also, sneaker companies make significant sums of money from the illicit gains of drug dealers.

Moreover, while sneaker companies have exploited black cultural expressions of cool, hip, chic, and style, they rarely benefit the people who both consume the largest quantity of products and whose culture redefined the sneaker companies' raison d'être. This situation is severely compounded by the presence of spokespeople like Jordan, Spike Lee, and Bo Jackson, who are either ineffectual, defensive about, or indifferent to the lethal consequences (especially in urban black-on-black violence over sneaker company products) of black juvenile acquisition and consumption of products that these figures have helped make culturally desirable and economically marketable.

Basketball is the metaphoric center of black juvenile culture, a major means by which even temporary forms of cultural and personal transcendence of personal limits are experienced. Michael Jordan is at the center of this black athletic culture, the supreme symbol of black cultural creativity in a society of diminishing tolerance for the black youth whose fascination with Jordan has helped sustain him. But Jordan is also the iconic fixture of broader segments of American society who see in him the ideal figure: a black man of extraordinary genius on the court and before the cameras, who by virtue of his magical skills and godlike talents symbolizes the meaning of human possibility while refusing to root it in the specific forms of culture and race in which it must inevitably make sense or fade to ultimate irrelevance.

Jordan also represents the contradictory impulses of the contemporary culture of consumption, where the black athletic body is deified, reified, and rearticulated within the narrow meanings of capital and commodity. But there is both resistance and consent to the exploitation of black bodies in Jordan's explicit cultural symbolism, as he provides brilliant glimpses of black culture's ingenuity of improvisation as a means of cultural expression and survival. It is also partially this element of black culture that has created in American society a desire to dream Jordan, to "Be like Mike."

The pedagogy of desire that Jordan embodies, although at points immobilized by its depoliticized cultural contexts, is nevertheless a remarkable achievement in contemporary American culture: a six-foot-six American man of obvious African descent is the dominant presence and central cause of athletic fantasy in a sport that twenty years ago was denigrated as a black man's game and hence deemed unworthy of wide attention or support. Jordan is therefore the bearer of meanings about black culture larger than his individual life, the symbol of a pedagogy of style, presence and desire that is immediately communicated by sight of his black body before it can be contravened by reflection.

In the final analysis, his big black body—graceful and powerful, elegant and dark—symbolizes the possibilities of other black bodies to at least remain safe long enough to survive within the limited but significant sphere of sport, since Jordan's achievements have furthered the cultural acceptance of at least the black athletic body. In that sense, Jordan's powerful cultural capital has not been exhausted by narrow understandings of his symbolic absorption by the demands of capital and consumption. His body is still the symbolic carrier of racial and cultural desires to fly beyond limits and obstacles, a fluid metaphor of mobility and ascent to heights of excellence secured by genius and industry. It is this power to embody the often conflicting desires of so many that makes Michael Jordan a supremely instructive figure for our times.

NOTES

1. I do not mean here a theory of commodification that does not accentuate the forms of agency that can function even within restrictive and hegemonic cultural practices. Rather, I think that, contrary to elitist and overly pessimistic Frankfurt School readings of the spectacle of commodity within mass cultures, common people can exercise "everyday forms of resistance" to hegemonic forms of cultural knowledge and practice. For an explication of the function of everyday forms of resistance, see Scott, *Domination and the Arts of Resistance*.

2 For a critical look at Jordan behind the myth, see Smith, *The Jordan Rules*.

WORKS CITED

Boers, Terry. "Getting Better All the Time." *Inside Sports* (May 1990): 30–33.
Bradley, Michael. "Air Everything." *Basketball Forecast* (1991–92) 60–67.
Editors. "How Does Michael Fly?" *Chicago Tribune* February 27, 1990: 28.
Giroux, Henry. *Border Crossings: Cultural Workers and the Politics of Education*. New York: Routledge, 1992.
McCallum, Jack. "His Highness." *Sports Illustrated* June 17, 1991: 28–33.
Patton, Paul. "The Selling of Michael Jordan." *New York Times Magazine* November 9, 1986: 48–58.
Scott, James. *Domination and the Arts of Resistance*. New Haven: Yale University Press, 1990.
Smith, Sam. *Jordan Rules*. New York: Simon and Shuster, 1992.
Vancil, Mark. "Playboy Interview: Michael Jordan." *Playboy Magazine* (May 1992): 51–164.

CHAPTER 7

FORMS OF INSURGENCY

IN THE PRODUCTION OF

POPULAR MEMORIES:

THE COLUMBUS

QUINCENTENARY AND

THE PEDAGOGY OF

COUNTER-

COMMEMORATION

ROGER I. SIMON

The aim of judgment in historical or literary-critical discourse . . . is not
that of determining guilt or innocence. It is to change history to memory:
to make a case for what should be remembered, and how it should be
remembered. This responsibility converts every judgment into a judgment
on the person who makes it. (Hartman, 1989: 80)

Addressed to 'current resident', I recently received a mail-order catalog inviting
me to acquire an assorted set of trendy American middle-class kitsch. Amid the
plethora of procurable objects, which included audio cassettes of 'Classic Bob and
Ray', Sterling Silver Teddy Bear Earrings with Matching Necklace, a book entitled
The Best of the Old Farmer's Almanac, and my choice of three different M. C. Escher
Silk Neckties, was a T-shirt on which appears a picture of a fifteenth-century
sailing ship and the inscription 'How could Columbus have discovered America
when Native Americans were already here?' Accompanying the catalog image was
the following text: 'This shirt poses an intriguing question—and reminds us all

that our continent's heritage goes back a lot further than 1492.' The counter-commemoration[1] has clearly not eluded commodification.

Yet commodification does not necessarily imply trivialization. Indeed, I will argue that consideration of this simple T-shirt can serve as a strategically productive entry into the study of a problem of crucial and current concern: the construction of a pedagogy that may help elicit the reformation of historical memory, consciousness and imagination (Kaye, 1991). To begin, one must locate the shirt in its undeniable context. In the last eighteen months the occurrence of the Columbus quincentenary has launched an extensive production and marketing of books, films, TV and radio programs, theatre performances, and rap songs as well as buttons, decorative and declarative fabrics, calendars, puzzles and games. While most of these commodities are intended to exploit the commemorative interest in either its celebratory or contentious forms, it would be a mistake to dismiss their cultural significance. No doubt, it is important to reserve a degree of cynicism for the interest in history promoted by educators and entrepreneurs on the major anniversaries of past events.[2] However, such reservations do not negate what should be grasped about the Columbian commodities mentioned above. As constructions within the field of historical representation, they are all attempts to make claims on our understanding of the past. In other words, they represent a portion of a complex process of the production of social memory; a process whose form and substance is simultaneously pedagogical and political.

In the North America of the late twentieth century, there is little doubt that cultural commodity forms have become integral to the formation of popular memories. Yet an interest in the formation of popular memories requires a consideration of the complementarity and contradictions among *all* the ways in which a sense of the past is constructed. A contested terrain, the past is traversed by competing and contradictory constructions. Cultural workers intending to initiate pedagogies of historical reformation need an understanding of the topography on which these struggles are taking place. A simple (yet incomplete) list of the sites[3] of popular memory production indicates the complexity at hand.

- Government rituals which reference national origins; literally the theatre of the state, e.g., the traditions of parliament and the monarchy

- State-sponsored commemorations either declared or enacted in law, e.g., holidays or national days of remembrance

- National and local archives which not only select what is considered important to preserve but define the retrieval codes which will provide access to stored documents and artifacts

- Public and private schools which mediate the relation between communities and state sanctioned historical representations

- Academic journals and books

- Museums and galleries, both state sponsored and private

- Fiction and non–fiction, adult and children's books produced for the 'general public'
- Newspapers, magazines and television news programs and documentaries
- Fictional narratives produced for either television or cinema
- Prints, posters, postcards and T–shirts
- Story quilts and arpelleras
- Performance spaces: theatres, community centers, etc.
- Public art ranging from state-commissioned monuments to community murals
- Photo albums and diaries
- Collections of memorabilia
- Orally produced and reproduced family or community narratives
- Ritualized, expressive speech forms

Taken together these sites constitute the field within which the practice of historical representation takes place; the locus of the social production of collective memory. Of course, this field is not homogenous in either its occupancy nor in the pedagogical potential of its commemorative practices (although this non-homogeneity is more complex than it first might appear). Obviously, some sites (national rituals, broadcast television, public schools) incorporate a capability for reaching far more people than others (theatre productions, gallery exhibitions). Furthermore, not all citizens have equal access to the use of sites, thus creating circumstances within which certain groups/agencies defined by particular communities of interest have control of commemorative practices enabling certain memories and forms of remembrance to become dominant across a public sphere. Additionally, it is quite evident that such groups/agencies have been successful in defining some sites as more legitimate than others in regard to their propensity to represent the truth. All of this, of course, points to the construction of hegemonic memories which, most often through what they omit or suppress remembrances which might call into question existing forms of social production and distributions of material wealth.

Of course, there are complications in the dynamics within this field that make the practice of hegemony unstable. First of all, the truth value accorded representations in any given site is not evenly distributed across complexly organized communities. Secondly, people do at times ignore dominant semiotic conventions and make of such representations what they will. Hence, representations may become unintentional parodies or be appropriated into contexts which shift their meaning.[4] Third, some of the more marginal sites of representations have considerable accessibility and greater potential for becoming living memories in people's everyday lives (posters placed in one's office or home). Fourth, while it is certainly the case that groups of people who have long been marginalized both in cultural representations and in their access to social wealth find themselves using sites with an undervalued truth status and a limited distribution capacity; all sites mentioned above are the loci of possible contestation. Fifth, because people who work in/ have access to different sites throughout the field can and do contest dominant memories, this initiates considerable cross-circulation of texts and images. The result is a field filled with the potential for aggregated relations which may function (within the sphere of cultural politics) as alliances working in favor of broadly based reformation.[5]

REMEMBRANCE, COMMEMORATION AND CULTURAL POLITICS

None of us can know of past events beyond our immediate experience outside of the ways they are taught to us. As James Young suggests, the truths of events inhere in the ways we understand, interpret, and write their histories: 'This is not to deny the historical facts of events outside of narrative framing, but to emphasize the difficulty of interpreting, expressing, and acting on these facts outside of the ways we frame them' (1988: 3) In this, Young is acknowledging that the past is not simply passed from generation to generation but regenerated within the contemporary forms through which its story is told. In other words, historical representations have an inherent pedagogical function and hence potentially matter a great deal.

Whether in the form of a T-shirt inscription, poster, print document or film, historical representations are practices that deliberately attempt to shape social memory. Such practices seek to either maintain or reinterpret dominant narratives, revive marginal ones, or bring to light those formerly suppressed, unheard or unarticulated. Historical representations are provocations aimed at altering our ongoing *processes of collective remembrance*. Central to these processes is a procedure within which images and stories of a shared past are woven together with a person (or group's) feelings and comprehension of their embodied presence in time and space. These processes of remembrance are organized and produced within *practices of commemoration* which initiate and structure the relation between a representation of past events and that constellation of affect and information which define a standpoint from which various people engage such representations.

It is in this sense the commemorative practices are pedagogical not only in function but in their very character. Pedagogy is a term which signals the practical synthesis of the questions 'what should be taught and why' with considerations as to how that teaching should take place [Simon, 1992: 55–7]. As a pedagogical form, commemoration incorporates a set of evaluations that structure what memories should inform our social imagination as well as a detailed, structured set of operations for presenting and engaging historical representations intended to provoke and sediment affect and meaning (Giroux, 1992; Trend, 1992). Historical monuments and high-school history texts are different versions of commemorative practices; likewise are poems, plays, films, videos and novels written to re-present aspects of past events. Ritual practices such as the Passover Seder which includes both oral and performative dimensions are also commemorative. In the fall of 1991, a replica of Leif Erickson's Viking ship completed a cross-Atlantic voyage by landing in Canada. This event too was a deliberate practice of commemoration timed to contest, not the notion of the 'discovery' of America, but the historical figure to be claimed as the 'discoverer'.

While the pedagogy of commemoration deserves the widest form of possible scrutiny, this paper is focused on a particular form of pedagogy, attempting to understand its conditions of possibility. My interest is in what I will be calling 'insurgent commemoration'; attempts to construct and engage representations that rub taken–for–granted history against the grain so as to revitalize and rearticulate what one sees as desirable and necessary for an open, just and life-sustaining future. In other words, my concern is with the ongoing dialectic between the present and the past as it is constituted in practices of commemoration, practices implicitly or explicitly organized within a political problematic.

The pedagogical and political [i.e., ethical] character of commemoration is centered[6] in the range of options for practical action defined and legitimated by a particular way a past is remembered, understood and linked to the present. In other words, we must be sensitive to the range of modalities through which the present makes an *educational* claim on the past. Such concerns proceed from the very human response that the past has something to teach us, but as well gives full recognition to the fact that there are alternative ways, each with a distinct pedagogical and political character, of constituting its lessons. I am not here concerned with the myriad of reasons which justify the full exercise of an historical imagination. I am also bypassing the educational argument that the teaching of history as a method is of importance in formulating critical thinking skills. My focus is the claim that *knowledge* of the past is important because it can make a difference in the present. Acknowledging and grappling with the complexity of this assumed educative relation between present and past is important to those of us who—as cultural workers and teachers—create, organize, distribute and structure engagements with commemorations.

Rather than engage in an extensive topological discussion of the various ways the present makes an educational claim on the past, I simply want to stress that the pedagogic action embedded in various forms of counter-commemoration receives direction from the type of assumption one makes about the social function of historical memory. As I will argue in detail below, much of the counter-commemorative work focused on the Columbus quincentenary articulates pedagogies which combine four different assumed insurgent qualities of historical memory: (1) that social memories form the basis for communal existence and are part of the contested terrain of national identities and the legitimating assumptions and policies which regulate and normalize sets of relations within a community (Hobsbawn and Ranger, 1983; Anderson, 1991); (2) that one can fabricate valid homologies between situations across time and that these must be attended to if we are to avoid mistakes and be inspired by the actions of previous historical actors; (3) that the provision of information and interpretations which demand the revision of the accepted histories can be used to call into question the guiding interests and public legitimacy of institutions which have provided a prevailing social truth; (4) that extermination, theft, fraud and seizure mark the terrain of history and the memories of such acts raise basic questions regarding the rectification of injustice.

These four qualities form a powerful, insurgent mode of pedagogic action when constituted in commemorative practices. Yet, to me, they remain insufficient for constituting the educational work that needs to be done. As I elaborate below, there is also a need for practices premised on two quite different functions of historical memory. The first rejects a form of historical reductionism which renders contemporary events as determinate phenomena of previously established structures and patterns. Instead, accounts of the past are utilized in order to examine the historical specificity within which a current problem exists. What is at stake here is made clear by Hobsbawn:

> You've got to recognize what is new in a situation and what is, therefore, unprecedented and to what extent old ways of handling it are inadequate or not . . . these things require historical perspective and that is essentially the capacity to see how society changes and when things are different and when they are the same (quoted in Kaye, 1991: 155).

At the core of this practice is the denaturalization of existing structures and practices. This denaturalization stems from historical representations which emphasize that the 'way things are is not the way they have always been nor the way they will, or must necessarily be, in the future' (Kaye, 1991: 154).

The second addition to the variety of ways the past can press insurgently on the present assumes a more personal level. That is, through an understanding of how my actions are structured within my circumstantial standpoint—which itself is constituted in a particular relation to the past—I may become more conscious of my complicity with historically constituted forms. Indeed, this is the meeting of the interrogation of popular memory and the practice of consciencization (Haug, 1986). The point, of course, is that through a recovery of the origins of current values and beliefs—their origins and tendencies known—they may be consciously adopted, rejected or modified.

Suggesting the above insurgent potentials of historical memory is not intended as an exercise in academic abstraction. If one's interest is in the question of how best to develop practices of insurgent commemoration, sorting out the different ways in which the present and past make educative claims on each other is important for clarifying what is at stake in the concrete details of a variety of pedagogic actions. However, before I develop this issue by clarifying its substance more specifically in the context of current attempts to contest the celebratory mode of the Columbus quincentenary, it is important to further clarify the agenda.

TOWARDS 'GRINGOSTROIKA'

Societies have differed in the degree to which their citizens have been able to contest the hegemonic practices of commemoration. In democratic communities we at least acknowledge *in principle* that previously established commemorative practices should be open to critique and contestation. Thus, democracy entails an ongoing tension between a retention of affirmed shared memories and the preservation of the possibility that such memories can be open to contestation. In other words, democrats cherish rather than dismiss practices of counter-memory which can call into question both the social imagination previously secured by particular commemorations and the social interests and ethical vision supported by such an imagination. In North America, such a practice might valuably take the form of what Guillermo Gomez-Peña (Martinez, 1991) has, humorously but seriously, called 'gringostroika'; a process of self-criticism and renewal which opens possibilities for change in the basic terms of reference of the relation among citizens, their environment and their state. Such a process does not mean mindlessly accepting all contesting counter-memories, but it does mean learning how to hear what is being asserted within them and seriously considering the claim they make on our understanding of the present.

Considering remembrance as a contested activity, it is virtually self-evident why the controversy over how to commemorate the quincentenary of Columbus's landfall is so important. At minimum the struggle here is over how the event is to be defined, what and whose stories and images are worth remembering in relation to the event under consideration, as well as what it might mean to learn from a past given our particular situated standpoints in the present, and what it might mean to learn about our present given our social organization of representations of the past.

REFUSING APPROPRIATIONS—ACCEPTING RESPONSIBILITY

This said, it is important that I identify my own present standpoint in relation to the Columbus quincentenary. This is especially so given the respect due commitments made at the intercontinental meetings of indigenous peoples to resist non-'Indian' groups that attempt to exploit the cause of 'Indian' people in 1992. There is a long history of the subsumption of concern for the peoples of the 'New World' into both dominant and resistant European agendas (e.g., England's propaganda against Spain during the period of enmity between these two countries; Bartolome' de la Casas' attempts at Catholic reformation by overturning policies legitimating the exploitation of indigenous people; contemporary New Age appropriations of First Nations spirituality). Clearly, 1992 is a time of mobilization of indigenous communities in North and South America for long-term constructive political action. Moreover, First Nations activists are working hard to develop public awareness and support for a variety of concrete actions in regard to native land claims, constitutional acceptance of inherent right of self-government, religious freedom, protection of sacred sites, community economic development and control of education. Given the ongoing process of learning what it means to be in solidarity with each other, perhaps then, for non-natives like myself, 1992 should be a time not for speaking and writing but for supportive listening.

The importance of such listening cannot be overstated. Yet self-limitation to such a posture would be an unfortunate restriction regulated by a focus on the question, 'who speaks?'—unfortunate because it suppresses the corollary questions of 'who is listening and what are they hearing?' Non-native educators have a responsibility to recognize that we have a role to play in influencing what is heard in our communities. Indeed, the question of how to initiate 'gringostroika' is *our* question. Recovered histories and the availability of stories previously suppressed do not ensure they will be incorporated into communal identities. While there is potential in such voices to challenge dominant memories and the social order they underwrite, if commemorative practice is simply concerned with 'correcting memory' and not explicitly concerned with renewing a reconstructed living history for a community, the potential insurgency in such practice will be greatly diminished. For me, recaptured and recreated textual and visual memories must be situated in communities in ways that enable remembering and living from within the standpoint of those memories. Thus it is that I am here concerned with the pedagogy of counter-commemoration.

MISSING STORIES AND NARRATIVE RE/VISIONS

It is at this point that I want to return to the T-shirt mentioned at the beginning of this paper. This rather modest image-text is part of the widespread effort to contest the dominant narrative of 'discovery' which for centuries has been rooted in the popular memories of non-indigenous North Americans. By considering the various pedagogical implications of what may at first seem a rather simple example, I intend to demonstrate the complexity inherent in the practice of insurgent commemoration.

Compared to books, films and more complex art forms, the inscribed T-shirt might seem trivial; a rather bare iconographic statement with a minimum of narrative and always in danger of reduction to a commodity cliché. Yet such apparel has become pervasive in North America and shirts with images and text designed to instigate forms of remembrance are now a cultural commonplace. Indeed, the form sustains its own dynamic as a pedagogical practice. A sign carried by bodies, the inscribed T-shirt brings its referent close to us; it declares the entry of history into our lives and confronts others we meet with our declared relation to the past. Intersecting with other circulating discourses, it makes history topical within the everyday and attempts to define an image-text which has the power of mediating relations between people.[7] As an act of public remembrance, it participates in the re-generation of our collective historical imagination.

To begin to grasp the substance of the pedagogy this particular T-shirt attempts to mobilize, consider for a moment the variety of reasons why many people now reject the use of the term 'discovery'.[8] The most common reason is to factually assert that the lands Columbus visited were quite well known to thousands if not millions of people and thus to declare his landfall as a discovery is both pompous and silly. The strongest versions of this position are suitably ironic. Take for instance the classic commentary by Roberto Fernandez Retamar.

> Madrid, Paris, Venice, Florence, Rome, Naples and Athens were all discovered by me in 1955 (having already discovered New York in 1947), and in 1956 I also discovered London, Antwerp and Brussels. Nevertheless, outside of a few of my own poems and letters, I have not found any other text which describes these interesting discoveries. I suppose that this clamorous silence has resulted from the fact that when I first arrived in these glamorous cities they were already full of people. A similar line of thought has always stopped me from accepting that the arrival of a few Europeans—soon to be five centuries ago—to the continent where I was born and where I live should be pompously referred to as the 'Discovery of America' (Retamar, 1991).[9] Translation of this passage by Michael Hoechsman—personal communication.

In this light, the 500-year-old use of the 'discovery' is a Eurocentric conceit which ignores the fact that the history of the peoples of the Americas began long before the arrival of Columbus. In addition, it is argued that the very logic of discovery constituted an acquisitive relationship between the discoverer and the people who met him on the shore. Humans, animals and plants were collapsed into passive objects; the wonders of both European gaze and desire (Greenblatt, 1991). Hence, discovery denies the possibility of a reciprocal encounter in which human dignity could be acknowledged and affirmed. This denial is not just a historical misfortune but persists as a contemporary concern. It is a legacy which has not passed and whose disruption requires (as one of its first moments) a radical reframing of the story. Thus, narratives of discovery must be rejected and replaced not simply with the problematic notion of an encounter which initiated reciprocal exchange, but with the realities of what happened from the indigenous point of view.

Recall that the counter-commemorative shirt described above reads: 'How could Columbus have discovered America when Native Americans were already here?' Other counter–commemorative shirts proclaim 500 years of indigenous resistance to European invasion. This shirt instead asks a question. It is a question posed from within the North American landscape and it is clearly addressed to those responsible for creating and circulating the texts and images proclaiming 'discovery' as well as those of us who have been subject to the truth claims of such representations.

The wearing of this shirt thus initiates a double pedagogical purpose. In relation to its membership in the genre of current texts which dismiss European notions of 'New World' discovery, the public wearing of such a shirt functions not so much as a question than as an assertion of solidarity with indigenous people who are increasingly gaining a wide hearing for a different story. In this sense, the wearing of the shirt is an act of commemoration which is intended to remind us of that which we previously hadn't the chance to remember. For centuries we have missed the 'view from the shore'; we have missed, in the words of Deborah Small, 'what it is like to be discovered' (Small, 1992). Thus we are made to be attentive, to hear that we are being asked to listen and, in the first moment of solidarity, we must do so.[10]

What we are asked to hear is that the past is being reclaimed as a site of injustice. Instead of the language of discovery we are asked to hear the language of invasion, occupation, attempted genocide and resistance. As indigenous communities in both hemispheres rename the time period since Columbus's arrival as '500 Years of Resistance'—reconstituting communal identities in this moment of historical agency—members of non-indigenous communities are being asked to respond to the question: what does the rectification of past injustice require us to do both in 1992 and beyond? Thus is constituted the first pedagogic moment initiated by the wearing of this shirt.

But the wearing of the shirt potentially does something more. Through challenging those it addresses to question received 'truths' and revise the narrative through which we have historically understood the genesis of our collective present, 'we' are also being asked to reflect on the status of the people and texts who promulgated these 'truths' in the first place. In other words, the image-text of the shirt also initiates the conditions from which the practice of the uncovering and demythification of power relations takes place. Indeed, this has not been lost on many teachers who are now 'rethinking' the way the history of Columbus's landfall has been taught in schools. Indeed, students are being asked to respond to such questions as 'What other stories in your history texts display similar interpretive biases?' 'Why have you used these texts?' 'Who has authorized them?' 'What and whose interests are served by their continued use?' (Bigelow, 1991)

For the above reasons, this T-shirt stands as an example of how specific pedagogies are articulated from within particular modes of constituting the educative relation between past and present. The historically pervasive notion of discovery is framed within a practice of ideological hegemony designed to ensure dominant interests. Indeed, the critique of discovery as a hegemonic lie is used pedagogically to call into question the entire apparatus of historical representation which has presented this and other stories central to the formation of the West. New narratives are offered which raise questions of what collectively needs to be done to redress the legacy of colonialism while those struggling against current structures and agents of that colonialism are given 'heart' by the rewritten stories of the past.

Yet I think if we construct our counter-commemorative pedagogies on these terms alone, we are missing an important dimension of the educational work that needs to be done. The weakness of a commemorative pedagogy that discredits the dominant narratives of discovery is the failure to interrogate the basis for their intelligibility in the first place. In words suitable to occasions of history and judgment, Geoffrey Hartman makes clear the issue: 'denunciation is not enough; it tends to foster a paranoid style of localizing evil that removes the issues too far from our time' (Hartman, 1989: 55–84) and, may I add, ourselves.

RETHINKING THE DISMISSAL OF THE LANGUAGE OF DISCOVERY

It is for the above reason that I have been spending some time rethinking the importance of maintaining the notion of the European 'discovery' of the Americas while simultaneously shifting it out of its mythic abstract encrustation. Instead of dismissing the notion of discovery, it seems to me it must be made problematic. At stake is the potential of additional insurgent commemorations, representational practices built with a cognizance of how particular ways of apprehending the past might be implicated in our understanding of and complicity with current unjust social relations and the prospects for a personal and communal renewal of identities and the possibilities which structure our everyday lives.

This alternative perspective on the European notion of discovery acknowledges that the phrase can be used to indicate a revealing of something that was previously unknown. As Mary C. Fuller points out in English texts about the 'New World':

> 'Discover' frequently carried the sense of revealing, laying open something previously hidden, bringing to light something previously dark . . . Discovery makes what exists at a distance . . . visible, accessible, understood. Discovery is the project of moving what is 'in there', the inwardness of the New World, to 'out here'—the public space of England—in a simple motion of unveiling (Fuller, 1991: 45).

This perspective makes partially intelligible the use of the term by Europeans who chose to narrate the consequences of Columbus's voyage as a tale of discovery.[11] Columbus did initiate (as others who reached the Americas before him did not) an unveiling of that which was previously unknown to the European world.

In Europe prior to 1500, the ocean was both a sign signifying the unknown as well as a physical barrier preventing knowledge. Crossing this barrier initiated a process of revelation. A revealing of a reality not immediately available in experience but requiring mediation through representation. This meant the telling of stories, the description of people, events and places, and the display of artifacts (including people made objects) all previously outside of European experience. The event of discovery required the symbolic rendering of that which was not previously known into text and image; a practice always limited by existing epistemological frames. Thus was formed through text, picture and 'artifact' a set of image-landscapes of a 'new world'; ones that entered into the formation of the plans, desires, actions of Europeans both on their own continent and in the 'Americas'.

This argument does not justify the historically hegemonic narrative of discovery but rather seeks to interrogate the form and consequences of its associated representational requirements. As Michel de Certeau (1986) has emphasized, at stake here is an inquiry into *how a 'new world' was made visible, accessible and understood* BY WHOM, FOR WHOM and WITH WHAT CONSEQUENCES both for *legitimation of action and interest* and in *concordance with* WHAT NOTIONS of WHOSE DESIRE?

Such inquiries can form the basis of commemorations which provoke remembrance of the European response to what Stephen Greenblatt calls the sensation of 'wonder'—'the decisive emotional and intellectual experience in the presence of radical difference' (1991: 14). Undeniably, this response was both *physical and discursive*. While the remembrance of the physical response—what Europeans did— must remain the prime focus of commemorative practice, I want to emphasize the pedagogical importance of practices which continue to rearticulate a collective memory of the discursive response. Initially, this may seem arcane; a call for a practice which incorporates the remembrance of a discourse as a discourse. Greenblatt is helpful in clarifying what is at stake.

> If microbes lie altogether beyond the grasp of Renaissance discourse, the other forces that we have cited as brute facts should under no circumstances be naturalized. The possession of weapons and the will to use them on defenseless people are cultural matters that are intimately bound up with discourse: with the stories that a culture tells itself, its conceptions of personal boundary and liability, its whole collective system of rules. And if gold is a natural phenomenon, the all-consuming craving for gold most assuredly is not. (63—4)

This is not a statement of linguistic omnipotence. The comprehension of events is rarely exhausted in a consideration of their discursive referents. In his focus on discourse, what Greenblatt is emphasizing is the interrelation of the denaturalization of history and the recognition that 'the drive to bring experience under discursive control is inseparable from the task of ethical justification and legitimation' (fn37: 170). In other words, a commemoration of the discursive response to the experience of 'wonder' is, at root, a remembrance of the presumptions, values and regulating forms which articulate a constructed moral framework.

This is the decisive point for the cultural work of insurgent commemoration. At stake is a pedagogy which moves away from the exclusive concern with historically isolated discussions of who did what to whom. Such discussions are too easily dismissed as a 'pious, self-serving moralizing . . . of no good whatever to the dead, and of dubious good to us the living, who are, as it is, altogether too prone to think ourselves kinder, wiser, and certainly less infectious' (Mays, 1991). What moves more centrally into focus are the forms through which relationships with those who are Other to ourselves are established and negotiated. While this may entail some degree of focus on motives and assumptions of individual historical actors, this is not the chief concern.[12] Instead, such commemorations would ask us to grasp the ways the encounter between indigenous and non-indigenous peoples were structured and continue to be structured and whether one can recognize the discursive continuities and transformations in this continuance. What is at stake is whether or not 'we can come to a recognition of the ethical relation between self and other in the narratives we tell'.[13] It would be a mistake to characterize this as an obsessive 'detailing of the sins of Europe that has become a perverse form of narcissism' (Miller, 1992). This is anything but narcissism. Assumed here is that we situate ourselves in certain relations to the Other within narratives that orient our actions toward the Other. But also assumed is an agency within which we can initiate the reconstruction of this relation aided in part by narratives which redefine the basic terms of relation among citizens, their environment and their state. Indeed, at stake here is nothing less than Gomez-Peña's notion of gringo-stroika; a search for the conditions necessary in order to secure social forms and institutional structures which will initiate a life-sustaining, nonsubordinate interdependency.

To illustrate the pedagogical importance of this perspective, I think it important to point to an example of counter-commemorative work which takes as its point of departure the language of discovery. A number of recent studies make clear the extensive way, in both Spanish and English texts, the language of the discovery of the 'New World' by Europeans was relentlessly gendered (Montrose, 1991: 1—41; Zamora, 1990—1: 127—49). In a very different site of historical representation, Karen Atkinson has been developing commemorative practices that are centered on this issue. Atkinson, an artist, writer, curator and teacher, has been creating images and installations which superimpose contemporary photographs from Caribbean travel brochures with original woodcuts depicting indigenous peoples experiencing the European invasion. Juxtaposed with these images are texts from tourist magazines, travel brochures, Columbus's diary and letters, as well as from a variety of Renaissance books—poetic and geographic—which extol the wonders of the 'New World'. What Atkinson's work makes clear is a remarkable continuity in the way in which the Caribbean is textually constituted for a population not indigenous to its islands (Atkinson, 1992). These lands (in the words of promotional tourism) remain *virgin, unspoiled, seductive, refined, laid back . . . they wait just for you*. Without collapsing the specificity of different historical eras, what Atkinson is asking us to recognize is the continuity of the tropes of desire which organize so much of the North American popular representation of the Caribbean. These are desires which promise fulfillment in a particular form of relationship, where the Other is the exotic, but available and willing object, who is open to being taken.

The insurgent character of the historical images and text employed by Atkinson is mobilized within their function as a form of perverse ethical referent. From the standpoint of the Other (indigenous/women), Atkinson's work attempts to force a re-recognition of historical discourse in order to expose its moral frameworks but in a manner that encourages us to use such a re-recognition as a basis for an interrogation and evaluation of the present and our standpoint in it. Contextualized in the current circulation of discourse contesting the meaning of the quincentenary, through her image constructions and text juxtapositions Atkinson has created a pedagogical form in which remembrance becomes a process through which we are asked, by recognizing our complicity in historically gendered forms, to reconsider the desires and associated assumptions that structure the eros which informs both our human encounters and our ecological interrelation with the environments through which we move.

If one accepts this form of pedagogy as a valuable addition to the notion of insurgent commemoration, the question occurs as to how should the voices and histories of those who have not been previously heard be positioned together within a project where the main focus is to 'work on ourselves'? The answer, I think is that they must proceed in parallel. One emphasis provokes remembrance of invasion, resistance and survival as an insurgent critique of the idea that any of the nation-states of the Americas should continue to be informed through narratives which propose a common identity linked within a single unifying culture and history. The other emphasizes that past forms of encounter are not to be grasped as inevitable consequences of history—as simply casualties in the early construction of the modern world—but were constituted through the actions of people. It is able to take seriously the perspective of those made victim and refuse the obscenity of accepting their suffering in the name of history. Instead of offering the deadening mantle of guilt, it challenges us to act in the name of a collective responsibility to continue the quest for justice and the establishment of new forms of interdependency which honor the dignity of the Other.

NOTES

1. By 'counter-commemoration' I am here referring to the widespread struggle to resist celebrating the 500th anniversary of the Columbus landfall as either a discovery or, alternatively, a mutually beneficial encounter between peoples.

2. In a recent interview, Artist James Luna has made this point abundantly clear. In 1992, 'curators want a certain kind of Indian and a certain kind of Indian art. They want you to be angry, they want you to be talking it up. It's the same rush to say let's have a multiculturalism show. Now everyone is saying let's have an Indian show or let's have a colonialism show. So when people call me [to participate] I have to ask why didn't you call me before? You're calling me now but are you going to call me in '93?' (Durland, 1991:34—9)

3. The notion of 'site' refers here to a specific material form with a particular relationship to time and space within which modes of production and distribution of representations are accomplished.

4. I recently experienced this when, for purposes of contrast, three Columbus Day celebration posters were included in a Berkeley counter-commemoration poster exhi-

bition held in conjunction with the Columbus quincentenary. In this context, their status as ideological constructions were highlighted rendering the image/text as virtual parody.

5. For example, national public broadcasting is distributing to its local affiliates a videotape of *Columbus Re-Visited* made by a television station in San Diego. This video itself is based on the art exhibition *Counter-colonialismo* which has toured the United States for twelve months. The tape is also being sold to schools and shown in classrooms across the country. Individual works in the exhibition will later be placed in other exhibition spaces. A catalog which elaborates on the themes of the exhibition is to be published and made available.

6. Any commemorative practice is also political in character by dint of the economy of sign production within which it is produced. Whether in the form of a poster, text or television program, commemorative practices are inevitably discursively and materially organized and regulated within real sets of social relations and their associated complex of convergent and divergent interests. The implication here is that specific commemorative practices name and narrate, juxtapose and explain within a limited structure of relevance whose correspondence to the assumptions of the framework of dominant relations is always a political question.

7. The classic commentary which condemns the image as the dominant mode within which relations among people are mediated is Debord (1977). While here I am focusing at the moment of progressive possibility made present by this mediation, I do not wish to diminish the still contemporary value of Debord's critique.

8. The issue here is not that there is evidence for previous landfalls by other mariners prior to the arrival of Columbus but rather how Columbus's landfall is to be understood. The voyage of Columbus was indeed significantly different from any prior contact with the peoples of 'the Americas' in that it initiated a set of events which were a significant turning point in the lives of millions of people. Whether or not Columbus made first contact is a deflection of what is centrally up for revision: the nature of the foundational event for the contemporary 'civilization' in which we live.

9. Translation of this passage by Michael Hoechsman—personal communication.

10. Of course the question is not just whether we are going to listen but how. What horror is to be grasped as we read with hands over eyes peering through the gaps made by our fingers (Reynolds, 1991).

11. This does not however explain why in the nineteenth century certain groups, most notably Irish Catholics and Italian immigrants in the United States sought to enshrine Columbus as the discoverer of the New World. See Trouillot (1990).

12. This is not simply a matter of representing Columbus in his historical context. To take seriously questions which pose queries about the motives, justifications and assumptions of historical actors has been one of the dictums of historical research. Thus the well-known importance of the search for an 'imaginative understanding' of the historical actor. This seems like a positive step although, by focusing on individual actors, such work may produce a distancing: a 'them/not me' character to the study of history. It quite often becomes a way of avoiding any serious educative dialectic between the past and the present.

13. Michael Bach, personal communication.

WORKS CITED

Anderson, Benedict (1991) *Imagined Communities* [revised edition], London: Verso.

Atkinson, Karen (1992) 'Tales of desire', *New Observations,* No. 88, March/April, 4–9.

Bigelow, Bill (1991) 'Discovering Columbus: re-reading the past', in Bill Bigelow, Barbara Miner and Bob Peterson (1991) editors, *Rethinking Columbus,* Milwaukee: Rethinking Schools Ltd.

Debord, Guy (1977) *Society of the Spectacle,* Detroit: Black and Red.

de Certeau, Michel (1986) *Heterologies: Discourse on the Other,* Minneapolis: University of Minnesota Press.

Durland, Steven (1991) 'Call me in '93: an interview with James Luna', *High Performance,* No. 56, Winter, 34–9.

Fuller, Mary C. (1991) 'Ralegh's fugitive gold: reference and deferral in *The discoverie of Guiana'*, *Representations,* 33, Winter, 42–64.

Giroux, Henry A. (1992) *Border Crossings: Cultural Workers and the Politics of Education,* New York: Routledge.

Greenblatt, Stephen (1991) *Marvelous Possessions: The Wonder of the New World,* Chicago: University of Chicago Press.

Hartman, Geoffrey (1989) 'History and judgment: the case of Paul de Man', *History and Memory,* Vol. 1, No. 1, Spring/Summer, 5–84.

Haug, Frigga (1986) *Female Sexualization: A Collective Work of Memory* [trans. Erica Carter], London: Verso.

Hobsbawm, Eric and Ranger, Terence (eds) (1963) *The Invention of Tradition,* Cambridge: Cambridge University Press.

Kaye, Harvey J. (1991) *The Powers of the Past: Reflections on the Crisis and Promise of History,* Minneapolis, University of Minnesota Press.

Martinez, Ruben (1991) 'On the North–South Border patrol, in Art and Life' *New York Times,* Sunday 15 October, Section H, 1, 35.

Mays, John Bentley (1991) 'The end of innocence or a new beginning?' *The Globe and Mail* [Toronto] 19 Oct., Section C Arts Weekend, 1, 15.

Miller, Laura (1992) 'Columbus and the quest for truth' *SF (San Francisco) Weekly,* April 1, 21–2.

Montrose, Louis (1991) 'The work of gender in the discourse of discovery', *Representations,* 33, Winter, 1–4.

Retamar, Roberto Fernandez (1991) 'America, Descubrimientos, Dialogos', in Dietrich S. Heinz (ed.) *Nuestra America: Contra el v centenario,* Navarra: Txalaparta Editorial.

Reynolds, Anna 'Review of Children of the Flames', *The Times Saturday Review,* London, 5 Oct., 1991.

Simon, Roger I. (1992) *Teaching Against the Grain: Texts for a Pedagogy of Possibility,* New York: Bergin & Garvey.

Small, Deborah with Jaffe, Maggie (1991) 1492: *What Is It Like To Be Discovered?* New York, Monthly Review Press.

Trend, David (1992) *Cultural Pedagogy: Art/Education/Politics,* New York: Bergin & Garvey.

Trouillot, Michel-Rolph (1990) 'Good day Columbus: silences, power and public history (1492–1892)', *Public Culture,* Vol. 3, No. 1, Fall, 1–24.

Young, James (1988) *Writing and Rewriting the Holocaust: Narrative and the Consequence of Interpretation,* Bloomington: Indiana University Press.

Zamora, Margarita (1990–1) 'Abreast of Columbus: gender and discovery', *Cultural Critique,* No. 17, Winter, 127–49.

INSURGENT

MULTI-

CULTURALISM

AND THE JOURNEY

INTO DIFFERENCE

CHAPTER 8

ON RACE AND VOICE:

CHALLENGES FOR

LIBERAL EDUCATION

IN THE 1990S

CHANDRA TALPADE
MOHANTY

FEMINISM AND THE LANGUAGE OF DIFFERENCE

"Isn't the whole point to have a voice?" This is the last sentence of a recent essay by Marnia Lazreg on writing as a woman on women in Algeria.[1] Lazreg examines academic feminist scholarship on women in the Middle East and North Africa in the context of what she calls a "Western gynocentric" notion of the difference between First and Third World women. Arguing for an understanding of "intersubjectivity" as the basis for comparison across cultures and histories, Lazreg formulates the problem of ethnocentrism and the related question of voice in this way:

> To take intersubjectivity into consideration when studying Algerian women or other Third World women means seeing their lives as meaningful, coherent, and understandable instead of being infused "by us" with doom and sorrow. It means that their lives like "ours" are structured by economic, political, and cultural factors. It means that these women, like "us," are engaged in the process of adjusting, often shaping, at times resisting and even transforming their environment. It means that they have their own individuality; they are "for themselves" instead of being "for us." An appropriation of their singular individuality to fit the generalizing categories of "our" analyses is an assault on their integrity and on their identity.[2]

In my own work I have argued in a similar way against the use of anlaytic categories and political positionings in feminist studies that discursively present Third World women as a homogeneous, undifferentiated group leading truncated lives, victimized by the combined weight of "their" traditions, cultures, and beliefs, and "our" (Eurocentric) history.[3] In examining particular assumptions of feminist scholarship that are uncritically grounded in Western humanism and its modes of "disinterested scholarship," I have tried to demonstrate that this scholarship inadvertently produces Western women as the only legitimate subjects of struggle, while Third World women are heard as fragmented, inarticulate voices in (and from) the dark. Arguing against a hastily derived notion of "universal sisterhood" that assumes a commonality of gender experience across race and national lines, I have suggested the complexity of our historical (and positional) differences and the need for creating an analytical space for understanding Third World women as the *subjects* of our various struggles *in history*. Other scholars have made similar arguments, and the question of what we might provisionally call "Third World women's *voices*" has begun to be addressed seriously in feminist scholarship.

In the last decade there has been a blossoming of feminist discourse around questions of "racial difference" and "pluralism." While this work is often an important corrective to earlier middle-class (white) characterizations of sexual difference, the goal of the analysis of difference and the challenge of race was not pluralism as the proliferation of discourse on ethnicities as discrete and separate cultures. The challenge of race resides in a fundamental reconceptualization of our categories of analysis so that differences can be historically specified and understood as part of larger political processes and systems.[4] The central issue, then, is not one of merely *acknowledging* difference; rather, the more difficult question concerns the kind of difference that is acknowledged and engaged. Difference seen as benign variation (diversity), for instance, rather than as conflict, struggle, or the threat of disruption, bypasses power as well as history to suggest a harmonious, empty pluralism.[5] On the other hand, difference defined as asymmetrical and incommensurate cultural spheres situated within hierarchies of domination and resistance cannot be accommodated within a discourse of "harmony in diversity." A strategic critique of the contemporary language of difference, diversity, and power thus would be crucial to a femininst project concerned with revolutionary social change.

In the best, self-reflexive traditions of feminist inquiry, the production of knowledge about cultural and geographical Others is no longer seen as apolitical and disinterested. But while feminist activists and progressive scholars have made a significant dent in the colonialist and colonizing feminist scholarship of the late seventies and early eighties, this does not mean that questions of what Lazreg calls "intersubjectivity," or of history vis-à-vis Third World peoples, have been successfully articulated.[6]

In any case, *scholarship,* feminist, Marxist, or Third World, is not the only site for the production of knowledge about Third World women/peoples.[7] The very same questions (as those suggested in relation to scholarship) can be raised in relation to our teaching and learning practices in the classroom, as well as the discursive and managerial practices of American colleges and universities. Feminists writing about race and racism have had a lot to say about scholarship, but perhaps our pedagogical and institutional practices and their relation to scholarship have not been examined with quite the same care and attention. Radical educators have long argued that the academy and the classroom itself are not mere sites of instruction. They are also political and cultural sites that represent accommodations and contestations over knowledge by differently empowered social constituencies.[8] Thus teachers and students produce, reinforce, recreate, resist, and transform ideas about race, gender, and difference in the classroom. Also, the academic institutions in which we are located create similar paradigms, canons, and voices that embody and transcribe race and gender.

It is this frame of institutional and pedagogical practice that I examine in this essay. Specifically, I analyze the operation and mangement of discourses of race and difference in two educational sites: the women's studies classroom and the workshops on "diversity" for upper-level (largely white) administrators. The links between these two educational sites lie in the (often active) *creation* of discourses of "difference." In other words, I suggest that educational practices as they are shaped and reshaped at these sites cannot be analyzed as merely transmitting already codified ideas of difference. These practices often produce, codify, and even rewrite histories of race and colonialism in the name of difference. But let me begin the analysis with a brief discussion of the academy as the site of political struggle and transformation.

KNOWLEDGE AND LOCATION IN THE U.S. ACADEMY

A number of educators, Paulo Freire among them, have argued that education represents both a struggle for meaning and a struggle over power relations. Thus, education becomes a central terrain where power and politics operate out of the lived culture of indivdals and groups situated in asymmetrical social and political positions. This way of understanding the academy entails a critique of education as the mere accumulation of disciplianry knowledges that can be exchanged on the world market for upward mobility. There are much larger questions at stake in the academy these days, not the least of which are questions of self and collective knowledge of marginal peoples and the recovery of alternative, oppositional histories of domination and struggle. Here, disciplinary parameters matter less than questions of power, history, and self-identity. For knowledge, the very act of knowing, is related to the power of self-definition. This definition of knowledge is central to the pedagogical projects of fields such as women's studies, black studies, and ethnic studies. By their very location in the academy, fields such as women's studies are grounded in definitions of difference, difference that attempts to resist incorporation and appropriation by providing a space for historically silenced peoples to construct knowledge. These knowledges have always been fundamentally oppositional, while running the risk of accommodation and assimilation and the consequent depoliticization in the academy. It is only in the late twentieth century, on the heels of domestic and global oppositional political movements, that the boundaries dividing knowledge into its traditional disciplines have been shaken loose, and new, often hereitcal, knowledges have emerged modifying the structures of knowledge and power as we have inherited them. In other words, new anlaytic spaces have been opened up in the academy, spaces that make possible thinking of knowledge as praxis, of knowledge as embodying the very seeds of transformation and change. The appropriation of these analytic spaces and the challenge of radical educational practice are thus to involve the development of critical knowledges (what women's, black, and ethnic studies attempt), and simultaneously, to critique knowledge itself.

Education for critical consciousness or critical pedagogy, as it is sometimes called, requires a reformulation of the knowledge-as-accumulated-capital model of education and focuses instead on the link between the historical configuration of social forms and the way they work subjectively. This issue of subjectivity represents a realization of the fact that who we are, how we act, what we think, and what stories we tell become more intelligible within an epistemological framework that begins by recognizing existing hegemonic histories. The issue of subjectivity and voice thus concerns the effort to understand our specific locations in the educational process and in the institutions through which we are constituted. Resistance lies in self-conscious engagement with dominant, normative discourses and representations and in the active creation of oppositional analytic and cultural spaces. Resistance that is random and isolated is clearly not as effective as that which is mobilized through systemic politicized practices of teaching and learning. Uncovering and reclaiming subjugated knowledges is one way to lay claim to alternative histories. But these knowledges need to be understood and defined *pedagogically,* as questions of strategy and practice as well as of scholarship, in order to transform educational institutions radically. And this, in turn, requires taking the questions of experience seriously.

To this effect, I draw on scholarhsip on and by Third World educators in higher education, on an analysis of the effects of my own pedagogical practices, on documents about "affirmatiave action" and "diversity in the curriculum" published by the adminstration of the college where I work, and on my own observations and conversations over the past three years.[9] I do so in order to suggest that the effect of the proliferation of ideologies of pluralism in the 1960s and 1970s, in the context of the (limited) implementation of affirmative action in institutions of higher education, has been to create what might be called the Race Industry, an industry that is responsible for the management, commodification, and domestication of race on American campuses. This commodification of race determines the politics of voice for Third World peoples, whether they/we happen to be faculty, students, administrators, or service staff. This, in turn, has long-term effects on the definitions of the identity and agency of nonwhite people in the academy.

There are a number of urgent reasons for undertaking such an analysis: the need to assess the material and ideological effects of affirmative action policies within liberal (rather than conservative—Bloom or Hirsch style) discourses and instititutions that profess a commitment to pluralism and social change, the need to understand this management of race in the liberal academy in realtion to a larger discourse on race and discrimination within the neoconservatism of the U.S., and the need for Third World feminists to move outside the arena of (sometimes) exclusive engagment with racism in white women's movements and scholarship and to broaden the scope of our struggles to the academy as a whole.

The management of gender, race, class, and sexuality are inextricably linked in the public arena. The New Right agenda since the mid-1970s makes this explicit: busing, gun rights, and welfare are clearly linked to the issues of reproductive and sexual rights.[10] And the links between abortion rights (gender-based struggles) and affirmative action (struggles over race and racism) are becoming clearer in the 1990s. While the most challenging critiques of hegemonic feminism were launched in the late 1970s and the 1980s, the present historical moment necessitates taking on board institutional discourses that actively construct and maintain a discourse of difference and pluralism. This in turn calls for assuming responsibility for the politics of voice as it is institutionalized in the academy's "liberal" response to the very questions feminism and other oppositional discourses have raised.[11]

BLACK/ETHNIC STUDIES AND WOMEN'S STUDIES: INTERSECTIONS AND CONFLUENCES

For US, THERE IS NOTHING OPTIONAL ABOUT "BLACK EXPERIENCE" AND/OR "BLACK STUDIES": WE MUST KNOW OUR-SELVES. —JUNE JORDAN

....

Unlike most academic disciplines, the origins of black, ethnic, and women's studies programs can be traced to oppositional social movements. In particular, the civil rights movement, the women's movement, and other Third World liberation struggles fueled the demande for a knowledge and history "of our own." June Jordan's claim that "we must know ourselves" suggests the urgency embedded in the formation of black studies in the late 1960s. Between 1966 and 1970 most American colleges and universities added courses on Afro-American experience and history to their curriculums. This was the direct outcome of a number of sociohistorical factors, not the least of which was an increase in black student enrollment in higher education and the broad-based call for a fundamental transformation of a racist, Eurocentric curriculum. Among the earliest programs were the black and African-American studies programs at San Francisco State and Cornell, both of which came into being in 1968, on the heels of militant political organizing on the part of students and faculty at these institutions.[12] A symposium on black studies in early 1968 at Yale University not only inaugurated African-American studies at Yale, but also marked a watershed in the national development of black studies programs.[13] In Spring 1969, the University of California at Berkeley instituted a department of ethnic studies, divided into Afro-American, Chicano, contemporary Asian-American, and Native American studies divisions.

A number of women's studies programs also came into being around this time. The first women's studies program was formed in 1969 at San Diego State University. Today 520 such programs exist across the United States.[14] Women's studies programs often drew on the institutional frameworks and structures of existing interdisciplinary programs such as black and ethnic studies. In addition, besides sharing political origins, an interdisciplinary project, and foregrounding questions of social and political inequality in their knowledge base, women's, black, and ethnic studies programs increasingly share pedagogical and research methods. Such programs thus create the possibility of a counter-hegemonic discourse and oppositional analytic spaces within the institution. Of course, since these programs are most often located within the boundaries of conservative or liberal-white-male institutions, they face questions of co-optation and accommodation.

In an essay examining the relations among ethnicity, ideology, and the academy, Rosaura Sanchez maintains that new academic programs arise out of specific interests in bodies of knowledge.[15] Sanchez traces the origins of ethnic and women's studies programs, however, to a defensive political move: the state's institutionalization of a discourse of reform in response to the civil rights movement.

> [E]thnic studies programs were instituted at a moment when the university had to speak a particular language to quell student protests and to ensure that university research and business could be conducted as usual. The university was able to create and integrate these programs administratively under its umbrella, allowing on the one hand, for a potential firecracker to diffuse itself and, on the other, moving on to prepare the ground for future assimilation of the few surviving faculty into existing departments.[16]

Sanchez identifies the pressures (assimilation and co-optation versus isolation and marginalization) that ethnic studies programs have inherited in the 1990s. In fact, it is precisely in the face of the pressure to assimilate that questions of political strategy and of pedagogical and institutional practice assume paramount importance.

For such programs, progress (measured by institutional power, number of people of color in faculty and administration, effect on the general curricula, etc.) has been slow. Since the 1970s, there have also been numerous conflits between ethnic, black, and women's studies programs. One example of these tensions is provided by Niara Sudarkasa. Writing in 1986 about the effect of affirmative action on black faculty and administrators in higher education, she argues: "As a matter of record, however, both in the corporate world and in higher education, the progress of white females as a result of affirmative action has far out-stripped that for blacks and other minorities."[17] Here Sudarkasa is pointing to a persistent presence of racism in the differential access and mobility of white women and people of color in higher education. She goes on to argue that charges of "reverse discrimination" against white people are unfounded because affirmative action has had the effect of privileging white women above men and women of color. Thus, for Sudarkasa, charges of reverse discrimination leveled at minorities "amount to a sanction of continued discrimination by insisting that inequalities resulting from privileges historically reserved for whites as a *group* must now be perpetuated in the name of 'justice' for the *individual.'*[18] This process of individualization of histories of dominance is also characteristic of educational institutions and processes in general, where the experiences of different constituencies are defined according to the logic of cultural pluralism.

In fact, this individualization of power hierarchies and of structures of discrimination suggests the convergence of liberal and neoconservative ideas about gender and race in the academy. Individualization, in this context, is accomplished through the fundamentally class-based process of professionalization. In any case, the post-Reagan years (characterized by fiancial cutbacks in education, the consolidation of the New Right and the right-to-life lobby, the increasing legal challenges to affirmative action regulations, etc.) suggest that it is alliances among women's, black, and ethnic studies programs which will ensure the survival of such programs. This is not to imply that these alliances do not already exist, but, in the face of the active corrosion of the collective basis of affirmative action by the federal government in the name of "reverse discrimination," it is all the more urgent that our institutional self-examinations lead to concrete alliances. Those of us who teach in some of these programs know that, in this context, questions of voice—indeed, the very fact of claiming a voice and wanting to be heard—are very complicated indeed.

To proceed with the first location or site, I attempt an analysis of the effect of my own pedagogical practices on students when teaching about Third World peoples in a largely white institution. I suggest that a partial (and problematic) effect of my pedagogy, the location of my courses in the curriculum and the liberal nature of the institution as a whole, is the sort of attitudinal engagement with diversity that encourages an empty cultural pluralism and domesticates the historical agency of Third World peoples.

CLASSROOM PEDAGOGIES OF GENDER AND RACE

How do we construct oppositional pedagogies of gender and race? Teaching about histories of sexism, racism, imperialism, and homophobia potentially poses very fundamental challenges to the academy and its traditional production of knowledge, since it has often situated Third World peoples as populations whose histories and experiences are deviant, marginal, or inessential to the acquisition of knowledge. And this has happened systemically in our disciplines as well as in our pedagogies. Thus the task at hand is to decolonize our disciplinary and pedagogical practices. The crucial question is how we teach about the West and its Others so that education becomes the practice of liberation. This question becomes all the more important in the context of the significance of education as a means of liberation and advancement for Third World and postcolonial peoples and their/our historical belief in education as a crucial form of resistance to the colonization of hearts and minds.

However, as a number of educators have argued, decolonizing educational practices requires transformations at a number of levels, both within and outside the academy. Curricula and pedagogical transformation has to be accompanied by a broad-based transformation of the culture of the academy, as well as by radical shifts in the relation of the academy to other state and civil institutions. In addition, decolonizing pedagogical practices requires taking seriously the relation between knowledge and learning, on the one hand, and student and teacher experience, on the other. In fact, the theorization and politicization of experience is imperative if pedagogical practices are to focus on more than the mere management, systematization, and consumption of disciplinary knowledge.

I teach courses on gender, race, and education, on international development, on feminist theory, and on Third World feminisms, as well as core women's studies courses such as "Introduction to Women's Studies" and a senior seminar. All of the courses are fundamentally interdisciplinary and cross-cultural. At its most ambitious, this pedagogy is an attempt to get students to think critically about their place in relation to the knowledge they gain and to transform their worldview fundamentally by taking the politics of knowledge seriously. It is a pedagogy that attempts to link knowledge, social responsibility, and collective struggle. And it does so sby emphasizing the risks that education involves, the struggles for institutional change, and the strategies for challenging forms of domination and by creating more equitable and just public spheres within and outside educational institutions.

Thus, pedagogy from the point of view of a radical teacher does not entail merely processing received knowledges (however critically one does this) but actively transforming knowledges. In addition, it involves taking responsibility for the material effects of these very pedagogical practices on students. Teaching about "difference" in relation to power is thus extremely complicated and involves not only rethinking questions of learning and authority but also questions of center and margin. In writing about her own pedagogical practices in teaching African-American women's history, Elsa Barkley Brown[19] formulates her intentions and method in this way:

> How do our students overcome years of notions of what is normative? While trying to think about these issues in my teaching, I have come to understand that this is not merely an intellectual process. It is not merely a question of whether or not we have learned to analyze in particular kinds of way, or whether people are able to intellectualize about a variety of experiences. It is also about coming to believe in the possibility of a variety of experiences, a variety of ways of understanding the world, a variety of frameworks of operation, without imposing consciously or unconsciously a notion of the norm. What I have tried to do in my own teaching is to address both the conscious level through the material, and the unconscious

level through the structure of the course, thus, perhaps, allowing my students, in Bettina Apthekar's words, to "pivot the center: to center in another experience."[20]

Clearly, this process is very complicated pedagogically, for such teaching must address questions of audience, voice, power, and evaluation, while retaining a focus on the material being taught. Teaching practices must also combat the pressures of professionalization, normalization, and standardization, the very pressures of expectations that implicitly aim to manage and discipline pedagogies so that teacher behaviors are predictable (and perhaps controllable) across the board.

Barkley Brown draws attention to the centrality of experience in the classroom. While this is an issue that merits much more consideration than I can give here, a particular aspect of it ties into my general argument. Feminist pedagogy has always recognized the importance of experience in the classroom. Since women's and ethnic studies programs are fundamentally grounded in political and collective questions of power and inequality, questions of the politicization of individuals along race, gender, class, and sexual parameters are at the very center of knowledges produced in the classroom. This politicization often involves the "authorization" of marginal experiences and the creation of spaces for multiple, dissenting voices in the classroom. The authorization of experience is thus a crucial form of empowerment for students—a way for them to enter the classroom as speaking subjects. However, this focus on the centrality of experience can also lead to exclusions—it often silences those whose "experience" is seen to be that of the ruling-class groups. This "more authentic-than-thou" attitude to experience also applies to the teacher. For instance, in speaking *about* Third World peoples, I have to watch constantly the tendency to speak *for* Third World peoples. For I often come to embody the "authentic" authority and experience for many of my students; indeed, they construct me as a native informant in the same way that left-liberal white students sometimes construct all people of color as the authentic voices of their people. This is evident in the classroom when the specific "differences" (of personality, posture, behavior, etc.) of one woman of color stand in for the difference of the whole collective, and a collective voice is assumed in place of an individual voice. In effect, this results in the reduction or averaging of Third World peoples in terms of individual personality characteristics: complex ethical and political issues are glossed over, and an ambiguous and more easily manageable ethos of the "personal" and the "interpersonal" takes their place.

Thus, a particularly problematic effect of certain pedagogical codifications of difference is the conceptualization of race and gender in terms of personal or individual experience. Students often end up determining that they have to "be more sensitive" to Third World peoples. The formulation of knowledge and politics through these individualistic, attitudinal parameters indicates an erasure of the very politics of knowledge involved in teaching and learning about difference. It also suggests an erasure of the structural and institutional parameters of what it means to understand difference in historical terms. If all conflict in the classroom is seen and understood in personal terms, it leads to a comfortable set of oppositions: people of color as the central voices and the bearers of all knowledge in class, and white people as "observers," with no responsibility to contribute and/or with nothing valuable to contribute. In other words, white students are constructed as marginal observers and students of color as the real "knowers" in such a liberal or left classroom. While it may seem like people of color are thus granted voice and agency in the classroom, it is necessary to consider what particular kind of voice it is that is allowed them/us. It is a voice located in a different and separate space from the agency of white students.[21] Thus, while it appears that in such a class the histories and cultures of marginalized peoples are now "legitimate" objects of study and discussion, the fact is that this legitimation takes place purely at an attitudinal, interpersonal level rather than in terms of a fundamental challenge to hegemonic knowledge and history. Often the culture in such a class vacillates between a high level of tension and an overwhelming desire to create harmony, acceptance of "difference," and cordial relations in the classroom. Potentially this implicitly binary construction (Third World students versus white students) undermines the understanding of co-implication that students must take seriously in order to understand "difference" as historical and relational. Co-implication refers to the idea that all of us (First and Third World) share certain histories as well as certain responsibilities: ideologies of race define both white and black peoples, just as gender ideologies define both women and men. Thus, while "experience" is an enabling focus in the classroom, unless it is explicitly understood as historical, contingent, and the result of interpretation, it can coagulate into frozen, binary, psychologistic positions.

To summarize, this effective separation of white students from Third World students in such an explicitly politicized women's studies classroom is problematic because it leads to an attitudinal engagement that bypasses the complexly situated politics of knowledge and potentially shores up a particular individual-oriented codification and commodification of race. It implicitly draws on and sustains a discourse of cultural pluralism, or what Henry Giroux calls "the pedagogy of normative pluralism,"[22] a pedagogy in which we all occupy separate, different, and equally valuable places and where experience is defined not in terms of individual *qua* individual, but in terms of an individual as representative of a cultural group. This results in a depoliticization and dehistoricization of the idea of culture and makes possible the implicit management of race in the name of cooperation and harmony.

However, cultural pluralism is an inadequate response because the academy as well as the larger social arena are constituted through *hierarchical* knowledges and power relations. In this context, the creation of oppositional knowledges always involves both fundamental challenges and the risk of co-optation. Creating counter-hegemonic pedagogies and combating attitudinal, pluralistic appropriations of race and difference thus involves a delicate and ever-shifting balance between the analysis of experience as lived culture and as textual and historical representations of experience. But most of all, it calls for a critical analysis of the contradictions and incommensurability of social interests as individuals experience, understand, and transform them. Decolonizing pedagogical practices requires taking seriously the different logics of cultures as they are located within asymmetrical power relations. It involves understanding that culture, especially academic culture, is a terrain of struggle (rather than an amalgam of discrete consumable entities). And finally, within the classroom, it requires that teachers and students develop a critical analysis of how experience itself is named, constructed, and legitimated in the academy. Without this analysis of culture and of experience in the classroom, there is no way to develop and nurture oppositional practices. After all, critical education concerns the production of subjectivities *in relation* to discourses of knowledge and power.

THE RACE INDUSTRY AND
PREJUDICE-REDUCTION WORKSHOPS

In his incisive critique of current attempts at minority canon formation, Cornel West locates the following cultural crises as circumscribing the present historical moment: the decolonization of the Third World which signaled the end of the European Age; the repoliticization of literary studies in the 1960s; the emergence of alternative, oppositional, subaltern histories; and the transformation of everyday life through the rise of a predominantly visual, technological culture. West locates contests over Afro-American canon formation in the proliferation of discourses of pluralism in the American academy, thus launching a critique of the class interests of Afro-American critics who "become the academic superintendents of a segment of an expanded canon or a separate canon."[23] A similar critique, on the basis of class interests and "professionalization," can be leveled against feminist scholars (First or Third World) who specialize in "reading" the lives/experiences of Third World women. However, what concerns me here is the predominately white upper-level administrators at our institutions and their "reading" of the issues of racial diversity and pluralism. I agree with West's internal critique of a black managerial class but think it is important not to ignore the power of a predominantly white managerial class (men and women) who, in fact, frame and hence determine *our* voices, livelihoods, and sometimes even our political alliances. Exploring a small piece of the creation and institutionalization of this Race Industry, prejudice-reduction workshops involving upper-level administrators, counselors, and students in numerous institutions of higher education—including the college where I teach—shed light on a particular aspect of this industry. Interestingly, the faculty often do not figure in these workshops at all; they are directed either at students and resident counselors or at administrators.

To make this argument, I draw upon my own institution, a college that has an impressive history of progressive and liberal policies. But my critique applies to liberal/humanistic institutions of higher education in general. While what follows is a critique of certain practices at the college, I undertake this out of a commitment and engagement with the academy. The efforts of the college to take questions of difference and diversity on board should not be minimized. However, these efforts should also be subject to rigorous examination because they have far-reaching implications for the institutionalization of multiculturalism in the academy. While multiculturalism itself is not necessarily problematic, its definition in terms of an apolitical, ahistorical cultural pluralism needs to be challenged.

In the last few years there has been an increase in this kind of activity—often as a response to antiracist student organization and demands, or in relation to the demand and institutionalization of "non-Western" requirements at prestigious institutions—in a number of academic institutions nationally. More precisely, however, these issues of multiculturalism arise as a response to the recognition of changing demographics in the United States. For instance, the fact that by the year 2000 almost 42 percent of all public school students will be minority children or other impoverished children, and that by the year 2000 women and people of color will account for nearly 75 percent of the labor force is crucial in understanding institutional imperatives concerning "diversity."[24] As Sanchez suggests, for the university to conduct "research and business as usual" in the face of the overwhelming challenges posed by even the very presence of people of color, it has to enact policies and programs aimed at accommodation rather than transformation.

In response to certain racist and homophobic incidents in the spring of 1988, this college instituted a series of "prejudice-reduction" workshops aimed at students and upper- and middle-level administrative staff. These workshops sometimes took the form of "unlearning racism" workshops conducted by residential counselors and psychologists in dorms. Workshops such as these are valuable in "sensitizing" students to racial conflict, behavior, and attitudes, but an analysis of the historical and ideological bases of such workshops indicates their limitations.

Briefly, prejudice-reduction workshops draw on the psychologically based "race relations" analysis and focus on "prejudice" rather than institutional or historical domination. The workshops draw on co-counseling and the reevaluation counseling techniques and theory and often aim for emotional release rather than political action. The name of this approach is itself somewhat problematic, since it suggests that "prejudice" (rather than domination, exploitation, or structural inequality) is the core problem and that we have to "reduce" it. The language determines and shapes the ideological and political content to a large extent. In focusing on "the healing of past wounds" this approach also equates the positions of dominant and subordinate groups, erasing all power inequities and hierarchies. And finally, the location of the source of "oppression" and "change" in individuals suggests an elision between ideological and structural understandings of power and domination and individual, psychological understandings of power.

Here again, the implicit definition of experience is important. Experience is defined as fundamentally individual and atomistic, subject to behavioral and attitudinal change. Questions of history, collective memory, and social and structural inequality as constitutive of the category of experience are inadmissible within this framework. Individuals speak as representatives of majority or minority groups whose experience is predetermined within an oppressor/victim paradigm. These questions are addressed in A. Sivanandan's incisive critique of the roots of Racism Awareness Training (RAT) in the United States (associated with the work of Judy Katz et al.) and its embodiment in multiculturalism in Britain.

Sivanandan draws attention to the dangers of the actual degradation and refiguration of antiracist, black political struggles as a result of the RAT focus on psychological attitudes. Thus, while these workshops can indeed be useful in addressing deep-seated psychological attitudes and thus creating a context for change, the danger resides in remaining at the level of personal support and evaluation, and thus often undermining the necessity for broad-based political organization and action around these issues.[25]

Prejudice-reduction workshops have also made their way into the upper echelons of the administration at the college. However, at this level they take a very different form: presidents and their male colleagues don't go to workshops; they "consult" about issues of diversity. Thus, this version of "prejudice reduction" takes the form of "managing diversity" (another semantical gem which suggests that "diversity" [a euphemism for people of color] will be out of control unless it is managed). Consider the following passage from the publicity brochure of a recent consultant:

> *Program in Conflict Management Alternatives:* A team of applied scholars is creating alternative theoretical and practical approaches to the peaceful resolution of social conflicts. A concern for maximizing social justice, and for redressing major social inequities that underlie much social conflict, is a central organizing principle of this work. Another concern is to facilitate the implementation of negotiated settlements, and therefore contribute to long-term change in organizational and community relations. Research theory development, organizational and community change efforts, networking, consultations, curricula, workshops and training programs are all part of the Program.[26]

This quote foregrounds the primary focus on conflict resolution, negotiated settlement, and organizational relations—all framed in a language of research, consultancy, and training. All three strategies—conflict resolution, settlement negotiation, and long-term organizational relations—can be carried out between individuals and between groups. The point is to understand the moments of friction and to resolve the conflicts "peacefully"; in other words, domesticate race and difference by formulating the problems in narrow, interpersonal terms and by rewriting historical contexts as manageable psychological ones.

As in the example of the classroom discussed earlier, the assumption here is that individuals and groups, as individual atomistic units in a social whole composed essentially of an aggregate of such units, embody difference. Thus, conflict resolution is best attempted by negotiating between individuals who are dissatisfied *as individuals.* One very important ideological effect of this is the standardization of behaviors and responses so as to make them predictable (and thus manageable) across a wide variety of situations and circumstances. If complex structural experiences of domination and resistance can be ideologically reformulated as individual behaviors and attitudes, they can be managed while carrying on business as usual.

Another example of this kind of a program is the approach of a company called "Diversity Consultants": "Diversity Consultants believe one of the most effective ways to manage multi-cultural and race awareness issues is through assessment of individual environments, planned educational programs, and management strategy sessions which assist professionals in understanding themselves, diversity, and their options in the workplace."[27]

The key ideas in this statement involve an awareness of race issues (the problem is assumed to be cultural misunderstanding or lack of information about other cultures), understanding yourself and people unlike you (diversity—we must respect and learn from each other; this may not address economic exploitation, but it will teach us to treat each other civilly), negotiating conflicts, altering organizational sexism and racism, and devising strategies to assess and manage the challenges of diversity (which results in an additive approach: recruiting "diverse" people, introducing "different" curriculum units while engaging in teaching as usual— that is, not shifting the normative culture versus subcultures paradigm). This is, then, the "professionalization" of prejudice reduction, where culture is a supreme commodity. Culture is seen as noncontradictory, as isolated from questions of history, and as a storehouse of nonchanging facts, behaviors, and practices. This particular definition of culture and of cultural difference is what sustains the individualized discourse of harmony and civility that is the hallmark of cultural pluralism. Prejudice-reduction workshops eventually aim for the creation of this discourse of civility. Again, this is not to suggest that there are no positive effects of this practice—for instance, the introduction of new cultural models can cause a deeper evaluation of existing structures, and clearly such consultancies could set a positive tone for social change. However, the baseline is still "maintaining the status quo"— diversity is always and can only be added on.

So what does all this mean? Diversity consultants are not new. Private industry has been utilizing these highly paid management consulting firms since the civil rights movement. However, when upper-level administrators in higher education inflect discourses of education and "academic freedom" with discourses of the management of race, the effects are significant enough to warrant close examination. There is a long history of the institutionalization of the discourse of management and control in American education. However, the management of race requires a somewhat different inflection at this historical moment. Due to historical, demographic, and educational shifts in the racial makeup of students and faculty in the last twenty years, some of us even have public voices that have to be "managed" for the greater harmony of all. The hiring of consultants to "sensitize educators to issues of diversity" is part of the postsixties proliferation of discourses of pluralism. But it is also a specific and containing response to the changing social contours of the U.S. polity and to the challenges posed by Third World and feminist studies in the academy. By using the language of the corporation and the language of cognitive and affectional psychology (and thereby professionalizing questions of sexism, racism, and class conflict) new alliances are consolidated. Educators who are part of the ruling administrative class are now managers of conflict, but they are also agents in the construction of "race"—a word that is significantly redefined through the technical language used.

RACE, VOICE, AND ACADEMIC CULTURE

The effects of this relatively new discourse in the higher levels of liberal arts colleges and universities are quite real. Affirmative action hires are now highly visible and selective; now every English department is looking for a black woman scholar to teach Toni Morrison's writings. What happens to such scholars after they are hired, and particularly when they come up for review or tenure, is another matter altogether. A number of scholars have documented the debilitating effects of affirmative action hiring policies that seek out and hire only those Third World scholars who are at the top of their fields—hence the pattern of musical chairs where selected people of color are bartered at very high prices. Our voices are carefully placed and domesticated: one in history, one in English, perhaps one in the sociology department. Clearly these hiring practices do not guarantee the retention and tenure of Third World faculty. In fact, while the highly visible bartering for Third World "stars" serves to suggest that institutions of higher education are finally becoming responsive to feminist and Third World concerns, this particular commodification and personalization of race suggests there has been very little change since the 1970s—both in terms of a numerical increase of Third World faculty and our treatment in white institutions.

In a recent article on the racism faced by Chicano faculty in institutions of higher education, Maria de la Luz Reyes and John J. Halcon characterize the effects of the 1970s policies of affirmative action:[28]

In the mid-1970s, when minority quota systems were being implemented in many non-academic agencies, the general public was left with the impression that Chicano or minority presence in professional or academic positions was due to affirmative action, rather than to individual qualifications or merit. But that impression was inaccurate. Generally [Institutions of Higher Education] responded to the affirmative action guidelines with token positions for only a handful of minority scholars in nonacademic and/or "soft" money programs. For example, many Blacks and Hispanics were hired as directors for programs such as Upward Bound, Talent Search, and Equal Opportunity Programs. Other minority faculty were hired for bilingual programs and ethnic studies programs, but affirmative action hires did not commonly extend to tenure-track faculty positions. The new presence of minorities on college campuses, however, which occurred during the period when attention to affirmative action regulations reached its peak, left all minority professionals and academics with a legacy of tokenism—a stigma that has been difficult to dispel.[29]

De la Luz Reyes and Halcon go on to argue that we are still living with the effects of the implementation of these policies in the 1980s. They examine the problems associated with tokenism and the ghettoization of Third World people in the academy, detailing the complex forms of racism that minority faculty face today. To this characterization, I would add that one of the results of the Reagan/Bush years has been that black, women's, and ethnic studies programs are often further marginalized, since one of the effects of the management of race is that individuals come to embody difference and diversity, while programs that have been historically constituted on the basis of collective oppositional knowledges are labeled "political," "biased," "shrill," and "unrigorous."[30] Any inroads made by such programs and departments in the seventies are being slowly undermined in the eighties and the nineties by the management of race through attitudinal and behavioral strategies, with their local dependence on individuals seen as appropriate representatives of "their race" or some other equivalent political constituency. Race and gender are reformulated as individual characteristics and attitudes, and thus an individualized, ostensibly "unmarked" discourse of difference is being put into place. This shift in the academic discourse on gender and race actually rolls back any progress made in carving institutional spaces for women's and black studies programs and departments.

Earlier, it was these institutional spaces that determined our collective voices. Our programs and departments were by definition alternative and oppositional. Now they are often merely alternative—one among many. Without being nostalgic about the good old days (and they were problematic in their own ways), I am suggesting that there has been an erosion of the politics of collectivity through the reformulation of race and difference in individualistic terms. By no means is this a conspiratorial scenario. The discussion of the effects of my own classroom practices indicates my complicity in this contest over definitions of gender and race in discursive and representational as well as personal terms. The 1960s and 1970s slogan "The personal is political" has been recrafted in the 1980s as "The political is personal." In other words, all politics is collapsed into the personal, and questions of individual behaviors, attitudes, and life-style stand in for political analysis of the social. Individual political struggles are seen as the only relevant and legitimate form of political struggle.

However, there is another, more crucial reason to be concerned about (and to challenge) this management of race in the liberal academy. And the reason is that this process of the individualization of race and its effects dovetails rather neatly with the neoconservative politics and agenda of the Reagan-Bush years— an agenda that has constitutively recast the fabric of American life in a pre-1960s mold. The recent Supreme Court decisions on "reverse discrimination" are based on precisely similar definitions of "prejudice," "discrimination," and "race." In an essay which argues that the U.S. Supreme Court's rulings on reverse discrimination are fundamentally tied to the rollback of reproductive freedom, Zillah Eisenstein discusses the individualist framework on which these decisions are based:

> The court's recent decisions pertaining to affirmative action make quite clear that existing civil rights legislation is being newly reinterpreted. Race, or sex (gender) as a collective category is being denied and racism, and/or sexism, defined as a structural and historical reality has been erased. Statistical evidence of racial and/or sexual discrimination is no longer acceptable as proof of unfair treatment of "black women as a group or class." Discrimination is proved by an individual only in terms of their specific case. The assault is blatant: equality doctrine is dismantled.[31]

Eisenstein goes on to analyze how the government's attempts to redress racism or sexism are at the core of the struggle for equality and how, in gutting the meaning of discrimination and applying it only to individual cases and not statistical categories, it has become almost impossible to prove discrimination because there are always "other" criteria to excuse discriminatory practices. Thus, the recent Supreme Court decisions on reverse discrimination are clearly based on a particular individualist politics that domesticates race and gender. This is an example of the convergence of neoconservative and liberal agendas concerning race and gender inequalities.

Those of us who are in the academy also potentially collude in this domestication of race by allowing ourselves to be positioned in ways that contribute to the construction of these images of pure and innocent diversity, to the construction of these managerial discourses. For instance, since the category of race is not static but a fluid social and historical formation, Third World peoples are often located in antagonistic relationships to each other. Those of us who are from Third World countries are often played off against Third World peoples native to the United States. As an Indian immigrant woman in the United States, for instance, in most contexts, I am not as potentially threatening as an African-American woman. Yes, we are both nonwhite and Other, subject to various forms of overt or disguised racism, but I do not bring with me a history of slavery—a direct and constant reminder of the racist past and present of the United States. Of course my location in the British academy would be fundamentally different because of the history of British colonization, because of patterns of immigration and labor force participation, and because of the existence of working-class, trade union, and antiracist politics—all of which define the position of Indians in Britain. An interesting parallel in the British context is the recent focus on and celebration of African-American women as the "true" radical black feminists who have something to say, while black British feminists ("black" in contemporary Britain refers to those British citizens who are of African, Asian, or Caribbean origin) are marginalized and rendered voiceless by the publishing industry and the academy. These locations and potential collusions thus have an impact on how our voices and agencies are constituted.

CRITICAL PEDAGOGY AND CULTURES OF DISSENT

To conclude, if my argument in this essay is convincing, it suggests why we need to take on board questions of race and gender as they are being managed and commodified in the liberal U.S. academy. One mode of doing this is actively creating public cultures of dissent where these issues can be debated in terms of our pedagogies and institutionalized practices.[32] Creating such cultures in the liberal academy is a challenge in itself, because liberalism allows and even welcomes "plural" or even "alternative" perspectives. However, a public culture of dissent entails creating spaces for epistemological standpoints that are grounded in the *interests* of people and which recognize the *materiality* of conflict, of privilege, and domination. Thus creating such cultures is fundamentally about making the axes of power transparent in the context of academic, disciplinary, and institutional structures as well as in the interpersonal relationships (rather than individual relations) in the academy. It is about taking the politics of everyday life seriously as teachers, students, administrators, and members of hegemonic academic cultures. Culture itself is thus redefined as incorporating individual and collective memories, dreams, and history that are contested and transformed through the political praxis of day-to-day living.

Cultures of dissent are also about seeing the academy as part of a larger sociopolitical arena which itself domesticates and manages Third World people in the name of liberal capitalist democracy. The struggle to transform our institutional practices fundamentally also involves the grounding of the analysis of exploitation and oppression in accurate history and theory, seeing ourselves as activists in the academy—drawing links between movements for social justice and our pedagogical and scholarly endeavors and expecting and demanding action from ourselves, our colleagues, and our students at numerous levels. This requires working hard to understand and to theorize questions of knowledge, power, and experience in the academy so that one effects pedagogical empowerment as well as transformation. Racism, sexism, and homophobia are very real, day-to-day practices in which we all engage. They are not reducible to mere curricular or policy decisions—that is, to management practices.

I said earlier that what is at stake is not the mere *recognition* of difference. The sort of difference which is acknowledged and engaged has fundamental significance for the decolonization of education practices. Similarly, the point is not simply that one should have *a voice;* the more crucial question concerns the sort of voice one comes to have as the result of one's location—both as an individual and as part of collectives.[33] I think the important point is that it be an active, oppositional, and collective voice which takes seriously the current commodification and domestication of Third World people in the academy. And this is a task open to all—people of color as well as progressive white people in the academy.

NOTES

This paper was published in *Cultural Critique,* 1990. I would like to thank Gloria Watkins (bell hooks), Satya Mohanty, and Jacqui Alexander for numerous passionate discussions on these issues. All three have helped sharpen the arguments in this essay; all faults, however, are mine.

1. Marnia Lazreg, "Feminism and Difference: The Perils of Writing as a Woman on Women in Algeria," *Feminist Studies* 14, no. 1 (Spring 1988): 81–107.

2. Ibid., 98.

3. See especially my "Under Western Eyes: Feminist Scholarship and Colonial Discourses," *Feminist Review* 30 (Autumn 1988): 61–88, and "Feminist Encounters: Locating the Politics of Experience," in the special issue, "Fin de Siecle 2000," of *Copyright* 1 (Fall 1987): 30–44. The present essay continues the discussion of the politics of location that I began in "Feminist Encounters" and can, in fact, be seen as a companion text to it.

4. I am referring here to a particular trajectory of feminist scholarship in the last two decades. While scholarship in the 1970s foregrounded gender as *the* fundamental category of analysis and thus enabled the transformation of numerous disciplinary and canonical boundaries on the basis of the recognition of sexual difference as hierarchy and inequality, scholarship in the 1980s introduced the categories of race and sexuality in the form of internal challenges to the earlier scholarship. These challenges were introduced on both political and methodological grounds by feminists who often considered themselves disenfranchised by the 1970s' feminism: lesbian and heterosexual women of color, postcolonial, Third World women, poor women, etc. While the recent feminist turn to postmodernism suggests the fragmentation of unitary assumptions of gender and enables a more differentiated analysis of inequality, this critique was prefigured in the earlier political analyses of Third World feminists. This particular historical trajectory of the political and conceptual categories of feminist analysis can be traced by analyzing developments in feminist journals such as *Signs* and *Feminist Studies,* feminist publishing houses, and curriculum "integration" projects through the 1970s and 1980s.

5. For instance, Jessie Bernard's *The Female World from a Global Perspective* (Bloomington: Indiana University Press, 1987) codifies difference as the exclusive relation of men to women, and women to women: difference as variation *among* women and as conflict *between* men and women.

6. It is clear from Lazreg's reliance on a notion like intersubjectivity that her understanding of the issue I am addressing in this essay is far from simple. Claiming a voice is for her, as well as for me, a complex historical and political act that involves understanding the interrelationships of voices. However, the term intersubjectivity, drawing as it does on a phenomenological humanism, brings with it difficult political problems. For a nonhumanist, alternative account of the question of "historical agencies" and their "imbrication," see S. P. Mohanty's recent essay "Us and Them: On the Philosophical Bases of Political Criticism," *Yale Journal of Criticism* 2, no. 2 (Spring 1989): 1–31, and his forthcoming *Literary Theory and the Claims of History* (Cambridge, Mass.: Basil Blackwell, 1990), especially the introduction and chapter 6. Mohanty discusses the question of agency and its historical imbrication (rather than "intersubjectivity") as constituting the fundamental theoretical basis for comparison across cultures.

7. In spite of problems of definition, I retain the use of the term "Third World," and in this particular context (the U.S. academy), I identify myself as a "Third World" scholar. I use the term here to designate peoples from formerly colonized countries, as well as people of color in the United States. Using the designation "Third World" to identify colonized peoples in the domestic as well as the international arena may appear reductive because it suggests a commonality and perhaps even an equation

among peoples with very diverse cultures and histories and appears to reinforce implicitly existing economic and cultural hierarchies between the "First" and the "Third" World. This is not my intention. I use the term with full awareness of these difficulties and because these are the terms available to us at the moment. In addition, in the particular discursive context of Western feminist scholarship and of the U.S. academy, "Third World" is an oppositional designation that can be empowering even while it necessitates a continuous questioning. For an elaboration of these questions of definition, see my "Cartographies of Struggle: Third World Women and the Politics of Feminism," in the volume I have co-edited with Lourdes Torres and Ann Russo (*Third World Women and the Politics of Feminism* [Bloomington: Indiana University Press, 1991).

8.   See especially the work of Paulo Freire, Michael Apple, Basil Bernstein, Pierre Bour-dieu, and Henry Giroux. While a number of these educational theorists offer radical critiques of education on the basis of class hierarchies, very few do so on the basis of gender or race. However, the theoretical suggestions in this literature are provocative and can be used to advantage in feminist analysis. The special issue "On Racism and American Education," *Harvard Educational Review* 58, no. 3 (1988) is also an excellent resource. See also Paulo Freire, *Pedagogy of the Oppressed,* trans. Myra Bergman Ramos (New York: Seabury Press, 1973), Paulo Freire and Donaldo Macedo, *Literacy: Reading the Word and the World* (South Hadley, Mass.: Bergin and Garvey, 1985), Michael Apple, *Ideology and the Curriculum* (London: Routledge and Kegan Paul, 1979), Basil Bernstein, *Class, Codes, and Control,* vol. 3 (London: Routledge and Kegan Paul, 1975), Henry Giroux, *Theory and Resistance in Education: A Pedagogy for the Opposition* (South Hadley, Mass.: Bergin and Garvey, 1983), Henry Giroux, *Teachers as Intellectuals: Toward a Critical Pedagogy of Learning* (South Hadley, Mass.: Bergin and Garvey, 1988), and Pierre Bourdieu and J. C. Passeron, *Reproduction in Education, Society and Culture,* trans. Richard Nice (Beverly Hills, Calif.: Sage Publications, 1977). For feminist analyses of education and the academy, see Charlotte Bunch and Sandra Pollack, eds., *Learning Our Way: Essays in Feminist Education* (Trumansburg, N.Y.: Crossing Press, 1983), Elizabeth Minnich et al., eds., *Reconstructing the Academy: Women's Education and Women's Studies* (Chicago: University of Chicago Press, 1988), Marilyn Schuster and Susan Van Dyne, *Women's Place in the Academy: Transforming the Liberal Arts Curriculum* (Totowa, N.J.: Rowan and Allenheld, 1985), and Elizabeth Minnich, *Transforming Knowledge* (Philadelphia: Temple University Press, 1990). See also back issues of the journals *Women's Studies Quarterly, Women's Studies International Forum,* and *Frontiers: A Journal of Women's Studies.*

9.   I am fully aware of the fact that I am drawing on an extremely limited (and some might say atypical) sample for this analysis. Clearly, in the bulk of American colleges and universities, the very introduction of questions of pluralism and difference is itself a radical and oppositional gesture. However, in the more liberal institutions of higher learning, questions of pluralism have had a particular institutional history, and I draw on the example of the college I currently teach at to investigate the implications of this specific institutionalization of discourses of pluralism. I am concerned with raising some political and intellectual questions that have urgent implications for the discourses of race and racism in the academy, not with providing statistically significant data on U.S. institutions of higher learning, nor with claiming "representativeness" for the liberal arts college I draw on to raise these questions.

10.   For analyses of the intersection of the race and sex agendas of the New Right, see

essays in the special double issue of *Radical America* 15, nos. 1 and 2 (1981). I have utilized Zillah Eisenstein's "Feminism v. Neoconservative Jurisprudence: The Spring '89 Supreme Court"(unpublished manuscript, 1990). I am indebted to her for sharing this essay with me and for our discussions on this subject.

11. Some of the most poignant and incisive critiques of the inscription of race and difference in scholarly and institutional discourses have been raised by Third World scholars working outside women's studies. See Cornel West, "Minority Discourse and the Pitfalls of Canon Formation," *Yale Journal of Criticism* 1, no. 1 (Fall 1987): 193–202. A Sivanandan, "RAT and the Degradation of Black Struggle," *Race and Class* 26, no. 4 (Spring 1985); 1–34, and S. P. Mohanty, "Us and Them."

12. Information about the origins of black studies is drawn from Nathan I. Huggins, *Afro-American Studies, A Report to the Ford Foundation* (n.p.: ford Foundation, July 1985). For provocative analyses and historic essays on black studies in the 1960s and 1970s, see John W. Blassingame, ed., *New Perspectives on Black Studies* (Urbana: University of Illinois Press, 1973).

13. For a documentation of this conference, see Armstead L. Robinson, Craig C. Foster, and Donald H. Ogilvie, eds., *Black Studies in the University, A Symposium* (New York: Bantam Books, 1969).

14. This information is culled from the National Women's Studies Association Task Force Report on *The Women's Studies Major* (unpublished manuscript, 1990). See also essays in Minnich et al. eds., *Reconstructing the Academy.*

15. Rosaura Sanchez, "Ethnicity, Ideology and Academia," *Americas Review* 15, no. 1 (Spring 1987): 80–88.

16. Ibid., 86.

17. Niara Sudarkasa, "Affirmative Action or Affirmation of Status Quo? Black Faculty and Administrators in Higher Education," *AAHE Bulletin* (February 1987): 3–6.

18. Ibid., 4.

19. Elsa Barkley Brown, "African-American Women's Quilting: A Framework for Conceptualizing and Teaching African-American Women's History," *Signs* 14, no. 4 (Summer 1989): 921–29.

20. Ibid., 921.

21. As a contrast, and for an interesting analysis of similar issues in the pedagogical context of a white woman teaching multicultural women's studies, see Peggy Pascoe's "At the Crossroads of Culture," *Women's Review of Books* 7, no. 5 (February 1990): 22–23.

22. Giroux, *Teachers as Intellectuals,* 95.

23. West, "Minority Discourse," 197.

24. See the American Council on Education, Education Commission of the States, *One-Third of a Nation. A Report of the Commission on Minority Participation in Education and American Life* (Washington, D.C.: American Council on Education, 1988). See also articles on "America's Changing Colors," in *Time,* April 9, 1990, especially, William A. Henry III, "Beyond the Melting Pot," for statistics on changing demographics in U.S. economic and educational spheres.

25. This discussion of the ideological assumptions of "prejudice reduction" is based on Patti DeRosa's presentation at the "Society for International Education, Training, and Research Conference" in May 1987.

26. From "Towards Prejudice Reduction: A Resource Document Consultants, Audio/

Visual Aids, and Providers of Workshops, Training and Seminars," a document prepared by Sue E. Prindle, Associate Director of Personnel and Affirmative Action Officer at Oberlin College (Oberlin, Ohio: 1988), 1.

27. Ibid., 8.

28. Maria de la Luz Reyes and John J. Halcon, "Racism in Academia: The Old Wolf Revisited," *Harvard Educational Review* 58, no. 3 (1988): 299–314.

29. Ibid., 303.

30. This marginalization is evident in the financial cutbacks that such programs have faced in recent years. The depoliticization is evident in, for instance, the current shift from "women's" to "gender" studies—by all measures, a controversial reconstitution of feminist agendas.

31. Eisenstein, "Feminism v. Neoconservative Jurisprudence," 5.

32. Gloria Watkins (bell hooks) and I have attempted to do this in a collegewide faculty colloquium called "Pedagogies of Gender, Race and Empire" that focuses on our practices in teaching and learning about Third World people in the academy. While the effects of this colloquium have yet to be thoroughly examined, at the very least it has created a public culture of dialogue and dissent where questions of race, gender, and identity are no longer totally dismissed as "political" and thus extraneous to academic endeavor, nor are they automatically ghettoized in women's studies and black studies. These questions are seen (by a substantial segment of the faculty) as important, constitutive questions in revising a Eurocentric liberal arts curriculum.

33. See my "Feminist Encounters" for an elaboration of these issues.

CHAPTER 9

....

SCHOOL'S OUT

....

SIMON WATNEY

HOW CHILDHOOD TRIES TO REACH US,
AND DECLARES THAT WE WERE ONCE WHAT TOOK IT SERIOUSLY.—RAINER MARIA
RILKE[1]

THE MOST CRUCIAL ASPECT OF PSYCHO-
ANALYSIS . . . IS THE INSISTANCE THAT CHILDHOOD IS SOMETHING IN WHICH
WE CONTINUE TO BE IMPLICATED AND WHICH IS NEVER SIMPLY LEFT BEHIND. . . .
IT PERSISTS AS SOMETHING WHICH WE ENDLESSLY REWORK IN OUR ATTEMPT TO
BUILD AN IMAGE OF OUR OWN HISTORY.—JACQUELINE ROSE[2]

....

INTRODUCTION

The American artist Tim Rollins has recently argued that "one of the most cherished ideas in America, the rationale for compulsory education and public schooling in this country, is the belief that a genuine democracy cannot exist without the full education of all its citizens."[3] Much the same could be said of most people's attitudes toward education in the United Kingdom. Yet when I was at school in the 1960s the subject of homosexuality only existed as a pretext for sniggers and insults. Little has significantly changed in either country. Two subsequent decades of debate and action in the direction of multiculturalism in the classroom have had, at best, only uneven results. But the question of homosexuality remains in total abeyance. Which is to say that the question of *sexuality* remains in abeyance, since our respective education systems manifestly fail to acknowledge the actual diversity of human sexuality within the curriculum or outside it. In effect, children are taught that homosexuality is beyond consideration. This is bad for everyone in education, but most especially for lesbian and gay teachers, and lesbian and gay students. In this article I want to consider briefly the immediate legal and ideological circumstances that frame the subject of homosexuality in schools, for unless we understand the historical and institutional dimensions of antigay prejudice, we will not be able to develop effective counterstrategies.

SECTION 28 AND THE "WOLFENDEN STRATEGY"

On May 24, 1988, Section 28 of the Local Government (Amendment) Act came into force in the United Kingdom. The Act states that

(1) A local authority shall not
   (a) intentionally promote homosexuality or publish material with the intent of promoting homosexuality;
   (b) promote the teaching in any maintained school of the acceptability of homosexuality as a pretended family relationship.
(2) Nothing in subsection (1) above shall be taken to prohibit the doing of anything for the purpose of treating or preventing the spread of disease.

This was the culmination, to date, of more than a decade of increasingly polarized debate and controversy focused around so-called "family values," which has involved a special emphasis on education in the broadest sense, from the formal curriculum in schools, to plays, films, and art exhibitions housed or in any way financed or supported by local government. In other words, we are witnessing an increasing acknowledgment of the role that culture plays in the construction of sexual identities, and it is the field of cultural production that is ever more subject to frankly political interventions, in Britain as in the United States.[4]

Yet it would be a mistake to regard Section 28 as something entirely new. On the contrary, in many respects it may be seen to stand in the mainstream of modern British legislation concerning homosexuality, which has never aimed to establish or protect the rights of lesbians and gay men. Rather, it has always aspired to protect our imaginary victims—those whom the law regards as especially "vulnerable," including the feeble-minded, women, and above all children. However, the concept of childhood remains highly elastic in relation to all aspects of homosexuality, as in the most obvious example of the legal age of consent for sex between men, which is still firmly fixed at 21, five years more than the age set for heterosexuals.[5] Far from ushering in a new age of sexual enlightment, the famous Sexual Offences Act of 1967 paved the way for the implementation of what Beverley Brown has named the Wolfenden Strategy, which has established ever more effective control of sex and sexuality by the state, but also by many other nonstate institutions, from the mass media to clinical medicine. Indeed, the Sexual Offenses Act of 1967 clearly enacted the legal moralism of the Report of the Wolfenden Committee on which it was belatedly modeled, which explicitly regretted the "general loosening of former moral standards."

Sadly, there has never been any question of English law turning its archaic attention to the rising tide of antigay prejudice and discrimination and actual violence in contemporary Britain. This is largely a result of the absence of any effective discourse of civil rights within parliamentary politics in the U.K.[6] On the contrary, the workings of the Wolfenden Strategy have consistently, if unconvincingly, attempted to define "acceptable" human sexuality in strict relation to reproductive sex between married couples, and to contain all forms of nonreproductive sex, from homosexuality to prostitution, in a legally defined private sphere where they are permitted to exist, but not to be culturally validated in any way. Hence it is no surprise that British lesbians and gay men are at the very bottom of the line in terms of available police protection, way behind women or racial minorities. In 1989 the Metropolitan Police launched a major poster campaign in London to combat racism. Yet a parallel campaign against antigay discrimination remains entirely unthinkable. In the meantime, police prosecutions of gay men in Britain in 1990 have reached the worst levels of the notorious witch-hunts of the mid-1950s.[7] This wider question of antigay prejudice in Britain, and the United States, must also be related to the worsening tragedy of HIV/AIDS in both countries, which are distinguished in international terms by governmental refusal to establish proper national policies which would take the epidemic seriously, and by the constant harassing of health education and nongovernment AIDS service organizations whose work is deemed to "promote homosexuality" or "drug abuse."[8] And in both countries the political opposition party has equally failed to challenge official government policies, or their absence, for fear of association with the dreaded "electoral liability" of lesbian and gay issues. The assault against lesbians and gay men in the field of education, whether as students or as teachers, must be viewed in this wider perspective if its full significance is to be understood, and if effective strategies are to be developed to remedy the situation. Section 28 simply put into law the previous recommendations of the Department of Education, which published an official Circular in November 1987 that baldly stated: "There is no place in any school in any circumstances for teaching which advocates homosexual behaviour, which presents it as 'the norm,' or which encourages homosexual experimentation by pupils."[9]

These brief yet densely written clauses already speak volumes about the attitudes and beliefs that constitute antigay prejudice, and the laws it brings about and sanctions. Indeed, they provide a startlingly clear insight into the world that the prejudiced inhabit, a world that is mainly defined by *fear*—fear of gay couples being accepted just like other couples, a world in which homosexuality is a perpetual and terrifying menace, a world in which the young are always thought to be in danger of corruption, and in which they can never be sufficiently protected. If we want to understand the force of antigay prejudice, and the role that it plays across the entire field of modern education, we must begin by considering the ways in which heterosexual adults are encouraged to identify with children. This required a close understanding of the discourse of "promotion" that unites both Section 28 in Britain and the Helms Amendment which banned safer sex education for gay men in the USA for several years in the late 1980s.[10] Yet at the same time, such laws also serve paradoxically to draw attention to the fact that fundamental definitions of sexual identity and sexual morality are historically contingent, and by no means "natural." They also further demonstrate the confidence of the institutions which insist that the existing power relations of sexuality and of gender must be vigorously defended, preemptively if necessary.

Certainly no area of social life has been subjected to more violent ideological contestation in the modern period than sex education, and the whole vexed question of homosexuality in schools. As we have already seen, this has now culminated in the state's claim to distinguish between supposedly "real" and "pretended" families. At a time when a third of babies in Britain are born into single-parent families, it would appear that underlying, long-term changes in the nature of adult sexual relations and patterns of childraising are encouraging ever stronger patterns of resistance, retrenched around a powerful fantasy of how "family life" used to be, and should be in future. Sex is the central and heavily overdetermined focus of such fantasies, which involve a sharp distinction between the world of marriage and the home, and the lives of lesbians and gay men. Since homosexuality cannot be acknowledged within the ordinary workaday world, it must of necessity be thought of as the completely different inversion of the heterosexually known and familiar. Indeed, it is vitally important that lesbians and gay men should be able to understand the mechanisms of displacement and denial that inform heterosexual projections about us as people, for these projections determine the world in which we must live our lives. Furthermore, as public attitudes gradually change over time, it would appear that there has been a consolidation of prejudice at the level of institutional politics, where the subject of homosexuality can easily be exploited, or else ignored as a supposed electoral "liability." Hence the need for broad cultural strategies in relation to "public opinion," as well as specific strategies targeting the state, and the very concept of "politics."

PROMOTING HOMOSEXUALITY

Throughout the long debate which accompanied the publication and the eventual passing into law of Section 28, journalists and other commentators frequently referred to the bill's aim to prevent the promotion of homosexuality in schools. The concept of "promotion" behind the bill was rarely questioned, except in legal opinions sought by the teaching trade unions and others in order to oppose it. Thus by analogy with British company law, Lord Gifford concluded his written Opinion with the observation that " 'promote homosexuality' involves active advocacy directed by local authorities towards individuals in order to persuade them to become homosexual, or to experiment with homosexual relationships."[11] While Section 28 does not supersede the legal authority of previous legislation concerning sex education in Britain, it has nonetheless had a wide cultural impact— not least in establishing the notion of homosexual "promotion" as never before. In this respect it is helpful to note the way in which the wording of Section 28 binds together a theory of the formation of sexual identity with a theory of representation. On the one hand it is assumed, within the wider terms of the

Wolfenden Strategy, that "the vulnerable" may be easily seduced into sexual experimentation, and into a rejection of supposedly "natural" heterosexuality. On the other hand it explicitly targets representations in any medium that depict lesbian or gay relationships as equivalent to heterosexual families. The unconscious logic thus runs that homosexuality can only exist as a result of the seduction of minors by predatory older perverts. This seduction may, however, be indirect, and effected via *cultural* means. In other words, there is a clear recognition that sexual identities are culturally grounded, and an acknowledgment that gay identity does not follow automatically from homosexual desire or practice. Something else is needed—the active presence of a confident, articulate lesbian and gay culture that clothes homosexual desire in a stable, collective *social* identity.

In this respect, the strategic significance of Section 28 lies in the way it harnesses a theory of (homo)sexual identity to a theory of representation which is remarkably like crude "copy-cat" theories concerning the supposed influence of pornography on its users, and especially on those who supposedly come across pornography "by accident." What in effect is acknowledged is the *pedagogic value* of gay culture in developing and sustaining gay identities. In all of this, it is the imagined vulnerability of heterosexuality that is more significant, together with the assumed power of homosexual pleasure to corrode the "natural" order of social and sexual relations. This is evidently a response to the long-term impact of gay culture in modern Britain, where the Government's Inspectorate of Schools concluded in 1986 that "given the openness with which homosexuality is treated in society now it is almost bound to arise as an issue in one area or another of a school's curriculum."[12] They therefore concluded that

> Information about the discussion of homosexuality, whether it involves a whole class or an individual, needs to acknowledge that experiencing strong feelings of attraction to members of the same sex is a phase passed through by many young people, but that for a significant number of people these feelings persist into adult life. Therefore it needs to be dealt with objectively and seriously, bearing in mind that, while there has been a marked shift away from the general condemnation of homosexuality, many individuals and groups hold sincerely to the view that it is morally objectionable. This is difficult territory for teachers to traverse, and for some schools to accept that homosexuality may be a normal feature of relationships would be a breach of the religious faith upon which they are founded. Consequently LEA'S [Local Education Authorities] voluntary bodies, governors, heads and senior staff in schools have important responsibilities in devising guidance and supporting teachers dealing with this sensitive issue.[13]

In all of this it should be noted that there is no consideration of the consequences for lesbian and gay teachers or students. Indeed, it is the very open-endedness of the Inspectors' report, published by the Department of Education, which seems to have been an immediate trigger behind the lobby that orchestrated Section 28.

For the report unambiguously recognizes a reality, "a marked shift away from the general condemnation of homosexuality," that the authors of Section 28 equally unambiguously wish to deny.

Section 28 thus exemplifies an extreme registration of the changing sexual politics of the past twenty years. In one sense it evidently belongs to the long tradition of anti-Freudian thought that denies infantile sexuality, whilst at the same time it is almost *too* eager to concede that sexuality may be "artificially" conjured into being via sexual "experimentation." This sense of homosexual desire as a kind of omni-present potential contagion is wholly in keeping with Michel Foucault's prophetic observation in 1980 that, in the future,

> sexuality will no longer be a form of behaviour with certain precise prohibitions but rather a kind of danger that lingers. . . . Sexuality will become the threat looming over all social bonds, relations among generations as among individuals. On this shadow, on this phantom, on this fear the power structure will assume control by means of a seemingly generous and blanket legislation thanks largely to a series of timely interventions that will probably involve judicial institutions supported by the medical profession. And there will arise a new order of sexual control. . . . Sex will be decriminalized only to reappear as a danger, and an universal one at that. There lies the real danger.[14]

Certainly we are presently witnessing an unparalleled struggle between values and identities forged within the sexual categories of the late nineteenth century and rival values and identities that have emerged in the twentieth century. This struggle is waged with special ferocity in those areas of social life where sexual identity is most contested, of which education is perhaps the most significant. Education has clearly long been targeted by antigay traditionalists because it is identified as the site at which the supposed "threat" of homosexuality is most acute, and where preemptive maneuvers are most needed. Yet public opinion polls in both Britain and the United States suggest that broad levels of prejudice are actually in decline. For example, 71% of Americans recently polled thought that lesbians and gay men should have equal job opportunities to heterosexuals, compared to only 59% in 1982.[15] Meanwhile in Britain a still more recent survey suggests that 60% of heterosexual men and 62% of women think that gay men should be allowed to adopt children, while over 60% of men and over 80% of women think that no gay person should be barred from any job on the grounds of his or her sexuality.[16] It is thus far from clear that popular consent could actually be won in relation to any attempt to recriminalize homosexuality as such, and it is highly significant that there has been no serious attempt in either Britain or the U.S. to introduce legislation to proscribe specific "sexual acts," in the manner of premodern laws. The contestation that is currently being fought out in relation to education involves a fight to the death between the diverse forces of radical sexual pluralism, including single-parent families, proabortion campaigners, and all whose lives are invalidated by "family values," and those who devotedly subscribe and submit themselves to "family values." Insofar as school represents a double threshold, between the privacy of the home and public space, as well as between the categories of child and adult, it is inevitable that education would find itself caught in the crossfire between fundamentally incompatible definitions of what it means to be a man or a woman in the late twentieth century, an adult or a child. In this context it is imperative that we appreciate the new significance of the discourse of "promotion," whether it is employed to justify attacks on gay culture as in Britain, or on safer sex education, as in the United States.[17]

For gay identity can undoubtedly be promoted, in circumstances where homosexual desire might otherwise have little opportunity of providing the ground for an integrated sense of self. Section 28 aims to restore a world of exclusively heterosexual values, identities, and institutions, in which homosexual desire could only be lived within the compliant, subservient terms of "homosexual" identity. "Homosexuals" are thus envisaged as a discrete number of invisible individuals, who preferably do not act on the basis of their desires. This is the picture of homosexuality and "homosexuals" that traditionalists wish to impose on young people and, as far as possible, throughout the rest of society. "Homosexuals" are thus depicted as a uniform type, an abstract, generalized, and thus dehumanized menace—especially dangerous because they cannot necessarily be readily identified. Unlike people of color, lesbians and gay men cannot immediately be recruited to constitute a visible, immediate definition of Otherness in relation to which Heterosexuality can be positively contrasted. It is therefore imperative that the cultural iconography of "the homosexual" have precedence over any representations that might reveal the actual diversity and complexity of sexual choice. Hence the traditionalists' obsession with the *representation* of family life, and their violent iconoclasm in relation to images that contravene their codes of "acceptable" gender imagery. It is precisely at this point that antipornography campaigners often unwittingly find themselves in alliance with another, parallel social-purity movement, rooted in antigay prejudice and strict patriarchal values. Ultimately, the conflict of contemporary sexual politics concerns the unreconcilable conflict between power relations that seek increasingly to define and divide people along the lines of sexual object choice, and a politics which aspires to transcend the power relations of the categories of sexuality altogether, along with the identities they produce. This conflict is currently being waged with special ferocity around rival definitions of the meaning of childhood. On the one hand, there is evidently a growing demand that sexual diversity should be acknowledged in schools, while, on the other, it is insisted that homosexuality should only be represented as a hideous perversion of heterosexuality, understood as a "natural" domain of unassailable, rigidly gendered characteristics organized around the prime purpose of sexual reproduction and the "protection" of asexual children.

THEORIZING CHILDHOOD

In his celebrated *Introductory Lectures on Psychoanalysis,* Freud succinctly argued that

to suppose that children have no sexual life—sexual excitations and needs and a kind of satisfaction—but suddenly acquire it between the ages of twelve and fourteen, would (quite apart from any observations) be as improbable, and indeed senseless, biologically as to suppose that they brought no genitals with them into the world and only grew them at the time of puberty. What *does* awaken in them at this time is the reproductive function, which makes use for its purposes of physical and mental material already present.[18]

Those who refuse to accept this "are committing the error of confusing sexuality and reproduction and by doing so you are blocking your path to an understanding of sexuality, the perversions and the neuroses."[19]

It is important at once to note that, for Freud, "perversion" was simply a descriptive term used to theorize all aspects of sexuality that do not have a reproductive aim, and one of the most productive tensions within his work concerns the way he often contradicts himself in relation to the supposed reproductive ends of adult sexuality. For elsewhere he insists that "in man the sexual instinct does not originally serve the purpose of reproduction at all, but has as its aim the gaining of particular kinds of pleasures."[20]

From Freud's perspective, it is above all *education* which serves to restrict the aim of sexual pleasure, and to channel it into socially and culturally acceptable directions—in other words, into familiar patterns of marriage and, we must note, of homophobia. Nor is this aim simply that of sexual reproduction. On the contrary, for Freud education aims

to tame and restrict the sexual instinct when it breaks out as an urge to reproduction, and to subject it to an individual will which is identical with the bidding of society. It is also concerned to postpone the full development of the instinct till the child shall have reached a certain degree of intellectual maturity, for, with the complete irruption of the sexual instinct, educatability is for practical purposes at an end.[21]

In other words, according to Freud, perhaps the central aspect of education is the inculcation of certain specific rules and attitudes toward sex, which will guarantee the subsequent sexual workings of (patriarchal) society, including the familiar double standards of sexual morality in relation to women and men of which he was a particularly bitter critic. With the benefit of hindsight we can also recognize that attitudes toward homosexuality are also thus an indispensable target of education, since it is always at least potentially available as a site of alternative sexual satisfaction to heterosexual sex, a site moreover which must therefore be rigorously controlled. In all of this, however, we should also note that neither Freud nor his followers have ever demonstrated much concern for the fate of young lesbian and gay people within a pedagogic environment which has as its central business the production of compliant heterosexual identities, largely by means of demonizing homosexuality. This is precisely where we pick up psychoanalysis in the late twentieth century. For the vital point is that young people do not lack sexuality: what they are frequently *denied* is an identity in relation to their sexuality.

This is largely effected by means of the establishment of the widely pervasive belief that there indeed exists a distinct "world of childhood," quite separate from and independent of adult life. While this is generally felt to be in the child's own best interests, it actually dooms children—and especially gay children—to very considerable misery, since the ordinary relations between adults and children are arbitrarily severed. As Hannah Arendt has pointed out, this can easily have disastrous consequences for the child for, by being "emancipated" from the authority of adults, he or she

> has not been freed but has been subjected to a much more terrifying and truly tyrannical authority, the tyranny of the majority . . . either thrown back upon themselves or handed over to the tyranny of their own group, against which, because of its numerical superiority, they cannot rebel, with which, because they are children, they cannot reason, and out of which they cannot flee to any other world because the world of adults is barred to them.[22]

This strikes me as a peculiarly accurate depiction of the dilemmas facing most young gay people at school.

Nor can most gay children expect any understanding of this dilemma at home, where their marginalization and vulnerability is only likely to be reinforced. Hence the familiar strategies such children so frequently develop as self-defense mechanisms—the semblance of ultraconformism to conventional gender roles, excessive zealousness in competitive sports or academic pursuits, and so on. Somehow we have to develop ways to defend young lesbians and gay children from the consequences of their own defensive strategies, with which they will often closely identify for obvious reasons. Much later unhappiness is undoubtedly rooted in such common childhood experience. This is one clear reason why we should not lie to children about the (homo)sexuality of historical or contemporary cultural

figures, including scientists, writers, artists, and athletes. For good education involves helping children to learn how to make and exercise choices. This is not to
say that one's sexuality is in any simple sense "chosen," at least in the same way
that one might choose a career. However, the choices one makes on the basis of
one's sexuality should be respected and encouraged, and this must include sexual
experimentation, which in turns involves (for most of us) both success and failure.
What we have to end is a world in which young lesbian and gay students often
feel no real sense of belonging, and where they have precious little opportunity
to develop a sustaining sense of their own self-esteem. Given the grotesque denial
of safer sex education to young gay men in schools, and our increasing understanding of the role of self-esteem in relation to preventing the transmission of HIV,
this is now more urgently important than ever. We must never forget that great
violence is routinely perpetrated against all young lesbians and gay men in the
name of "education," violence which is generally continuous with the emotional
violence of heterosexual domesticity and "family values" which would deny our
very existence, let alone the dignity and significance of our particular emotional
and sexual needs, whether as young people or as adults.

From this perspective we may invert the usual question of what children
supposedly want or need from education, and ask what it is that adults want or
need of children in the name of "education." For it is in relation to theories of
childhood that the practices of adult power relations may be very productively
analyzed, and nowhere more so than in the wholesale denial of children's sexuality.
As Michel Foucault has pointed out, "When it comes to children, the first assumption is that their sexuality can never be directed towards an adult. Secondly they
are deemed incapable of self-expression. Thus no one ever believes them. They
are believed to be immune to sexuality, and unable to discuss it."[23] It is especially
ironic that this position is generally presented within the context of a heavily
vulgarized version of psychoanalysis itself, harnessed to the most reactionary (and
anti-Freudian) purpose of denying children's sexuality altogether. In this respect
we should recognize the high priority of targeting the domain of "educational
psychology" that underpins so many aspects of the training of teachers. This in
turn involves acknowledging the erotic component that plays so central part in *all*
educational environments. As long as education is imagined to be entirely nonsexual, the actual erotics of the pedagogic situation can be displaced away in the
imaginary likeness of the evil pervert, "promoting" his or her sexuality with
"innocent" children. The question is *not* whether or not children are sexual beings,
but how adults respond to children's sexuality, in ways that range from total denial
to an untroubled acceptance.

CONCLUSION

Behind the rhetoric that identifies the supposedly widespread and perilous "promotion" of homosexuality lies a particularly dense core of fantasy and denial that

needs to be carefully unpacked if the rhetoric is to be successfully countered. On a descriptive level we may easily detect deep-seated fears that cross over the familiar social barriers of class, gender, and culture. These fears constitute a narrative, according to the logic of which "vulnerable" (i.e., nonsexual) children are in constant danger of being seduced into homosexuality via sexual "experimentation" stimulated by the depiction of gay and lesbian relationships as fully equivalent to "family" (i.e., heterosexual) relations. The discourse of "promoting homosexuality" thus articulates real anxieties on the part of many people, as well as providing an imagined solution to the problem in the form of new laws and other extraordinary measures. These are rationalized as forms of defense against what is perilous, yet they are in fact transparently aggressive and preemptive, since powerful legislation already exists to deal with the complex realities of actual child abuse. We may therefore be justified in suspecting that the "reality" that this discourse addresses is not that of concrete social relations but of the unconscious.

In a sense this should already be apparent from the sheer tenacity of the ways in which the narrative returns to the imagined spectacle of the child's seduction, and his or her *acceptance* of the seducer, which is most dreaded. In other words, the narrative of "homosexual promotion" should be regarded as a powerful fantasy which permits some heterosexuals to legitimately dwell on the image of children's bodies as objects of (homo)sexual desire, and, moreover, as its active *subjects*. In this respect the narrative reveals significant parallels to other fantasy narratives that also possess widespread contemporary currency, from those of satanic child abuse, to demonic possession, and so on. All of these share a heavily overdetermined investment in the "innocence" of childhood, and the depravity of the surrounding adult world, from which it is considered to be the primary responsibility of parents to protect the young. In all these respects the discourse of the "promotion" of homosexuality should be recognized as an essentially premodern construction, that is only able to conceptualize homosexual desire in the likeness of sinister, predatory perverts, luring innocent victims to their doom, having corrupted them from within. It articulates "the homosexual" in the image of nineteenth-century Christian popular culture as an essentially *immoral* figure against which "the heterosexual" is left to define "morality." In these terms, homosexuality is to all extents and purposes a metaphysical force rather than a human characteristic, and the resurgence of the discourse of "promotion" may best be explained as a last-ditch attempt to resist the larger implications of the emergence of gay politics, which insist on giving lesbians and gay men ordinary human features. This perhaps is what is most terrifying of all to those who conceptualize themselves and other people in brutally archaic terms. For as long as "the homosexual" is not regarded as human, individual lesbians and gay men can continue to be marginalized and persecuted. The greatest threat that gay politics offers to this ideological formation is the risk of acknowledging that, on the contrary, we are as human as everyone else. It is precisely this threat that the discourse of "promotion" therefore aims to forestall. What is new is the tacit recognition that there is no going back to the strategy of criminalizing sexual acts, and with this we witness a displaced concern with the role of *representation,* as in so many other areas of contemporary moralism. The discourse of "promition" therefore aims to saturate the image of "the homosexual" with the raditional connotations of depraved sexual acts, and to prevent the cultural acceptability of gay identity, and sexual diversity rooted in the principle of sexual choice. It is choice that the discourse of "promotion" wishes to deny, and it is on this level and around these terms that gay politics will undoubtedly have to fight its major battles in the 1990s.

NOTES

1. Rainer Maria Rilke, "How Childhood tries to reach us," *Selected Works Volume 2, Poetry,* ed. J. B. Leishman (London: Hogarth Press, 1967), 322.

2. Jacqueline Rose, *The Case of Peter Pan, or The Impossibility of Children's Fiction* (London: Macmillan, 1984), 12.

3. Tim Rollins, Education and Democracy," in *Democracy: A Project by Group Material,* ed. B. Wallis (Seattle: Bay Press, 1990), 47.

4. For example, see Lisa Duggan, "On Sex Panics," *Artforum 28,* no. 2 (October 1989): 26–27.

5. See Simon Watney, *Policing Desire: Pornography, AIDS, and the Media* (Minneapolis: University of Minnesota Press, 1989).

6. See Simon Watney, "Practices of Freedom: 'Citizenship' and the Politics of Identity in the Age of AIDS," in *Identity: Community, Culture, Difference,* ed. J. Rutherford (London: Lawrence and Wishart, 1990).

7. Indecency prosecutions against gay men in the U.K. have risen from 857 in 1985 to an astonishing 2,022 in 1989.

8. See Simon Watney, "Introduction," in *Taking Liberties: AIDS and Cultural Politics,* ed. Erica Carter and Simon Watney (London: Serpent's Tail Press, 1989).

9. Department of Education and Science, *Circular 11* (1987).

10. See Douglas Crimp, "How to Have Promiscuity in an Epidemic," in *AIDS: Cultural Analysis, Cultural Activism,* ed. Douglas Crimp (Cambridge, MA: MIT Press, 1988).

11. Quoted in Madeleine Colvin with Jane Hawksley, *Section 28: A Practical Guide to the Law and Its Implications* (London: National Council for Civil Liberties, 1989), 12.

12. *Health Education from 5 to 16* (London: Her Majesty's Stationery Office, 1986).

13. *Health Education from 5 to 16.*

14. Michel Foucault, *Semiotext(e) Special, Intervention Series 2: Loving Children* (Summer 1980): 41–42.

15. Michael R. Kagay, "Homosexuals Gain More Acceptance," *New York Times,* 25 October, 1989, A24.

16. "Is It Still OK to Be Gay?" *New Woman* (October, 1990): 16–20.

17. See Crimp "How to Have Promiscuity," 10.

18. Sigmund Freud, "The Sexual Life of Human Beings," in *Introductory Lectures on Psychoanalysis* (Harmondsworth: Penguin, 1972), 353.

19. Ibid.

20. Sigmund Freud, "Civilised' Sexual Morality and Modern Nervous Illness," *Penguin Freud Library Vol. 12* (Harmondsworth: Penguin, 1977).

21. Freud, "The Sexual Life," 353.

22. Hannah Arendt, "The Crisis In Education," *Between Past and Future: Eight Exercises in Political Thought* (Harmondsworth: Penguin, 1977), 181–82.

23. Foucault, *Semiotext(e),* 42.

CHAPTER 10

MULTICULTURALISM

AND

OPPOSITIONALITY

MICHELE WALLACE

Many individual events on the current cultural landscape conspire to make me obsessed with contemporary debates over "multiculturalism" in both the art world and the culture at large, but my concern is grounded first and foremost in my observation of the impact of present material conditions of an increasing sector of the population. These material conditions, which include widespread homelessness, joblessness, illiteracy, crime, disease (including AIDS), hunger, poverty, drug addiction, alcoholism, as well as the various habits of ill health, and the destruction of the environment are (let's face it) the myriad social effects of late multinational capitalism.

In New York City where I live the population most affected by these conditions consists largely of people of African, Latino, or Asian descent, some of whom are gay—blacks either from, or one or two generations removed from, the South, the Caribbean, or Africa, or Latinos of mixed race from the Caribbean or Central or South America, or Asians from Korea, the Philippines, or China. In other parts of the country, the ethnic composition of the population that is most economically and politically disenfranchised may vary to include more poor whites, women, and children of all races and ethnicities, gays, Native Americans, and Chicanos. In New York City this population, which accounts for more than half the population of the city, is menaced in very specific ways by inadequate and formidably expensive housing and medical care, by extremely shoddy and bureaucracy-ridden systems of social services and public education, by an inefficient, militaristic police force, and by increasing street violence and crime promoted by drug trafficking and high rates of drug addiction.

One of the immediate consequences of this system is that most people who are not rich, white, and male (and therefore virtually never leave the Upper Eastside) live in fear in New York City. And contrary to the impression that one might get based on the overreporting of those incidents that involve black-on-white crime, it is women, children, and old people, and especially young men of color, who live under the greatest and most constant threat. Last spring and summer, even as multiculturalism was being debated in the cultural pages of the Sunday *New York Times* and celebrated by a variety of cultural events in the art world, New York City's nonwhite community was being doubly menaced by a series of events, the symbolic and/or political weight of which tended to endow them with a certain quality of hyperreality, however fleeting.

These events were 1) the black boycott of the Korean fruit market in Flatbush, held in response to high prices and the alleged ill treatment of a Haitian woman; 2) the trials of the murderers of Yusef Hawkins; 3) the trials of the Central Park rapists; and 4) the story of producer Cameron MacKintosh's resistance to the American Actor's Equity's decision that the white British actor Jonathan Pryce should be replaced by an Asian as the lead in the Broadway version of the musical *Miss Saigon*. Perhaps the media representation of each of these events deserves its own analysis at some point, although I'm not sure that any one of them significantly departs from well-established media patterns in racializing various kinds of "news" stories, especially those stories that include underlying gender issues.[1] Rather in this instance I wish to invoke them, and their extraordinary coverage in the mainstream media, as a background to the present discussion of "multiculturalism."

The character of the response—in the media and in the streets—to the trials of the Central Park rapists and the murders of Yusef Hawkins, the *Miss Saigon* debate, and the Korean store boycott begins to give us some idea of the complex and contradictory attitudes in the dominant culture toward events that take place at the interstices of racial and social difference. The Central Park rape incident was first portrayed as "wilding" by New York City newspapers, a term apparently relevant only to the gang violence of black male youths, for it was not used to describe the attack by white male youths on Yusef Hawkins in Bensonhurst.

As for the black boycott of the Korean store in Flatbush and the refusal of producer Cameron MacKintosh to bring *Miss Saigon* to Broadway given the insistence on the part of Actor's Equity that Pryce be replaced by an Asian, the former event was handled by the New York City press as though it were a transparent case of black-on-Asian racism, whereas the latter event was reported as a blow for "artistic freedom," "freedom of expression," and even "multiculturalism." In the process, a mockery was made of the history of Asians in the American theater; Yul Brynner in *The King and I,* as well as the white actor who played Charlie Chan, were paraded as positive examples of "nontraditional casting."

While it is not surprising to encounter these contradictory attitudes in the mainstream, it is interesting to note how related ideological conflicts are played out in the programming and attitudes of the art world and the cultural left. Thus far this particular area of multicultural discourse has centered around attempts by writers, artists, and others to establish relationships or kinships between issues of gender, sexuality, and ethnicity. In the past, the problem for cultural activitists has been how to theorize links between the establishment commonalities among diverse constituencies. The current left cultural and art world versions of multiculturalism respond to this problem by circumventing theoretical discourse altogether in favor of a virtually unrestricted inclusiveness. I suspect that the link that multiculturalism is trying to establish between discourses on feminism, sexual preference, and ethnicity could be more usefully viewed as a pragmatic political coalition: the cultural left version of Jesse Jackson's Rainbow Coalition against the rising tide of the conservative Right.

While multiculturalism's inclination toward unrestricted inclusiveness as opposed to hierarchical exclusiveness doesn't automatically lead to significant structural changes in existing aesthetic and critical priorities and institutional discourses of power, it could and thus far has offered more opportunities for critical discussion outside the dominant discourse, and dissent and debate within, than its present aesthetic and critical alternatives. These alternatives I see as 1) a "color-blind" cultural homogeneity which originates in liberal humanist ideology; 2) separatist aesthetics and politics such as "Afrocentrism"; and 3) racist/sexist aesthetics, which range from the cultural fascism of a Hilton Kramer in the *New Criterion* to the social fascism of such right-wing vigilantes as the Ku Klux Klan and the youth gangs that attacked Yusef Hawkins in Bensonhurst and the female jogger in Central Park. Thus, despite my reservations about multiculturalism, I have become a reluctant supporter of it. At the same time it is crucial to its usefulness that we view multiculturalism not as an obdurate and unchanging ideological position, but as an opportunity for ongoing critical debate.[2]

In an essay on "Endangered: Art and Performance by Men of Color" (a series of performances and exhibitions that included Marlon Riggs and Essex Hemphill at Intermedia Arts Minneapolis in 1990), Asian (Sansei) cultural critic and poet David Mura Juxtaposes the exemplary multiculturalism of this series with Richard Bernstein's remarks on the threat of multiculturalism in a recent *New York Times* article entitled "The Arts Catch Up with a Society in Disarray" (Sept. 2, 1990). In reading Mura's essay, I am reminded that my remarks about multculturalism are designed to invert Bernstein's. Mura summarizes Bernstein, who characterizes multiculturalism as "the new tribalism," in this way:

> Bernstein quotes Arthur Schlesinger's remark that the melting pot has yielded to the "Tower of Babel." In a seeming effort to complicate Schlesinger's observation, Bernstein admits there is a necessary connection between "artistic matters and the harsh world of the streets, where things seem to be getting conspicuously worse." What follows is a litany of the recent racial cases which have rocked New York—the rape and assault of the Central Park Jogger, the incident in Bensonhurst, Tawana Brawley, the picketing of Korean grocers, Washington, D.C. Mayor Barry's drug trial. Through such a listing, Bernstein creates an unspoken association in the reader's mind: minority artists find their sources in the violence of the streets; this is the main difference between minority artists and mainstream tradition. A further implication: minority arts represent the anger and violence of the barbarians at the gate, figures of chaos and dissolution.

While Mura goes on to talk about other issues around multiculturalism, I would like to reclaim here Bernstein's image of social chaos as the basis for any successful multiculturalism. The politicization of art that he is railing against is precisely what is absolutely necessary. As for a society in disarray: when has American society ever been in order for people of color and people of sensitivity, for those who are visibly and invisibly other? For the poor, the gay, the women, the children, the disabled, the elderly, the not-white? "society" is now in disarray for Bernstein only because he, and those of his cast of mind, have been forced to recognize that they are not the only ones on this planet, that they are, in fact, a distinct although not yet endangered "minority."

In the following remarks I want to analyze three contemporary instances of multicultural programming and art work: the panel and film series "Sexism, Colonialism, Misrepresentation: A Corrective Film Series," held at the Dia Art Foundation and the Collective for Living Cinema in New York City and organized by the feminist film critic Bérénice Reynaud and filmmaker Yvonne Rainer; *The Decade Show,* a joint exhibition of the New Museum of Contemporary Art and the Museum of Contemporary Hispanic Art, which are across the street from each other in Soho, and The Studio Museum in Harlem; and Yvonne Rainer's film *Privilege* (1990).

These events exemplify an interrelated set of issues relevant to current multicultural practice in the art world: the problematic elision of race within dominant psychoanalytic models of criticism, the accompanying lack of work by people of color that theorizes the relation of race to issues of class and gender, and finally, the tendency in multicultural programming to rely on artists and writers of color as the "subject matter" whose experience is then reconstituted through the theoretical elaboration of white intellectuals.

I want to begin by considering the controversy surrounding the coverage of "Sexism, Colonialism, Misrepresentation" by the Cuban American critic and curator Coco Fusco in the pages of *Afterimage* and *Screen* (she also reviewed the Celebration of Black Cinema Conference in Boston in the same articles). The event consisted of a series of three panels and the screening of 40 films from Africa, Australia, the Middle and Far East, Latin America, and Europe. These films included, in addition to many films by people of color, films by white feminists and even one film by a white male on the French Left. Instead of discussing the films—a possibly endless discussion given the range of aesthetic and critical issues arising from any series of independent films—or even all three of the panels, I would like to focus on Fusco's criticism of one of the panels—"The Visual Construction of Sexual Difference"—and on the defense of the series by Rainer and Reynaud. Before going any further, I should say that not only was I involved in the "Sexism, Colonialism, Misrepresentation" conference, but I am recently acquainted and friendly with Reynaud and Rainer and a close friend of Fusco. As such, it would be both impossible and ill-advised for me to attempt to engage in a thorough critique of their works or their intentions, especially since I am wholly sympathetic to their various endeavors. It is my assumption that Coco, Bérénice, Yvonne, and I are on the same side in matters having to do with gender, culture, and the mythologies and realities of "race."

Fusco begins her discussion by reminding us that "the blossoming of multicultural media events" is a response to the "perceived need to redress the effective ethnic segregation of the art world." The particular division of labor that she describes is one in which white, "avant-garde" intellectuals "theorize about racism while ethnic film and video producers supply 'experiential' materials in the form of testimony and documentation, or in which the white intelligentsia solicits token third world intellectuals to theorize about the question—that is, the problem of the 'other'—for the white intelligentsia."

Much more insidious to me than the problem of white intellectuals theorizing nativist "data" is the problem of "whiteness' itself as an unmarked term in such conferences and discussions. This was particularly noticeable in the discussions that followed the panel on "The Visual Construction of Sexual Difference." A large portion of time was given over to arguing about what could be expected of psychoanalysis in terms of cultural resistance, whether or not psychoanalysis could be historicized, and whether it could be made to do political readings of cultural production. For the most part, the participants seemed thoroughly convinced that such a combination would be unthinkable.

What Fusco says about the problem of this panel is that, first, "to ignore white ethnicity is to redouble its hegemony by naturalizing it. Without specifically addressing white ethnicity there can be no critical evaluation of the construction of the other." Second, she says, "it did not officially include any interrogation of the eurocentric prioritization of sexual difference." Of the conference overall, she further says, "there operated a eurocentric presumption that sexual difference could be separated from other forms of difference and that the theoretical models that privilege gender-based sexual difference could be used to understand other differ- ence."

My view, however, is that the challenge of multicultural criticism cannot be met simply by prioritizing other kinds of difference to the exclusion of gender but rather by theorizing sexuality, the body, and gender from other cultural perspec- tives. The solution is not to reject Freudian, Lacanian, and Foucauldian discourses about sexual difference out of hand in order to return to the pragmatics of race and class, for then we confront the old problem of a reductive "social realism" hamstringing critical analysis. Moreover, we don't want to neglect the contribution that feminist thought on the left (in both cultural studies and psychoanalytic film criticism) has made to thinking about cultural responsibility—specifically the idea that gender and sexuality are socially and culturally constructed, yet individual desire is never fully described or subsumed or determined by such constructions.

It is true that the left feminist avant-garde has had a rocky and uneven history (which needs to be recorded) in dealing with its own tendencies toward racism, elitism, and cultural apartheid. But it is also true that this sector, unlike any other, has been instrumental in foregrounding a political discourse on art and culture, thus fostering a climate in which it becomes at least hypothetically possible to publicly review and interrogate that very history of exclusion and racism.

The problem remains, however, that within the various progressive political and cultural positions there is an almost total lack of theoretical discourse that relates "race" to gender and sexuality. It is not often recognized that bodies and psyches of color have trajectories in excess of their socially and/or culturally constructed identities. What is needed to achieve effective social change is some intervention in the present deployment of these bodies and psyches, an intervention that demands a sophisticated level of theorization of racial and social identity. This is where the extra extraordinary, thus far insuperable difficulty arises in effecting concrete social transformation through discussions of cultural interpretation. In the rush to analyze, many of us not only reinscribe eurocentric dominance and hegemony but also stifle the possibility of more pragmatic interpretations based on the belief that psychoanalytic and other forms of theory simply can't deal with racial differences.

For me, the most interesting thing said in the panel was Joan Copjec's commentary drawing from the work of Frantz Fanon, the African psychoanalyst in *Black Skins, White Masks:* ". . . the most insidious effect of the colonizing enterprise is that it constructs the very desires of the colonizing subject. The danger lies in the implied assumption that the content of desire is defined by the apparatuses of domination" and "Psychoanalysis has never claimed that the subject is totally mastered by the social order. Psychoanalysis is the discourse which obliges us to think the subversion of mastery—not only of the subject by itself, but also the subject by the social."

Such ideas seem crucial to reconceptualizing the black female subject, black feminist cultural resistance, and a multicultural consciousness. And yet the discussion that followed Copjec's remarks seemed extremely uneasy about the relevance of such a discourse to other than middle-class white feminist women, as though a culturally relativist perspective would preclude any attempt at psychoanalytic interpretations of subjectivity.

The problem arises in panels such as this from a basic misunderstanding. Despite the general critique of essentialism in many feminist discussions, when Reynaud asks the panelists and the audience, "So which father are we talking about? Are we talking about the heterosexual, repressive father, about the white father, about the master of language, about the colonialist father, the capitalist father? We are constructing these fathers, and we are constructed by them. When we talk about patriarchy, what are we talking about? Who is the enemy?" she implicitly identifies herself and other white feminists on the left with the "colonized." Yet neither bell hooks, nor Isaac Julien and Kobena Mercer in their subsequent comments, felt as though they could afford to confuse the position of white women in discourse with the position of the racially and ethnically colonized. "How does the canon of psychoanalytic discourse deal with the absence of black women in these new forms (TV, film) of representation?" Julien asks: "I think the Law of the Father is different from the Law of the Land," Julien further proposes, "and this is an inseparable identity for black subjectivity."

In such exchanges everyone is far too polite to come out and say the thing that needs to be said first—women are not to be trusted just because they're women, any more than blacks are to be trusted because they're black, or gays because they're gay and so on. Unfortunately what proves this position, besides the glaring examples of women, blacks, or gays who are profoundly reactionary, is precisely such superficially progressive discourses as feminist psychoanalytic film criticism which one can read for days on end without coming across any lucid reference to, or critique of, "race."

How am I to understand this discourse as oppositional if it seems to do even less than the classic film tradition it reflects upon to challenge or interrogate racial/cultural apartheid? If racism (racial stereotyping and/or the confinement of black characters to the margins of the plot) is one of the most fundamental features of the Hollywood classic film tradition and, moreover, if the way in which such racism was imposed upon black female characters is eminently describable, how are we to regard the exclusion of such material altogether from what purports to be an ideological critique?

When Constance Penley suggests in a discussion that "we have to accept psychoanalysis in terms of its quite modest claim. It is a theory of sexual difference. It may not be easily articulable to the other kinds of differences discussed today," I can only respond that I am unwilling to cede sexual difference to white women. Sexual difference is something that women of color, poor women, and gay women share with white middle-class women. How am I supposed to regard a theory of sexual difference that doesn't apply to women of color? To my mind such theoretical discourses, in which "race" is marginalized, trivialized, and excluded, provide the component parts for the structure of racism in the dominant discourse. It has meant and continues to mean that as you turn to the cultural left you are greeted by the emphatic symbolic representation of your own invisibility. At least "race" is real to the reactionary Right.

I'd like to suggest that there may be opportunities for control and theorizing that are not being adequately seized by people of color. People of color need to be engaged in critical and/or theorizing practices around multiculturalism as it is currently being developed in cultural institutions, in universities, and in public schools. Where I see the most intensive theorizing going on among African-American critics, for example, is in academia and in response to texts, particularly historical literary texts. Although such activity is important and necessary, I also think that given the political/economic context in which we're living we have a responsibility to reach a broader audience by making connections between the interpretation of canonical texts, tradition building, and what is happening in the Supreme Court and the Middle East today.

Yvonne Rainer's film *Privilege* is a laudable effort on the part of a white, feminist avant-garde filmmaker to integrate issues of race and ethnicity into her work. Yet, however intriguing the result is, the film is still depressing for its inability to take seriously the subjectivities of women of color. Again, I want to emphasize that what is at issue here is not whether or not bodies of color are included on the set or in the film (or on the panel). In this case, the shortcoming of multiculturalism is a structural dilemma. In order for me to believe that the subjectivities of women of color have been taken seriously, I have to see a structural change in the ways in which their voices are incorporated into the cultural discourse.

I am also disturbed by the feeling that I need to do this kind of postmortem on a work of art because, right or wrong, I still believe that artists are special and that the cult status of the work of art is not all bullshit. And I definitely don't believe in censorship. To the contrary, I wish more white feminist cultural producers and artists would foreground "race" in their work. On the other hand, if I haven't the right as a black feminist to critique what they've done, then the positive effects of the effort are canceled.

Although *Privilege* is in an entirely different league from such mainstream filmic attempts to deal with race as *Long Walk Home, Cry Freedom, Betrayed, Mississippi Burning, Round Midnight,* or *Bird* in that Rainer allows women of color to speak from a variety of positions, the filmmaker still shows no concrete interest in having the women of color themselves theorize race, or class, or gender. The positions from which women of color speak in the film are qualitatively different from, and inferior to, the positions from which white women, white men, and men of color speak.

The ideological positions from which white men speak are the least complex and interesting. Although the lawyer who works in the D.A.'s office is portrayed as a humane character, he's still a racist and a sexist. The "white male" medical authorities (some of whom are women) that pervade the film in its documentary sections are almost comic in their inflexible pathologizing and palpable ignorance of female sexuality. Nevertheless and needless to say, white men come across with as much authority as ever.

The white women—from the white female, Jenny, whose storytelling structures the film's plot to the former anarchists who are interviewed about their experience of menopause—are repeatedly humanized through close-ups, point-of-view shots, and dialogue. As viewers we are encouraged to identify with Jenny's anxiety about aging, her fantasies about men, her guilty admission that she lied under oath in order to get the Latino Carlos convicted. The interviews with the former anarchists in which they weave aspects of their political lives into their reflections on menopause are equally fascinating. The women emerge completely triumphant over the symptoms the white male doctors describe.

The men of color, much like the white men, are highly inflexible and one-dimensional. Almost everything they say is from a text by a male author of color—Piri Thomas, Eldridge Cleaver, Frantz Fanon, etc—selected precisely for its author's inability to conceptualize black female subjectivity. Moreover the film dwells on the issue of whether black men or Latino men want to rape white women, a question that is both irritating and uninteresting to me. Rainer's film attempts to deal with issues of race and gender but ignores the historical rape of the black woman—which literally founded the African-American race and the African diaspora. What interests me is the larger issue of how dominant ideologies and discourses of power continue to structure desire. This is particularly true for men, black, white, and brown, but it is also true for women.

Which brings us to the women of color in the film. The film begins with a documentary-style interview with a nameless black woman, a "native," about menopause. That woman is my mother, Faith Ringgold. Ringgold is an important African-American artist and one of the key early black feminist voices in antiwar, antiracist, and feminist art-world activism. Yet she isn't asked to talk about the impact of race on menopause, or race in the art world or the film world, or anything that might identify her as who and what she is—a highly opinionated and influential black female subject. Three other interviews with black women, at least two of whom were recommended by Ringgold, are interspersed within the main narrative. Ringgold's statement that "Getting older is a bitch" opens the film since it foreshadows the main character Jenny's perspective on aging, not because it problematizes racial privileges. Rainer admits in a recent interview to having "missed an opportunity to ask the women of color in the film how they felt race impinged on their aging and on their treatment by the medical establishment."[3]

Novella Nelson plays the black Yvonne Washington whom we are supposed to conceive as a kind of alter ego of the white Yvonne Rainer. The black Yvonne, we are told, is the "author" of the documentary on menopause for which Ringgold and other black women are interviewed but not asked about race. But despite the apparent promotion of a fully developed alternative subjectivity, or alternative position in discourse, Yvonne serves largely as a foil or straight man for Jenny's narcissistic reveries. In interviews, Rainer has credited Novella Nelson with having impacted on the final form of the film by improvising lines which she chose to leave in. Nelson's desire to intervene in the script doesn't surprise me at all, given the film's equation, at one point, of race and gender with feces and blood, as an explanation for why white men find "blacks and women" equally contemptible. As far as I'm concerned, this theory of racism, which she borrows from Joel Kovel, is thoroughly inadequate because it discounts the historical accomplishments of African-American culture and other cultures of the African diaspora. For the most part, the alternative subjectivities of women of color are a product of precisely such cultures.

Finally, the representation of Digna (Gabriella Farrar), the Latino woman who is beaten up by Carlos and subsequently incarcerated in Bellevue, is perhaps the most deeply problematic. The antithesis of madness to "voice" is not sufficiently interrogated. Digna "speaks" from Bellevue in a straightjacket about how Latino women are more likely to be diagnosed as schizophrenic. But not only is the viewer never told where this information comes from; there is no suggestion that this Latino woman might be able to resist or subvert such a deadly cultural hegemony. More to the point: women of color don't generally speak from madhouses. Is the voice and visualization of Digna, a Latino woman, so deeply problematic for Rainer that she can only be figured "speaking" under the profound erasure of a straightjacket and incarceration in a mental hospital?

Does this mean that Digna is the most oppressed? Is she meant to represent a kind of extreme antitheses to "privilege": the subject who is completely without privilege? Rainer establishes a hierarchical continuum along which the individual's potential capacity for racial and gendered privilege and victimization is carefully calibrated. According to this view white men can't be victims any more than a Latino woman of color can have privilege. In summation, my point is that, while women of color were ostensibly allowed "to speak in their own voices" in *Privilege,* they were not empowered to structure the discourse of the film. Nor will women viewers of color be empowered to imagine themselves as structuring subjects of film discourse. Or if they are (and this would be the best scenario) it will be to rebel against the invisible but nevertheless real authority of Rainer as a preeminent feminist filmmaker, and other well-meaning artists, theorists, and academic intellectuals.

If we move from the Rainer film to the *Decade Show* we encounter an instance of "multicultural" programming that seems intensely engaged by issues of authority, authenticity, who speaks for whom, and how discourses that flatten and trivialize difference are constructed. But there is a level of failure in this exhibition that demonstrates the failure of the present potential for multicultural discourses as processed by white feminists.

The *Decade Show* is an example of programming and theorizing by white feminists. When I speak of white feminists I am talking about Marsha Tucker, the director of the New Museum, whose background in the left art world goes back to the 1960s, and about Laura Trippi and Gary Sangster, who were the New Museum's curators for this exhibition. Although curators and personnel were involved at the other two institutions, in their catalog statements they made clear that what they hoped to achieve is distinctly pragmatic. In contrast, the New Museum's conception of the show is self-consciously theoretical. Sharon Patton, the curator from the Studio Museum for the *Decade Show* begins by writing:

For the Studio Museum in Harlem, the **Decade Show** is a curatorial endeavor to insert artists of color, especially African American artists, into the history of contemporary art in the U.S. The institutional agendas were clear: first, to present in a national arena African American artists; and second, to affirm cultural pluralism within the theatre of the art world. The exhibition is a response, albeit not unique nor the first, to the exclusion of many African American artists from the critical literature, art history, and exhibitions on American art. Many of the presented artists have been denied, or have had limited access to "mainstream" modernist and postmodernist documentation in terms of professional recognition (other than peers) and legitimization."[4]

In the context of "socially conscious art," which Patton says is the "agenda of the eighties," she is talking about African-American artists getting their piece of the economic pie, sharing in the enormous wealth of the art world. Except in regard to her critique of racial exclusion, Patton is not suggesting any profound alteration in the structure of the mainstream.

The same is true of the essay by the curator from the Museum of Contemporary Hispanic Art. While Julia Herzberg invokes the necessity for "meaningful crosscultural dialogue" and "comprehensive inclusion," her essay, even more than the essay by Patton, provides an inventory of Latin American artists that focuses intensively on the value and originality of their art, in other words, on their ability to produce the transcendent art object upon which the cult value and the market value of art are based.

It is Laura Trippi and Gary Sangster, curators at the New Museum, who take on the task of providing the conjunction of cultural practices, cultural production, and economic, the theoretical overview, the context for interpreting political, and social realities.

> A cornerstone of modern Western aesthetics—with its impressionisms and expressionisms, on the one hand, and its ideals of disinterested, universal judgement on the other—the idea of the autonomous self helped provide a base for the larger edifice of modernity, an edifice built for the benefit of a largely white, largely male few, at the expense of the many. The application of dialogic models to considerations of identity suggested that the self be understood not as an entity but as a provisional construction, a weave of differing dialogic, or discursive, threads.[5]

This exhibition, Trippi and Sangster argue, whether the artist is gay, or feminist, or a person of color, or some combination, is not really about "identity" as a unified, monological field but about "identities." They quote from and heavily rely upon Stuart Hall for this observation. As Hall says in ICA Document 6 in an essay called "Minimal Selves,"

> It may be true that the self is always, in a sense, a fiction, just as the kind of "closures" which are required to create communities of identification— nation, ethnic group, families, sexualities, etc.—are arbitrary closures; and the forms of political action, whether movements, or parties, or classes, those too, are temporary, partial, arbitrary. It is an immensely important gain when one recognizes that all identity is constructed across difference.

The extraordinary and ironic thing about the authority of Hall's remarks in this context is that although the ideas come from poststructuralist thought, they are filtered through the imagination of a very committed political activist who happens to also be black and originally from the Caribbean. Needless to say, he is not identified as such by the Trippi/Sangster essay. So Hall speaks here not only about ideas but also about material realities. In a very concrete and specific sense, the so-called "identity" of the diasporic subject is constructed out of a plurality of "wheres" and "whats," as well as where and what one is not. As Gayatri Spivak, West, Hall, Hortense Spillers, hooks, Trinh Minh-ha and so many other people of color who are interested in what is vaguely called "theory" might remind us, the nature of the "overview" changes depending upon "the politics of location" of the "author." For instance, in the Trippi/Sangster essay, the reality of the art world in the 1980s is described in terms of the metaphor of a board game called "Trivial Pursuit," and the art of making a deal is discussed in the sense that Donald Trump might use the word "deal." How real is this picture for artists of color or for critics or museum administrators of color? Where is the overview of artists and cultural critics of color on the left emanating from marginal theories and practices themselves? Don't we need one? Who will write it?

NOTES

1. In each case, gender provides an underlying impetus for an explicitly racial story: in the Korean fruit market boycott, a black woman is allegedly struck by an asian male; in the Central Park rape a white woman is raped by black and Puerto Rican boys and men; in the Yusef Hawkins murder, we are told the initial provocation had to do with the suspicion that a white Bensonhurst girl was dating a black boy. In the case of the Cameron MacIntosh/*Ms. Saigon* debacle, the part that Jonathan Pryce will play is a pimp who sells sex with Vietnamese women to mostly white American GIs.

2. As last year's debates on culture in the mainstream press tended to center on censorship, this year's round of debates has centered on the notion of "political correctness." Interestingly enough, if one sees the censorship debate and the political correctness debate as stages in a larger, ongoing multiculturalism debate, then one will also see the continuous underlying motivation of the dominant discourse is to delay and/or forego the validation of alternative subjectivities and discourses as long as possible in favor of reconsolidating the center as one in which all debates are between "the left" and "the right," both of whom are viewed as white (they have no ethnicity or "race"). Of course, racial issues are continually subsumed by the so called larger debates of censorship or political correctness and, in the process, blacks are neatly objectified (from the naked, black male bodies in Mapplethorpe to the black female college student who gloats over having been able to function as a racist for a semester in Jules Feiffer's cartoon about political correctness).

3. Yvonee Rainer: *Declaring States* (San Francisco: San Francisco Cinematheque, 1990), 9.

4. Sources: Coco Fusco, "Fantasies of Oppositionality," *Afterimage* 16, no. 5 (Dec. 1988), 6–9 and *Screen* 29, no. 4 (Winter 1988) "The Last Special Issue on Race?" which also includes Coco Fusco's "Fantasies of Oppositionality-Reflections on Recent Conferences in Boston and New York," as well as other pivotal essays such as "De Margin and De Centre," the introduction by Isaac Julien and Kobena Mercer, Jane Gaines, "White Privilege and Looking Relations-Race and Gender in Feminist Film Theory," Mathia Diawara's "Black Spectatorship-Problems of Identification and Resistance," and Judith Williamson's "Two Kinds of Otherness: Black Film and the Avant-Garde," Yvonne Rainer's response, "More Oppositionality," and Coco Fusco's reply, *Afterimage* 17, 2 (Sept. 1989) 2–3, and *Screen* 30, no. 3 (Summer 1989), which includes Bernice Reynaud's and Yvonne Rainer's responses to Fusco's essay, as well as a reply to them by Fusco. Lucy R. Lippard, *Mixed Blessings: New Art in a Multicultural America* (New York: Pantheon, 1990).

5. Eunice Lipton et. al., *The Decade Show: Frameworks of Identity in the 1980s* (New Museum of Contemporary Art, 1990). "Sexism, Colonialism, Misrepresentation," in *Motion Picture* 3 no. 3–4 (Summer-Autumn 1990), Collective for Living Cinema.

CHAPTER 11

···

MULTICULTURALISM

AND THE POST-

MODERN CRITIQUE:

TOWARD A PEDAGOGY

OF RESISTANCE AND

TRANSFORMATION

···

PETER MCLAREN

FOR THE PROLETARIAT DOES NOT NEED
ALL THE THOUSANDS OF LITTLE WORDS BY WHICH THE BOURGEOISIE MASKS CLASS
STRUGGLES IN ITS OWN PEDAGOGY. THE "UNPREJUDICED," "UNDERSTANDING," "EM-
PATHETIC" BOURGEOISIE PRACTICES, THE "CHILD-LOVING" TEACHERS—THESE WE
CAN DO WITHOUT. —WALTER BENJAMIN, "PROGRAM FOR A PROLETARIAN CHIL-
DREN'S THEATER"

···

SOCIAL JUSTICE UNDER SIEGE

We inhabit skeptical times, historical moments spawned in a temper of distrust, disillusionment, and despair. Social relations of discomfort and diffidence have always preexisted us but the current historical juncture is particularly invidious in this regard, marked as it is by a rapture of greed, untempered and hypereroticized consumer will, racing currents of narcissism, severe economic and racial injustices, and heightened social paranoia. The objective conditions of Western capitalism now appear so completely incompatible with the realization of freedom and libera- tion that it is no understatement to consider them mutually antagonistic enterprises. Situated beyond the reach of ethically convincing forms of accountability, capitalism has dissolved the meaning of democracy and freedom into glossy aphorisms one finds in election campaign sound bytes or at a bargain basement sales in suburban shopping malls. The American public has been proffered a vision of democracy that is a mixture of Sunday barbecue banality, American Gladiator jocksniffery, AMWAY enterprise consciousness, and the ominous rhetoric of "New World Order" jingoism.

The heroic cult of modernism which has naturalized the power and privilege of "dead white men" and accorded the pathology of domination the status of cultural reason has all but enshrined a history of decay, defeat, and moral panic. As illustrated so vividly in Oliver Stone's television mini-series, *Wild Palms,* greed, avarice, and cynicism have insinuated themselves into virtually every aspect of cultural life, and have become rationalized and aestheticized as necessary resources that must be fed into a vast technological machine known as Western civilization. It is history that has installed Willie Horton into our structural unconscious and helped make possible and desirable the legal torture and dehumanization of Rodney King and peoples of color in general. That the fortified, postmodern *noir* metropolises of this fin-de-siècle era have grown more Latinophobic, homophobic, xenophobic, sexist, racist, and bureaucratically cruel is not reflective of the self-understanding of the public at large but of the way that the public has been constructed through a politics of representation linked to the repressive moralism of the current conservative political regime and current counterattacks on cultural democracy from the Right. We should not forget, as well, the spectatorial detachment of those postmodern free-floating intellectuals who, despite their claim to be part of a collective deconstructive project, often fail to mobilize intellectual work in the interest of a liberatory praxis.

The present moral apocalypse, perhaps most vividly represented by the maelstrom of anger and violence under the smoke-filled skies of Los Angeles—what Mike Davis calls the "L.A. Intifada" (Katz and Smith, 1992)—has not been brought on simply by the existence of midnight hustlers, the drug trade, skewered ambition, or gang members taking advantage of public outrage over the justice system but by shifting economic, political, and cultural relations that have worsened over the last two decades. We have been standing at the crossroads of a disintegrating culture for the last two decades where we have witnessed a steady increase in the disproportionate level of material wealth, economic dislocation, and intergenerational poverty suffered by African-Americans, Latinos, and other minorities. Such conditions have been brought about by the frenetic and, at times, savage immorality of the Reagan and Bush administrations, as evidenced in their direct attacks on the underclass, the disintegration of social programs, and the general retreat from civil rights that occurred during their tenure in office.

Other characteristics of this current juncture include: changes in the structure of the U.S. economy; the declining inner-city job market; growing national "unemployment rates; a drastic decline in the number of unskilled positions in traditional blue-collar industries in urban areas; the increasing numbers of youth competing for fewer and fewer entry-level unskilled jobs; the automation of clerical labor; the movement of the African-American middle class out of the once multiclass ghetto; the shifting of service-sector employment to the suburbs (Kasinitz 1988);

the destructive competition among nations that results from a free-trade policy fueled by the retrograde notion that other nations can achieve economic growth by unbalanced sales to the U.S. market; increased global competition provoking capitalist manufacturing firms to reduce costs by exploiting immigrant workers in U.S. cities or "out-sourcing" to Third World countries; and a post-Fordist demonopolization of economic structures and the deregulation and globalization of markets, trade, and labor as well as deregulated local markets "that [make] local capital vulnerable to the strategies of corporate raiders" (Featherstone 1990, 7).

In addition, we are faced with an increasing assault on human intelligence by the architects of mass culture, an increasing dependency on social cues manufactured by the mass media to construct meaning and build consensus on moral issues, and the strengthening of what Piccone (1988, 9) has called the "unholy symbiosis of abstract individualism and managerial bureaucracies." The white-controlled media (often backed by victim-blaming white social scientists) have ignored the economic and social conditions responsible for bringing about in African-American communities what Cornel West has called a *"walking nihilism* of pervasive drug addiction, pervasive alcoholism, pervasive homicide, and an exponential rise in suicide" (cited in Stephanson 1988, 276).

Furthermore, the white media have generated the racially pornographic term "wilding" to account for recent acts of violence in urban centers by groups of young African-Americans (Cooper 1989). Apparently the term "wilding," first reported by New York City newspapers in relation to the Central Park rapists, was relevant only to the violence of black male youth, since it was conspicuously absent in press reports of the attack of white male youths on Yusef Hawkins in Bensonhurst (Wallace 1991). Thus, the postmodern image which many white people now entertain in relation to the African-American underclass is one constructed upon violence and grotesquery—a population spawning mutant Willie Horton–type youths who, in the throes of bloodlust, roam the perimeter of the urban landscape high on angel dust, randomly hunting whites with steel pipes (see Giroux's discussion of *Grand Canyon* in this volume). Latino youth fare no better in the public eye.

THE DILEMMA OF POSTMODERN CRITIQUE AND THE DEBATE OVER MULTICULTURALISM

I have foregrounded the social and cultural situatedness of oppression as a background for my discussion of multiculturalism since I share Michele Wallace's conviction that the debates over multiculturalism cannot afford to have their connection to wider material relations occulted by a focus on theoretical issues divorced from the lived experiences of oppressed groups. She is worth quoting on this issue:

Many individual events on the current cultural landscape conspire to make me obsessed with contemporary debates over "multiculturalism" in both the art world and the culture at large, but my concern is grounded first and foremost in my observation of the impact of present material conditions on an increasing sector of the population. These material conditions, which include widespread homelessness, joblessness, illiteracy, crime, disease (including AIDS), hunger, poverty, drug addiction, alcoholism as well as the various habits of ill health, and the destruction of the environment are (let's face it) the myriad social effects of late multinational capitalism. (1991, 6)

A focus on the material and global relations of oppression can help us to avoid reducing the "problem" of multiculturalism to simply one of attitudes and temperament or, in the case of the academy, to a case of textual disagreement and discourse wars. It also helps to emphasize the fact that in the United States the concoction called "multiculturalism," which has resulted from a forensic search for equality and the political ladling of the long-brewing "melting pot," has produced an aversion to rather than a respect for difference. Regrettably, multiculturalism has been too often transformed into a code word in contemporary political jargon that has been fulsomely invoked in order to divert attention from the imperial legacy of racism and social injustice in this country and the ways in which new racist formations are being produced in spaces culturally dedifferentiated and demonized by neoconservative platforms that anathematize difference through attacks on the concept of heterogeneous public cultures (see Ravitch 1990, 1991; Kimball 1991; Browder 1992).

In the sections that follow, I want to discuss recent articulations of the postmodern critique in order to examine the limitations of current conservative and liberal formulations of multiculturalism. In doing so, I would like to pose an alternative analysis. I shall argue that, despite its limitations for constructing an emancipatory politics, postmodern criticism can offer educators and cultural workers a means of problematizing the issue of difference and diversity in ways that can deepen and extend existing debates over multiculturalism, pedagogy, and social transformation. Certain new strands of postmodern critique that fall under the rubric of "political" and "critical" postmodernism deserve serious attention in this regard.

More specifically, I shall redraw the discussion of multiculturalism from the perspective of new strands of postmodern critique that emphasize the construction of "a politics of difference." I will conclude by urging critical educators to reclaim the importance of relational or global critique—in particular the concept of "totality"—in their efforts to bring history and materiality back into theoretical and pedagogical discourses.

SUBALTERN AND FEMINIST CHALLENGES TO THE POSTMODERN CRITIQUE

Enlightenment reason mocks us as we allow it to linger in our educational thinking and policies; for some of the most painful lessons provided by postmodern criticism have been that a teleological and totalizing view of scientific progress is antipathetic to liberation; that capitalism has posited an irrecuperable disjunction between ethics and economics; and that, paradoxically, modernity has produced an intractable thralldom to the very logic of domination which it has set out to contest and in doing so has reproduced part of the repression to which it has so disdainfully pointed.

The riot of contradictory perspectives surrounding the lush profusion of rival claims about what exactly constitutes the postmodern condition is perhaps one of the ironic outcomes of the condition itself. Broadly speaking, the postmodern critique concerns itself with a rejection or debunking of modernism's epistemic foundations or metanarratives; a dethronement of the authority of positivistic science that essentializes differences between what appear to be self-possessing identities, an attack on the notion of a unified goal of history, and a deconstruction of the magnificent Enlightenment swindle of the autonomous, stable, and self-contained ego that is supposed to be able to act independently of its own history, its own indigenist strands of meaning-making and cultural and linguistic situatedness, and free from inscriptions in the discourses of, among others, gender, race, and class.

Postmodern social theory has rightly claimed that we lack a vocabulary or epistemology that is able to render the world empirically discoverable or accurately mappable, and that experience and reason cannot be explained outside of the social production of intelligibility. It emphasizes the indissociability of language, power, and subjectivity. Meaning does not inhere stratigraphically within a text or in the abstract equivalence of the signified. The labyrinthian path of Enlightenment rationality has been shown to function not as an access to but rather as a detour from the iterability of meaning—from its connection to human suffering and oppression. Further, the postmodern critique has been exemplary in revealing the hopelessness of attempts by empiricists to transcend the political, ideological, and economic conditions that transform the world into cultural and social formations. While postmodern social theory has advanced our understanding of the politics of representation and identity formation, the fashionable apostasy of ceratin postmodern articulations and inflections of critical social theory have noticeably abandoned the language of social change, emancipatory practice, and transformative politics. In fact, many of them carry in their intoxication with the idea of cultural surplus a mordantly pessimistic and distinctively reactionary potential.

Postmodern criticism's shift in the concept of the political through its emphasis on signification and representation, its preoccupation with the dispersion of history into the afterimage of the text, and its challenge to logocentric conceptions of truth and experience has not gone uncontested. For instance, Paul Gilroy has made clear some of the problems with theorizing under the banner of postmodernism— if under such a banner one assumes one has constructed a politics of refusal, redemption, and emancipation. Gilroy writes:

> It is interesting to note that at the very moment when celebrated Euro-American cultural theorists have pronounced the collapse of "grand narra-

tives" the expressive culture of Britain's black poor is dominated by the need to construct them as narratives of redemption and emancipation. This expressive culture, like others elsewhere in the African diaspora, produces a potent historical memory and an authoritative analytic and historical account of racial capitalism and its overcoming. (1990, 278)

What some prominent cultural critics view as the constituent features of post-modernism—depthlessness, the retreat from the question of history, and the disappearance of affect—do not, in Gilroy's view, take seriously enough what is going on in African-American expressive culture. Blatantly contradicting this supposed "cultural dominant" of postmodernism is "the repertoire of 'hermeneutic gestures' " emanating from black expressive cultures. Gilroy points out that widely publicized views of the postmodern condition held by such prominent critics as Fredric Jameson may simply constitute another form of Eurocentric master narrative since black expressive cultures use all the new technological means at their disposal "not to flee from depth but to revel in it, not to abjure public history but to proclaim it" (1990, 278). Similarly, Cornel West (1989, 96) qualifies black cultural practices in the arts and intellectual life as examples of a "potentially enabling yet resisting postmodernism" that has grown out of

an acknowledgement of a reality that [black people] cannot *not know*—the ragged edges of the real, of necessity; a reality historically constructed by white supremacist practices in North America during the age of Europe. These ragged edges—of not being able to eat, not to have shelter, not to have health care—all this is infused into the strategies and styles of black cultural practices. (1989, 93)

Important concerns about the postmodern critique have also been posed by feminist theorists. They have questioned why men, in particular, find the new gospel of postmodernism to be so significantly compelling at this current historical moment. Not the least of their objections is related to the fact that a theoretical conversion to the postmodern critique in many instances allows men to retain their privileged status as bearers of the Word precisely because it distracts serious attention from the recent concentration on feminist discourse (Kaplan 1987, 150–52). Dominant strands of the postmodern critique also tend to delegitmize the recent literature of peoples of color, black women, Latin Americans, and Africans (Christian 1987, 55). In addition, we are reminded that just at a time in history when a great many groups are engaged in "nationalisms" which involve redefining them as marginalized Others, the academy has begun to legitimize a critical theory of the "subject" which holds the concept of agency in doubt, and which casts a general skepticism on the possibilities of a general theory which can describe the world and institute a quest for historical progress (Harstock 1987, 1989; Di Stephano, 1990).

It is difficult to argue against these calls to decapitalize the registers of Patriarchy,

Manhood, and Truth as they manifest themselves within dominant variants of the postmodern critique. And with such a consideration in mind, I would ask if it is at all possible to recuperate and extend the project of postmodernist critique within the context of a critical pedagogy of multiculturalism in a way that remains attentive to the criticisms posed above. To attempt to answer such a question demands that I establish at the outset both my own convergences with and departures from the discourse genre of postmodernism.

LUDIC AND RESISTANCE POSTMODERNISM

My general sympathy with the postmodern critique does not come without serious qualifications. Postmodernist criticism is not monolithic and for the purposes of this essay I would like to distinguish between two theoretical strands. The first has been astutely described by Teresa Ebert (1991, 115) as "ludic postmodernism"— an approach to social theory that is decidedly limited in its ability to transform oppressive social and political regimes of power. Ludic postmodernism generally focuses on the fabulous combinatory potential of signs in the production of meaning and occupies itself with a reality that is constituted by the continual playfulness of the signifier and the heterogeneity of differences. As such, ludic postmodernism (e.g., Lyotard, Derrida, Baudrillard) constitutes a moment of self-reflexivity in deconstructing Western metanarratives, asserting that "meaning itself is self-divided and undecidable" (Ebert forthcoming).

Politics, in this view, is not an unmediated referent to action that exists outside of representation. Rather, politics becomes a textual practice (e.g., parody, pastiche, fragmentation) that unsettles, decenters, and disrupts rather than transforms the totalizing circulation of meaning within grand narratives and dominant discursive apparatuses (Ebert forthcoming; Zavarzadeh and Morton 1991). While ludic postmodernism may be applauded for attempting to deconstruct the way that power is deployed within cultural settings, it ultimately represents a form of detotalizing micropolitics in which the contextual specificity of difference is set up against the totalizing machineries of domination. The contingent, in this case, determines necessity as ludic postmodernism sets up a "superstructuralism" that privileges the cultural, discursive, and ideological over the materiality of modes and relations of production (Zavarzadeh and Morton 1991).

I want to argue that educators should assume a cautionary stance toward ludic postmodernism critique because, as Ebert notes, it often simply reinscribes the status quo and reduces history to the supplementarity of signification or the free-floating trace of textuality (1991, 115). As a mode of critique, it rests its case on interrogating specific and local enunciations of oppression but often fails to analyze such enunciations in relation to larger, dominating structures of oppression (McLaren forthcoming; Aronowitz and Giroux 1992).

Ludic postmodernism is akin to what Scott Lach (1990) calls "spectral postmodernism"—a form of critique that deals with the dedifferentiation and blurring of disciplinary knowledge and genres (e.g., literature and criticism) and involves the implosion of the real into representation, the social into the mediascape, and exchange value into sign value. For the spectral postmodernists, the social is sucked up and dissolved into the world of signs and electronic communication while depth of meaning is imploded into superficiality. Pauline Marie Rosenau (1992) refers to this as "skeptical postmodernism"—a strand of postmodernism that reflects not only an ontological agnosticism that urges a relinquishing of the primacy of social transformation but also an epistemological relativism that calls for a tolerance of a range of meanings without advocating any one of them. Ludic postmodernism often takes the form of a triumphalistic and hoary dismissal of Marxism and grand theory as being hopelessly embroiled in a futile project of world-historical magnitude that is out of place in these postmodern new times. Such an endeavor often brings new forms of "totalization" into the debate through the conceptual back door of antifoundationalist theorizing.

The kind of postmodern social theory I want to pose as a counterweight to skeptical and spectral postmodernism has been referred to as "oppositional postmodernism" (Foster 1983), "radical critique-al theory" (Zavarzadeh and Morton 1991), "postmodern education" (Aronowitz and Giroux 1991), "resistance postmodernism" (Ebert 1991, forthcoming) and "critical postmodernism" (McLaren forthcoming; Giroux 1992; McLaren and Hammer 1989). These forms of critique are not alternatives to ludic postmodernism but appropriations and extensions of this critique. Resistance postmodernism brings to ludic critique a form of materialist intervention since it is not solely based on a textual theory of difference but rather on one that is social and historical. In this way, postmodern critique can serve as an interventionist and transformative critique of U.S. culture. Following Ebert, resistance postmodernism attempts to show that "textualities (significations) are material practices, forms of conflicting social relations" (1991, 115). The sign is always an arena of material conflict and competing social relations as well as ideas, and we can "rewrite the sign as an ideological process formed out of a signifier standing in relation to a matrix of historically possible or suspended signifieds" (Ebert forthcoming). In other words, difference is politicized by being situated *in* real social and historical conflicts rather than simply textual or semiotic contradictions.

Resistance postmodernism does not abandon the undecidability or contingency of the social altogether; rather, the undecidability of history is understood as related to class struggle, the institutionalization of asymmetrical relations of power and privilege, and the way historical accounts are contested by different groups (Zavarzadeh and Morton 1991; Giroux 1992; McLaren and Hammer 1989). On this matter Ebert remarks: "We need to articulate a theory of difference in which the differing, deferring slippage of signifiers is not taken as the result of the immanent logic of language but as the effect of the social conflicts traversing signification" (1991, 118). In other words, to view difference as simply textuality, as a formal, rhetorical space in which representation narrates its own trajectory of signification, is to ignore the social and historical dimensions of difference (Ebert forthcoming). Ebert elaborates this point as follows:

A postmodern analytics of difference would enable us to move beyond the theory of difference as reified experience, and to critique the historical, economic, and ideological production of difference itself as a slipping, sliding series of relations that are struggled over and which produce the significations and subjectivities by which we live and maintain existing social relations. (1991, 118)

She further describes resistance postmodernism as a politics of difference, as a theory of practice and a practice of theory:

A resistance postmodern cultural critique—interrogating the political semiosis of culture—would be an oppositional political practice produced through the activity of reading, of making sense of cultural texts. However, opposition does not lie within—in other words it is not inherent in—a text or individual but is produced out of the practice of critique itself. Moreover the critic herself is always already interpellated in the hegemonic subject positions of the culture, and contestation derives not from some will to resist but again is produced through the practice of critique. (1991, 129)

Resistance postmodernism takes into account both the macropolitical level of structural organization and the miropolitical level of different and contradictory manifestations of oppression as a means of analyzing global relations of oppression. As such, resistance postmodernism bears a considerable degree of affinity to what Scott Lash has recently termed "organic postmodernism." Organic postmodernism tries to move beyond epistemic skepticism and explanatory nihilism to concern itself with issues related not just to the commodification of language but to the commodification of labor and the social relations of production. According to Lash, it attempts to reintegrate the cultural into the natural, material environment. From this perspective, rationality is not panhistorical or universal but is always situated in particular communities of discourse. In addition, organic postmodernism argues that high modernism articulates reality in a way that often serves as a cover for validating a Cartesian universe of discrete parts disconnected from wider economies of power and privilege. In other words, high modernism is accused of collapsing difference into the uneasy harmony we know as white patriarchal privilege—a privilege inextricably bound up with nationalism, imperialism, and the state.

MULTICULTURALISM AND THE POSTMODERN CRITIQUE

In this section I want to bring a critical or resistance postmodernist perspective to bear on the issue of multiculturalism. For me, the key issue for critical educators is to develop a multicultural curriculum and pedagogy that attends to the specificity (in terms of race, class, gender, sexual orientation, etc.) of difference (which is in keeping with ludic postmodernism) yet at the same time addresses the commonality of diverse Others under the law with respect to guiding referents of freedom and liberation (which is in keeping with resistance postmodernism).

Viewed from the perspective of resistance postmodernism, the liberal and conservative attacks on multiculturalism as separatist and ethnocentric carry with them the erroneous assumption that North American society fundamentally constitutes social relations of uninterrupted accord. This view furthermore underscores the idea that North American society is largely a forum of consensus with different minority viewpoints simply accretively added on. This constitutes a politics of pluralism which largely ignores the workings of power and privilege. More specifically, it "involves a very insidious exclusion as far as any structural politics of change is concerned: it excludes and occludes global or structural relations of power as 'ideological' and 'totalizing' " (Ebert forthcoming). In addition, it presupposes harmony and agreement—an undisturbed space in which differences can coexist. Yet such a presupposition is dangerously problematic. Chandra Mohanty (1989/90) notes that the difference cannot be formulated as negotiation among culturally diverse groups against a backdrop of presumed cultural homogeneity. Difference is the recognition that knowledges are forged in histories that are riven with differentially constituted relations of power; that is, knowledges, subjectivities, and social practices are forged within "asymmetrical and incommensurate cultural spheres" (1989/90, 181).

Too often liberal and conservative positions on diversity constitute an attempt to view culture as a soothing balm—the aftermath of historical disagreement—some mythical present where the irrationalities of historical conflict have been smoothed out. This is not only a disingenuous view of culture, it is profoundly dishonest. The liberal and conservative positions on culture also assume that justice already exists and needs only to be evenly apportioned. However, both teachers and students need to realize that justice does not already exist simply because laws exist. Justice needs to be continually created, constantly struggled for. The question that I want to pose to teachers is this: Do teachers and cultural workers have access to a language that allows them to sufficiently critique and transform existing social and cultural practices that are defended by liberals and conservatives as democratic?

THE SUBJECT WITHOUT PROPERTIES

The critical postmodernist critique provides us with a way of understanding the limitations of a multiculturalism trapped within a logic of democracy that is under the sway of late capitalism. One of the surreptitious perversions of democracy has been the manner in which citizens have been invited to empty themselves of all racial or ethnic identity so that, presumably, they will all stand naked before the law.

In effect, citizens are invited to become little more than disembodied consumers. As Joan Copjec points out,

> Democracy is the universal quantifier by which America—the "melting pot," the "nation of immigrants"—constitutes itself as a nation. If *all* our citizens can be said to be Americans, this is not because we share any positive characteristics, but rather because we have all been given the right to *shed* these characteristics, to present ourselves as disembodied before the law. I divest myself of positive identity, therefore I am a citizen. This is the peculiar logic of democracy. (1991, 30)

Renato Rosaldo (1989) refers to this process as "cultural stripping," wherein individuals are stripped of their former cultures in order to become "transparent" American citizens. While the embodied and perspectival location of any citizen's identity has an undeniable effect on what can be said, democracy has nevertheless created formal identities which give the illusion of identity while simultaneously erasing difference. David Lloyd (1991, 70) refers to this cultural practice as the formation of the "subject without properties." As the dominated are invited to shed their positive identities, the dominators unwittingly serve as the regulating principle of identity itself by virtue of their very indifference.

The universality of the position of dominator is attained through its literal indifference and it "becomes representative in consequence of being able to take anyone's place, of occupying any place, of a pure exchangeability" (Lloyd 1991, 70). Such a subject without properties governs the distribution of humanity into the local (native) and the universal by assuming the "global ubiquity of the white European" which, in turn, becomes the very "regulative idea of Culture against which the multiplicity of local cultures is defined" (Lloyd 1991, 70). Lloyd notes that the domination of the white universalized subject "is virtually self-legitimating since the capacity to be everywhere present becomes an historical manifestation of the white man's gradual approximation to the universality he everywhere represents" (1991, 70).

Against this peculiar logic of democracy, resistance postmodernism argues that individuals need always to *rethink the relationship between identity and difference.* They need to understand their ethnicity in terms of a politics of location, positionality, or enunciation. Stuart Hall argues, rightly in my view, that "there's no enunciation without positionality. You have to position yourself *somewhere* in order to say anything at all" (1991, 18). One's identity, whether as black, white, or Latino, has to do with the discovery of one's ethnicity. Hall calls this process of discovery the construction of "new ethnicities" or "emergent ethnicities." Entailed in such a discovery is the

> need to honor the hidden histories from which . . . [people] . . . come. They need to understand the languages which they've been taught not to speak. They need to understand and revalue the traditions and inheritances

of cultural expression and creativity. And in that sense, the past is not only a position from which to speak, but it is also an absolutely necessary resource in what one has to say. . . . So the relationship of the kind of ethnicity I'm talking about to the past is not a simple, essential one—it is a constructed one. It is constructed in history, it is constructed politically in part. It is part of narrative. We tell ourselves the stories of the parts of our roots in order to come into contact, creatively, with it. So this new kind of ethnicity—the emergent ethnicities—has a relationship to the past, but it is a relationship that is partly through memory, partly through narrative, one that has to be recovered. It is an act of cultural recovery. (Hall 1991, 18–19)

While the discourse of multiculturalism has tended to oppose hierarchical exclusiveness with arguments in favor of unrestricted inclusiveness (Wallace 1991, 6), a resistance postmodernist critique further problematizes the issue of exclusion and inclusion by articulating a new relationship between identity and difference. Not only can a resistance postmodernist articulation of difference theorize a place where marginalized groups can speak *from* but it can also provide groups a place from which to move *beyond* an essentialized and narrow ethnic identity since they also have a stake in global conditions of equality and social justice (Hall 1991).

Homi Bhabha (1990) has articulated an important distinction between "difference" and "diversity." Working from a poststructuralist perspective, Bhabha breaks from the social-democratic version of multiculturalism where race, class, and gender are modeled on a consensual conception of difference and locates his work within a radical democratic version of cultural pluralism which recognizes the essentially contested character of the signs and signifying apparatuses that people use in the construction of their identities (Mercer 1990, 8).

Bhabha is critical of the notion of diversity used in liberal discourse to refer to the importance of plural, democratic societies. He argues that with diversity comes a "transparent norm" constructed and administered by the "host" society that creates a false consensus. This is because the normative grid that locates cultural diversity at the same time serves to *contain* cultural difference: The "universalism that paradoxically permits diversity masks ethnocentric norms" (Bhabha 1990, 208). Differences, on the other hand, do not always speak to consensus but are often incommensurable. Culture, as a system of difference, as symbol-forming activity, must in Bhabha's view be seen as "a process of translations" (1990, 210). From this follows the observation that while cultures cannot be simply reduced to unregulatable textual play, neither do they exist as undisplaceable forms in the sense that they possess "a totalized prior moment of being or meaning—an essence" (1990, 210).

Otherness in this sense is often internal to the symbol-forming activity of that culture and it is perhaps best to speak of culture as a form of "hybridity." Within this hybridity, there exists a "third space" that enables other discursive positions to emerge—to resist attempts to normalize what Bhabha refers to as "the time-lagged colonial moment" (1991a, 211). This "third space" opens up possibilities for new structures of authority, and new political vistas and visions. Identity from this perspective is always an arbitrary, contingent, and temporary suturing of identification and meaning. Bhabha's distinction makes it clear why people such as Ravitch, Bloom, Hirsch, and Bennett are so dangerous when they talk about the importance of building a common culture. Who has the power to exercise meaning, to create the grid from which Otherness is defined, to create the identifications that invite closures on meanings, on interpretations and translations?

This essay has suggested that conservative and liberal multiculturalism is really about the politics of assimilation because both assume that we really do live in a common egalitarian culture. Such an understanding of difference implies, as Iris Marion Young (1990, 164) notes, "coming into the game after the rules and standards have already been set, and having to prove oneself according to those rules and standards." These standards are not seen as culturally and experientially specific among the citizenry at large because within a pluralist democracy privileged groups have occluded their own advantage by invoking the ideal of an unsituated, neutral, universal common humanity of self-formation in which all can happily participate without regard to differences in race, gender, class, age, or sexual orientation. Resistance postmodernism, in particular, unsettles such a notion of universal common humanity by exploring identity within the context of power, discourse, culture, experience, and historical specificity.

DIFFERENCE AND THE POLITICS OF SIGNIFICATION

Resistance postmodernism has been especially significant in reformulating the meaning of difference as a form of signification. Differences in this view do not constitute clearly marked zones of autointelligible experience or a unity of identity as they do within most conservative and liberal forms of cultural pluralism. Rather, differences are understood through a politics of signification, that is, through signifying practices that are both reflective and constitutive of prevailing economic and political relations (Ebert 1991). Against the conservative multiculturalist understanding of difference as "self-evident cultural obviousness," as a "mark of plurality," or "the carefully marked off zones of experience—the privileged presence—of one group, one social category against another that we faithfully cultivate and reproduce in our analyses," Teresa Ebert defines difference as

> culturally constituted, made intelligible, through signifying practices. [For postmodern theories] "difference" is not a clearly marked zone of experience, a unity of identity of one social group against another, taken as cultural pluralism. Rather, postmodern differences are relations of opposing signifiers. (1991, 117)

According to Ebert, our current ways of seeing and acting are being disciplined for us through forms of signification, that is, through modes of intelligibility and ideological frames of sense making. Rejecting the Saussurian semiotics of signifying practices (and its continuing use in contemporary poststructuralism) as "ahistorical operations of language and tropes," Ebert characterizes signifying practices as "an ensemble of material operations involved in economic and political relations" (1991, 117). She maintains, rightly in my view, that socioeconomic relations of power require distinctions to be made among groups through forms of signification in order to organize subjects according to the unequal distribution of privilege and power.

To illustrate the politics of signification at work in the construction and formation of racist subjects, Ebert offers the example of the way in which the terms "negro" and "black" have been employed within the racial politics of the United States. Just as the term "negro" became an immutable mark of difference and naturalized the political arrangements of racism in the 1960s, so too is the term "black" being refigured in the white dominant culture to mean criminality, violence, and social degeneracy. This was made clear in the Willie Horton campaign ads for George Bush and in the current Bush and David Duke position on hiring quotas. And in my view it was evident in the verdict of the Rodney King case in Los Angeles.

Carlos Munoz (1989) has revealed how the term "Hispanic" in the mid-1970s became a "politics of white ethnic identity" that deemphasized and in some cases rejected the Mexican cultural base of Mexican-Americans. Munoz writes that the term "Hispanic" is derived from "Hispania" which was the name the Romans gave to the Iberian peninsula, most of which became Spain, and "implicitly emphasizes the white European culture of Spain at the expense of the nonwhite cultures that have profoundly shaped the experiences of all Latin Americans" (1989, 11). Not only is this term blind to the multiracial reality of Mexican-Americans through its refusal to acknowledge "the nonwhite indigenous cultures of the Americas, Africa, and Asia, which historically have produced multicultural and multiracial peoples in Latin America and the United States" (Munoz 1989, 11), it is a term that ignores the complexities within these various cultural groups. Here is another example of the melting pot theory of assimilation fostered through a politics of signification. We might ask ourselves what signifieds (meanings) will be attached to certain terms, such as "welfare mothers." I think we know what government officials mean when they refer derisively to "welfare mothers." They mean black and Latino mothers.

The examples discussed above confirm the observation of resistance postmodernism that differences are produced according to the ideological production and reception of cultural signs. As Mas'ud Zavarzadeh and Donald Morton point out, "Signs are neither eternally predetermined nor pan-historically undecidable: they are rather 'decided' or rendered as 'undecidable' in the moment of social conflicts" (1990, 156). Difference is not "cultural obviousness" such as black versus white or Latino versus European or Anglo-American; rather, differences are historical and cultural constructions (Ebert 1991).

Just as we can see the politics of signification at work in instances of police brutality, we can see it at work in special education placement where a greater proportion of black and Latino students are considered for "behavioral" placements whereas white, middle-class students are provided, for the most part, with the more comforting and comfortable label of "learning disabled" (McLaren 1989a). Here, a resistance postmodernist critique can help teachers explore the ways in which students are differentially subjected to ideological inscriptions and multiply organized discourses of desire through a politics of signification. For instance, a resistance postmodernist critique helps to understand how student identities are produced by a type of discursive ventriloquism in that they are creatures of the languages and knowledges that they have inherited and which unconsciously exert control over their thinking and behavior. As James Donald (forthcoming) points out, social norms often surface as personal and guilt-provoking desires since they have gone through a process that Foucault referred to as *folding*. Donald points out that the

> norms and prohibitions instituted within social and cultural technologies are folded into the unconscious so that they "surface" not just as "personal desires" but in a complex and unpredictable dynamic of desire, guilt, anxiety and displacement. Subjects have desires that they do not want to have; they reject them at the cost of guilt and anxiety.

While subjects are invariably prisoners of a male monopoly on language and knowledge production (Grosz 1990, 332), they are also active agents who are capable of exercising deliberate historical actions in and on the world (Giroux 1992). The point, of course, is that conscious knowledge is not exhaustive of either identity or agency. We need to acknowledge what is not so obvious about how difference is constitutive of *both identity and agency*.

Attempting to abandon all vestiges of the dominant culture in the struggle for identity can lead to a futile search for premodern roots that, in turn, leads to a narrow nationalism, as in the case of what Hall calls the "old ethnicity." Refusing to attempt to decolonize one's identity in the midst of the prevailing ideological and cultural hegemony can serve as a capitulation to assimilation and the loss of forms of critical historical agency. Needed is a view of multiculturalism and difference that moves beyond the "either-or" logic of assimilation and resistance. To make a claim for multiculturalism is not, in the words of Trinh T. Minh-ha (1991, 232), "to suggest the juxtaposition of several cultures whose frontiers remain intact, nor is it to subscribe to a bland 'melting pot' type of attitude that would level all differences. [The struggle for a multicultural society] lies instead, in the intercultural acceptance of risks, unexpected detours, and complexities of relation between break and closure."

ALWAYS TOTALIZE!

In this section I want to focus my analysis of multiculturalism on the concept of totality. I would like to emphasize that while educators must center their pedagogies on the affirmation of the "local" knowledges of students within particular sociopolitical and ethnic locations, the concept of totality must not be abandoned altogether. Not all forms of totalization are democratically deficient. Not all forms truncate, oppress, and destroy pluralism. As Fredric Jameson remarks, "Local struggles . . . are effective only so long as they remain figures or allegories for some larger systemic transformation. Politics has to operate on the micro—and the macro— levels simultaneously; a modest restriction to local reforms within the system seems reasonable, but often proves politically demoralizing" (1989, 386). George Lipsitz underscores this idea, arguing that while totality can do violence to the specificity of events, a rejection of all totality would likely "obscure real connections, causes, and relationships—atomizing common experience into accidents and endlessly repeated play . . . [and that] only by recognizing the collected legacy of accumulated human actions and ideas can we judge the claims to truth and justice of any one story" (1990, 214).

Without a shared vision (however contingent or provisional) of democratic community, we risk endorsing struggles in which the politics of difference collapses into new forms of separatism. As Steven Best points out, poststructuralists rightly deconstruct essentialist and repressive wholes, yet they often fail to see how crippling the valorizing of difference, fragmentation, and agonistics can be. This is especially true of ludic postmodernism. Best writes: "The flip side of the tyranny of the whole is the dictatorship of the fragment. . . . [W]ithout some positive and normative concept of totality to counter-balance the poststructuralist/postmodern emphasis on difference and discontinuity, we are abandoned to the seriality of pluralist individualism and the supremacy of competitive values over communal life" (1989, 361). Best is correct in suggesting that what needs to be abandoned is the reductive use of totality, not the concept of totality itself. Otherwise, we risk undermining the very concept of democratic public life.

Teresa Ebert (forthcoming) argues—brilliantly in my mind—that we need to reassert the concept of totality not in the Hegelian sense of an organic, unified, oppressive unity, but rather "as both a system of relations and *overdetermined structure of difference.*" Difference needs to be understood as social contradictions, as difference in relation, rather than dislocated, free-floating difference. Systems of differences, notes Ebert, always involve patterns of domination and relations of oppression and exploitation. We need to concern ourselves, therefore, with economies of relations of difference within historically specific totalities that are always open to contestation and transformation. As structures of difference that are always multiple and unstable, the oppressive relations of totalities (social, economic, political, legal, cultural, ideological) can always be challenged within a pedagogy of liberation. Ebert argues that totalities shouldn't be confused with Lyotard's notion of universal metanarratives.

Only when they are used unjustly and oppressively as all-encompassing and all-embracing global warrants for thought and action in order to secure an oppressive regime of truth, should totality and universality be rejected. We need to retain some kind of moral, ethical, and political ground—albeit a provisional one—from which to negotiate among multiple interests. Crucial to this argument is the important distinction between universal metanarratives (master narratives) and metacritical narratives. The resistance postmodernist critique that I am suggesting educators consider repudiates the necessity or choice of any one master narrative because master narratives suggest that there is only one public sphere, one value, one conception of justice that triumphs over all others. Resistance postmodernism suggests, on the contrary, that "different spheres and rival conceptions of justice must be accommodated to each other" (Murphy 1991, 124). In other words, "[t]he communitarian, the liberal or social democrat, the developmental liberal or humanist, the radical, and the romantic must find ways of living together in the same social space" (Murphy 1991, 124). This does not mean trying to press them all into a homogeneous cultural pulp but to suggest that there must be a multiplication of justices and pluralistic conceptions of justice, politics, ethics, and aesthetics.

Again, the crucial question here is one that deals with the notion of *totality*. While I would argue against one grand narrative, I believe that there exists a primary metadiscourse that could, in fact, offer a *provisional* engagement with discourses of the Other in a way that can be unifying without dominating and that can provide for supplementary discourses. This is the metacritical narrative of rights or freedom. Peter Murphy distinguishes between a master discourse and a metadiscourse, arguing that "a master discourse wants to impose itself on all the other discourses—it is progressive, they are reactionary; it is right, they are wrong. A metadiscourse, on the other hand, seeks to understand society as a *totality*" (1991, 126). Murphy, like Ebert, argues against a Lyotardian rejection of the grand narrative of emancipation. Instead, he embraces the idea of totality as set forth by Charles Jencks. This distinction is worth emphasizing.

> Postmodernism, Jencks, following Venturi, argues is concerned with complexity and contradiction, and precisely because it is concerned with complexity and contradiction, it in fact has a special obligation to the whole. This is not the "harmonious whole" of canonic classicism, but rather the "difficult whole" of a pluralized and multi-dimensional world. Postmodernism, Jencks argues, is committed to synthesizing a "difficult whole" out of fragments, references, and approaches. Its truth lies not in any part, but, as Venturi puts it, *in its totality or implications of totality*. (Murphy 1991, 126; italics original)

Here I am not reclaiming or rewriting totality as a synonym for political economy or suggesting that a critical postmodernism resist narrating the location of the theorist or abandon local struggles. I am not setting up a Manichean contest between the *méta récits* of liberation and social justice and the polyvocality and positionality of an antifoundational approach to difference. I also want to make clear that I am not using the concept of "totalizing" to mean an act of generalizing from the law of intelligibility of one phenomenon to the level of all social or cultural phenomena (Zavarzadeh and Morton 1991). Nor I am using it to mean some forgotten plenitude, formalized auratic experience, or bygone world that needs to be recovered for the sake of some noble nostalgia. Rather, I am using "totalizing" in the manner that Zavarzadeh and Morton (1991) have described as "global." Global understanding is a "form of explanation that is *relational* and *transdisciplinary* and that produces an account of the 'knowledge-effects' of culture by *relating* various cultural series" (155). It is a mode of inquiry that attempts to address how the ludic postmodernist critique serves as a strategy of political containment by privileging forms of "local" analysis which center the subject in experience as the Archimedean site of truth and posit ideology as the sole "reader" of experience.

Global or relational knowledge points to the existence of an underlying logic of domination within the signifying practices that constitute the cultural products of late capitalism and for this reason it sets itself against ludic postmodernism's dismissal of knowledge as integrative and political because of the supposed incommensurability of cultural, political, and economic phenomena. It moves beyond the cognitivism and empiricism of the dominant knowledge industry by dispossessing individuals of their imaginary sense of the autointelligibility of experience. Further, it reveals that *différance* is not an inherent condition of textuality but a socially overdetermined historical effect that acquires its tropicity only within given historical and cultural modes of intelligibility. Zavarzadeh and Morton argue that

> in the ludic space of playfulness, the social relations of production are posited not as historically necessary but as subject to the laws of the alea: chance and contingency. In ludic deconstruction chance and contingency perform the same ideological role that "native" (i.e., non-logical, random, inscrutable) difference plays in traditional humanistic discourses. Both posit a social field beyond the reach of the logic of necessity and history. (1991, 194)

Resistance postmodernism offers teachers working in multicultural education a means of interrogating the locality, positionality, and specificity of knowledge (in terms of the race, class, and gender locations of students) and of generating of a plurality of truths (rather than one apodictic truth built around the invisible norm of Eurocentrism and white ethnicity), while at the same time situating the construction of meaning in terms of the material interests at work in the production of "truth effects"—that is, in the production of forms of intelligibility and social practices. Consequently, teachers working within a resistance postmodernism are able to call into question the political assumptions and relations of determination upon which social truths are founded in both the communities in which they work and the larger society of which they are a part. Ludic postmodernism, in contrast, effectively masks the relationship between dominant discourses and the social relations that they justify through an immanent reading of cultural texts (reading texts on their own terms) in which their internal and formal coherence takes priority over the social relations of their production. In fact, Zavarzadeh and Morton (1991) go so far as to suggest that ludic postmodernism gained ascendancy in the academy just at the time when capitalism became deterritorialized and multinational. In effect, they are arguing that the ludic postmodern critique has suppressed forms of knowing that "could explain multi-national capitalism's trans-territoriality and its affiliated phenomena" (Zavazadeh and Morton 1991, 163).

Viewed from the perspective of constructing a global or relational understanding, the idea of organizing postmodern critique around the referents of freedom and emancipation is an attempt to avoid a unifying logic that monolithically suppresses or forecloses meaning. Conversely, it is a determined effort to retain and understand the "difficult whole" of a pluralistic and global society. It is to take up a position against reactionary pluralists such as William Bennett, Diane Ravitch, and Allan Bloom, who embrace and advocate the idea of a harmonious common culture.

I have tried to argue that in order to have a liberating narrative informing our pedagogies, educators need to address the concept of totality. The idea of a master narrative's "phallic projectory" into the telos of historical destiny needs to be discredited, yet the idea of totality as a heterogeneous and not homogeneous temporality must be recuperated. The concepts of totality and infinity need to be dialectically positioned within any pedagogy of liberation. Emmanuel Levinas (1969, 25) notes that "the idea of infinity delivers subjectivity from the judgement of history to declare it ready for judgement at every moment" (cited in Chambers 1990, 109). Isn't this precisely what Frantz Fanon was trying to describe when he urged us to *totalize infinitely* as a communicative act (Taylor 1989, 26)? For me, spaces for rewriting dominant narratives come into being by the very fact of the patience of infinity, the diachrony of time which, observes Levinas, is produced by our situatedness as ethical subjects and our responsibility to the Other. The problem, of course, is that the remaking of the social and the reinvention of the self must be understood as dialectically synchronous—that is, they cannot be conceived as unrelated or only marginally connected. They are mutually informing and constitutive processes.

According to Patrick Taylor (1989, 25), the essential ingredient of a narrative of liberation is the recognition of freedom in necessity. In this sense, the necessity of freedom becomes a *responsible totalization*. Not in the sense of a master narrative but in the sense of a metadiscourse or discourse of possibility (Giroux 1992). If we talk about totalization in the sense of a master narrative, we are referring to a type of discursive homogenization, a premature closure on meaning, a false universalism (what Taylor calls an "ordered totality") that leads to a categorical utopia—that leads, in other words, to various inflections of fascism. Infinite totalization, which is an asymptotical approach, refers to a hypothetical or provisional utopia. As P.B. Dauenhauer (1989) notes, the hypothetical embrace of utopian representation must be distinguished from the categorical embrace. To embrace ideology or utopia categorically is a form of "bad infinity" by denying alternatives to the present reality. Of course, in saying this, attention must be given to the specific structural differences that exist in various national contexts today.

Teachers need to stress in their teaching (following Ernst Bloch, 1986) the hypothetical or provisional and not the categorical embrace of utopia. Paradoxically, hypothetical utopias based on infinite totalization are the most concrete of all because they offer through their negative content (i.e., the concrete negation of domination) *the end of ordered totalities*. Patrick Taylor, citing Jameson, notes that "the ultimate interpretive task is the understanding of symbolic works in relation to a demystifying, open-ended narrative of liberation that is grounded in the imperative of human freedom" (1989, 19). Ann Game makes a similar point when she locates inquiry as a "disturbing pleasure" in which "the risks of infinity, with hints of madness. . . . are far preferable to the safety (and possibly, bad faith) of closure" (1991:191).

Narratives of freedom are ways of transcending those social myths (with their pregiven narrative orders) that reconcile us, through the resolution of binary oppositions, to lives of lived subordination. Narratives of liberation are those that totalize infinitely, but not by integrating difference into a monolithic executive identity produced by modernity's colonial or neocolonial situation—by forcing difference into silence precisely when it is asked to speak (Sáenz 1991, 158). They do not simply negate the difference produced by identity secreted in a situation of domination, because this simply saps the sustenance of the identity of the dominator (Sáenz 1991). Narratives of liberation do not simply construct an identity that "runs counter Eurocentric identity; for such would be a mere resurrection of the racist European myth of the 'noble savage'—a millenarianism in reverse, the expression of Eurocentric self-dissatisfaction and self-flagellation over its own disenchantment with the 'modernity' produced by its project of 'possessive individualism' " (Sáenz 1991, 159). Rather, narratives of liberation point to the possibility of new, alternative identities contemporaneous with modernity but not simply through inverting its normative truths.

As historical agents, educators are positioned within the tension produced by modernist and postmodernist attempts to resolve the living contradiction of being both the subject and the object of meaning. But their mode of critical analysis needs to move beyond the tropological displacement of discursive familiarity or a highjacking of meaning in the back alleys of theory (as is the case with ludic postmodernism). Educators require narratives of liberation that can serve a *metacritical* function—that can metaconceptualize relations of everyday life—and that do not succumb to the transcendental unity of subject and object or their transfiguring coalescence (Saldivar 1990, 173). In other words, such narratives promote a form of analectic understanding in addition to a dialectical understanding. As Enrique Dussel (1985) has argued, analectics reaches exteriority not through totality (as does dialectics) but rather *beyond* it. But Sáenz (1991, 162) remarks that the "beyond" that Dussel speaks about must not be interpreted as an absolute beyond all criticism (i.e., God) but rather as a "beyond" that has its roots "in the midst of domination," that is, in the suffering of the oppressed "understood within its colonial textuality." Analectics could be thus described as a form of "pluritopic" dialectical critique aimed at revealing the monotopic understanding of Eurocentrism as merely contingent to its own cultural traditions (Sáenz 1991).

Through a praxis of infinite totalization educators can provide analectically a new vision of the future that is latent in the present, immanent in this very moment of reading, in the womb of the actual. Such a praxis can help us understand that subjective intentions do not constitute the apodictical site of truth. Subjectivities and identities of students and teachers are always the artifacts of discursive formations; that is, they are always the products of historical contexts and language games (Kincheloe 1991; Carspecken 1991). Students and teachers are all actors in narrative configurations and employments that they did not develop but that are the products of historical and discursive struggles that have been folded back into the unconscious. Teachers need to learn to recognize those internalized discourses that not only inform the ritualization of their teaching practices, but those that organize their vision of the future. They must recall, too, that human agency is not a substrate that props them up like the crutches in a Dali painting, but has *imperative force*. The theater of agency is *possibility*.

Agency is informed by the stereotypical ways in which subjectivities have been allegorized by historical discourses which have been gridded in the subject positions teachers and students take. These discourses differentially enable and enact specific forms of practice. Yet while there is a logos immanent to the discourses that constitute teachers that makes them functionaries within modern technologies of power, this does not mean that educators and cultural workers cannot foster and realize potentialities within the discursive and material conditions of their own communities. Educators have a heritage of possibilities from which to work. While these possibilities affect the ground of teachers' subjectivities, they do not saturate their will, nor do they prevent them from struggling against the constraints that bind freedom and justice. Identities may thus be considered both mobilely structured and structured mobilities and as such are dialectically re-initiating. David Trend speaks to this issue when he emphasizes the importance of understanding the productive character of knowledge. While one's influence on the process of knowledge production is always partial, cultural workers do exert considerable influence:

> Acknowledging the role of the "learning subject" in the construction of culture, we affirm processes of agency, difference, and, ultimately, democracy. We suggest to students and audiences that they have a role in the making of their world and that they need not accept positions as passive spectators or consumers. This is a position that recognizes and encourages the atmosphere of diverse and contradictory opinions so dreaded by the conservative proponents of a "common culture." It functions on the belief that a healthy democracy is one that is always being scrutinized and tested. (1992, 150)

Exerting an influence over cultural production means finding ways of speaking and acting outside the totalizing systems of logocentric thought by creating metacritical and relational perspectives linked to the imperative of a unifying project (in Sartre's sense). Educators need to get outside the admixtures and remnants of languages—the multiplicity of stereotypical voices that already populate their vocabulary and fill up all the available linguistic spaces—in order to find different ways of appropriating or mediating the real. Educators and cultural workers need to cross borders into zones of cultural difference rather than construct subjectivities that simply reassert themselves as monadic forms of totality facilitated by a consumerist ethics and marketplace logic (Giroux 1992; McLaren forthcoming). This means developing a more effective theory for understanding pedagogy in relation to the workings of power in the larger context of race, class, and gender articulations. It means advancing a theory that does not elevate the teacher-other as individual knower and devalue the student as an objectified, unknowing entity. Students must not be constructed as the zombified ideal "always already" open to manipulation for passive acquiescence to the status quo. We should not forfeit the opportunity of theorizing both teachers and students as historical agents of resistance.

CRITICAL PEDAGOGY: TEACHING FOR A HYBRID CITIZENRY AND MULTICULTURAL SOLIDARITY

"THERE'S ROOM FOR ALL AT THE RENDEZ-VOUS OF VICTORY"

—CÉSAIRE

....

Resistance postmodernism has figured prominently in the development of new forms of pedagogical praxis concerned with rethinking educational politics in a multicultural society (Giroux 1992; McLaren and Leonard, forthcoming; McLaren forthcoming; Aronwitz and Giroux 1991). Of particular significance is Giroux's concept of a "border pedagogy" which enables educators to affirm and legitimate local meanings and constellations of meanings that grow out of particular discursive communities but at the same time interrogate the interests, ideologies, and social practices that such knowledges serve when viewed from the perspective of more global economies of power and privilege.

A pedagogy informed significantly by resistance postmodernism suggests that teachers and cultural workers need to take up the issue of "difference" in ways that don't replay the monocultural essentialism of the "centrisms"—Anglocentrism, Eurocentrism, phallocentrism, androcentrism, and the like. They need to create a politics of alliance building, of dreaming together, of solidarity that moves beyond the condescensions of, say, "race awareness week," which actually serves to keep forms of institutionalized racism intact. A solidarity has to be struggled for that is not centered around market imperatives but develops out of the imperatives of freedom, liberation, democracy, and critical citizenship.

The notion of the citizen has been pluralized and hybridized, as Kobena Mercer notes, by the presence of a diversity of social subjects. Mercer is instructive in pointing out that "solidarity does not mean that everyone thinks the same way, it begins when people have the confidence to disagree over issues because they

'care' about constructing a common ground" (1990, 68). Solidarity is not imperme-
ably solid but depends to a certain degree on antagonism and uncertainty. Timothy
Maliqualim Simone calls this type of multiracial solidarity "geared to maximizing
points of interaction rather than harmonizing, balancing, or equilibrating the distribution of bodies, resources, and territories" (1989, 191).

While guarding against the privileging of a false universalism, a false unity that
denies the internal rifts of bodily desire, both teachers and students need to open
themselves to the possibility of Otherness so that the particularity of individual
being can become visible in relation to larger relations of power and privilege.
Students especially need to be provided with opportunities to devise different
assemblages of the self by dismantling and interrogating the different kinds of
discursive segmentarity that inform their subjectivities, subverting those stratified
and hierarchized forms of subjectivity that code the will, and developing nomadic
forms of individual and collective agency that open up new assemblages of desire
and modes of being-in-the-world (Grossberg 1988).

Educators must examine the development of pedagogical discourses and practices that demonize Others who are different (through transforming them into
absence or deviance). A resistance postmodernism that takes multiculturalism seriously calls attention to the dominant meaning systems readily available to students—
most of which are ideologically stitched into the fabric of Western imperialism
and partriarchy. It challenges meaning systems that impose attributes on the Other
under the direction of sovereign signifiers and tropes. And this means not directing
all our efforts at understanding ethnicity as "other than white," but interrogating
the culture of whiteness itself. This is crucial because unless we do this—unless
we give white students a sense of their own identity as an emergent ethnicity—
we naturalize whiteness as a cultural marker against which Otherness is defined.
Coco Fusco warns that "to ignore white ethnicity is to redouble its hegemony by
naturalizing it. Without specifically addressing white ethnicity there can be no
critical evaluation of the construction of the other" (cited in Wallace 1991, 7).
White groups need to examine their ethnic histories so that they are less likely to
judge their own cultural norms as neutral and universal. "Whiteness" does not
exist outside of culture but constitutes the prevailing social texts in which social
norms are made and remade. As part of a politics of signification that passes
unobserved into the rhythms of daily life, and a "politically constructed category
parasitic on 'Blackness' " (West 1990, 29), "whiteness" has become the invisible
norm for how the dominant culture measures its own civility.

With this in mind, a critical pedagogy that embraces a resistance postmodernism
needs to construct a politics of refusal that can provide both the conditions for
interrogating the institutionalization of formal equality based on the prized imperatives of a white, Anglo male world and for creating spaces to facilitate an investiga-
tion of the way in which dominant institutions must be transformed so that they
no longer serve simply as conduits for a motivated indifference to victimization
for a Euroimperial aesthetics, for depredations of economic and cultural dependency, and for the production of asymmetrical relations of power and privilege.

Here it is important to contest the charge made by some liberal humanist educators that teachers should only speak for themselves and not for others. Those who claim that teachers can and should only speak for themselves—a claim that is at the very least implied by many critics of critical pedagogy—forget that "when I 'speak for myself' I am participating in the creation and reproduction of discourses through which my own and other selves are constituted" (Alcoff 1991–92, 21). Linda Alcoff notes that we need to promote a *dialogue with* rather than a *speaking for* others (although this does not preclude us from speaking for others under certain restricted circumstances). Drawing upon the work of Gayatri Chakravorty Spivak, Alcoff maintains that we can adopt a "speaking to" the other that does not essentialize the oppressed as nonideologically constructed subjects. Summarizing Spivak, Alcoff stresses how important it is that the intellectual "neither abnegates his or her discursive role nor presumes an authenticity of the oppressed but still allows for the possibility that the oppressed will produce a 'countersentence' that can then suggest a new historical narrative" (cited in Alcoff 1991–92, 23). As educators we need to be exceedingly cautious about our attempts to speak for others, questioning how our discourses as *events* position us as authoritative and empowered speakers in ways that unwittingly constitute a reinscription of the discourse of colonization, of patriarchy, of racism, of conquest—"a reinscription of sexual, national, and other kinds of hierarchies" (Alcoff 1991–92, 29). Educators also need to avoid a "tolerance" that appropriates the difference of the Other in the name of the colonizer's own self-knowledge and increased domination.

Critical pedagogy does not work toward some grandiose endpoint of an ideo-logically perceived world history but rather attempts to make understandable the indefinite and to explore other modes of sociality and self-figuration that go beyond dominant language formations and social organizations. In doing so, it has often been accused of being inaccessible to rank-and-file teachers. Trinh T. Minh-ha (1991) issues a very telling warning against such calls for accessibility of language. She writes that resistance to the language of complex theory can reinstitute "common sense" as an alternative to theory—that is, it can usher in a new dictatorship of pretheoretical nativism in which experience supposedly speaks for itself. To be "accessible," writes Minh-ha, often suggests

> one can employ neither symbolic and elliptical language, as in Asian, African, or Native American cultures (because Western ears often equate it with obscurantism); nor poetic language (because "objective" literal thinking is likely to identify it with "subjective" aestheticism). The use of dialogical language is also discouraged (because the dominant worldview can hardly accept that in the politics of representing marginality and resist-ance one might have to speak at least two difference things at once). (1991, 228)

Minh-ha further notes, after Isaac Julien, that resistance to theory is embodied in white people's resistance to the complexity of black experience. Not only does such resistance point to the illusion that there exists a natural, self-evident language but such a call for accessibility can also lead to forms of racism and intolerance and the politics of exclusion. The "diversely hybrid experiences of heterogeneous contemporary societies are denied" by such a form of binary thinking, which would reduce the language of analysis to white, hegemonic forms of clarity (Minh-ha 1991, 229).

INTENSIFYING THE OBVIOUS AND ACCELERATING THE MUNDANE

A pedagogy that takes resistance postmodernism seriously does not make the nativist assumption that knowledge is preontologically available and that various disciplinary schools of thought may be employed in order to tease out different readings of the same "commonsense" reality in a context of impartiality. Rather, the discourses that inform the educator's problematics are understood as constitutive of the very reality that he or she is attempting to understand. Consequently, the classroom is the site of the teacher's own embodiment in theory/discourse, ethical disposition as moral and political agent, and situatedness as a cultural worker within a larger narrative identity. In recognizing the important role played by "place" in any critical pedagogy, it should be clear that we are talking not about the physical milieu where knowledge is made visible within preordained and circumscribed limits but rather the textual space that one occupies and the affective space one creates as a teacher. In other words, the discursive practice of "doing pedagogy" does not simply treat knowledge outside of the way that it is taken up by both teachers and students *as a form of dialogue*. I am referring here to the multi-voicedness of democratic discourse not in the sense of unrestrained intersubjective exchange but rather as challenging "the logic of dialogue as equal linguistic exchange." Such a challenge involves interrogating the ediological interests of the speaker, the social overdeterminations of utterances, and the social context in which utterances are both historically produced and culturally understood (Hitchcock, 1993, 7). Knowledge can never be treated as a cultural artifact or possession that serves as a pristine, prefigurative source of cultural authenticity inviting unbiased analysis.

The project of critical pedagogy means bringing the laws of cultural representation face to face with their founding assumptions, contradictions, and paradoxes. It also means encouraging teachers to participate in the affective as well as intellectual cultures of the oppressed, and to challenge in the spirit of Ernst Bloch's "militant optimism" ethical and political quietism in the face of operating homilies such as "progress is inevitable" or what might seem like historical inevitability—a perspective that leads to the cult of the mausoleum. Educators can no longer project onto the student-as-Other that part of themselves that out of fear and loathing they rejected or subtracted from their identities in their attempt to become unified subjects—that "split-off" part of themselves which prevents them from becoming whole, that disfiguring surplus that they have cast out in order to become white or live in the thrall of racelessness, that metaphysical double that guarantees their own self-regarding autonomy. From this point of view, liberation is never an encapsulated fulfillment of some prefigured end constructed in the temple of memory but a lived tension between the duration of history and the discourse of possibility. It resides in an approach to the *"Aufhebung"*—our passing *into* the "not-yet," and seeking the immanent utopia in the crisis of meaning and the social relations that inform it. It is found, too, in the proleptic consciousness of liminality—the liberating intention of the reflective will caught in the "subjunctive" moment of the "ought" and disabused of metaphysical illusion. It is formed out of an ethical intent commensurate with the love that Paulo Freire and Che Guevara both argue constitutes the ground from which all revolutionary action should take place.

Neither the academy nor the public school system needs to sow the seeds of future priests of deconstruction in the desacralized institutional spaces of the postmodern scene by turning the college classroom into a prewar Europe Nietzschean cafe or Cabaret Voltaire for leftist educators who wish to reap no real political consequences for their semiotic revolution. Rather, the more pressing need is to transform present social practices and institutional relations because history compels us to do so, because the present historical juncture in which we witness so much misery and suffering necessitates it. History compels us because our dreams and our suffering are forged in it; it is what houses the furnace of our will. In the iron womb of history we create the shape of our longings, and to reclaim history is to be fully present in its making.

Educators need to do more than to help students redescribe or represent themselves in new ways—although the way we seek to imagine ourselves is an important step in the struggle for liberation. As Sander L. Gilman has pointed out in his study of stereotypes of sexuality, race, and madness, "we view our own images, our own mirages, our own stereotypes as embodying qualities that exist in the world. And we act upon them" (1985, 242). More specifically, a pedagogy must be made available to teachers that will enable them along with their students to outface the barrenness of postmodern culture by employing a discourse and set of social practices that will not be content with infusing their pedagogies with the postmodern élan of the ludic metropolitan intellectual, with resurrecting a nostalgic past which can never be reclaimed, or with redescribing the present by simply textualizing it, leaving in place its malignant hierarchies of power and privilege, its defining pathologies. For these latter acts only stipulate the lineage of and give sustenance to those social relations responsible for the very injustice critical educators are trying to struggle against. Educators need to stare boldly and unflinchingly into the historical present and assume a narrative space where conditions may be created where students can tell their own stories, listen closely to the stories of others, and dream the dream of liberation. Identity formation must be understood in terms of how subjectivity is contextually enacted within the tendential forces of history (Grossberg, 1992). The exploration of identity should consist of mapping one's subject position in the field of multiple relationships and should be preceded by a critique of hegemony (San Juan, Jr. 1992, 128). This suggests that educators and students need to uncouple themselves from the "disciplined mobilizations" that regulate their social lives and rearticulate the sites of their affective investments in order to create new strategies and alliances of struggle.

A critical pedagogy also demands political and cultural tactics that can fight multiple forms of oppression yet achieve a cohesiveness with divergent social groups working toward liberatory goals. To this end, Chela Sandoval (1991) suggests that cultural workers develop "tactical subjectivities" which she describes as forms of oppositional and differential consciousness and counterhegemonic praxis (which she discusses in the context of feminism). Tactical subjectivity enables teachers as social agents to recenter their multiple subjectivities with respect to the kind of oppression that is being confronted and "permits the practitioner to choose tactical positions, that is, to self-consciously break and reform ties to ideology, activities which are imperative for the psychological and political practices that permit the achievement of coalition across differences" (Sandoval 1991, 15).

RESISTANCE AS "LA CONCIENCIA DE LA MESTIZA"

The invitation posed by critical pedagogy is to bend reality to the requirements of a just world, to decenter, deform, disorient, and ultimately transform modes of authority that domesticate the Other, that lay siege to the power of the margins. Educators would do well to consider Gloria Anzaldúa's (1987) project of creating *mestizaje* theories that create new categories of identity for those left out or pushed out of existing ones. Critical pedagogy calls for the construction of a praxis where peripheralized peoples such as African-Americans and Latinos are no longer induced to fear and obey the White Gaze of Power, where bonds of sentiment and obligation can be formed among diverse groups of oppressed peoples, where resistance can enable schools to become more than instruments of monitorization and social replication, where contrasting cultural styles and cultural capital among diverse groups cease to be tokens of estrangement that separate them but rather become the very impetus that invites them as liminal travelers to create an arch of social dreaming. We need to move beyond pedagogies of protest, which Houston Baker reminds us only reinforces the dualism of "self" and "other" and reinstates the basis of dominant racist evaluations, and preserves the "always already" arrangements of white patriarchal hegemony (1985, 388). We need to develop a praxis that gives encouragement to those who, instead of being content with visiting history as curators or custodians of memory, choose to live in the furnace of history where memory is molten and can be bent into the contours of a dream and perhaps even acquire the immanent force of a vision.

The sites of our identity within postmodernity are various; as seekers of liberation, we recognize the heterogeneous character of our inscription into colonial texts of history and cultural discourses of empire. New sites of agency are erupting at the borderlines of cultural instability, in the transgressive act of re-membering, and through the disavowal and refashioning of consciousness in the in-between spaces of cultural negotiation and translation. Marcos Sanchez-Tranquilino and

John Tagg (1991) refer to this as the borderland, the "in-between" space that Gloria Anzaldúa calls *la frontera*. It is a space of borders where teachers may be able to recognize

> another narration of identity, another resistance. One that asserts a difference, yet cannot be absorbed into the pleasures of the global marketing culture. One that locates its different voice, yet will not take a stand on the unmoving ground of a defensive fundamentalism. One that speaks its location as more than local, yet makes no claim to universality for its viewpoint of language. One that knows the border and crosses the line. (1991, 105)

The rhythm of the struggle for educational and social transformation can no longer be contained in the undaunted, steady steps of the workers' army marching toward the iron gates of freedom but is being heard in the hybrid tempos of bordertown bands; in the spiraling currents of an Aster Aweke Kabu vocal, in the percussive polyrhythms of prophetic black rap, in meanings that appear in the folds of cultural life where identities are mapped not merely by diversity but through difference.

WORKS CITED

Alcoff, Linda (1991–92). "The Problem of Speaking for Others." *Cultural Critique* no. 20: 5–32. No volume no.

Anzaldúa, Gloria (1987). *Borderlands/La Frontera: The New Mestiza.* San Francisco: Spinsters/ Aunt Lute.

Aronowitz, Stanley, and Giroux, Henry (1991). *Postmodern Education.* Minneapolis, Minn.: University of Minnesota Press.

Baker, Houston A. (1985). "Caliban's Triple Play." In Henry Louis Gates, Jr., (ed.) *"Race," Writing and Difference.* Chicago, Illinois: The University of Chicago Press, 381–395.

Benjamin, Walter (1973). "Program For a Proletarian Children's Theater." *Performance* 1, no. 5 (March–April): 28–32. Trans. Susan Buck-Morss from Benjamin, "Programm eines proletarischen Kindertheaters" (1928), in *Ober Kinder, Jugend und Erziehung,* ed. Suhrkamp 391. Frankfurt am Main: Suhrkamp Verlag, 1969.

Best, Steven (1989). "Jameson, Totality and Post-Structuralist Critique." In Doug Kellner (ed.), *Postmodernism/Jameson/Critique.* Washington: Maisonneuve, 233–368.

Bhabha, Homi (1990). "Introduction: Narrating the Nation." In Homi K. Bhabha (ed.), *Nation and Narration.* London and New York: Routledge. 291–322.

Bhabha, Homi (1991a). " 'Race,' Time, and the Revision of Modernity." *Oxford Literary Review* 13, nos. 1–2:193–219.

Bhabha, Homi (1991b). "The Third Space," In Jonathan Rutherford (ed.). *Identity: Community, Culture, Difference.* London: Lawrence and Wishart. 207–37.

Bloch, Ernst (1986). *The Principle of Hope* (3 vols.) Translated by Neville Plaice, Stephen Plaice and Paul Knight. Cambridge, Mass.: The MIT Press.

Browder, Leslie H. (1992). "Which America 2000 Will Be Taught in Your Class, Teacher?" *International Journal of Educational Reform* 1, no. 2:111–33.

Carspecken, Phil Francis (1991). *Community Schooling and the Nature of Power: The Battle for Croxteth Comprehensive.* London and New York: Routledge.

Chambers, Iain (1990). *Border Dialogues: Journeys in Postmodernity.* London and New York: Routledge.

Christian, Barbara (1987). "The Race for Theory." *Cultural Critique* no. 6:51–63.

Cooper, B. M. (1989). "Cruel and the Gang: Exposing the Schomburg Posse." *Village Voice* 34, no. 19:27–36.

Copjec, Joan (1991). "The Unvermogender Other: Hysteria and Democracy in America". *New Formations* 14:27–41.

Dauenhauer, P. B. (1989). "Ideology, Utopia, and Responsible Politics." *Man and World* 22:25–41.

DiStephano, Christine. (1990). "Dilemmas of Difference: Feminism, Modernity, and Post-modernism." In Linda J. Nicholson, (ed), *Feminism/Postmodernism.* New York and London: Routledge. 63–82.

Donald, James (forthcoming). "The Natural Man and the Virtuous Woman: Reproducing Citizens." In Chris Jencks (ed.), *Cultural Reproduction.* London and New York: Routledge.

Dussel, Enrique (1980). *Philosophy of Liberation.* Maryknoll, N.Y.: Orbis Books.

Ebert, Teresa (1991). "Political Semiosis in/of American Cultural Studies." *American Journal of Semiotics* 8, no. ½:113–35.

Ebert, Teresa (forthcoming). "Writing in the Political Resistance (Post) Modernism."

Featherstone, Mike (1990). "Global Culture: An Introduction." *Theory, Culture, and Society* nos. 2–3:1–14.

Foster, Hal (ed.) (1983). *The Anti-Aesthetic: Essays on Postmodern Culture.* Port Town-send, Wash. Bay Press.

Frank, Arthur W. (1990). "Bringing Bodies Back In: A Decade Review." *Theory, Culture, and Society* 7, no. 1:131–62.

Game, Ann. (1991). *Undoing the Social: Towards a Deconstructive Sociology.* Toronto and Buffalo: University of Toronto Press.

Gilman, Sander L. (1985). *Difference and Pathology.* Ithaca, New York: Cornell University Press.

Gilroy, Paul (1990). "One Nation under a Groove: The Cultural Politics of 'Race' and Racism in Britain." In Goldberg 1990. 263–82.

Giroux, Henry (1992). *Border Crossings.* London and New York: Routledge.

Goldberg, David Theo (1990). *Anatomy of Racism.* Minneapolis: University of Minnesota Press.

Grossberg, Larry (1988). *It's a Sin.* University of Sydney, Australia: Power Publications.

Grossberg, Larry. (1992). *We Gotta Get Out of This Place.* New York and London: Routledge.

Grosz, Elizabeth (1990). "Conclusion: Notes on Essentialism and Difference." In Sneja Gunew (ed.), *Feminist Knowledge: Critique and Construct.* London, Routledge. 332–44.

Hall, Stuart (1991). "Ethnicity: Identity and Difference." *Radical America* 23, no. 4:9–20.

Harstock, Nancy. (1987). "Rethinking Modernism: Minority vs. Majority Theories", *Cultural Critique* 7: 187–206.

Harstock, Nancy (1989). "Foucault on Power: A Theory for Women?" In Linda J. Nicholson (ed.), *Feminism/Postmodernism.* New York and London, Routledge. 157–75.

Hitchcock, Peter (1993). *Dialogics of the Oppressed.* Minneapolis and London: University of Minnesota Press.

Jameson, Fredric (1989). "Afterword—Marxism and Postmodernism." In Doug Kellner (ed.), *Postmodernism/Jameson/Critique.* Washington: Maisonneuve. 369–87.

Kaplan, E. Ann (1987). *Rocking around the Clock: Music, Television, Postmodernism and Consumer Culture.* New York: Methuen.

Kasinitz, P. (1988). "Facing Up to the Underclass." *Telos* 76:170–80.

Katz, Cindi and Smith, Neil. (1992). "L.A. Intifada: Interview with Mike Davis." *Social Text.* 33:19–33.

Kimball, Roger (1991). "Tenured Radicals: A Postscript." *The New Criterion* 9, no. 5:4–13.

Kincheloe, Joe (1991). *Teachers as Researchers: Qualitative Inquiry as a Path to Empowerment.* London: Falmer.

Larsen, Neil (1990). Modernism and Hegemony: *A Materialist Critique of Aesthetic Agencies.* Minneapolis, MN: University of Minnesota Press.

Lash, Scott (1990). "Learning from Leipzig . . . or Politics in the Semiotic Society." *Theory, Culture, and Society* 7, no. 4:145–58.

Levinas, Emmanuel (1969). *Totality and Infinity.* Pittsburgh: Duquesne University Press.

Lippard, Lucy R. (1990). *Mixed Blessings: New Art in a Multicultural America.* New York: Pantheon Books.

Lipsitz, George (1990). *Time Passages.* Minneapolis: University of Minnesota Press.

Lloyd, David (1991). "Race under Representation." *Oxford Literary Review* 13, nos. 1–2:62–94.

McLaren, Peter (1989a). *Life in Schools.* White Plains, N.Y.: Longman.

McLaren, Peter (1989b). "Schooling the Postmodern Body: Critical Pedagogy and the Politics of Enfleshment." *Journal of Education* 170:53–58.

McLaren, Peter (ed.) (forthcoming). *Postmodernism, Postcolonialism and Pedagogy.* Albert Park, Australia: James Nicholas Publishers.

McLaren, Peter and Hammer, Rhonda. (1989). "Critical Pedagogy and the Postmodern Challenge," *Educational Foundations,* 3, no. 3:29–69.

McLaren, Peter, and Leonard, Peter (1993). *Paulo Freire: A Critical Encounter.* London and New York: Routledge.

Mercer, Kobena (1990). "Welcome to the Jungle: Identity and Diversity in Postmodern Politics." In Jonathan Rutherford (ed.), *Identity: Community, Culture, Difference.* London: Lawrence and Wishart. 43–71.

Minh-ha, Trinh T. (1991). *When the Moon Waxes Red: Representation, Gender, and Cultural Politics.* New York and London: Routledge.

Mohanty, Chandra (1989/90). "On Race and Voice: Challenges for Liberal Education in the 1990s." *Cultural Critique* 19:179–208.

Munoz, Carlos (1989). *Youth, Identity, Power.* London and New York: Verso.

Murphy, Peter (1991). "Postmodern Perspectives and Justice." *Thesis Eleven* no. 30:117–32.

Piccone, Paul (1988). "Roundtable on Communitarianism." *Telos* no. 76:2–32.

Ravitch, Diane (1990). "Multiculturalism: E Pluribus Plures." *The American Scholar* 59, no. 3:337–54.

Ravitch, Diane (1991). "A Culture in Common." *Educational Leadership* (December): 8–16.

Rosaldo, Renato (1989). *Culture and Truth: The Remaking of Social Analysis.* Boston: Beacon.

Rosenau, Pauline Marie (1992). *Post-Modernism and the Social Sciences: Insights, Inroads, and Intrusions.* Princeton, N.J.: Princeton University Press.

Sáenz, Mario (1991). "Memory, Enchantment and Salvation: Latin American Philosophies of Liberation and the Religions of the Oppressed." *Philosophy and Social Criticism* 17, no. 2:149–73.

Saldivar, Ramon (1990). *Chicano Narrative: The Dialectics of Difference.* Madison WI: University of Wisconsin Press.

Sanchez-Tranquilino, Marcos, and Tagg, John (1991). "The Pachuco's Flayed Hide: The Museum, Identity, and Buenas Garvas." In Richard Griswold de Castillo, Teresa McKenna, and Yvonne Yarbro-Bejarano (eds.), *Chicano Art: Resistance and Affirmation.* Los Angeles: Wright Art Gallery. 97–108.

Sandoval, Chela (1991). "U.S. Third World Feminism: The Theory and Method of Oppositional Consciousness in the Postmodern World." *Genders* no. 10:1–24.

San Juan, Jr., E. (1992). *Racial Formations/Critical Formations.* New Jersey and London: Humanities Press.

Simone, Timothy Maliqualim (1989). *About Face: Race in Postmodern America.* Brooklyn, NY: Autonomedia.

Stephanson, Anders (1988). "Interview with Cornel West." In Andrew Ross (ed), *Universal Abandon? The Politics of Postmodernism.* Minneapolis: University of Minnesota Press. 269–86.

Taylor, Patrick (1989). *The Narrative of Liberation: Perspectives on Afro-Caribbean Literature, Popular Culture, and Politics.* Ithaca, N.Y.: Cornell University Press.

Trend, David (1992). *Cultural Pedagogy: Art/Education/Politics.* New York: Bergin and Garvey.

Wallace, Michele (1991). "Multiculturalism and Oppositionality." *Afterimage* (October): 6–9.

West, Cornel (1989). "Black Culture and Postmodernism." In Barbara Kruger and Phil Mariani (eds.), *Remaking History.* Seattle: Bay Press. 87–96.

West Cornel (1990). "The New Cultural Politics of Difference." In Russell Ferguson, Martha Gever, Trinh T. Minh-ha, and Cornel West (eds.), *Out There: Marginalization and Contemporary Cultures.* Cambridge, Mass.: MIT Press and the New Museum of Contemporary Art, New York. 19–36.

Young, Iris Marion (1990). *Justice and the Politics of Difference.* Princeton, NJ: Princeton University Press.

Zavarzadeh, Mas'ud, and Morton, Donald (1990). "Signs of Knowledge in the Contemporary Academy." *American Journal of Semiotics* 7, no. 4:149–60.

Zavarzadeh, Mas'ud, and Morton, Donald (1991). *Theory, (Post)Modernity, Opposition.* Washington, D.C.: Maisonneuve.

NATIONALISM,
POST-
COLONIALISM,
AND THE BORDER
INTELLECTUAL

C H A P T E R   1 2

···

NATIONALITIES,

PEDAGOGIES,

AND MEDIA

···

D A V I D   T R E N D

Nationality is a fiction. It is a story people tell themselves about who they are, where they live, and how they got there. As such, it is a complicated and highly contested text. In the contemporary U.S., issues of national identity resonate in debates over educational reform, literary canons, multiculturalism, political correctness, and artistic freedom. All of these result, at least in part, from the paradoxical manner that "nations, like narratives, lose their origins in the myths of time and only fully realize their horizons in the mind's eye" (Bhabha 1990, 1). One's location in this narrative, one's ability to write oneself into the text of nationality, constitutes a form of literacy. It is an acquired language of belonging in space and time to an imaginary community. Increasingly, both the Left and the Right have recognized the educational importance of this process of national identification, as young people are socialized to understand their roles as citizens. Opinions differ radically over both the form and the content of this language. Some argue that in an increasingly complex and multicultural society there is a need for a common literacy; others propose that we are moving toward a culture of many literacies.

Media figure prominently in all of these debates. Without doubt, substantial ingredients in the process of national identification are delivered through newspapers, magazines, television, and movies—not to mention the plethora of instructional materials, catalogues, billboards, and junk mail that bombard citizens daily. There is a growing sense that these media constitute the primary source of identity formation, supplanting roles formerly held by school, church, and the family. Rather than seeing this as a negative phenomenon, educators and parents should acknowledge the importance of media in cultural life, and work to harness this power in productive ways. Like it or not, young people are as much educated, albeit informally, through daily encounters with media as they are in the formal environment of school (Lusted 1991b, 5).

It is even argued that a national identity is itself a product of media. Some historians link the development of the modern nation-state to the evolution of

European "print capitalism" (Anderson 1983). Prior to the mass dissemination of newspapers, books, and pamphlets it was difficult for people to imagine a collectivity on a broader than local scale. It doesn't take much insight to recognize the current role of network television and movies in constructing the illusion of connectedness among citizens thousands of miles apart. As Benedict Anderson puts it, "an American will never meet, or even know the names of more than a handful of his fellow Americans. He has no idea of what they are up to at any one time. But he has complete confidence in their steady, anonymous, simultaneous activity" (1983, 16).

Moreover, the reach of contemporary electronic media is hardly bound by a country's geographical borders. The ability to broadcast across national boundaries, even in the face of government resistance, motivated the electronic warfare waged by programs like Radio Free Europe. Not that media imperialism is typically so belligerent. On the contrary, the mass marketing of U.S. productions throughout the world is customarily portrayed as a positive function of the "free market." Due to the scale and technical sophistication of the American media industry, Hollywood films and television programs constitute the nation's second largest source of foreign income, just behind aerospace technology (Morley and Robins 1989, 12). Although this ability to profit in the media trade helps the nation's sagging economy, the massive influx of U.S. images into other nations is not always viewed as a positive phenomenon. The now-familiar figure of "Dallas" glowing on television screens throughout Europe, Africa, and Asia has triggered mass resentment about the transmission of American culture throughout the globe. As a consequence, government-sponsored media education programs in nations that import significant amounts of film and television are far more advanced than in the U.S.

People at home aren't entirely thrilled by media either. Almost since the inception of television, a diverse assortment of educators, parents, and religious groups has warned of the corrupting influence of commercial media. Like critics of media dissemination overseas, domestic opponents believe it exerts an irresistible control over its consumers. To those on the Right, the media are seen as conveyors of moral depravity. On the Left, they are believed to transmit oppressive ideologies. Both are unified by their belief that media must be resisted at all costs (Buckingham 1991, 12). All of these arguments assign a range of social problems to the media that originate elsewhere. They make the error of believing that representations invariably correspond to outcomes and that viewers exert no license in the viewing process. In part the problem stems from a lack of understanding about how media are received and interpreted. Intellectuals, parents, and clergy make judgments about the media practices of the less powerful. This results in a condescending series of assumptions about the capabilities of viewers to evaluate what they see. The solutions to this perceived tyranny lie in turning off the tube or girding oneself to resist its mendacity. This has been the premise of traditional media education, the rationale for the development of public broadcasting, and even the motivation for several United Nations resolutions.

In what follows I will review media attitudes both in the U.S. and elsewhere, by raising questions specifically focused on issues of national identity. How do contemporary media define public perceptions of nationality? What role do media play in developing citizenship and collective agency? How do media influence relationships among global powers? Addressing these questions will entail both institutional and textual analysis of the way nationality has been constructed in an international context. Such analyses are particularly needed at a time when the U.S. is asserting its right as the only legitimate superpower in the "New World Order." My central premise is that, while the material and textual power of the communications industry is indisputable, the authority of media is clearly not absolute. But just because audiences possess the ability to mediate the texts they receive, they do not necessarily exercise that option with skill or consistency. Through a concerted media literacy program such capacities can be cultivated. Models for such pedagogies already exist, but they are few and far between. In describing the ways some of these new media curricula operate I will also explain why they have been so poorly received, particularly in U.S. schools. In an era in which schooling is increasingly driven by a corporatist agenda of basic skills, interdisciplinary studies like media are seen as both frivolous and subversive. Nevertheless, arguments for media education can be made that are both powerful and progressive.

THE BIG PICTURE: INTERNATIONAL PERSPECTIVES ON MEDIA IMPERIALISM

The problems started after World War II. What began with the seemingly innocent export of commercial media products evolved over time into a global ideological offensive. Of course, U.S. business interests had long promoted American capitalism with a religious zeal. But it wasn't until the Cold War era that politicians and entrepreneurs like publishing magnate Henry Luce began urging Americans to spread the gospel of capitalism throughout the globe by accepting "wholeheartedly our duty and our opportunity as the most powerful and vital nation in the world and in consequence to exert upon the world the full impact of our influence, for such purposes as we see fit and by such means as we see fit."[1]

Complementing such attitudes was a U.S. diplomatic policy promoting a "free flow of information" throughout the world. This transparently self-interested stance was asserted as a protection against the resurgence of fascism and the outbreak of future wars. Yet it also represented a direct assault on the protectionism practiced by the Eastern Bloc. The resulting fusion of profit and policies fed a news and entertainment complex that was already the largest in the world—and one of the first domestic industries to restructure itself along transnational lines. By the 1960s concerns about American media hegemony had reached such a magnitude worldwide, that the United Nations convened a special series of conferences to investigate the media market and establish a corrective "New World Information Order." At one of those early meetings Finnish president Urho Kekkonen expressed the sentiments of many gathered when he asked, "could it be that the prophets who preach unhindered communication are not concerned with equality among nations, but are on the side of the stronger and wealthier?" (Schiller 1970, 44).

The UNESCO consensus related to two fundamental tenets of national self-definition: concepts of limits (the ability to maintain clear boundaries) and sovereignty (the authority to govern within these boundaries) (Anderson 1983, 14–15). Hence, a 1972 Free Flow of Information declaration pertaining to broadcast technology stated that nations must reach "prior agreements concerning direct satellite broadcasting to the population of countries other than the country of origin of the transmission" (Schiller 1976, 40). Nations like the U.S. ignored such declarations in part due to lack of enforcement, and both the U.S. and Britain subsequently withdrew from UNESCO.

In the years since the U.N. withdrawal matters have worsened. As borders continue to soften within the Americas, the European community, and throughout the world, the occurrence of cultural imperialism—led by a few dominant nations—continues to increase. A global economy may indeed open the door to an electronic global village. The question is, what can be done about this? Part of the answer lies in education, in the recognition that the cross-cultural exchange of media is not an inherently negative phenomenon. Old nations about the unilateral imposition of ideology from the strong to the weak need to be rethought. Understandings need to be developed of the complex and often contradictory ways that weak and strong powers enable each other. Assertions of cultural sovereignty are difficult to maintain in nations whose populations are clamoring for Madonna tickets. This is because typical cultural imperialism discourse fails to adequately theorize viewing/consuming subjects, their needs, desires, and pleasures. Instead of mediating the oppressive logics of capitalism and modernization, conventional cultural imperialism discourse offers a reactionary mix of humanism, chauvinism, and nostalgia.

Take the case of Great Britain. Since the end of World War II values of "Americanization" were widely regarded as a threat to the purity of British national culture and tradition. Speaking of soap operas, George Orwell and Richard Hoggart both wrote of the erosion of working-class strength that might result from such a "feminine" medium (Morely and Robins 1989, 20). To F. R. Leavis, the danger was less specified, but more sinister. Leavis pointed to "the rootlessness, the vacuity, the inhuman scale, the failure of organized cultural life, and the anti-human reductionism [of] the American neo-imperialism of the computer" (Morley and Robins 1989, 22). Such criticisms of the media were justified, but misdirected. In Leavis's comments, one finds a nostalgic yearning for authenticity that often characterizes cultural nationalism. This is a longing for common origins in a world seemingly run amok with difference (Anderson 1983, 129–41). Such romanticism is patently antimodernist, more pitted against notions of change than of media. Like many cultural nationalists, Leavis was lamenting the threat to such traditions posed by an American media of rock and roll, fast cars, and plastic plates. Ironically, this disposable modern culture was a great deal more appealing to the British working class than the pastoral nostalgia it associated with British aristocracy. It wasn't Leavis's dusty traditions that Britons wanted, but the newness offered by icons like Elvis and Marilyn Monroe.

Similarly, it has been argued that much of what is customarily identified as cultural imperialism is really a function of time itself. John Tomlinson asserts that national identities defined purely in spatial terms fail to come to terms with the temporal character of culture (Tomlinson 1991, 68–99). Simply put, there is no such thing as a single national culture that remains the same year after year. Nations are constantly assimilating, combining, and revising their national "characters." Moreover, even spatial boundaries rarely correspond to the demarcations between racial and ethnic groups, speakers of various languages, and even families. Thus, the heterogeneous and changing nature of nations raises the question of who is authorized to speak on behalf of a national identity and when.

HOME VIEWING: DOMESTIC MEDIA
AND NATIONAL IDENTITY

No one needs reminding that similar debates over media texts continue to be waged within the U.S., as antagonists on both the Left and the Right have recognized the capacity of images to assume a symbolic meaning in the national consciousness. Domestic complaints about media fall into three categories.[2] The first might be called the moral crisis argument. Its proponents assert that the violent and sexual content of television, movies, and recordings causes deviant behavior in viewers. This position insistently overlooks the absence of any empirical validation of such beliefs, despite countless studies on the subject. It also refuses to recognize both the complexity of young people's viewing practices and the kinds of pleasure derived from such viewing. Most significantly, by blaming social problems on the media, moral panickers divert attention from root causes of crime and violence like racism and structural poverty.

The second criticism frames the activity of television viewing as a form of narcotic that dulls the senses, encourages laziness, and confuses the viewer's sense of reality. This is the well-known labeling of TV as "mind candy," the "idiot box," or the "plug-in drug." The medium is blamed for ills ranging from poor academic performance to obesity to voter apathy. Not only do the media become a scapegoat for other problems, but they are condemned for their very functions as relaxation and entertainment that bring people pleasure.

The third argument relates to ideology by posing media as extensions of a consciousness industry that exerts a virtual authority over consumers. Viewers are seen as passive recipients of instructions that they are powerless to challenge. Like the moral panic stance, this position chooses to overlook the growing body of research suggesting that audiences use media in extremely diverse and complex ways. It fails to see that there is no such thing as a homogeneous "public" for media, but instead a variety of audience configurations with different needs and desires.

It's worth remembering that recent debates over media censorship were not initiated by popular outrage or scholarly concern but by religious extremists and headline-hungry politicians. Even though the potential has always existed for partisan misreadings of cultural signs, until the late 1980s the political incentive (and strategic wherewithal) was insufficient to elevate the practice above name calling (Mattick 1990, 354). Religious fundamentalists and political conservatives linked their accusations of immorality to a populist resentment of artists, intellectuals, and the "minority" interests the cultural community represented. Rather than proferring an inherently "false" message, the Right successfully linked its program to existing attitudes by associating Martin Scorcese, Karen Finley, and Two Live Crew with such perceived threats to traditional values as atheism, socialism, homosexuality, racial difference, and gender nonconformity.

Ironically, while the conservative program makes surface appeals to a nationalistic populism, it simultaneously promotes a cultural elitism that excludes the identities and histories of most citizens. This is a function of the often contradictory deployment of power in contemporary society. As Homi K. Bhabha has suggested, the continuing renewal of national identity—the will to nationhood that is reaffirmed anew each day—requires a form of forgetting past origins, ethnicities, and places. The obligation to forget in the name of unity is a form of "violence involved in establishing the national writ" (Bhabha 1990, 310). It is a matter to which national subjects consent and with which they struggle. Culture can no longer be seen as simply rooted in the kinds of "functionalist" views of social reproduction to which the Right has clung for much of the past century. Instead, it needs to be seen as a set of social transactions that are negotiated and exchanged over time.

At the same time, as important as it is to see culture as a network of negotiated texts, it would be foolish to discount the role of the political economy in which they reside. The sustenance of academic and political conservativism lies in the consolidated corporate strength supporting it. No amount of theorizing by itself will place an alternative record album on a store shelf or an independent video on television. Those institutions are firmly under the thumb of an economic power structure that functions strictly in its own interest. This effect of economic reproduction across a range of productive fields has been well documented. Less than 20 companies (Westinghouse, Gulf and Western, Time, ABC, CBS, McGraw-Hill, the New York Times, and Harcourt Brace Jovanovitch, among others) control all leading television networks, 70% of the major book publishers, 45% of the dominant magazine companies, 75% of the leading movie companies, and 70% of the major radio networks (Bagdikian 1990, 4).

In orthodox Marxist analysis, this monopolistic control of media was believed to promote an ever-increasing textual homogenization that promoted the consumption of mass-produced goods and the delegitimization of alternative thinking. At the other extreme, the Right argued that the expansion and differentiation of capitalist production ensured an ever-widening set of choices. Both positions failed to account adequately for differences among consuming groups in their willingness and ability to engage in consumption.

Further analysis has recognized that media address an ideal spectator who possesses a particular set of interpretive capacities and preferences. The appeal to an ideal spectator is made in the form of a preferred reading that asks the viewer to identify with particular values and beliefs. As a subset of this process, television has its own special forms of address, related to its ability to communicate to national and international audiences.[3] This address assumes three basic functions in national identity formation. First, it replicates and thereby reinforces hierarchies of capital within a given society. Major media networks are owned and controlled by a small elite who dispense information to multitudes. Second, television is structured into what Raymond Williams termed a "flow." This is the tendency of viewers to watch a chain of programs, commercials, and news without switching from discrete program to program. Over time this flow creates the impression of a unified theme. Third, television's direct address to viewers (who are often isolated) positions them as "the public" looking over a commentator's shoulder. This positioning implies a controlling gaze through which viewers survey and control a world of difference.

Because communications industries are predicated on maximizing audience shares, they tend to address a normative spectator profile. Yet, particularly in recent years, this approach has been problematized with a growing recognition of different audiences identified by such factors as age, race, gender, and region. Further exacerbating this fragmentation has been the consumer flexibility afforded by cable television and home cassette viewing. These factors have encouraged large-scale producers to search for issues that transcend audience divisions. And indeed, many of the highest grossing films address themes with a national—or nationalist—appeal. One form this national chauvinism takes is the nostalgic appeal to origins mentioned earlier. From the misty romanticism of *Driving Miss Daisy (1989)* to the soft-core social critique of *Dances with Wolves* (1990) filmmakers seek to conjure up a shared national past. Literally or symbolically the specter of an ominous Other often lurks in the background, encouraging viewers to draw their nationalistic wagons in a circle of defense. Not surprisingly, media villains and political scapegoats are often indistinguishable, whether it is in the implied ethnic criminality of *Boyz n the Hood* (1991) and *Bugsy* or the foreign menace of *Shining Through* and *The Hunt For Red October* (1990). On one level, it is argued that such films help to coalesce an audience around the fear of a common demon that throws national parochialism into relief. But this analysis fails to adequately account for the complex economies of attraction and desire that also characterize constructions of difference. As Ernesto Laclau has suggested, any entity is both defined and limited by objects of alterity (Laclau, 1991). Because the externalized Other is simultaneously a figure of antago-nism and radical possibility, it constitutes a part of the self that the self both wants and fears.

This ambivalence toward otherness finds its most instrumental expression in colonial narratives. Here, difference is both material substance and textual sign. The short distance from nationalistic pride to imperialistic aggression, from patriotism to racism, is demonstrated in a comparable range of films celebrating colonialism past and present such as *Heat and Dust* (1983), *The Gods Must Be Crazy* (1981), *A Passage to India* (1984), *Out of Africa* (1985), *Indiana Jones* (1984), or *Club Paradise* (1986). In each instance the world becomes a stage for an alternating program of benevolence and conquest.[4] Often this ideology is written directly on the surface of the consumer items, as in "Banana Republic" clothing, which evokes the name given to nations exploited in the 1920s by the United Fruit Company, or the Ralph Lauren perfume "Safari," which celebrates a comparable legacy of colonial trophy hunting. These sentiments are perhaps best summarized by a recent ad for the fragrance, featuring travel postcard images of foreign deserts and tropical beaches captioned with the phrases "Safari by Ralph Lauren," "A world without boundaries," "A personal adventure and a way of life."

In an age increasingly defined by limits, the commercial discourse of the West anxiously calls for continued expansion in the name of social betterment. This compulsive drive for the proliferation of Western capital is manifest in a plethora of recent ads baying at the threat of international competition. The U.S. trade deficit mounts ever higher as Buick touts its "Commitment to World-Class Quality" and AT&T urges U.S. business to "Take on the World." While the pressure from foreign trade competition continues to grow, the rhetoric of global domination heightens. This obsession with expansion even in an age of limits is part of a long legacy of American colonization and control. From the War of 1812 to the present, the U.S. has maintained an image of military invulnerability and global sovereignty. Sharon D. Welch has attributed this seemingly aggressive imaginary to a utopian vision of world peace enforced through the benevolence of a single superpower. Despite its utopian intentions, the U.S. has carried out this program with an irrational ruthlessness with three primary characteristics: a desire for absolute freedom from any outside control, a privileging of unilateral action over extended diplomacy, a tendency to use military force to resolve political or economic problems.[5] Although this patriarchal attitude has been manifest in recent U.S. interventions in Central America and the Middle East, it culminated in its most explicit form in the 1992 Pentagon plan for a "New World Order" calling for all nations except the U.S. to demilitarize.[6]

Implicit in this American attitude of benevolent world domination is a vision of global agreement and sameness similar to that purportedly existing within the U.S. itself. This is a world of total conformity to a single standard of beliefs and principles—as represented in a presumably perfect U.S. system. As Ronald Reagan put it, the ethos "for which America and all democratic nations stand represents the culmination of Western Civilization."[7] Whether the subject is education or foreign policy, in such an environment dissent becomes no longer appropriate or acceptable. Agreement to standardized norms, held in place by elaborate social technologies, becomes the only permissible option. Unilateral action on the international front is therefore always permissible because the U.S. is always correct. The spread of U.S. culture throughout the world is viewed as healthy and just.

BACK TO SCHOOL: THE EVOLUTION OF MEDIA
IN THE CLASSROOM

Television entered the pedagogical picture in the decade following the Second World War, but critical viewing was the last thing on its proponents' minds. As the first wave of the baby boom hit the classroom in the 1950s, video was instantly seized upon as a means of increasing teacher productivity. By simply eliminating the need for duplicate presentations, video was credited with reductions in labor of up to 70 percent (Diamond 1964a, 3). It was also recognized as a powerful tool for observation and evaluation (Hofstrand 1964, 149). Concurrent advances in computer and telecommunications industries prompted more elaborate speculation. While in residence at New York's Fordham University during the late 1960s, Marshall McLuhan attracted a quasi-religious following based on his vision of a global telecommunications network designed on biological (and therefore "natural") principles that would undermine all hierarchical structures. At the core of McLuhan's program lay a concept of media as "information without content" that defined international turmoil as the result of failed communication rather than ideological confrontation (McLuhan 1964, 23).

This pop-philosophy approach to new technology fit perfectly into 1960s educational reformism, while also complementing U.S. cultural policy. In a domestic atmosphere of desegregation, urban renewal, and other liberal initiatives, efforts were made to eliminate the biases inherent in standard pedagogies. As a means of deemphasizing differences of race, gender, and class, theories of educational formalism were introduced into many schools to stress the structure of learning over culturally specific content. As John Culkin put it in 1970, "one doesn't have to know all about a subject, but one should know what a subject is all about" (28). Educators saw photographic media as tools for directly engaging student experience.

With the economic downturns of the 1980s and the ascendancy of the Reagan/ Bush government came sweeping indictments of liberal programs. Supply-side analysts blamed schools for the nation's inability to compete in world markets, while ironically arguing for reductions in federal education and cultural budgets. Because they often required expensive equipment, media programs were terminated in the name of cost reduction, as renewed emphasis was placed on a "back to basics" curriculum. This did not mean that television disappeared from the classroom, only that its more complicated, hands-on, applications were replaced by simple viewing.

The reemergence of the television as teacher in the 1980s paralleled distinct shifts in media production and distribution. These were outgrowths of large-scale changes in the film and television industry brought about by the emergence of affordable consumer videocassette equipment. For the viewer, home recording and tape rental allowed hitherto unknown control over what was watched. The same was true in the classroom. For the instructional media industry, the hitherto costly process of copying 16mm films was quickly supplanted by inexpensive high-speed video duplication. The entire concept of educational media products began to change, as films could be mass-produced on a national scale (in effect "published") like books. Market expansion in this type of video was exponential.

There is a negative side to the video boom, particularly in what tend to be regressive classroom applications. Beyond obvious arguments that pit time efficiency against human interaction lie the more subtle issues of subjective address. Unlike home viewing that affords a degree of flexibility and choice, the use of educational media does indeed position students as passive receivers of information, while at the same time validating an intellectual process based on stereotyping.[8] This replicates the most conservative forms of transmission learning and teacher-centered pedagogy. Such an approach is typified in the flood of slickly produced and moralistic videos for the school market from such entities as the Children's Defense Fund, the Center for Humanities, and Guidance Associates, among others. These latter organizations offer an enormous range (the current Guidance Associates catalogue lists over 500 filmstrips, slide series, and tapes) on topics from drug abuse to "values clarification," all stressing a prescriptive and normative ideology.

The renewed use of such instructional aids has again increased in the 1990s, as corporate educational reformers reach for technological solutions to school problems. Witness the phenomenon of Channel One. Since going on line in 1990, the Whittle Communication Corp. Channel One has been piping its MTV-style blend of news programming and commercials for corn chips and acne medicine into 8,600 secondary schools. In exchange for up to $50,000 in free video equipment, schools agree to present the 15-minute programs to their students. As explained by company president Chris Whittle, normally "you can't make people who don't watch television watch television" (Kleinfield 1991, 79). In school you can.

Clearly, the importance of audiovisual materials will continue to grow in school, in the workplace, and at home. With the proliferation of videocassette equipment, added cable channels, home shopping networks and computer information services, telecommunications link-ups, interactive texts and games. We should not delude ourselves that these new technologies by themselves have the capability of changing social relationships or economic structures. As quickly as a new gimmick is developed, Madison Avenue finds a way to turn a profit from it. Yet these new tools offer potential for innovative use and subversion, for the establishment of new forms of alliance, and for the creation of new strains of cultural production.

THE NEW MEDIA LITERACY MOVEMENT

As with regressive written texts, the key for an emancipatory use of media materials in the classroom lies in helping students to locate oppositional readings to those offered. Particularly in settings with students from diverse backgrounds, it is important to stress that culture isn't limited to what is legitimated in books and other instructional materials. It is also a sociological substance produced every day by each of us.[9] This is especially true with everyday texts, and it is what makes a static view of national identity problematic. Narrative relationships are constantly in flux—both those found in books and the diverse narratives encountered in such items as movies, television, clothing, appliances, food, and housing. Our understandings of many of these texts are always in need of some revision to adapt them to change and circumstance. As people continue to adjust their interpretations, they are making the meaning that is culture.

In progressive circles of education a growing body of literature has developed in recent decades to contest hierarchical models of schooling.[10] This critical pedagogy movement has sought to reconcile students and teachers as partners in an educational relationship that can serve as a model for broader social compacts. At the same time, because so much of subjectivity is shaped through the media, the effects of communications industries have become the object of intense scrutiny. Partly informed by critical pedagogy and cultural studies, the new "media literacy" movement is an amalgam of reader response theories and institutional analyses. While acknowledging the persuasive properties of images, practitioners in the new media literacy movement emphasize ways that viewers use media in individualized ways.

In textual terms, the media literacy movement argues that the ability to mediate dominant readings and spectator positionings in media can be improved with study and that these skills can be taught to children regardless of age or grade level. One can teach young people to use the media for their own ends by actively interpreting how it functions and choosing how to read it. This is done by encouraging viewers to look beyond specific texts by asking critical questions like "Who is communicating and why?" "How is it produced?" "Who receives it and what sense do they make of it?" A characteristic exercise for younger children might ask what TV programs they like and dislike. In the course of the discussion the class quickly divides into groups of Voltrons, Noozles, and Smurfs. What becomes apparent is the relatively simple, yet important, notion that media texts are not uniformly received. By examining their own preferences, children come to recognize that mass media do not define a unified national audience, but a heterogeneous universe of spectator groups. From this a discussion can evolve on the ways advertisers and media producers tailor their programming based on media use.

In a class conducted by the San Francisco–based group Strategies for Media Literacy, students compare pictures of their own families with ones they find on TV (Lloyd-Kolkin and Tyner 1991). By making visual comparisons between the Huxtables, the Keatons, and themselves kids are asked to ponder "which is real?" Of course the answer is none, because depictions—private and public—are fictional. Through this exercise youngsters begin to learn not only how they are interpellated by the forces of media myth making, but also the ways they have internalized received narratives of family. Again, the lesson is that children are not part of a unified "national family" but of many different communities and affinity groups. By drawing attention to their own attitudinal biases and stereotypes the lesson underscores the relationship of self to image. In doing so, it introduces young children to a set of concepts about the ideological unconscious that many adults have trouble grasping. Because youngsters occupy an early stage of ego development, they can face this notion of an unstable self without the anxieties of their older counterparts.[11] Young children have not developed the same investment in personal identity as teenagers.

On the other hand, older students can accommodate a broader range of topics ranging—from discipline-oriented inquiry and values education to cross-media studies and critical thinking. Through technical, linguistic, and sociological discussions one can convey the ways government and corporate interests construct reality through media, as well as the audience's role in creating these meanings. Although the U.S. has been slow to address these issues, our neighbors to the north have not. This is partly a function of the extent to which nations like Canada are inundated by U.S. media and have responded to this cultural imperialism. The Canadian Ministry of Education workbook *The Media Literacy Resource Guide* characterizes reception in the following manner: "When we look at a media text, each of us finds meaning through a wide variety of factors: personal needs and anxieties, the pleasures and troubles of the day, racial and sexual attitudes. . . . In short, each of us finds or 'negotiates' meaning in different ways." (Ontario Ministry of Education 1989).

In practice such lessons can often be quite explicit in discussing the ideological implications of commercial (and noncommercial) media practices, even going so far as to point out the ways that Hollywood obscures its ideological messages to hide its political intent. Educators can use media to describe the way values are conveyed both directly, in the specific contents of works, and indirectly, through the "structured absences" that systematically exclude certain viewpoints. This point is illustrated most explicitly in *Media Literacy* in relation to U.S. media imperialism. ("For Canadians, our domination by American media has obvious cultural implications. The struggle for a distinctive Canadian identity will continue to be difficult, a challenge that media-literacy programs need to address" [Ontario Ministry of Education 1989, 33]).

Beyond such textual issues media education can also interrogate the very concrete ways that television, radio, and movies structure audiences and their material surroundings. For example, the address of TV has evolved in part to cater to a domestic audience and to encourage certain patterns of television use within the home. It serves as breakfast entertainment, evening family ritual, or weekend sports gathering. These functions have influenced the layout and use of spaces within the home as well as appointments within individual rooms. Consequently TV has both a direct and an indirect impact on a broad range of commodities— a point hardly lost on the merchandisers of goods ranging from popcorn poppers to easy chairs. John Fiske has written of the way people use television to modulate the "texture" of living environments, which people create and alter as a means of laying claim to social space: "Television is used to increase, enrich and further densify the texture. It is typically left on all the time, adding color, sound and action to apartment life; it is used to frame and cause conversations, to fill gaps and silences. It can provide both a means of entering and intensifying this dense everyday culture and a way of escaping it" (Fiske 1992, 156). This function is especially important to a sense of human agency in the face of alienating social technologies. These include the many institutions of health, law, education, and media that inscribe the body in webs of material overdetermination. The consumption of television and other media can represent both a response and a resistance to these social technologies.

Such consumer activism hardly characterizes most media literacy curricula. All too often in conventional pedagogies such emancipatory forms of media literacy are discounted as inconsequential, banal, or unhealthy. Offered instead is a program of viewer "empowerment," suggesting a free-market attitude of audience "choice" in which viewers become reconciled to the options available to them. This has been the rationale of numerous recent prescriptions from educational conservatives, most notably the authors of the National Endowment for the Arts's *Toward Civilization: A Report on Art Education*. In it NEA pedagogues suggested that the value of media studies lay in creating smarter shoppers:

> Every child growing up in the United States is bombarded from birth with popular art and artful communication over the airways and on the streets. The purpose of arts education is not to wean young people from these arts (an impossible task even if it were desirable) but to enable them to make reasoned choices about them and what is good and bad. Art education can help make discriminating consumers. (National Endowment for the Arts 1988, 18)

Toward Civilization's attitude toward media is quite consistent with its view of culture in general, which promotes a single, "good" standard of visual literacy to which all Americans should subscribe. The overall goal is the production of a national identity of verisimilitude, wherein all citizens share the same competencies, values, and rights. Difference is only tolerated to the degree it can be ameliorated into a shared sameness. Even in the Canadian *Media Literacy* volume, despite its brave words on media imperialism (hardly a point of controversy within the Canadian electorate), the book is decidedly understated in explaining the political implications of its contents. It rarely mentions the human consequences of corporate media hegemony (structural poverty, racism, homophobia) or the potential means of its restructuring (independent publishing, community television, legislative initiatives).

In part this political ambivalence is due to the relative intransigence of North American education markets and to the low status of media studies within school districts. In such a conservative environment media texts can hardly do much boat rocking. As an interdisciplinary field largely devoted to popular culture, media literacy is often dismissed by school administrators as an educational frill. Such courses are vehemently opposed by "back to basics" advocates, who claim that they undermine traditional culture and values. (The difficulty, of course, is that the popular appeal of mass cultural texts comes largely from their *antieducational* character.) Also, it hardly goes unnoticed that media courses are by definition student-centered and subversive in their critiques of capitalism and patriarchy.

When media literacy does find its way into the school curriculum it generally emerges as either a form of vocational education or an enhancement of an existing course in another discipline. As media education is introduced in a vocational context it is generally driven by a job-preparation mandate lacking in any critical consciousness. At Cincinnati's Hughes High School for the Communications, a Scripps-Howard Foundation–sponsored national model in vocational media education, students engage a rigorous four-year curriculum of media writing and production. In addition to producing cable television programs, photography projects, and public relations materials, students also participate in a special school newspaper covering such controversial issues as student race relations, homosexuality, and drug use.

Yet while providing technical training and a forum for airing social issues, the overall curriculum promotes an unexamined image of commercial media and journalism. As with the U.S. "free flow of information" doctrine and the government's *Toward Civilization* cultural prescriptions, the media landscape is presented as an inherently even terrain, where choice is open and access unstymied. Little acknowledgment is given to the extremely unequal positions from which people enter this terrain, the continuing discriminations they suffer, and the power structures that benefit from these arrangements. An unproblematic image is promoted of a nation where all citizens have equal opportunities, if only they have the gumption to follow their dreams. Failure is thus personalized as an individual shortcoming rather than an institutionally programmed necessity.

As enhancements to existing courses, studies of television, movies, or print media are most likely to be found in English, art, or social studies classes where textual reading and production already have a footing. Unfortunately this atmosphere is often locked into canonical regimens that can stultify critical thinking. Consequently, as media education has been constituted as an add-on to existing courses, it has been extremely limited in its ability to challenge forms of identity— national or otherwise—perpetuated in schools. This needn't be the case, but change requires effort. One place to begin this process is within schools of education, where the curricula of teacher preparation continues to reproduce very traditional attitudes toward media. The introduction of media literacy into other courses need not rely on special texts or instructional materials. Like other critical pedagogies, it hinges more on the way a teacher handles existing materials. On a primary level, media education within a given curriculum entails a greater attention to photographs, films, or videos as producers of meaning. Although there is nothing new about this emphasis on media, the media literacy approach involves a greater emphasis on the way this meaning is made.

This entails abandoning assumptions that particular readings are self-evident or that the medium itself is a neutral carrier of information. Such views are rooted in the same subject/object dualisms that foster transmission theories of teaching. In contrast to these views, it needs to be pointed out that truth does not pass perfectly through a video to a student, nor knowledge through a teacher. Both require the engagement of students in receiving the messages and making sense of them. Therefore, beyond attention to course content and the forms of its delivery, emphasis needs to be placed on developing competencies of reception that permit students to make choices and exercise agency in learning.

This form of media education capitalizes on what students already know about the vocabulary and syntax of media, while encouraging them to become more critically conscious of "how they know what they know" (Moore 1991, 173). In history classes this might involve a content analysis of the images in a textbook. What kind of people are pictured and in what numbers? Who seems to be in control? Similar questions can be asked in geography. In social studies current events are often used as a springboard for discussion. But do newspapers and television report the facts with complete objectivity? What parts of the story have been highlighted or ignored? In an English class dealing with required texts, a teacher might spend time talking about the limits of specific genres, the economics of publishing, and the separation of "high" culture from the everyday (Moore 1991, 181).

In each of these instances media literacy begins when we ask students to question the way their identities have been shaped as subjects in the school, the neighborhood, the nation, and the world. The point is that whether or not viewers realize it (in fact because they often *don't* realize it) they are always being interpellated by the media into quite specific roles. Every movie, every textbook, and every magazine addresses an ideal audience that is not often defined in terms of a national collectivity. This interpellation is so ubiquitous that is seems nonexistent. It is simply assumed.

This national interpellation is more than the brazen chauvinism of Rambo and Ralph Lauren. It exists in an advertising industry that pictures the world as its playground, a commercial ethos of economic dominance rather than cooperation, and now, a military attitude of complete global control rather than negotiation. Images aside, the question these attitudes leave begging concerns the future role of the U.S. in the world community. Indeed, what is the relevance of any national identity in a world of transnational capital? The combined effects of the free flow of information and the breakdown of national boundaries have caused changes in the centers as well as the margins of international culture. U.S. media products now reach larger audiences abroad than at home. For this reason production companies (many of which are owned by non-U.S. companies) now tailor programs for international audiences. Increasingly the choices offered to American viewers are determined by audiences located elsewhere. As the U.S. loses strength as an economic power the influence of external culture will continue to grow.

These realities come into direct conflict with a foreign policy based on the eternal correctness of the U.S. and its "right" to unilateral action throughout the globe. Sooner or later the U.S. will need to recognize the inherent partiality of any single perspective and the need for cooperation in global affairs. One place where this awareness can begin to be introduced is the classroom. By stressing the limitation of any single viewpoint or reading, students can develop literacies that value difference. Such literacies recognize the necessity of difference in creating a moral vision that a single perspective can never offer.

NOTES

1. Henry Luce as quoted in Schiller 1969.
2. These issues are discussed at length in Bucki.

3. These three points of national and international communication are summarized in King and Rowse 1990. In elaborating this typology, the authors borrow the concept of "flow" introduced in Williams 1975.

4. A lengthy discussion of films glorifying the expansion of American capitalism is found in Williamson 1991.

5. Welch cites James Chace and Caleb Carr in her development of this typology of U.S. foreign policy.

6. The gendered character of national and international relations is discussed in Parker et al. 1992.

7. Ronald Reagan, as cited in Welch 1990.

8. These issues are taken up in depth in Ellsworth and Whatley 1990.

9. This banality of culture is taken up at length in the often-quoted William

10. A representative sampling of recent texts on critical pedagogy: Apple 1990; Aronowitz and Giroux 1990; Giroux 1992; McLaren 1989, 1992; Mohanty 1989; Simon 1992; and Trend 1992.

11. The problems of explaining the received character of identity to teenagers are taken up in Williamson 1981–82.

WORKS CITED

Alvarado, Manual, and Thompson, John O., eds. (1990). *The Media Reader*. London: British Film Institute.

Anderson, Benedict (1983). *Imagined Communities: Reflections on the Origin and Spread of Nationalism*. London: Verso.

Apple, Michael (1990). *Teachers and Texts*. New York: Routledge.

Aronowitz, Stanley, and Grioux, Henry A. (1990). *Postmodern Education: Politics, Culture, and Social Criticism*. Minneapolis: University of Minnesota Press.

Bagdikian, Ben J. (1990). *The Media Monopoly*. Boston: Beacon Press.

Bhabha, Homi K. (1990). *Nation and Narration*. London and New York: Routledge.

Buckingham, David (1991). "Teaching about the Media." In Lusted 1991b.

Corner, John, and Harvey, Sylvia, eds. (1991). *Enterprise and Heritage: Crosscurrents of National Culture*. London and New York: Routledge.

Culkin, John M. (1970). "Films Deliver". In Culkin and Schillaci 1970.

Culkin, John M. and Schillaci, (1970) eds. *Films Deliver*. New York: Citation Press.

Diamond, Robert M, ed. (1964a). *A Guide to Instructional Media*. New York: McGraw-Hill.

Diamond, Robert M. (1964b/c). "Single Room Television," in Diamond 1964a.

Ellsworth, Elizabeth, and Whatley, Miriamne (1990). *The Ideology of Images in Educational Media: Hidden Curriculums in the Classroom*. New York: Teachers College Press.

Fiske, John (1992). "Cultural Studies and the Culture of Everyday Life." In Grossberg et al. 1992. 154–64.

Giroux, Henry A. (1992). *Border Crossings: Cultural Workers and the Politics of Education*. New York and London: Routledge.

Grossberg, Lawrence; Nelson, Cary; and Treichler, Paula A., eds. (1992). *Cultural Studies*. New York and London: Routledge.

Hofstrand, John M. (1964). "Television and Classroom Observation." Diamond 1964a.

King, Noel, and Rowse, Thomas (1990). "Typical Aussies: Television and Populism in Australia." In Alvarado and Thompson 1990: 36–49.

Kleinfield, N. R. (1991). "What Is Chris Whittle Teaching Our Children?" *New York Times Magazine* May 19: 79.

Laclau, Ernesto (1991). *New Reflections on the Revolution of Our Time.* London: Verso.

Lloyd-Kolkin, Donna, and Tyner, Kathleen (1991). *Media and You: An Elementary Media Literacy Curriculum.* San Francisco: Strategies of Media Literacy.

Lusted, David (1991a). Introduction. In Lusted 1991b.

Lusted, David, ed. (1991b). *The Media Studies Book.* London and New York: Routledge.

Mattick, Paul Jr. (1990). "Art and the State: The NEA Debate in Perspective." *Nation* October 1 (251): 10.

McLaren, Peter (1989). *Life in Schools: An Introduction to Critical Pedagogy in the Foundations of Education.* New York and London: Longman.

McLaren, Peter, ed. (1992). *Postmodernism, Post-colonialism, and Pedagogy.* Albert Park, Australia: James Nicholas Publishers.

McLuhan, Marshall (1964). *Understanding Media: Extensions of Man.* New York: McGraw-Hill.

Mohanty, Chandra Talpade (1989 89–90). "On Race and Voice." *Cultural Critique* 14 (Winter): 179–200.

Moore, Ben (1991). "Media Education." In Lusted 1991: 171–190.

Morley, David, and Robins, Kevin (1989). "Spaces of Identity: Communications Technologies and the Refiguration of Europe." *Screen* (Autumn)30:4

National Endowment for the Arts (1988). *Toward Civilization: A Report on Arts Education.* Washington, National Endowment for the Arts.

Ontario Ministry of Education (1989). *Media Literacy Resource Guide.* Toronto: Ontario Ministry of Education.

Parker, Andrew; Russo, Mary; Sommer Dorris; and Yaeger, Patricia, eds. (1992). *Nationalisms and Sexualities.* New York and London: Routledge.

Schiller, Herbert I. (1969). *Mass Communications and American Empire.* New York: Beacon Press.

Schiller, Herbert I. (1976). *Communication and Cultural Domination.* White Plains, N.Y.: International Arts and Sciences Press.

Simon, Roger I. (1992). *Teaching against the Grain.* New York: Bergin and Garvey.

Tomlinson, John (1991). *Cultural Imperialism: A Critical Introduction.* Baltimore: Johns Hopkins.

Trend, David (1992). *Cultural Pedagogy: Art/Education/Politics.* New York: Bergin and Garvey.

Welch, Sharon D. (1990). *A Feminist Ethic of Risk.* Minneapolis: Fortress Press.

Williams, Raymond (1956). "Culture is Ordinary." In Williams 1989.

Williams, Raymond (1975). *Television: Technology and Cultural Form.* New York: Schocken Books.

Williams, Raymond (1989). *Resources of Hope.* London: Verso.

Williamson, Judith (1981–82). "How Does Girl Number 20 Understand Ideology?" *Screen Education.* (Autumn/Winter)40.

Williamson, Judith (1991). "Up Where You Belong: Hollywood Images of Big Business in the 1980s." In Corner and Harvey 1991: 151–61.

CHAPTER 13

SOME IMPLICATIONS

OF PAULO'S FREIRE'S

BORDER PEDAGOGY

ABDUL R. JANMOHAMED

As is well known, Paulo Freire's pedagogic theory eschews what he calls the "nutritionist" concept of knowledge, a view which implicitly construes literacy as a tool provided to an already formed and existing subjectivity that can therefore be modified only in a narrow technical sense by the acquisition of this skill. Instead, for Freire literacy is a process, "an act of knowing," which empowers the nonliterate and reactivates a moribund subjectivity (45). It might even be argued that his theory and procedures permit the nonliterate "peasants" (whom Freire does not identify specifically) to create themselves as new subjects, though he is rather cautious in claiming that those who have become literate are thereby radically transformed.

Yet such a claim needs to be investigated since a remarkable and powerful isomorphism links the two components of Freire's pedagogic method. These two components—the technical procedures that introduce the peasants to literacy, on the one hand, and what, for the sake of brevity, I will at present characterize as ideology critique—are so thoroughly intertwined that Freire does not seem willing to articulate theoretically their different moments. The isomorphism lies in the parallel structures of the method through which the peasants are introduced to written language and the procedure used for the analysis of what Freire calls their existential condition—that is, the technique of "decodifying" the "codified," sedimented reality of their mundane lives. Both these methods permit the peasants to understand that, from an analytic angle, linguistic and social structuration are based on differential relations of elements that can be separated and recombined, and therefore controlled, by the subject performing the operation. Thus, by revealing that the differential relations of elements in both realms are constitutive of the "meanings" of their lives and by providing the individuals with some sense of control over the analytic and synthesizing procedures, Freire's pedagogic strategies introduce them to knowledge as power and to the possibility of agency.

In the rest of this essay I would like to examine in some detail the nature of this isomorphic procedure as well as its social and political implications. I would also like to suggest that Freire empowers the nonliterate by encouraging them to focus on dislocation, a form of alienation, and to become nascent "border intellectuals" by crossing the boundary between what he calls semi-intransitive consciousness and naive transitive consciousness.[1]

In the appendix to the essay "Cultural Action and Consciencization," Freire describes his method, which contrasts markedly with the literacy primers based on a nutritionist theory of literacy (91–93). In the specific example provided, the program begins by examining the representation of a slum that constitutes a concrete and immediate aspect of the conditions of existence for the peasants. That is, the social, political, and economic "codifications" through which the slum has been created as a "natural" object—i.e., "natural" in that the peasants perceive and accept it as an inevitable part of their condition—are examined by the group as "the knowable object." This is then subjected to a process of "decodification," that is, to a "breaking down [of] the codified totality and putting it together again (retotalizing it)," which becomes "the process by which the knowing subject seeks to know" (Freire, 91). What is crucial in this deconstructive maneuver is that it "enables the students *to penetrate the whole in terms of the relationships among its parts,* which until then the [students] did not perceive" (Freire, 92; emphasis added). At this point, when the peasants have begun to understand the differential relations among the parts that constitute their sociopolitical experience, the signifier, *favela,* that codifies their experience is introduced and submitted to a scrutiny for the "semantic relations between the generative word and what it signifies" (Freire, 92). Thus a careful bridge is built between the referent, understood as an ensemble of differentially related and overdetermined sociopolitical elements, and the signifier, after which the latter is isolated and similarly deconstructed. *Favela* is divided into three syllables, each of which is then differentiated from its "family" members (fa, fe, fi, etc.) until a "horizontal and a vertical reading" of the elements permits the distinction between consonants and vowels. Finally the students are encouraged to recombine the syllables so that they constitute signifiers different from the one with which they began.

What is remarkable about this procedure is that both the referent and the signifier are subject to similar differential analysis. Moreover, the tacit symmetry involved in this analysis most probably conveys, or at least implies, to the students an important lesson about social reality, a lesson that in this instance is communicated through the "noise," through the form rather than the content of the procedure: just as they can master written communication through the control and manipulation of the discrete though related elements of the language so can they master their social condition through similar manipulation of its constituent elements. The demystification of the structure of language implies, through the symmetry in the analysis of referent and signifier, a parallel potential demystification of social-political-cultural structuration, and agential control over the elements of language intimates a similar control over social elements.

While Freire neither identifies the isomorphism of his procedure nor articulates theoretically its implications, he is clearly aware of the latter. In the dialectical interaction between reflection and action that, according to Freire, is central to the acquisition of literacy as an "act of knowing," the learner "must engage in an authentic process of abstraction by means of which he can reflect on the action-object whole, or, more generally, *on forms of orientation in the world*" (50–51; emphasis added). Thus the procedure, more or less a form of phenomenological meditation, necessitates a focus on the categories of experience and of social construction. Freire is quite insistent on this:

> The surface structure of codification makes the action-object whole explicit in a purely taxonomic form. The first stage of decodification—or reading— is descriptive. At this stage the "readers"—or decodifiers—focus on the relationship between the categories constituting the codification. . . .
>
> Codification represents a given dimension of reality as individuals live it, and this dimension is proposed for their analysis in a context other than that in which they live it. [Decodification] thus transforms what was a way of life in the real context into "objectum" in the theoretical context. The learners, rather than receive information about this or that fact, analyze aspects of their own existential experience represented in the codification. (52).

Two aspects of this method need particular emphasis. First, the procedure does not attempt to articulate or privilege for the peasants a specific set of lacks or demands, injustices or utopian programs, because such demands, once satisfied, would not necessarily alter their structural condition. Instead, Freire focuses on constitutive categories, which, when transformed, can produce epistemic shifts that in turn are capable of generating other categorical changes and developing specific demands, programs, goals, etc. These procedures, then, are also analogous to the acquisition of literacy in that they provide a set of rules and skills through which one can generate infinite specificity and negotiate a variety of concrete demands.

Second, the method is also phenomenological in that Freire's conception of "codification" and "decodification" closely parallels Husserl's definition of "sedimentation" and "reactivation": for Husserl the former denotes the routinization and forgetting of origins and the latter the process of recovering the "constitutive" activity of thought. However, "reactivation," as Ernesto Laclau points out, does not have to mean a search for a positive origin, which in any case is impossible (34–35). Rather, it implies a (re)discovery of the contingent nature of the sedimented, codified social condition that one has been induced to take for granted as the singular order of reality.

The efficacy of Freire's strategy of decodifying the codified becomes clearly evident in the light of Laclau's appropriation and rearticulation of Husserl's terms. For Laclau "the sedimented forms of 'objectivity' make up the field of what we will call the 'social.' The moment of antagonism where the undecidable nature of the alternatives and their resolution through power relations becomes fully visible constitutes the field of the 'political' " (35). Even if we modify Laclau's insistence on the "full" visibility of undecidability, or conversely of a completely coherent and rational program for achieving alternatives, the definition of the "political" as a *commencement* of the process of "reactivating" sedimented social structures permits us to see the profoundly political nature of Freire's literacy project. The very decision to focus on "categories constituting the codification" represents a shift from the "social/sedimented" to the "political/reactivated." Even the mastery of literacy represents for the peasants a shift from the codified society (which includes as one of its essential features the very illiteracy against which they are struggling) to a political subject position. To the extent that the dominant society that disfranchises the peasants is never a totally sutured and stable structure, it manages to sustain its coherence and power only by repressing the peasants who threaten it. Thus, for Freire to encourage them to study the conditions of their existence is implicitly to persuade them to study the power relations that define their current and future identities.

The reflection entailed in the decodification process leads to the creation of a distance that is also empowering. According to Freire, for "the learner to know what he did not know before, he must engage in an authentic process of abstraction by means of which he can reflect on the action-object whole, or, more generally, on forms of orientation in the world" (51). The abstraction produces a distance between the mundane practices in which the peasant is immersed and the new awareness opened up by reflection, in short, between what Freire calls the "semi-intransitive consciousness" and "naive transitive consciousness." This distance provides a space in which a new subjectivity can begin to articulate itself, and the process of reflection creates a degree of autonomy for the subject to the extent that the decision to begin the reflective process is not positively determined by the existing dominant social structure. Finally, the incipient constitution of a new identity implied by all this is an act of power. However, the power entailed in this action should not be confused as being in any way equivalent to the massive institutional and juridical power available to dominant society. The newly literate peasants exist at the point where their virtual powerlessness (in that they have little, if any, access to institutionalized power) intersects with the massive prohibitive power of various state and civil apparatuses, power that, it must be emphasized, is always underwritten by actual or potential use of coercive violence.

Freire's method also encourages the peasants to develop clearer antagonisms between themselves and the dominant group and to draw boundaries between them, a process which in turn further clarifies their nascent identities. Freire urges the cultivation of antagonism simultaneously at the levels of collective subjectivity and cultural formation. In the former case, he argues, "when the dominated classes reproduce the dominators' style of life, it is because the dominators live 'within' the dominated. The dominated can eject the dominators only by getting distance from them and objectifying them. Only then can they recognize them as their antithesis" (53). Secondly, "ejection must also be achieved by a type of cultural action in which culture negates culture. That is, culture, as an interiorized product that in turn conditions men's subsequent acts, must become the object of men's knowledge so that they can perceive its conditioning power" (52–53). Finally, he insists that the opposition "must express itself in a behavior that is equally antagonistic" (81).

This insistence on the clarification of antagonism has several important consequences. In the first instance, antagonism, which in this case emerges gradually from the peasants' contemplation of their social condition, returns them to the contingency of that condition. According to Laclau, antagonistic force simultaneously fulfills two crucial and contradictory functions:

> On the one hand, it "blocks" the full constitution of identity to which it is opposed and thus shows its contingency. But on the other hand, given that this latter identity, like all identities, is merely relational and would therefore not be what it is outside the relationship with the force antagonizing it, the latter is also part of the conditions of existence of that identity. (21).

To the extent that the peasants must understand that their situation is not preordained but a product of specific circumstances that can be changed, their freedom depends as much on the recognition of the contingency as of the necessity that constitutes their history.

The emphasis on antagonism developed through decodification also clarifies the paradox of what Henry Giroux calls "border pedagogy," which advocates the adoption of the viewpoint of "people moving in and out of borders constructed around coordinates of difference and power" and encourages students "to develop a relationship of non-identity with their own subject positions and the multiple cultural, political, and social codes that constitute established boundaries of power, dependency, and possibility" (Aronowitz and Giroux 199–200). Freire also implicitly urges his students to develop relationships of nonidentity with their own subject positions. Yet, in order to develop such a relationship, one would in effect have to adopt another subject position from which to critique and distance oneself from one's "own" subject position. A relationship of nonidentity with one's position amounts to the development of an antagonism with oneself, which can only be accomplished when one has already begun to identify, tacitly or deliberately, with another position, whether that position is fully formed or nascent. In short, such a procedure simultaneously requires disidentification and identification: it demands a shift away from the deeply cathected inertia of fixed, sedimented identities and toward an engagement in the process of reidentification. It is therefore also a process of forming affiliations with other positions, of defining equivalences and constructing alliances. To the extent that nonidentification is impossible without simultaneous alternate identification, such a process then becomes crucial for the possibility of forming counterhegemonic organizations.

It must be emphasized that this process of disidentification also requires an ejection of the introjected subject positions of dominant groups. Laclau is correct to insist that at the ontological level antagonism is based on a "constitutive outside":

> It is an "outside" which blocks the identity of the "inside" (and is, nonetheless, prerequisite for its constitution at the same time). With antagonism,

denial does not originate from the "inside" of identity itself but, in its most radical sense, *from outside;* it is thus pure facticity which cannot be referred back to any underlying rationality. (Laclau 17)

However, at the sociopolitical level it is not the antagonism of pure facticity but that of other individual and collective subjects that blocks one's identity. And denial of identity operates most effectively not simply by the imposition of external limitations, or by a prohibition against certain subjects occupying given subject positions within the dominant culture, but through the construction of hegemonic rules and regulations that are "internalized" as normal operating procedures. Thus, on the sociopolitical register antagonism exists on the "inside"; it cleaves the subject, or, to put it differently, it manifests itself as a fundamental incompatibility between the different subject positions that one occupies at a given point. And the need to expel the antagonistic forces produces explosive contradictions within the subject or between subject positions. Antagonism thus draws powerful boundaries not only between groups and between subjects but also "within" the subject.

If identity is based on the antagonism of a constitutive "outside" and an "inside," whether at the ontological or the sociopolitical levels, then antagonism defines identity only by creating borders. To be sure, these borders are always unstable, always shifting and realigning themselves, but they are crucial to the construction of identities, to group formations, and, indeed, to any negotiation of the "political" field. To the extent that the shift from existence in a sedimented state of society or subjectivity to a reactivated examination of that society or subjectivity constitutes a shift in the form of agency, the movement from the social to the political entails the crossing of an important boundary. This is precisely what Freire's pedagogy encourages the peasants to do; it is important to clarify that his method does not present them with anything like fully constituted alternate identities, but instead inspires them to cross the boundary between the social and the political and thereby to begin to redefine their subject positions.

In short, Freire's is a "border pedagogy," one which, however, has some other important implications that need to be explored. The pedagogic site in Freire's work is clearly utopian in character. However, its dimensions become clearer if one examines them in light of Michel Foucault's notions of utopia/heterotopia. Utopias and heterotopias are, according to Foucault, the two sites that "have the curious property of being in relation with all other sites, but in such a way as *to suspect, neutralize, or invert the set of relations that they happen to designate, mirror, or reflect"* (22; emphasis added). These two sites are linked with all other sites, but primarily by a relation of contradiction. Established "in the very founding of society," heterotopias, like boundaries, are "countersites" in which all the other real sites that can be found within a culture "are simultaneously represented, contested, and inverted" (Foucault, 22). Like Foucault's heterotopic site—cemeteries, fairs, libraries, prisons, etc.—the pedagogic site is also a social and institutional space. According to Foucault's description all these sites are defined as *inherently* heterotopic. However, it would seem more accurate to characterize them as constitutionally ambiguous sites, as spaces that dominant cultures can utilize for the purposes of hegemonic construction and that oppositional groups can employ for their heterotopian value: all these sites are *potentially* heterotopic, but need to be utilized in that manner for their potential to become manifest. This is true above all of pedagogic institutions, which, as sites centrally involved in the production and formation of subjectivity, agency, systems of value, regimes of truth, etc., are deeply invested spaces for hegemonic and counterhegemonic contestation.

As such, pedagogic institutions are sites where borders are constantly drawn and redrawn—borders that define epistemic, ethical, cultural, social, political, economic, gender, racial, and class spaces and that legitimate and valorize them positively or negatively. The pedagogic apparatuses will thus produce some subjects who are content to remain within the prescribed borders and others who will violate them, reluctantly or willfully, painfully or with pleasure, or, in practice, with complex, overdetermined combinations of affects. A specific variant of the transgressive subject, the "border intellectual" is simultaneously a "space" and a subject, is, indeed, a subject-as-space. The transformation of such a border subject, who is always constituted as a *potential* heterotopic site, into an *actual* heterotopic, specular border intellectual depends upon his/her own agency: only by directly or indirectly reading the self as a heterotopic border can the intellectual articulate his/her specular, antagonistic, transgressive potentiality.

Freire's pedagogy implicitly advocates the nurturing of intellectuals who will cross borders and in the process develop strong antagonisms. To the extent that Freire's (generic) peasants begin to reflect on the conditions of their existence and (judging from the evidence that Freire presents, they clearly do begin the long process), they become nascent specular border intellectuals. Caught between the dominant group's practices, which seek to disenfranchise them and appropriate their labor for a pittance, and the resultant poverty that forces them to exist on the edge of subsistence, the peasants turn, upon the inducement of Freire's pedagogy, to an examination of the borders that confine them. In so doing, they in effect become archeologists of the site of their own social formation; their new subject positions begin to cathect around the project of excavating and reading their own social and physical bodies, which are in fact texts of the history of their oppression. Thus their new subjectivity emerges in the process of drawing borders around their old subject positions, a process that constitutes them as nascent specular border intellectuals. Their contemplation of the condition of their lives represents a freedom, or at least an attempt to achieve freedom, from the politics of imaginary identification and opposition, from conflation of identity and location, and so on— in short, from the varied and powerful forms of suturing that are represented by and instrumental in the construction of their sedimented culture. The process of decoding as well as the emerging command of literacy permits them a gradual shift from the confines of the imaginary to the outer edges of the symbolic realm.

Their new status as border intellectuals, however, does not limit them entirely to specular reflection, for the drawing of boundaries has other implications as well. In order to articulate epistemic and sociopolitical differences, borders generate digital punctuation of analog differences, that is, they delineate highly valorized, stylized, and formulaic punctuation of infinite, continuous, and heterotopic differences that fill a given continuum. In contrast to the analog differences, borders (i.e., digitalized articulations of differences) introduce categorical gaps in a continuum. Such categorical gaps then become the basis on which antagonisms can be defined. However, the charged and exclusionary divisions instituted by digitalized boundaries, it must be emphasized, do not finally determine, at least in principle, the nature of social relations between the two groups. If digital differentiation is understood as a subset of analog differentiation, then both can be accurately characterized as oppositional but not binary. An analog border, which in principle defines an infinitely broad and permeable continuum, is designed not to exclude individual subjects as such (i.e., identities thought to be fully constituted) but to distinguish between a broad ensemble of interests and intentions.

Hence in advocating that the peasants understand themselves as the "antithesis" of the dominant group and that their practices manifest antagonisms, Freire implies a simultaneous transgression of one border and the establishment of another. First, through the process of decodification as well as through the acquisition of literacy, that is, in the movement from semi-intransitive to naive transitive consciousness, the peasants cross the border of their sedimented social existence, and then introduce, or, more accurately, "reactivate" the border between themselves and the dominant group.

The drawing or reactivation of this second boundary has several consequences that need elaboration. The first stems from the fact that the introduction of boundaries in human relations is an intentional act: boundaries are teleological, and their "meanings" and "functions" are more or less, though never totally, under the control of those who introduce and police them. Borders thus "belong" to those who control them, and the relations of other individuals or groups to these borders can be more or less active or passive. In relation to Freire's project, these distinctions permit a clarification of the peasants' actions. In drawing or "reactivating" the second boundary the peasants are changing their relation to it from a passive to an active one. In the process they are outlining broad differences and antagonisms between the utopian/heterotopic sociopolitical, economic, and cultural intentionalities of progressive forces and the opposed intentionalities of those who would prefer to confine the peasants to their disenfranchised, sedimented "culture of silence." In short, they are opening themselves up to the possibility of forming alliances. As such they become not only specular but, potentially, syncretic border intellectuals as well.

As one can judge from the above analysis of Paulo Freire's project, it is strongly influenced by the politics of radical hope. His vision is profoundly optimistic, without succumbing to naivete. Indeed, his work is characterized by a dialectic tension between radical optimism and a realistic caution, with the implications of the former, however, always remaining predominant.

Thus, for instance, he is quite explicit about powerful residual conservativeness and inertia in the consciousness of those who have begun the transition enabled by literacy. As he puts it,

> Although the qualitative difference between the semi-intransitive consciousness and the naive transitive consciousness can be explained by the

phenomenon of emergence due to structural transformations in society, there are no rigidly defined frontiers between the historical moments that produce qualitative changes in men's awareness. In many respects, the semi-intransitive consciousness remains present in the naive transitive conscious-ness. . . . Therefore, the transitive consciousness emerges as a naive con-sciousness, as dominated as the former. Nevertheless, it is now indisputably more disposed to perceive the source of its ambiguous existence in the objective conditions of society. (77).

This tendency to qualify a very realistic assessment of the situation with an immediate search for the site of interstitial or marginal optimism is typical of Freire. In this specific instance, the tension between the two is again packed with a series of implications that need elaboration. Freire is, of course, quite right to insist that "structural transformations in society" do not necessarily or automatically lead to articulations and negotiations of antagonism, which alone make social transforma-tion possible: for such transformation to take place, the unfolding of antagonisms in turn must be predicated on the development of systematic and deliberate resistance.

This realistic pessimism, however, is balanced by the implications, particularly concerning temporality and history, that are condensed in Freire's insistence on the value of the perceptual transformation which the semi-intransitive consciousness has experienced. The condensed optimism becomes more evident in his articulation of the tension that exists in a single moment wherein the "denunciation" of existence in sedimented society is simultaneously combined with the "annuncia-tion"—however implicit and as yet inarticulate that annunciation may be—of an alternate set of possibilities. Denunciation and annunciation together constitute "an historic commitment," claims Freire. And while the former demands an increasingly precise understanding of one's condition and the latter "increasingly requires a theory of its transforming action . . . neither act by itself implies the transformation of the denounced reality or the establishment of that which is announced. Rather, *as a moment in a historical process*, the announced reality is already present in the act of denunciation and annunciation" (57; emphasis added). What Freire seems to imply here is that the temporality entailed in the establishment of a "fully" achieved new reality must be distinguished from its inaugural moment, which as such is qualitatively different from the temporality that follows. Alternately, this moment can be approached through Freire's claim that dominant groups are characterized by an anxiety to maintain the identity of present social relations into the future. By contrast, Freire's pedagogy frees the peasants from their anxiety to reproduce the limitations of the present in the future. Thus the inaugural moment that announces, however vaguely, a new social reality opens up the future as pure possibility, and it is this pure possibility, when linked with a sense of agential control, that becomes crucial for sustaining radical hope, which in turn becomes essential for sustaining the work required to achieve a new reality. In short, the inaugural moment is decisive in its foundational capacity.

Finally, it must be pointed out that the inaugural moment has an equally strong effect on the peasants' relation to their present and past. The acquisition of literacy is, in a certain sense, a minimal, albeit necessary, first step in a series that could eventually alleviate the condition of peasants in a substantive manner. But it is also a major step in that it provides them with an entry into the symbolic realm. Of course, nonliterate peasants who live in chirographic cultures are already subsumed indirectly in the logic and economy of a chirographically ordered universe. However, direct access to literacy would significantly alter their condition, for a fundamental distinction between oral and chirographic cultures (or states) is that the latter provide the possibility of a much finer and more *determinate* control of the symbolic. As Walter Ong, Jack Goody, and other have pointed out, control of alphabetic literacy (as opposed to pictographic representation, for instance) enables a variety of changes: the codification and representation of finer distinctions in all realms of signification; the documentation of events and thus the development of a historical archive; the possibility of greater individuation; and so on. In short, literacy permits the development of a dense discursivity and the very concept of historicity. Documentation, predicated on literacy, enables the development, over a period of time, of a rich archive, which in turn eventually permits various interpretations of the specific changes that have occurred in the past. Contemplation of the history thus produced, that is, of the series of interpretations, then facilitates a theoretical consideration of the methods of historiography. However, from the present viewpoint it is more important to note that access to the construction and comprehension of one's history, enabled by literacy, implies a greater control of one's past and present. And that control, when combined with an understanding of the future as pure possibility, significantly enhances one's sense of agency and hence the possibility of changing one's present condition.

These, it seems to me, are some of the fundamental implications of Freire's pedagogy. But these ramifications are not necessarily confined to the site of his practice; they are portable and can have equally significant effects on other pedagogical sites, provided that Freire's methods are adapted to the specific circumstances of the new site.

NOTES

1. For a detailed discussion of the border intellectual see my article "Wordliness-without-World."

   As Henry Giroux has pointed out, Freire's own experience as a border intellectual informs his methodology. My aim in this essay is not to explore this fascinating parallel but simply to focus on how his method functions to produce border intellectuals.

WORKS CITED

Aronowitz, Stanley, and Henry A. Giroux. *Postmodern Education: Politics, Culture, and Social Criticism.* Minneapolis: University of Minnesota Press, 1991.

Foucault, Michel. "Of Other Spaces." *Diacritics* 16.1 (Spring 1986): 22–27.

Freire, Paulo. *The Politics of Education: Culture, Power, and Liberation*. Trans. Donaldo Macado. Boston: Bergin and Garvey, 1985.

Giroux, Henry. "Paulo Freire and the Politics of Postcolonialism." *Journal of Advanced Composition* 12.1 (1992): 15–26.

Goody, Jack. *The Domestication of the Savage Mind*. Cambridge: Cambridge University Press, 1977.

JanMohamed, Abdul R. "Worldliness-without-World, Homelessness-as-Home: Toward a Definition of the Specular Border Intellectual." *Edward Said: A Critical Reader* Ed. Michael Sprinker. Boston: Basil Blackwell, 1992: 96–120.

Laclau, Ernesto. *New Reflections on the Revolution of Our Time*. London: Verso, 1990.

Ong, Walter. *Orality and Literacy: The Technologizing of the Word*. London: Methuen, 1982.

CHAPTER 14

DECOLONIZATION AS

LEARNING: PRACTICE

AND PEDAGOGY IN

FRANTZ FANON'S

REVOLUTIONARY

NARRATIVE

KENNETH MOSTERN

THE THEORETICAL CONTEXT FOR A FANONIAN
INTERVENTION IN EDUCATION THEORY

This article offers a close reading of the later revolutionary texts of Frantz Fanon with close attention paid to the contemporary theoretical enterprises of "theories of practice," "critical pedagogy," and "social movement theory." In making this contribution to Frantz Fanon studies in the context of a book on critical pedagogy, it is necessary that I emphasize at the outset that I do not treat Fanon in the context of psychoanalysis—though psychoanalysis is his first professional and literary interest—but rather as a theorist of social revolution. I begin by noting this here because, while Fanon's work is seeing a tremendous growth of interest in the Western literary academy, the main interest has been in his early and most specifically psychoanalytical work *Black Skin, White Masks* (1967a), nearly to the exclusion of his later work.[1] As a result, it has tended to focus almost exclusively on the relationship of race to the process of intellectual production. *Black Skin, White Masks* is, in fact, largely a work of textual analysis, providing an important contribution to the discussion of the formation of the racialized intellectual (white as well as black). On the other hand, the later complete works, *A Dying Colonialism* (1967) and *Wretched of the Earth* (1963), are about a different (though not inconsistent) set of issues: the process of racialization, on the one hand, and national revolution, on the other, of large social groupings in the complicated interactions of the institutions of race, nation, class, and (with mixed success) gender.

In *Black Skin, White Masks,* the process of colonization and decolonization of the individual Caribbean intellectual or artist—the person who is defined by his or her position between cultures and nations—is the central issue. By contrast, in *Wretched of the Earth,* individuals participate in different social locations in a complicated social drama which is in various ways explicitly pedagogical. My intention in this paper, then, is to try to describe the dialectic of mass/political and individual decolonization, including how such individual decolonization differs among people of different classes and genders, as it appears in the later texts. This description, in turn, will imply a negotiation of the three sets of contemporary intellectual discourse I referred to above: theories of practice, critical pedagogy, and social movement theory. As we will see, in Fanon's work these three discourses are not separable; rather, each implies the other. However, for the purposes of introducing my analysis of Fanon, I will now turn to explaining what I mean when I refer to these discourses, and the places where I believe that a Fanonian analysis may make a contribution.

THEORIES OF PRACTICE

The idea of a theory of practice, or a theoretical description of the complicated ways in which subjectivity forms and performs, is best exemplified in the work of Pierre Bourdieu. For Bourdieu the reason for engaging in such a description is primarily to understand how systems of hierarchy and domination reproduce themselves. That is, his understanding of the formation of subjects in the practice of the educational institution is that "in any given social formation the different [pedagogic authorities] tend to reproduce the system of cultural arbitraries characteristic of that social formation, thereby contributing to the reproduction of the power relations" in the social formation (Bourdieu and Passeron 1990, 10). Needing a description of how this happens, Bourdieu details, in *Outline of a Theory of Practice,* the social conditions (of which the educational institution is one) in which apparently free choice results in actions which are consistent with the stated or unstated intentions of the pedagogic agents: "the whole trick of pedagogic reason lies precisely in the way it extorts the essential while seeming to demand the insignificant" (1977, 94–95). The claim that institutions and societies reproduce themselves should not be mistaken, however, for the idea that no changes occur in the process of reproduction, or that human subjects, caught in a predetermined web, are restricted to a single, predictable course:

> Because the habitus has an endless capacity to engender products—thought, perception, expressions, actions—whose limits are set by the historically and socially situated conditions of its production, the conditioned and socially situated freedom it secures is as remote from a creation of unpredict-

able novelty as it is from a simple mechanical reproduction of the initial conditionings. (Bourdieu 1977, 95)

Bourdieu's theory, then, is a theory of reproduction, but also a theory that provides a framework for social change. It allows us to choose among practices consistent with our social positions, since no historical context restricts individuals or groups to a single possible course. If this description of the conditions of practice (and thus learning) is accepted, then, the question for critical pedagogy must be to enunciate the possibilities for causing learners to participate in activities that will, within their context, not act toward the reproduction of a class-, race-, and gender-stratified social system.[2]

Most contemporary theorization of the formation of subjectivity in practice involves the description of practices of individuals in so-called "everyday" settings. In searching for an institutional locus of learning that is effective for the development and progression of lives, theorists assume a regular reproduction of the social body. Thus, Jean Lave and Etienne Wenger (1991) focus their theory of learning on the apprenticeship of individuals as they enter communities. The use of apprenticeship as a model has a number of terminological and conceptual advantages to the theorist of practice: It suggests that knowing and doing result from the embodiment of practices developed from what they call a "community of practice"; the apprentice is then a "legitimate peripheral participant" in such a community, who will later presumably become a "full participant" (Lave and Wenger 1991, 34–37). All practice is described in terms of the subjectivity of the community (autonomous action being conceivable only in terms of what one is autonomous from), and pedagogy as the activity designed to increase the community. I find it necessary to stretch this especially useful terminology, conceiving it in terms outside those that Lave and Wenger refer to as "legitimate"—in the setting of the social revolution, in which Fanon's description of the colonized "native," who does not participate in the world of power over his or her own existential situation, strives to become a full participant in a not yet existent community. Fanon will be useful in making the move, then, from the description of practice and pedagogy in the "everyday" to the description of practice and pedagogy in the special situation of forging new (but nevertheless consistent with the objective historical context) communities of practice.

CRITICAL PEDAGOGY

The attempt to achieve a critical pedagogy has two components which connect in specific ways to theories of practice and to the theorization of social movements. First, the critical pedagogue understands that the acquisition of knowledge is always dependent on the already given subjectivity of the student. In Paulo Friere's metaphor, the teacher is not a banker who deposits information into the student's account of "facts"; rather, the student is a developing (but never developed) human being embodying a history of knowledge and action that provides the context in which new information, ideas, and interactions (including pedagogic actions) take place (1989, chap. 2). For this reason, the critical pedagogue is always someone who teaches from were the student is at, rather than from where the teacher is at. This does not mean that the teacher denies his or her pedagogical intentions or specific expertise, but merely that s/he respects the myriad expertise of the students that s/he does not share. Second, the critical pedagogue works for social justice, and, living in a world of injustice, not only attempts to enact change in his or her classroom, but develops the strategies and confidence of students to work for social change beyond the classroom. Thus, the critical pedagogue does two things: s/he learns where the students in a class are coming from, and with them attempts to forge a strategy for social change. Any theoretical discourse that would describe such a practice needs to have within it the components of a theory of practice as already described—for only by understanding the objective situation ("habitus," in Bourdieu's word) of the student at the beginning of a pedagogical situation can the critical pedagogue attempt to promote learning within it; further, such a discourse needs to engage with social movement theory, because only by having a sense of the possibilities and past practices of movements for social change can the critical pedagogue know what s/he is trying to achieve.

Writing about critical pedagogy has had at least two different modes, which themselves tend to incorporate different aspects of these discourses. On the one hand, critical pedagogy has proponents and practitioners who have been largely involved in movements of social justice, into which pedagogical situations have been carved. Internationally the work of Paulo Freire (see esp. 1973) and within the United States the work of the Highlander Folk School, especially through the figures of Myles Horton, the school's founder, and Septima Clark, who as director of educational programs at Highlander built the educational component of the civil rights movement (Horton and Freire 1990; Clark and Brown 1989), are the best known of this group of critical pedagogues. On the other hand, in the United States a group of theorists of schooling have spoken of already pedagogical situations into which a radical practice has to be carved. This group, whose most prolific and accomplished member is Henry Giroux, has provided a body of theory that describes the objective situation of U.S. classrooms, though without making the specific links to social movement practice that I claim it is necessary for critical pedagogy to address.[3]

A narrative which can trace an objective situation of oppression (as, for example, experienced in colonialism), the process of learning implied by the overcoming of this oppression, and the positions of the pedagogical actors (whether teachers or other cultural workers) within the movement against oppression is necessary at this time. Below I will develop a reading of Frantz Fanon's revolutionary theory in terms of the way his work negotiates this complex of issues. But first, I need to describe the state of my other body of theoretical work, social movement theory.

SOCIAL MOVEMENT THEORY

Radical academic social movement theory has recently been dominated by the neo-Gramscian "new social movement" paradigm. "New social movement" theorists come initially from a Marxist theoretical framework but break from the economic determinism of Leninist Marxism through their emphasis on the ways that identities are formed and changed in the process of social movement. For Antonio Gramsci, the collective transformation of an economic system (i.e., capitalism) implies the creation of a collective subject including people with diverse affiliations that can overcome its material conditions of domination. This collective subject is the "historical bloc": "the complex, contradictory and discordant *ensemble* of the superstructures [which is] the reflection of the social relations of production" (Gramsci 1971, 366). What is appealing, then, about his concept, from the point of view of the new social movement theorists, is that it presumes the existence of multiple identities in the field of bloc formation, rather than an already given "objective" identity. From this starting point, one may theorize the contexts in which people from different locations in the social relationship of production may nevertheless be positioned with complementary identities.

Ernesto Laclau and Chantal Mouffe have provided the most extensive working out of what this process means for contemporary practice. For them, the creation of blocs and alliances among and between various practitioners of new social movements is the only form that activism can take, a position with which it is hard to disagree. Yet their account, relying on a notion of identity politics as "hegemonic articulation" (Laclau and Mouffe 1985, 177) rather than as the ongoing social practice of solidarity, assumes that such alliances will fundamentally change the identities of power between the participants in the alliance, merely through the articulation of a decision to do so. Lacking a theory of practice (or, concurrently, pedagogic intervention), Laclau and Mouffe have no argument for why certain identity formations remain central to their "multiplicity of social movements" long after supposedly "new identities" have been forged. To be specific, the way their theory runs together "the rise of the new feminism, the protest movements of ethnic, national, and sexual minorities, the anti-institutional ecology struggles waged by marginalized layers of the population, the anti-nuclear movement, the atypical forms of social struggle in countries on the capitalist periphery" (Laclau and Mouffe 1985, 1) as though all these were categorically similar prevents discussion of the differences between a given United States citizen who articulates an antinuclear politics and the impossibility of articulation for citizens—especially women—of the "capitalist periphery" (cf. Spivak 1988). Their statement that the elements making up the oppositional discourse in these social movements "never appear as crystallized" (176) must be challenged strongly—the point being precisely that in the case of systemic reifications like race, class, and gender, the identities under consideration do *appear* as crystallized (even though they demonstrably are not crystallized) because the people who claim these identities have spent lifetimes of practice in situations in which these specific identities are the arena of lifelong struggle and accomplishment.[4]

In the last several years a large number of theorists of color have produced nonessentialist, nonteleological accounts of the persistence of race and gender patterns and identities in social movements which imply significant qualifications within any generalized theory of practice proposed by a First World, white male academic theorist. Specifically, I am interested in Paul Gilroy's (1987) account of the persistence of racist and racialist themes across the political spectrum of England over two post–World War II generations even as the precise characteristics and content attributed to "blackness" by the white majority has changed drastically. His construction of racially based (though sometimes, as with Rock Against Racism, coalitional) social movements must be taken into account by any theorist of critical pedagogical practice. I am also interested in bell hooks's (1989, 1992) descriptions of the practical and existential dilemmas that black people, and especially black women, continue to face prior to "coming to voice"—developing the ability to achieve a hegemonic articulation that for Laclau and Mouffe is already assumed for participation in social movements.[5]

Fanon, then, is described below not merely for the depth his analyses of social revolution can add to the discourses of practice, pedagogy, and social movements, but for the fact that he describes a situation of *colonization*. Since actors within the Fanonian situation are not all equal, the sorts of practical participation available to them are not restricted merely to the categories of "peripheral" and "full" but are contingent on already given social identities, or habituses; coming to revolutionary voice necessitates the disaggregation of these identities and the additional questions of participation in what, when? Fanon's revolutionary narrative will thus provide a model not to be copied in its details (for the obvious reason that United States educators do not live in a decolonizing Africa) but that can suggest a method for constructing our own narrative of pedagogical and theoretical practice.

FRANTZ FANON: DECOLONIZATION AS LEARNING

NARRATIVES OF LIBERATION

We are told that one of the defining significances of the postmodern moment has been the decline in so-called "metanarratives," such as teleological versions of Marxism or various nationalisms, which attempt to explain the course of human history in teleological terms. As an attempt to speak scientific truth, the decline of metanarratives must be seen as a good thing; it has become impossible to justify truth claims based on their location within a preaccepted system. But, as Giroux points out, even after we learn to be suspicious of "universality,"

> metanarratives play an important theoretical role in placing the particular and the specific in broader historical and relational contexts. To reject all notions of totality is to run the risk of being trapped in particularistic theories that cannot explain how the various diverse relations that constitute larger social, political and global systems interrelate or mutually determine and constrain one another. (Giroux 1992, 68)

Any radical politics must *narrate*, not under the guise of universal truth but in order to understand current practices and also to provide a model of intervention and change. Frantz Fanon's books *A Dying Colonialism* and *Wretched of the Earth* provide two such narrative accounts. Precisely because they do narrate toward a telos of existential freedom which is itself historically produced, these accounts of decolonization may provide us with a theoretical model of pedagogical practice that combines the varying discourses I've been analyzing in this essay.

Patrick Taylor refers to Fanon's entire oeuvre as a "narrative of liberation." The course of the narrative is the movement from a historically situated moment of oppression, that being the European colonization of Africa, toward an ethical nation-state "based on the assumption of universal freedom and dignity" (Taylor 1989, 11). The notion of freedom in Fanon is largely that described in the existentialist Marxism enunciated by Sartre in the same period (the 1950s and early 1960s) in which Fanon was writing. (Sartre and Fanon corresponded during this period and they were mutually influential, as can be seen in Sartre's preface to *Wretched of the Earth*.) In Sartre's system, the telos of freedom is not universal, but arises historically out of the consciousness of its need in situations of colonial or class domination. That is, freedom becomes a problem precisely because of the accomplishment of cultural enslavement (Taylor 1989, 62–67; also Sartre 1968, 22 and passim chap. 1).

Fanon takes up this telos of freedom and places it in a narrative that, while not exactly a historical description of any particular set of events, is a totalization of the historical situation of Africa as he knows it. In this sense, Fanon's works are not, as has been claimed, "mythical":

Fanon [took] the tradition of liberating narrative and used it to understand the history of the Third World. . . . Fanon's works are practical and concrete totalizations of the anticolonial struggle. They reveal the interactions of individuals and groups in terms of the necessity of freedom. Their existential task is to comprehend and to communicate the categorical imperative in a particular social situation. (Taylor 1991, 25)

These categories of freedom and struggle are, in Fanon, conceived in both individual and communal terms; in fact, it is only through the dialectical understanding of these terms, where the individual is defined in relation to the community and the community has no existence except as the collection of individuals, that we can understand Fanon's narrative. His social psychology thus unifies the term "decolonization" as a process which can happen only to individuals and nations simultaneously. Any liberatory or pedagogical practice must be conscious both of the needs of individuals to attain a consciousness of freedom from domination, and to actually remove the material constraints on their actions. Thus, in contrast to the conventional notion that decolonization is a term that refers to a change in state power, Fanon states:

Decolonization never takes place unnoticed, for it influences individuals and modifies them fundamentally. It transforms spectators crushed with their inessentiality into privileged actors. . . . It brings a natural rhythm into existence, introduced by new men, and with it a new language and a new humanity. Decolonization is the veritable creation of new men. (1963, 36)

For the mass of people in Africa (then and now) a mere change in power at the top is of no avail in making them "privileged actors," the historical class of Marx's revolutionary theory. It will merely transform one situation of practical disempowerment to another. However, if the revolutionary movement is carried out in a fully democratic manner, each individual will participate in his or her own empowerment: "the 'thing' which has been colonized becomes man during the same process by which it frees itself" (Fanon 1963, 37). Thus decolonization is never simply a political problem, but a process of populations learning to become "men."[6] It is easy to see, then, that decolonization is a social and practical problem—requiring a theory of practice—about learning to "become oneself" in a material situation that denies one the social space to do so,[7] and derived from Marx's statement in the "Theses on Feuerbach" (1947) that "the coincidence of the changing of circumstances and of human activity or self-changing can be conceived and rationally understood only as *revolutionary practice*" (121; emphasis in original).

THE PROCESS OF LEARNING (NARRATIVE 1): WOMEN LEARNING IN THE ALGERIAN REVOLUTION

A Dying Colonialism is a book written by a propaganda officer in the midst of a revolution, so it should not surprise us that it is unflaggingly optimistic. I do not want to explore this case study of women in the Algerian revolution for the precision of its historical or ethnographical data, for there are many issues, details, and conflicts left out. (Some of these become central issues in *Wretched of the Earth*, as we will see below.) Rather, it is worth exploring for the idealized account of learning it provides. I would suggest that the eventual failure of this description of women's decolonization of Algeria after liberation[8] must be read not as a failure of Fanon's theory of practice but as the result of counterforces significant to the issue of learning present at the time of the writing of *A Dying Colonialism* but consciously ignored by the author, for the purposes of maintaining unity and secrecy within a liberation party fighting a war.

In *Black Skin, White Masks* Fanon explores in detail the dialectical relationship between white and black both as linguistic markers and enforceable definitions of people in the colonies. Color symbols have significance for everyone, powerful and powerless, growing up under African colonialism. These colors are not merely in dialectical relation, with the construction of the civilized white resting on the notion of a perfectly savage other—but also in Manichean relation, where the colors represent good and bad, refined and crude, and every level of value judgment that power can maintain (JanMohamed 1983). Here the racial distinction is reified such that class conflict *is* race conflict—the cause is the consequence; you are rich because you are white, you are white because you are rich" (Fanon 1963, 40). After several generations of this structure, the primary framework of political identity is racial identity. Though it will turn out, later in the narrative of liberation, that class unity among blacks was a false construct, at the outset it is entirely and necessarily assumed.

For this reason, at the start of *A Dying Colonialism,* the turf battle over dress— European appearance versus Algerian appearance, as identified by the dress of women—is entirely politicized. Whatever the cultural status of the veil worn by Arab women prior to colonization, under colonialism wearing the veil *exemplifies* resistance to colonial power, the more so because the French have a conscious policy of denouncing veil wearing.

> The officials of the French administration in Algeria, committed to destroy-ing the people's originality, and under instructions to bring about the disintegration, at whatever cost, of forms of existence likely to evoke a national reality directly or indirectly, were to concentrate their efforts on the wearing of the veil, which was looked upon at this juncture as a symbol of the status of Algerian women. (Fanon 1967b, 37)

The colonial government understands this cultural "originality" as one that subjects women to an unacceptable level of patriarchal oppression—conveniently overlook-ing its own patriarchal practices[9]—and for this reason it becomes particularly important for the resisting colonial subject, if a woman, to wear the veil: "The tenacity of the occupier in his endeavor to unveil the women, to make them an ally in the work of cultural destruction, had the effect of strengthening the traditional pattern of behavior" (Fanon 1967b, 49). The veil, for better or worse, becomes reinforced as the privileged sign of being an Algerian woman to the women and men of Algeria, precisely because of their resistance, female as well as male, to the cultural assumptions being imposed from an outside dominator. Women who have long worn veils are reinforced in the practice by the attempt at suppressing this aspect of their cultural identity.

A women's liberation movement internal to the revolutionary movement is possible—and indeed necessary—in spite of this. How such a movement comes about—the process by which Algerian women discover their need to be "un-veiled," and in collaboration with men (who must also come to accept that such an unveiling is desirable) begin to bring it about—is the theme of this chapter of *A Dying Colonialism.* Fanon thus uses the veil to illustrate, through a genealogical account of the participation of women in the FLN, that cultural change 1) must always be consistent with the practical situation (or habitus) in which it is occurring (thus, European rationalities for abandoning the veil, however apt in their own cultural context, are neither appropriate nor available to Algerian women within a Manichean colonial setting), and 2) that in the practice of decolonization of *all* colonial subjects, women and men, an indigenous sense of the need for women's emancipation develops.

The initial response of the colonized to explicit French attempts to change women's appearance in Algeria is, as one would expect in a dialectical/Manichean model of colonialism, violent reaction.

> To the colonialist offensive against the veil, the colonized opposes the cult of the veil. What was an undifferentiated element in a homogenous whole acquires a taboo character, and the attitude of a given Algerian woman with respect to the veil will be constantly related to her overall attitude with respect to the foreign occupation. The colonized, in the face of the emphasis given by the colonialist to this or that aspect of his traditions, reacts very violently. (Fanon 1967b, 47)[10]

Because of the colonizer's program to change the practice of veil wearing, this restriction on women's movement is not merely an issue internal to the culture, but is *representative* of it. At this stage of the narrative, the suggestion that the veil is in any way repressive is prima facie evidence of Western cultural influence, and therefore collaboration with an oppressive regime. An element of culture which has never before been significant in itself develops into an ontological category due to political circumstances: the cultural significance of wearing the veil changes as its ability to offend the colonial power is learned.

The acceptance of wearing the veil as a political act, however, will turn out to contain its own undoing. For once political liberation is a conscious choice among women, they will choose to engage with men in more direct forms of revolutionary struggle—if, of course, they can convince the patriarchal leadership of the FLN to let them. Indeed, during the course of 1955, Fanon reports, this is exactly what happened: women, first in positions of subordination (such as standing lookout at a house where men are meeting), but soon thereafter in responsible, independent positions, join the revolutionary movement.

Joining the revolution, in the beginning, means appearing "exposed" or "naked," especially around Europeans. For example, having a woman stand lookout is facilitated if she is not wearing a veil: a woman appearing in public in a given location with a veil (and thus in relative motionlessness) looks very suspicious; one dressed like a European woman and moving unrestrictedly is less so. But understanding the meaning of being unveiled cannot stop with understanding the political strategy engaged, for the unveiled woman is experiencing a materially new way of being. An entire change in consciousness accompanies it. The woman who is used to wearing heavily restrictive clothing, but who now walks "stark naked,"

> experiences a sense of incompleteness with great intensity. She has the anxious feeling that something is unfinished, and along with this a frightful sense of disintegrating. The absence of the veil distorts the Algerian woman's corporal pattern. She quickly has to invent new dimensions for her body, new means of muscular control. She has to create for herself an attitude

of unveiled-woman-outside. . . . The Algerian woman . . . relearns her body, re-establishes it in a totally revolutionary fashion. This new dialectic of the body and of the world is primary in the case of one revolutionary woman. (Fanon 1967b, 59)

This decolonization of the female body occurs in concert with the decolonization of the woman as an Algerian, for she

must overcome a multiplicity of inner resistances, of subjectively organized fears, of emotions. . . . She must consider the image of the occupier lodged somewhere in her mind and in her body, remodel it, initiate the essential work of eroding it, make it inessential, remove some of the shame that is attached to it, devalidate it. (Fanon 1967b, 52)

Thus her physical being—not merely her consciousness—is reformed, newly embodied, and thus dually decolonized, as woman and Algerian, through full participation in the practice of revolutionary movement. Neither decolonization would have been possible to learn without this active participation.

In *Outline of a Theory of Practice,* Bourdieu speaks of the body as "made" through a series of totalitarian (not in the political sense, consciously by a state, but rather in the sense of Fanon's "homogenous whole" cultural system) arrangements in such a way that knowledge goes beyond consciousness (Bourdieu 1977, 94; see also Foucault 1979). Further evidence for this as it concerns the liberation of women's bodies has been reported in the volume by the feminist working group around German theorist Frigga Haug, *Female Sexualization: A Collective Work of Memory* (Haug et al. 1987, 73–175). In this volume twelve women recount their experiences of learning what they call "sexualization"—the explicit and implicit training received, at various moments in their childhood development, about "proper" looks, posture, and manners. Through months of memory games, the women recall large numbers of events regarding societal enforcement of manners that, taken as a system, promote behavior "in the manner of slavegirls" (Haug et al 1987, 79). Liberation, according to Haug et al., does not come simply from the articulation of the stories in the book, for the embodied, automatic effects survive long after the feminist analysis of domination has occurred. Over time, through participation in feminist social action among feminist women and men, behavior does change, but it does so neither completely nor reliably. This is clearly consistent with Fanon's sense that the unlearning and change in bodily behavior is only possible through participation in an oppositional social movement. If anything, Fanon's position is too optimistic, the changes he describes happening too easily.[11]

VIOLENCE AND DEMOCRATIC PARTICIPATION

The case of Algerian women learning bodily freedom just described is typical of the process of decolonization in Fanon's writing. That is, full participation within a democratic social movement is the process by which decolonization, a specialized form of learning, occurs in Fanon's writing. Since (to pick up from the end of a passage quoted previously) "decolonization is the veritable creation of new men," we need to describe a practical and contextual mechanism by which these men are created. Fanon continues: "But this creation owes nothing of its legitimacy to any supernatural power; the 'thing' which has been colonized becomes man during the same process by which it frees itself" (Fanon 1963, 36–37). What sort of mechanism is available for participation by every person living in a colonial situation which will simultaneously permit the overthrow of the colonial mentality and the material condition of colonialism? Popular participation in armed struggle, rather than the specialized struggle of party-connected professional armies, is the only realistic answer to this question.

The emphasis on violence in Fanon's writing stems from this source. In a colonial situation which is by definition violent (and Fanon documents that the pervasive terrorism of the French, which was far greater than any the resistance was even technologically capable of), decolonization happens when each individual can participate in its overthrow. Fanon thus conceives participation in violence for the collective good as the surest way of democratizing the revolution and leading to true decolonization. In the chapter of *A Dying Colonialism* I have been examining, participation in the practice of revolutionary violence is one of the most significant new possibilities opened up for women once they are "unveiled." Women's co-participation in violence is not only the source of trust and freedom for the women, but also of men's growing confidence in women's autonomous ability (Fanon 1967b, 48). Thus violence is not intended to provide some sort of irrational catharsis, as in a writer like Georges Sorel; rather, it is a rational technique for struggle, and results in regeneration for a population in the same way that lifting a very heavy weight off the body (e.g., a veil) relieves an individual (see Jinadu 1986, 91–94). Violence is the most available resource in the formation of a community of practice which opposes colonial violence. The individual violent act is part and parcel of an individual's transformation, for it implies the participation in the national struggle for freedom. Communal violence is a strategy for engaging people in their own freedom, while peaceful transfer of power is just that—those who negotiate, colonized and colonizer, transfer power, among themselves.

Jinadu addresses at length this moral justification for violence in Fanon's work (1986, 66–95) but also insists that Fanon leaves open the possibility, if not the likelihood, of a peaceful decolonization process that is democratic (71–75). However, on the basis of an interpretation of the Algerian experience, where the French army fought particularly long and hard to retain power, and its extrapolation into other colonial settings, Fanon is convinced that democratic alternatives to popular massive violence are unlikely to be available if decolonization in all senses is to occur.

THE PROCESS OF DECOLONIZATION (NARRATIVE 2): THE DEVELOPMENT OF MEN AND NATIONS

We have already followed the Fanonian narrative of the individual in *A Dying Colonialism;* it is necessary at this point to follow the Fanonian narrative of the nation through *Wretched of the Earth*. This will take us beyond the mere recital of national identity and to the points where the unitary identity of the nation breaks up. Earlier I mentioned that in the anticolonial struggle, in the beginning, blackness is itself understood as a revolutionary identity. Significantly, the reason why this doesn't remain the case in *Wretched of the Earth* is the failure of the nationalist leaders (and the bourgeoisie they represent) to understand the conditions of their own popular support—as we will see, it is a *pedagogical* failure on their part. They misconstrue the dialectical relation between their practice of articulation and the revolutionary activities of the people.

According to Fanon, early in the revolutionary movement "in their political speech, the leaders give a name to the nation. In this way the native's demands are given shape" (1963, 68). This articulation is an important moment of identity formation because it conforms to the revolutionary struggle taking place; it is the necessary practical reification of a developing practice that permits and encourages nationalist activity. (Thus it may be thought of as one of Gayatri Spivak's "strategic essentialisms" around which political action takes place at a given moment [Spivak 1990, 51].) The bourgeois nationalist leader, however, misinterprets the positive response that his speeches receive. He believes that the response is the result of his *teaching* (or depositing the truth into, in the "banking" sense of education) the peasant community of their need to revolt, when in fact it is the result of his words' experienced conformity to the material realities of oppression, and their articulation of the ideals of the revolution being made by the people. Because of this misunderstanding, in the neocolonial regime,

> the leader pacifies the people. For years on end after independence has been won, we see him, incapable of urging on the people to a concrete task, unable really to open the future to them or of flinging them into the path of national reconstruction, that is to say, of their own reconstruction; we see him reassessing the history of independence and recalling the sacred unity of the struggle for liberation. . . . During the struggle for liberation the leader awakened the people and promised them a forward march. . . . Today he uses every means to put them to sleep.
>
> Now it must be said that the masses show themselves totally incapable of appreciating the long way that they have come. The peasant who goes on scratching out a living from the soil, and the unemployed man who never finds employment do not manage, in spite of public holidays and flags . . . to convince themselves that anything has really changed in their lives. (Fanon 1963, 168–69)

Decolonization has all along been a democratic project, with the leader playing the necessary role of reifying the national identity, providing the specific articulations which introduce the people into a community of revolutionary practice. But he has not appreciated the substantial limitations to his own actions. He believes that his speeches will continue to be internalized, though they no longer have relation to embodied practice. The population remains undeceived, and are again the victims of oppression.[12]

It is because of the existence of neocolonialism as a possibility that Fanon, at this stage of his narrative, backs off from the class-unified version of nationalism he has previously advocated. Nationalism is a necessary point of revolutionary articulation, but it is not a final one, for nationalism has within it the possibilities of class hegemony, a situation in which full decolonization has not reached the proletariat. It is this point at which a truly popular national culture, forged in the struggle for liberation, becomes the everyday means of resistance to challenge and circumvent bourgeois rule.

At this stage of the narrative, where the bourgeois leader refuses his earlier role as liberatory pedagogue, that it becomes the ethical responsibility of the revolutionary intellectual to continue to act in that role. The intellectual who would be part of the popular national culture under germination must continue to act in dialogical relation with the people whose nation s/he intends to articulate. In fact, the stages of African intellectual work, in Fanon's narrative, correspond exactly to the stages of national awakening in the narrative of liberation described above. In the generation preceding decolonization, artists and teachers largely mimic the styles and concerns of the occupying power; during the nationalist stage they create discourse which is oppositional to Europeans, but still reflects their class baggage, since its ties are to the revolutionary leadership's articulations. When, in the stage of neocolonialism, those articulations are no longer those of the people, the revolutionary intellectual must "turn himself into an awakener of the people; hence comes a fighting literature, and a national literature" (Fanon 1963, 223). Again, this is not missionary work, but dialogical engagement:

> The first duty of the native poet is to see clearly the people he has chosen as the subject of his work of art. He cannot go forward resolutely unless he first realizes the extent of his estrangement from them. . . . It is not enough to try to get back to the people in that past out of which they have already emerged; rather, we must join them in that fluctuating move-ment which they are just giving a shape to, and which, as soon as it has started, will be the signal for everything to be called in question. (226–27)

Finally, in this description of artistic (and pedagogical) practice, we see brought together all the discourses I have been addressing in this essay: an ethical theory and practice of critical pedagogy for intellectuals, engaged in radical social move-ment, based on a theory of practice that respects where people are at, and the borders they have to cross to achieve freedom.

TOWARD A FANONIAN ACADEMIC PRACTICE

Radical cultural studies accounts which would attempt to take specific situations of practice and turn them into strategies for pedagogical and social action are as yet relatively few. My call here is not merely to "teach from a position," but to join (and develop) communities of activist practice in which others may participate. The need for a critical pedagogy of the practice of social movements has never been stronger. The reawakening of interest in Frantz Fanon's work offers us the opportunity to think about one of the few writers who has crossed all the divisions of theoretical work described in this essay, and proposed an ethical theory of liberation that represents the varied situations of the individual in the historical setting of decolonization.

For a variety of fairly obvious reasons, we cannot simply transplant the guidelines of participation and change in identity through which Fanonian theory works to our own situation. Racial identity is not nearly so Manichean in my situation as in Fanon's, perhaps opening for me the possibility of antiracist solidarity; nevertheless, racial identity continues to affect my practice as a white man. The production of aversion which the colonial government effects with regard to the veil continues in its United States manifestations (see hooks 1992). My participation in antiracist social movements is no guarantee of solidarity with any given black student in my class; the history of our differences is too great. To be a successful teacher in my present situation I must define my present situation of practice in terms both similar to and different from Fanon's, developing strategies that acknowledge the significance of my own whiteness and maleness (and present professionalness, notwithstanding my class background) as cultural signs.

The incorporation of social movement theory into the pedagogy of schooling requires that we speak not merely of the classroom but of what we hope to accomplish in solidarity with our students when we all leave the classroom. It will be clear now, after my close reading of Fanon, that it is no denigration of the notions of process and participation (so central to all critical pedagogy) for me to assert that our goal now must be the positive articulation of a variety of possible identities that will provide the space for students to enter into a community of radical practice. Our articulations must be consistent with the practical situations of our students, and they must act in such a way that our students may "come to voice," as bell hooks says. It is in this context that I can think of no better way to end than by repeating Chandra Talpade Mohanty's call for the construction of "cultures of dissent." Given her analysis of liberal antiracism and the ways it is recouped by the forces of domination, we need to stress a pedagogy affirmative in its encouraging participation in challenging domination, negative in the necessary attention it pays to that domination, and serious about addressing the contributions of people of oppressed nations, classes, and genders to creating a democratic world. I thus end by quoting Mohanty, adding only that in our present context this seems to me a well-elaborated Fanonian project:

> Cultures of dissent are about seeing the academy as part of a larger sociopolitical arena which itself domesticates and manages Third World people in the name of liberal capitalist democracy. The struggle to transform our institutional practices fundamentally also involves the grounding of the analysis of exploitation and oppression in accurate history and theory, seeing

ourselves as activists in the academy . . . and expecting and demanding
action from ourselves, our colleagues, and our students at numerous levels.
(Mohanty in this book, 162)

NOTES

1.   Henry Louis Gates, Jr. (1991), helped me to see this point in his recent article on
     Fanon studies in *Critical Inquiry*. Noting this, however, does not stop him from
     conflating a critique of Fanon's FLN activities in the later period with commentary
     about recent critical appropriations of *Black Skin, White Masks*. Further, notwithstand-
     ing Gates's implicit suggestion that this regrowth of Western scholarly interest is
     inappropriate because Fanon has no readership in postindependence Africa, L. Adele
     Jinadu (1986) (whose work I cite below with respect to the idea of violence in Fanon)
     claims that Fanon studies is growing among theorists of neocolonialism there. With
     the exception of Jinadu's book, I am as yet unaware of the debates about Fanon's
     work within Africa; thus, my paper treats Fanonian theory as it currently exists in the
     Euro/American academy.

2.   It is my view that race, class, and gender provide central and deeply embodied
     discursive frameworks in which human subjectivity is expressed in individuals in the
     contemporary United States, the place in which I live and work. They are not the
     only such existing discursive formations, nor are they unitary within themselves;
     nevertheless, the tendency to deny their operationality in certain poststructuralist
     arguments—or the equivalent tendency to reduce the distinctiveness of each to mere
     categories of "difference" without substantial particular content—strikes me as an
     example of the unwillingness of many theorists from dominant groupings to interrogate
     the objective conditions of practice in which they themselves work.

3.   This description would imply that these two branches of critical pedagogy are entirely
     separate, though, of course, they are not. My intention is to point out the ways in
     which they remain more separate than is usually acknowledged. Certainly, Paulo
     Freire's work has been universally cited as influential within critical pedagogy; the
     notion of the dialectic of student-teacher and teacher-student (all participants in the
     learning situation are both teachers and students at all times), first described in *Pedagogy
     of the Oppressed* (1989), can be said to be the most consistent theory of practice within
     all versions of critical pedagogy, including those which describe situations of schooling.
     However, my claim here is that this dialectic, precisely because it has been accepted
     without specific comparison of the situations of peasant revolution and U.S. schooling,
     has often been misapplied. In the Frierean situation the literacy teacher is understood
     to be entering the peasant village in a position of absolute cultural authority. It is
     because Freire asks us to understand the inappropriateness of that authority that he
     makes his intervention into educational theory. The authority of the teacher often
     exists in schooling, but it can be complicated in a variety of ways, especially at American
     universities where the authority of anything "left" or even "liberal" can always be
     called into question by the students, who have heard that we're all communists before
     they show up. Students, in some situation, may actually have a great deal more wealth,
     authority, and power than their teachers. For a concrete example, think of bell hooks's
     comments on teaching at Yale and Oberlin (hooks 1989, esp. chaps. 8–11, and scattered
     throughout her work.)

4. For all these reasons I believe that the principles of "coalition," as developed by Barbara Smith and Bernice Johnson Reagon in separate essays in the early black feminist collection *Home Girls* (Smith 1983), continue to provide a more promising formulation for contemporary political practice than Laclau and Mouffe's "hegemonic articulation." These black feminists are sometimes cited as arguing the same position as, or being precursors to, new social movement theorists like Laclau and Mouffe. A careful comparison, however, will reveal that the black feminists place a great deal of emphasis on relations of power within a coalition, while Laclau and Mouffe's notion of "hegemony" acts without reference to power stratification among and between oppositional subject positions. It is easy to guess whose articulations will become "hegemonic." It is thus unclear, from my understanding of black feminist coalition politics, what the advantage of being part of a "hegemonic articulation" would be to someone without race and gender privilege.

5. I take as given that class identity, too, remains of particular importance, though many post-Marxists seem to have abandoned class analysis altogether. Fortunately this is not true of either Gilroy or hooks.

6. A note is necessary concerning gender-bias in Fanon's language: As with all appropriations of masculinist theory, there is a legitimate concern that what gets called learning in this essay, in Fanon's imagination and in fact, is characteristic of *men* in revolution, and not women. This problem is compounded by my sense that rhetorically, within the gender-biased English (and presumably French as well) language, there is no equivalence between the concepts of "becoming a man" and "becoming a person." "Becoming a man" has the connotation of maturity of consciousness; "becoming a person" sounds biological. For this reason my discussion is more than usually tied to the gender bias in the language, even while I want to argue for decolonization as becoming fully a person.

   Below I provide a case study in Fanonian learning which concerns the consciousness of women. This case study demonstrates that Fanon is concerned that women be revolutionaries so that they can, with men, engage in the process of becoming men/people; on the other, even here there are passages in which he constructs "Algerians" as a category separate from that of "women."

   In spite of this problem I believe that useful conclusions about a characteristic process of men and women learning can be drawn from an analysis of Fanon.

7. This formulation will, of course, offend poststructuralists who would deny an ontological category of "being oneself." My concern here is not whether there is a natural, essentialized or unified self, but the historical situation which engenders the consciousness that dominant *material* agents (be they "individuals," "discourses," or "armies") are determining one's own situation in such a way that the conditions of freedom (in Bourdieu's sense) permit no agency or definition (participation in the dialectic of freedom and constraint) to the oppressed self. On this issue please see bell hooks's essay "On Self-Recovery" (1989, 28–34).

8. The radical FLN leadership during the revolution, as exemplified by Ahmed Ben Bella, supported women's equality, as Fanon claims; after Ben Bella's assassination in 1966 a "moderate" and antifeminist faction took over (Morgan 1984, 45–49).

9. Gayatri Spivak refers to this in "Can the Subaltern Speak?" as "white men saving brown women from brown men" (1988, 297), a practice common to colonial rulers— the English outlawed sati in India for the same ostensible purpose.

10. Fanon takes no stand on the question of what place the veil has in North African

culture prior to colonial domination. In referring to it as "an undifferentiated element in a homogenous whole," he implies that there is no special point of contention over the veil prior to the French invasion. He makes no pretense to interpret, positively or negatively, the status of women in previously "homogenous" Algerian society.

Clearly, from a feminist point of view we would want to ask whether, and to what extent, there were heterodox views or resistances to the veil from within the culture prior to colonialism. Again, though, while this may be important research, it is Fanon's point to suggest that colonial domination results in nationalist (and thus orthodox) unity, possibly even at the expense of indigenous progressive movements. I will discuss this point more in the next section, when I look with some care at *Wretched of the Earth,* where Fanon is very clear about the limits of nationalism and speaks of the possibility of class conflict within the neocolonialist setting should a nondemocratic indigenous regime replace the colonial power—that is, should true decolonization not take place. The concept of neocolonialism can also, then, by the same argument, be applied to the present status of women in Algerian society.

11. It is not irrelevant for me to mention my own activism as a white male antiracist over the last five years, since the instincts with which I grew up—those of the segregated white working-class New York neighborhood where I grew up—have remained with me. In spite of engaging in a wide variety of actions and close friendships with people of color, and in spite of living in a predominantly black community, to this day I retain gut reactions of fear and loathing when I am alone and see a black man. This is a psychological ailment I am normally unwilling to admit, and which I believe only the possibility of revolutionary struggle will ever help me to overcome. This personal anecdote is, of course, the flip side of the description bell hooks gives of her continuing terror of being in white institutions described in the essay "Representing Whiteness in the Black Imagination" (hooks 1992). My recognition of this fact is perhaps the root of my belief that what she says there is true, unlike the predominantly white academics who she reports "jok[ed] about how ludicrous it was for me to say I felt terrorized" in academic settings (345).

12. This, of course, also provides a framework for understanding masculinist backlash. If the minds of the women who participate in the struggle are decolonized while the leadership who takes political control are unreconstructed, then oppression from the top may again be instituted. Unless the movement against all forms of domination can be sustained democratically, renewed repression is always a likelihood.

WORKS CITED

Bourdieu, Pierre (1977 [1972]). *Outline of a Theory of Practice.* New York: Cambridge University Press.

Bourdieu, Pierre, and Jean-Claude Passeron (1990 [1970]). *Reproduction in Education, Society and Culture.* 2d ed. London: SAGE Publications.

Clark, Septima, and Cynthia Stokes Brown (1990). *Ready from Within.* Trenton, N.J.: Africa World Press.

Fanon, Frantz (1963 [1961]). *Wretched of the Earth.* New York: Grove Press.

Fanon, Frantz (1967a [1952]). *Black Skin, White Masks.* New York: Grove Press.

Fanon, Frantz (1967b [1959]). *A Dying Colonialism.* New York: Grove Press.

Foucault, Michel (1979 [1975]). *Discipline and Punish: The Birth of the Prison.* New York: Vintage Books.

Freire, Paulo (1973 [1969]). *Education for Critical Consciousness.* New York: Continuum.

Freire, Paulo (1989 [1971]) *Pedagogy of the Oppressed.* New York: Continuum.

Gates, Henry Louis, Jr. (1991). "Critical Fanonianism." In *Critical Inquiry* 17:457–70.

Gilroy, Paul (1987). *There Ain't No Black in the Union Jack: The Cultural Politics of Race and Nation.* Chicago: University of Chicago Press.

Giroux, Henry (1992). *Border Crossings: Cultural Workers and the Politics of Education.* New York: Routledge.

Gramsci, Antonio (1971). *Selections from the Prison Notebooks.* New York: International Publishers.

Haug, Frigga and Others (1987). *Female Sexualization: A Collective Work of Memory.* London: Verso.

hooks, bell (1989). *Talking Back: Thinking Feminist, Thinking Black.* Boston: South End Press.

hooks, bell (1992). "Representing Whiteness in the Black Imagination." In *Cultural Studies,* ed. Lawrence Grossberg, Cary Nelson, and Paula Treichler. New York: Routledge.

Horton, Myles, and Paulo Freire (1990). *We Make the Road by Walking: Conversations on Education and Social Change.* Philadelphia: Temple University Press.

JanMohamed, Abdul R. (1983). *Manichean Aesthetics.* Amherst: University of Massachusetts Press.

Jinadu, L. Adele (1986). *Fanon: In Search of the African Revolution.* London: KPI Ltd.

Laclau, Ernesto, and Chantal Mouffe (1985). *Hegemony and Socialist Strategy: Towards a Radical Democratic Politics.* London: Verso.

Lave, Jean, and Etienne Wenger (1991). *Situated Learning: Legitimate Peripheral Participation.* New York: Cambridge University Press.

Marx, Karl (1947 [1847]). "Theses on Feuerbach." In Karl Marx and Frederick Engels, *The German Ideology,* edited and with an introduction by C. J. Arthur. New York: International Publishers.

Morgan, Robin, ed. (1984). *Sisterhood Is Global.* Garden City, N.Y.: Anchor Books, 1984.

Sartre, Jean-Paul (1968 [1960]). *Search for a Method.* New York: Vintage Books.

Smith, Barbara, ed. (1983). *Home Girls: A Black Feminist Anthology.* New York: Kitchen Table Press.

Spivak, Gayatri Chakravorty (1988). "Can the Subaltern Speak?" In *Marxism and the Interpretation of Culture,* ed. Cary Nelson and Lawrence Grossberg. Urbana, Ill.: University of Illinois Press.

Spivak, Gayatri Chakravorty (1990). *The Post-Colonial Critic: Interviews, Strategies, Dialogues.* New York: Routledge.

Taylor, Patrick (1989). *The Narrative of Liberation: Perspectives on Afro-Caribbean Literature, Popular Culture, and Politics.* Ithaca, N.Y.: Cornell University Press.

INDEX

CONTRIBUTORS

Carol Becker is Associate Dean for the School of Art Institute in Chicago.

Ava Collins is Chair of the Gender Studies Program at the University of Notre Dame.

Michael Eric Dyson teaches in the Afro-American Studies Department at Brown University.

Nancy Fraser teaches in the Philosophy Department at Northwestern University.

Henry A. Giroux holds the Waterbury Chair Professorship at Pennsylvania State University.

bell hooks is Professor of English and Women's Studies at Oberlin College.

Abdul R. JanMohamed teaches in the Department of English at the University of California, Berkeley.

Peter McLaren is Associate Professor, Graduate School of Education, University of California at Los Angeles.

Chandra Talpade Mohanty holds the Jane Watson Irwin Professorship in Women's Studies at Hamilton College.

Kenneth Mostern is a graduate student in the Department of English at the University of California, Berkeley.

Roger I. Simon is Professor of Education at the Ontario Institute for Studies in Education.

David Trend teaches at San Francisco State University.

Michele Wallace teaches at the City University of New York.

Simon Watney is Assistant Editor of the National AIDS Manual in the U.K. He is formerly Senior Lecturer in the History and Theory of Photography at the Polytechnic of Central London.